T0260587

Mastering Kafka Streams and ksqlDB

Building Real-Time Data Systems by Example

Mitch Seymour

Beijing · Boston · Farnham · Sebastopol · Tokyo

Mastering Kafka Streams and ksqlDB

by Mitch Seymour

Copyright © 2021 Mitch Seymour. All rights reserved.

Published by O'Reilly Media, Inc., 1005 Gravenstein Highway North, Sebastopol, CA 95472.

O'Reilly books may be purchased for educational, business, or sales promotional use. Online editions are also available for most titles (*http://oreilly.com*). For more information, contact our corporate/institutional sales department: 800-998-9938 or *corporate@oreilly.com*.

Acquisitions Editor: Jessica Haberman
Development Editor: Jeff Bleiel
Production Editor: Daniel Elfanbaum
Copyeditor: Kim Cofer
Proofreader: JM Olejarz

Indexer: Ellen Troutman-Zaig
Interior Designer: David Futato
Cover Designer: Karen Montgomery
Illustrator: Kate Dullea

February 2021:   First Edition

Revision History for the First Edition

2021-02-04:   First Release

See *http://oreilly.com/catalog/errata.csp?isbn=9781492062493* for release details.

The O'Reilly logo is a registered trademark of O'Reilly Media, Inc. *Mastering Kafka Streams and ksqlDB*, the cover image, and related trade dress are trademarks of O'Reilly Media, Inc.

The views expressed in this work are those of the author, and do not represent the publisher's views. While the publisher and the author have used good faith efforts to ensure that the information and instructions contained in this work are accurate, the publisher and the author disclaim all responsibility for errors or omissions, including without limitation responsibility for damages resulting from the use of or reliance on this work. Use of the information and instructions contained in this work is at your own risk. If any code samples or other technology this work contains or describes is subject to open source licenses or the intellectual property rights of others, it is your responsibility to ensure that your use thereof complies with such licenses and/or rights.

978-1-492-06249-3

[LSI]

Table of Contents

Part IV.   The Road to Production

Foreword

Businesses are increasingly built around events—the real-time activity data of what is happening in a company—but what is the right infrastructure for harnessing the power of events? This is a question I have been thinking about since 2009, when I started the Apache Kafka project at LinkedIn. In 2014, I cofounded Confluent to definitively answer it. Beyond providing a way to store and access discrete events, an event streaming platform needs a mechanism to connect with a myriad of external systems. It also requires global schema management, metrics, and monitoring. But perhaps most important of all is stream processing—continuous computation over never-ending streams of data—without which an event streaming platform is simply incomplete.

Now more than ever, stream processing plays a key role in how businesses interact with the world. In 2011, Marc Andreessen wrote an article titled "Why Software Is Eating the World." The core idea is that any process that can be moved into software eventually will be. Marc turned out to be prescient. The most obvious outcome is that software has permeated every industry imaginable.

But a lesser understood and more important outcome is that businesses are increasingly defined in software. Put differently, the core processes a business executes—from how it creates a product, to how it interacts with customers, to how it delivers services—are increasingly specified, monitored, and executed in software. What has changed because of that dynamic? Software, in this new world, is far less likely to be directly interacting with a human. Instead, it is more likely that its purpose is to programmatically trigger actions or react to other pieces of software that carry out business directly.

It begs the question: are our traditional application architectures, centered around existing databases, sufficient for this emerging world? Virtually all databases, from the most established relational databases to the newest key-value stores, follow a paradigm in which data is passively stored and the database waits for commands to retrieve or modify it. This paradigm was driven by human-facing applications in which a user looks at an interface and initiates actions that are translated into database queries. We think that is only half the problem, and the problem of storing data needs to be complemented with the ability to react to and process events.

Events and stream processing are the keys to succeeding in this new world. Events support the continuous flow of data throughout a business, and stream processing automatically executes code in response to change at any level of detail—doing it in concert with knowledge of all changes that came before it. Modern stream processing systems like Kafka Streams and ksqlDB make it easy to build applications for a world that speaks software.

In this book, Mitch Seymour lucidly describes these state-of-the-art systems from first principles. *Mastering Kafka Streams and ksqlDB* surveys core concepts, details the nuances of how each system works, and provides hands-on examples for using them for business in the real world. Stream processing has never been a more essential programming paradigm—and *Mastering Kafka Streams and ksqlDB* illuminates the path to succeeding at it.

— Jay Kreps
Cocreator of Apache Kafka,
Cofounder and CEO of Confluent

Preface

For data engineers and data scientists, there's never a shortage of technologies that are competing for our attention. Whether we're perusing our favorite subreddits, scanning Hacker News, reading tech blogs, or weaving through hundreds of tables at a tech conference, there are so many things to look at that it can start to feel overwhelming.

But if we can find a quiet corner to just think for a minute, and let all of the buzz fade into the background, we can start to distinguish patterns from the noise. You see, we live in the age of explosive data growth, and many of these technologies were created to help us store and process data at scale. We're told that these are modern solutions for modern problems, and we sit around discussing "big data" as if the idea is avantgarde, when really the focus on data volume is only half the story.

Technologies that only solve for the data volume problem tend to have batch-oriented techniques for processing data. This involves running a job on some pile of data that has accumulated for a period of time. In some ways, this is like trying to drink the ocean all at once. With modern computing power and paradigms, some technologies actually manage to achieve this, though usually at the expense of high latency.

Instead, there's another property of modern data that we focus on in this book: data moves over networks in steady and never-ending streams. The technologies we cover in this book, Kafka Streams and ksqlDB, are specifically designed to process these continuous data streams in real time, and provide huge competitive advantages over the ocean-drinking variety. After all, many business problems are time-sensitive, and if you need to enrich, transform, or react to data as soon as it comes in, then Kafka Streams and ksqlDB will help get you there with ease and efficiency.

Learning Kafka Streams and ksqlDB is also a great way to familiarize yourself with the larger concepts involved in stream processing. This includes modeling data in different ways (streams and tables), applying stateless transformations of data, using local state for more advanced operations (joins, aggregations), understanding the different time semantics and methods for grouping data into time buckets/windows, and more. In other words, your knowledge of Kafka Streams and ksqlDB will help you distinguish and evaluate different stream processing solutions that currently exist and may come into existence sometime in the future.

I'm excited to share these technologies with you because they have both made an impact on my own career and helped me accomplish technological feats that I thought were beyond my own capabilities. In fact, by the time you finish reading this sentence, one of my Kafka Streams applications will have processed nine million events. The feeling you'll get by providing real business value without having to invest exorbitant amounts of time on the solution will keep you working with these technologies for years to come, and the succinct and expressive language constructs make the process feel more like an art form than a labor. And just like any other art form, whether it be a life-changing song or a beautiful painting, it's human nature to want to share it. So consider this book a mixtape from me to you, with my favorite compilations from the stream processing space available for your enjoyment: Kafka Streams and ksqlDB, Volume 1.

Who Should Read This Book

This book is for data engineers who want to learn how to build highly scalable stream processing applications for moving, enriching, and transforming large amounts of data in real time. These skills are often needed to support business intelligence initiatives, analytic pipelines, threat detection, event processing, and more. Data scientists and analysts who want to upgrade their skills by analyzing real-time data streams will also find value in this book, which is an exciting departure from the batch processing space that has typically dominated these fields. Prior experience with Apache Kafka is not required, though some familiarity with the Java programming language will make the Kafka Streams tutorials easier to follow.

Navigating This Book

This book is organized roughly as follows:

- Chapter 1 provides an introduction to Kafka and a tutorial for running a single-node Kafka cluster.

- Chapter 2 provides an introduction to Kafka Streams, starting with a background and architectural review, and ending with a tutorial for running a simple Kafka Streams application.

- Chapters 3 and 4 discuss the stateless and stateful operators in the Kafka Streams high-level DSL (domain-specific language). Each chapter includes a tutorial that will demonstrate how to use these operators to solve an interesting business problem.

- Chapter 5 discusses the role that time plays in our stream processing applications, and demonstrates how to use windows to perform more advanced stateful operations, including windowed joins and aggregations. A tutorial inspired by predictive healthcare will demonstrate the key concepts.

- Chapter 6 describes how stateful processing works under the hood, and provides some operational tips for stateful Kafka Streams applications.

- Chapter 7 dives into Kafka Streams' lower-level Processor API, which can be used for scheduling periodic functions, and provides more granular access to application state and record metadata. The tutorial in this chapter is inspired by IoT (Internet of Things) use cases.

- Chapter 8 provides an introduction to ksqlDB, and discusses the history and architecture of this technology. The tutorial in this chapter will show you how to install and run a ksqlDB server instance, and work with the ksqlDB CLI.

- Chapter 9 discusses ksqlDB's data integration features, which are powered by Kafka Connect.

- Chapters 10 and 11 discuss the ksqlDB SQL dialect in detail, demonstrating how to work with different collection types, perform push queries and pull queries, and more. The concepts will be introduced using a tutorial based on a Netflix use case: tracking changes to various shows/films, and making these changes available to other applications.

- Chapter 12 provides the information you need to deploy your Kafka Streams and ksqlDB applications to production. This includes information on monitoring, testing, and containerizing your applications.

Source Code

The source code for this book can be found on GitHub at *https://github.com/mitch-seymour/mastering-kafka-streams-and-ksqldb*.

Instructions for building and running each tutorial will be included in the repository.

Kafka Streams Version

At the time of this writing, the latest version of Kafka Streams was version 2.7.0. This is the version we use in this book, though in many cases, the code will also work with older or newer versions of the Kafka Streams library. We will make efforts to update the source code when newer versions introduce breaking changes, and will stage these updates in a dedicated branch (e.g., kafka-streams-2.8).

ksqlDB Version

At the time of this writing, the latest version of ksqlDB was version 0.14.0. Compatibility with older and newer versions of ksqlDB is less guaranteed due to the ongoing and rapid development of this technology, and the lack of a major version (e.g., 1.0) at the time of this book's publication. We will make efforts to update the source code when newer versions introduce breaking changes, and will stage these updates in a dedicated branch (e.g., ksqldb-0.15). However, it is recommended to avoid versions older than 0.14.0 when running the examples in this book.

Conventions Used in This Book

The following typographical conventions are used in this book:

Italic
> Indicates new terms, URLs, email addresses, filenames, and file extensions.

`Constant width`
> Used for program listings, as well as within paragraphs to refer to program elements such as variable or function names, databases, data types, environment variables, statements, and keywords.

`Constant width bold`
> Shows commands or other text that should be typed literally by the user.

`Constant width italic`
> Shows text that should be replaced with user-supplied values or by values determined by context.

> This element signifies a tip or suggestion.

> This element signifies a general note.

> This element indicates a warning or caution.

Using Code Examples

Supplemental material (code examples, exercises, etc.) can be found on the book's GitHub page, *https://github.com/mitch-seymour/mastering-kafka-streams-and-ksqldb*.

If you have a technical question or a problem using the code examples, please email *bookquestions@oreilly.com*.

This book is here to help you get your job done. In general, if example code is offered with this book, you may use it in your programs and documentation. You do not need to contact us for permission unless you're reproducing a significant portion of the code. For example, writing a program that uses several chunks of code from this book does not require permission. Selling or distributing examples from O'Reilly books does require permission. Answering a question by citing this book and quoting example code does not require permission. Incorporating a significant amount of example code from this book into your product's documentation does require permission.

We appreciate, but generally do not require, attribution. An attribution usually includes the title, author, publisher, and ISBN. For example: "*Mastering Kafka Streams and ksqlDB* by Mitch Seymour (O'Reilly). Copyright 2021 Mitch Seymour, 978-1-492-06249-3."

If you feel your use of code examples falls outside fair use or the permission given above, feel free to contact us at *permissions@oreilly.com*.

O'Reilly Online Learning

For more than 40 years, *O'Reilly Media* has provided technology and business training, knowledge, and insight to help companies succeed.

Our unique network of experts and innovators share their knowledge and expertise through books, articles, and our online learning platform. O'Reilly's online learning platform gives you on-demand access to live training courses, in-depth learning paths, interactive coding environments, and a vast collection of text and video from O'Reilly and 200+ other publishers. For more information, visit *http://oreilly.com*.

How to Contact Us

Please address comments and questions concerning this book to the publisher:

O'Reilly Media, Inc.
1005 Gravenstein Highway North
Sebastopol, CA 95472
800-998-9938 (in the United States or Canada)
707-829-0515 (international or local)
707-829-0104 (fax)

We have a web page for this book, where we list errata, examples, and any additional information. You can access this page at *https://oreil.ly/mastering-kafka-streams*.

Email *bookquestions@oreilly.com* to comment or ask technical questions about this book.

For news and information about our books and courses, visit *http://oreilly.com*.

Find us on Facebook: *http://facebook.com/oreilly*.

Follow us on Twitter: *http://twitter.com/oreillymedia*.

Watch us on YouTube: *http://www.youtube.com/oreillymedia*.

Acknowledgments

First and foremost, I want to thank my wife, Elyse, and my daughter, Isabelle. Writing a book is a huge time investment, and your patience and support through the entire process helped me immensely. As much as I enjoyed writing this book, I missed you both greatly, and I look forward to having more date nights and daddy-daughter time again.

I also want to thank my parents, Angie and Guy, for teaching me the value of hard work and for being a never-ending source of encouragement. Your support has helped me overcome many challenges over the years, and I am eternally grateful for you both.

This book would not be possible without the following people, who dedicated a lot of their time to reviewing its content and providing great feedback and advice along the way: Matthias J. Sax, Robert Yokota, Nitin Sharma, Rohan Desai, Jeff Bleiel, and Danny Elfanbaum. Thank you all for helping me create this book, it's just as much yours as it is mine.

Many of the tutorials were informed by actual business use cases, and I owe a debt of gratitude to everyone in the community who openly shared their experiences with Kafka Streams and ksqlDB, whether it be through conferences, podcasts, blogs, or even in-person interviews. Your experiences helped shape this book, which puts a special emphasis on practical stream processing applications. Nitin Sharma also provided ideas for the Netflix-inspired ksqlDB tutorials, and Ramesh Sringeri shared his stream processing experiences at Children's Healthcare of Atlanta, which inspired the predictive healthcare tutorial. Thank you both.

Special thanks to Michael Drogalis for being a huge supporter of this book, even when it was just an outline of ideas. Also, thank you for putting me in touch with many of this book's reviewers, and also Jay Kreps, who graciously wrote the foreword. The technical writings of Yeva Byzek and Bill Bejeck have also set a high bar for what this book should be. Thank you both for your contributions in this space.

There have been many people in my career that helped get me to this point. Mark Conde and Tom Stanley, thank you for opening the doors to my career as a software engineer. Barry Bowden, for helping me become a better engineer, and for being a great mentor. Erin Fusaro, for knowing exactly what to say whenever I felt overwhelmed, and for just being a rock in general. Justin Isasi, for your continuous encouragement, and making sure my efforts don't go unrecognized. Sean Sawyer, for a suggestion you made several years ago, that I try a new thing called "Kafka Streams," which has clearly spiraled out of control. Thomas Holmes and Matt Farmer, for sharing your technical expertise with me on many occasions, and helping me become a better engineer. And to the Data Services team at Mailchimp, thanks for helping me solve some really cool problems, and for inspiring me with your own work.

Finally, to my friends and family, who continue to stick by me even when I disappear for months at a time to work on a new project. Thanks for sticking around, this was a long one.

## PART I

Kafka

## CHAPTER 1

A Rapid Introduction to Kafka

The amount of data in the world is growing exponentially and, according to the World Economic Forum (*https://oreil.ly/Avd2n*), the number of bytes being stored in the world already far exceeds the number of stars in the observable universe.

When you think of this data, you might think of piles of bytes sitting in data warehouses, in relational databases, or on distributed filesystems. Systems like these have trained us to think of data in its *resting state*. In other words, data is sitting somewhere, resting, and when you need to process it, you run some query or job against the pile of bytes.

This view of the world is the more traditional way of thinking about data. However, while data can certainly pile up in places, more often than not, it's moving. You see, many systems generate continuous streams of data, including IoT sensors, medical sensors, financial systems, user and customer analytics software, application and server logs, and more. Even data that eventually finds a nice place to rest likely travels across the network at some point before it finds its forever home.

If we want to process data in real time, while it moves, we can't simply wait for it to pile up somewhere and then run a query or job at some interval of our choosing. That approach can handle some business use cases, but many important use cases require us to process, enrich, transform, and respond to data incrementally as it becomes available. Therefore, we need something that has a very different worldview of data: a technology that gives us access to data in its *flowing state*, and which allows us to work with these continuous and unbounded data streams quickly and efficiently. This is where Apache Kafka comes in.

Apache Kafka (or simply, Kafka) is a streaming platform for ingesting, storing, accessing, and processing streams of data. While the entire platform is very interesting, this book focuses on what I find to be the most compelling part of Kafka:

the stream processing layer. However, to understand Kafka Streams and ksqlDB (both of which operate at this layer, and the latter of which also operates at the stream ingestion layer), it is necessary to have a working knowledge of how Kafka, as a platform, works.

Therefore, this chapter will introduce you to some important concepts and terminology that you will need for the rest of the book. If you already have a working knowledge of Kafka, feel free to skip this chapter. Otherwise, keep reading.

Some of the questions we will answer in this chapter include:

- How does Kafka simplify communication between systems?
- What are the main components in Kafka's architecture?
- Which storage abstraction most closely models streams?
- How does Kafka store data in a fault-tolerant and durable manner?
- How is high availability and fault tolerance achieved at the data processing layers?

We will conclude this chapter with a tutorial showing how to install and run Kafka. But first, let's start by looking at Kafka's communication model.

Communication Model

Perhaps the most common communication pattern between systems is the synchronous, client-server model. When we talk about systems in this context, we mean applications, microservices, databases, and anything else that reads and writes data over a network. The client-server model is simple at first, and involves direct communication between systems, as shown in Figure 1-1.

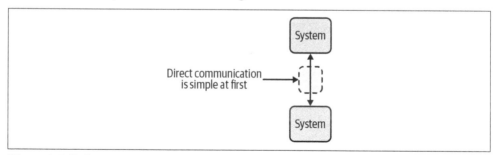

Figure 1-1. Point-to-point communication is simple to maintain and reason about when you have a small number of systems

For example, you may have an application that synchronously queries a database for some data, or a collection of microservices that talk to each other directly.

However, when more systems need to communicate, point-to-point communication becomes difficult to scale. The result is a complex web of communication pathways that can be difficult to reason about and maintain. Figure 1-2 shows just how confusing it can get, even with a relatively small number of systems.

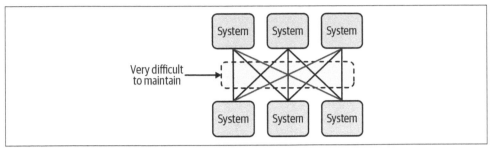

Figure 1-2. The result of adding more systems is a complex web of communication channels, which is difficult to maintain

Some of the drawbacks of the client-server model include:

- Systems become *tightly coupled* because their communication depends on knowledge of each other. This makes maintaining and updating these systems more difficult than it needs to be.

- Synchronous communication leaves little room for error since there are *no delivery guarantees* if one of the systems goes offline.

- Systems may use different communication protocols, scaling strategies to deal with increased load, failure-handling strategies, etc. As a result, you may end up with multiple species of systems to maintain (*software speciation*), which hurts maintainability and defies the common wisdom that we should treat applications like cattle instead of pets.

- Receiving systems can easily be overwhelmed, since they don't control the pace at which new requests or data comes in. *Without a request buffer*, they operate at the whims of the applications that are making requests.

- There isn't a strong notion for what is being communicated between these systems. The nomenclature of the client-server model has put too much emphasis on *requests* and *responses*, and not enough emphasis on the data itself. Data should be the focal point of data-driven systems.

- Communication is *not replayable*. This makes it difficult to reconstruct the state of a system.

Kafka simplifies communication between systems by acting as a centralized communication hub (often likened to a central nervous system), in which systems can send and receive data without knowledge of each other. The communication pattern it implements is called the *publish-subscribe pattern* (or simply, pub/sub), and the result is a drastically simpler communication model, as shown in Figure 1-3.

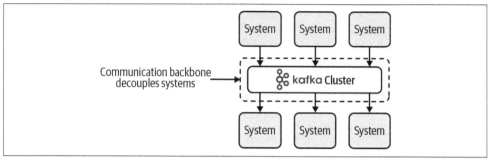

Figure 1-3. Kafka removes the complexity of point-to-point communication by acting as a communication hub between systems

If we add more detail to the preceding diagram, we can begin to identify the main components involved in Kafka's communication model, as shown in Figure 1-4.

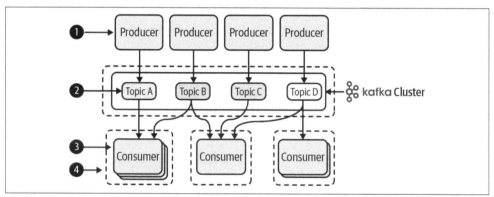

Figure 1-4. The Kafka communication model, redrawn with more detail to show the main components of the Kafka platform

❶ Instead of having multiple systems communicate directly with each other, *producers* simply publish their data to one or more topics, without caring who comes along to read the data.

❷ *Topics* are named streams (or channels) of related data that are stored in a Kafka cluster. They serve a similar purpose as tables in a database (i.e., to group related data). However, they do not impose a particular schema, but rather store the raw bytes of data, which makes them very flexible to work with.[1]

❸ *Consumers* are processes that read (or subscribe) to data in one or more topics. They do not communicate directly with the producers, but rather listen to data on any stream they happen to be interested in.

❹ Consumers can work together as a group (called a *consumer group*) in order to distribute work across multiple processes.

Kafka's communication model, which puts more emphasis on flowing streams of data that can easily be read from and written to by multiple processes, comes with several advantages, including:

- Systems become *decoupled* and easier to maintain because they can produce and consume data without knowledge of other systems.
- Asynchronous communication comes with *stronger delivery guarantees*. If a consumer goes down, it will simply pick up from where it left off when it comes back online again (or, when running with multiple consumers in a consumer group, the work will be redistributed to one of the other members).
- Systems can standardize on the communication protocol (a high-performance binary TCP protocol is used when talking to Kafka clusters), as well as scaling strategies and fault-tolerance mechanisms (which are driven by consumer groups). This allows us to write software that is broadly consistent, and which fits in our head.
- Consumers can process data at a rate they can handle. Unprocessed data is stored in Kafka, in a durable and fault-tolerant manner, until the consumer is ready to process it. In other words, if the stream your consumer is reading from suddenly turns into a firehose, the Kafka cluster will act as a buffer, preventing your consumers from being overwhelmed.
- A stronger notion of what data is being communicated, in the form of *events*. An event is a piece of data with a certain structure, which we will discuss in "Events" on page 11. The main point, for now, is that we can focus on the data flowing through our streams, instead of spending so much time disentangling the communication layer like we would in the client-server model.
- Systems can rebuild their state anytime by replaying the events in a topic.

---

1 We talk about the raw byte arrays that are stored in topics, as well as the process of deserializing the bytes into higher-level structures like JSON objects/Avro records, in Chapter 3.

One important difference between the pub/sub model and the client-server model is that communication is not bidirectional in Kafka's pub/sub model. In other words, streams flow one way. If a system produces some data to a Kafka topic, and relies on another system to do something with the data (i.e., enrich or transform it), the enriched data will need to be written to another topic and subsequently consumed by the original process. This is simple to coordinate, but it changes the way we think about communication.

As long as you remember the communication channels (topics) are stream-like in nature (i.e., flowing unidirectionally, and may have multiple sources and multiple downstream consumers), it's easy to design systems that simply listen to whatever stream of flowing bytes they are interested in, and produce data to topics (named streams) whenever they want to share data with one or more systems. We will be working a lot with Kafka topics in the following chapters (each Kafka Streams and ksqlDB application we build will read, and usually write to, one or more Kafka topics), so by the time you reach the end of this book, this will be second nature for you.

Now that we've seen how Kafka's communication model simplifies the way systems communicate with each other, and that named streams called *topics* act as the communication medium between systems, let's gain a deeper understanding of how streams come into play in Kafka's storage layer.

How Are Streams Stored?

When a team of LinkedIn engineers[2] saw the potential in a stream-driven data platform, they had to answer an important question: how should unbounded and continuous data streams be modeled at the storage layer?

Ultimately, the storage abstraction they identified (*https://oreil.ly/Y2Fe5*) was already present in many types of data systems, including traditional databases, key-value stores, version control systems, and more. The abstraction is the simple, yet powerful *commit log* (or simply, *log*).

 When we talk about *logs* in this book, we're not referring to *application logs*, which emit information about a running process (e.g., HTTP server logs). Instead, we are referring to a specific data structure that is described in the following paragraphs.

Logs are *append-only* data structures that capture an *ordered sequence* of events. Let's examine the italicized attributes in more detail, and build some intuition around logs, by creating a simple log from the command line. For example, let's create a log

---

2 Jay Kreps, Neha Narkhede, and Jun Rao initially led the development of Kafka.

called `user_purchases`, and populate it with some dummy data using the following command:

```
# create the logfile
touch users.log

# generate four dummy records in our log
echo "timestamp=1597373669,user_id=1,purchases=1" >> users.log
echo "timestamp=1597373669,user_id=2,purchases=1" >> users.log
echo "timestamp=1597373669,user_id=3,purchases=1" >> users.log
echo "timestamp=1597373669,user_id=4,purchases=1" >> users.log
```

Now if we look at the log we created, it contains four users that have made a single purchase:

```
# print the contents of the log
cat users.log

# output
timestamp=1597373669,user_id=1,purchases=1
timestamp=1597373669,user_id=2,purchases=1
timestamp=1597373669,user_id=3,purchases=1
timestamp=1597373669,user_id=4,purchases=1
```

The first attribute of logs is that they are written to in an append-only manner. This means that if `user_id=1` comes along and makes a second purchase, we do not update the first record, since each record is *immutable* in a log. Instead, we just append the new record to the end:

```
# append a new record to the log
echo "timestamp=1597374265,user_id=1,purchases=2" >> users.log

# print the contents of the log
cat users.log

# output
timestamp=1597373669,user_id=1,purchases=1 ❶
timestamp=1597373669,user_id=2,purchases=1
timestamp=1597373669,user_id=3,purchases=1
timestamp=1597373669,user_id=4,purchases=1
timestamp=1597374265,user_id=1,purchases=2 ❷
```

❶ Once a record is written to the log, it is considered immutable. Therefore, if we need to perform an update (e.g., to change the purchase count for a user), then the original record is left untouched.

❷ In order to model the update, we simply append the new value to the end of the log. The log will contain both the old record and the new record, both of which are immutable.

Any system that wants to examine the purchase counts for each user can simply read each record in the log, in order, and the last record they will see for user_id=1 will contain the updated purchase amount. This brings us to the second attribute of logs: they are ordered.

The preceding log happens to be in timestamp order (see the first column), but that's not what we mean by *ordered*. In fact, Kafka does store a timestamp for each record in the log, but the records do not have to be in timestamp order. When we say a log is ordered, what we mean is that a record's *position* in the log is fixed, and never changes. If we reprint the log again, this time with line numbers, you can see the position in the first column:

```
# print the contents of the log, with line numbers
cat -n users.log

# output
1       timestamp=1597373669,user_id=1,purchases=1
2       timestamp=1597373669,user_id=2,purchases=1
3       timestamp=1597373669,user_id=3,purchases=1
4       timestamp=1597373669,user_id=4,purchases=1
5       timestamp=1597374265,user_id=1,purchases=2
```

Now, imagine a scenario where ordering couldn't be guaranteed. Multiple processes could read the user_id=1 updates in a different order, creating disagreement about the actual purchase count for this user. By ensuring the logs are ordered, the data can be processed deterministically[3] by multiple processes.[4]

Furthermore, while the position of each log entry in the preceding example uses line numbers, Kafka refers to the position of each entry in its distributed log as an *offset*. Offsets start at 0 and they enable an important behavior: they allow multiple consumer groups to each read from the same log, and maintain their own positions in the log/stream they are reading from. This is shown in Figure 1-5.

Now that we've gained some intuition around Kafka's log-based storage layer by creating our own log from the command line, let's tie these ideas back to the higher-level constructs we identified in Kafka's communication model. We'll start by continuing our discussion of topics, and learning about something called *partitions*.

---

3 Deterministic means the same inputs will produce the same outputs.

4 This is why traditional databases use logs for replication. Logs are used to capture each write operation on the leader database, and process the same writes, *in order*, on a replica database in order to deterministically re-create the same dataset on another machine.

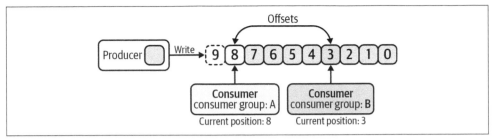

Figure 1-5. Multiple consumer groups can read from the same log, each maintaining their position based on the offset they have read/processed

Topics and Partitions

In our discussion of Kafka's communication model, we learned that Kafka has the concept of named streams called topics. Furthermore, Kafka topics are extremely flexible with what you store in them. For example, you can have *homogeneous topics* that contain only one type of data, or *heterogeneous topics* that contain multiple types of data.[5] A depiction of these different strategies is shown in Figure 1-6.

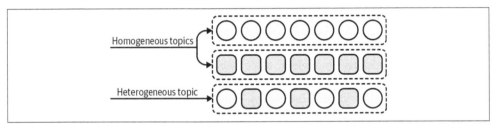

Figure 1-6. Different strategies exist for storing events in topics; homogeneous topics generally contain one event type (e.g., `clicks`) while heterogeneous topics contain multiple event types (e.g., `clicks` and `page_views`)

We have also learned that append-only commit logs are used to model streams in Kafka's storage layer. So, does this mean that each topic correlates with a log file? Not exactly. You see, Kafka is a distributed log, and it's hard to distribute just one of something. So if we want to achieve some level of parallelism with the way we distribute and process logs, we need to create lots of them. This is why Kafka topics are broken into smaller units called *partitions*.

---

5 Martin Kleppmann has an interesting article on this topic, which can be found at *https://oreil.ly/tDZMm*. He talks about the various trade-offs and the reasons why one might choose one strategy over another. Also, Robert Yokota's follow-up article (*https://oreil.ly/hpScS*) goes into more depth about how to support multiple event types when using Confluent Schema Registry for schema management/evolution.

Partitions are individual logs (i.e., the data structures we discussed in the previous section) where data is produced and consumed from. Since the commit log abstraction is implemented at the partition level, this is the level at which ordering is guaranteed, with each partition having its own set of offsets. Global ordering is not supported at the topic level, which is why producers often route related records to the same partition.[6]

Ideally, data will be distributed relatively evenly across all partitions in a topic. But you could also end up with partitions of different sizes. Figure 1-7 shows an example of a topic with three different partitions.

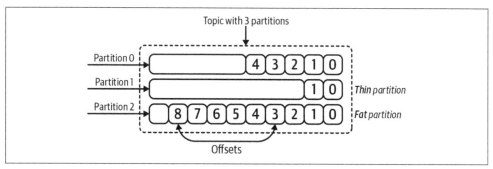

Figure 1-7. A Kafka topic configured with three partitions

The number of partitions for a given topic is configurable, and having more partitions in a topic generally translates to more parallelism and throughput, though there are some trade-offs of having too many partitions.[7] We'll talk about this more throughout the book, but the important takeaway is that only one consumer per consumer group can consume from a partition (individual members across different consumer groups can consume from the same partition, however, as shown in Figure 1-5).

Therefore, if you want to spread the processing load across N consumers in a single consumer group, you need N partitions. If you have fewer members in a consumer group than there are partitions on the source topic (i.e., the topic that is being read from), that's OK: each consumer can process multiple partitions. If you have more members in a consumer group than there are partitions on the source topic, then some consumers will be idle.

---

6 The partitioning strategy is configurable, but a popular strategy, including the one that is implemented in Kafka Streams and ksqlDB, involves setting the partition based on the record key (which can be extracted from the payload of the record or set explicitly). We'll djscuss this in more detail over the next few chapters.

7 The trade-offs include longer recovery periods after certain failure scenarios, increased resource utilization (file descriptors, memory), and increased end-to-end latency.

With this in mind, we can improve our definition of what a topic is. A topic is a named stream, composed of multiple partitions. And each partition is modeled as a commit log that stores data in a totally ordered and append-only sequence. So what exactly is stored in a topic partition? We'll explore this in the next section.

Events

In this book, we spend a lot of time talking about processing data in topics. However, we still haven't developed a full understanding of what kind of data is stored in a Kafka topic (and, more specifically, in a topic's partitions).

A lot of the existing literature on Kafka, including the official documentation, uses a variety of terms to describe the data in a topic, including messages, records, and events. These terms are often used interchangeably, but the one we have favored in this book (though we still use the other terms occasionally) is *event*. An event is a timestamped key-value pair that records *something that happened*. The basic anatomy of each event captured in a topic partition is shown in Figure 1-8.

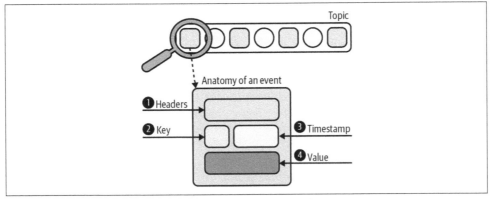

Figure 1-8. Anatomy of an event, which is what is stored in topic partitions

❶ Application-level headers contain optional metadata about an event. We don't work with these very often in this book.

❷ Keys are also optional, but play an important role in how data is distributed across partitions. We will see this over the next few chapters, but generally speaking, they are used to identify related records.

❸ Each event is associated with a timestamp. We'll learn more about timestamps in Chapter 5.

❹ The value contains the actual message contents, encoded as a byte array. It's up to clients to deserialize the raw bytes into a more meaningful structure (e.g., a JSON object or Avro record). We will talk about byte array deserialization in detail in "Serialization/Deserialization" on page 69.

Now that we have a good understanding of what data is stored in a topic, let's get a deeper look at Kafka's clustered deployment model. This will provide more information about *how* data is physically stored in Kafka.

Kafka Cluster and Brokers

Having a centralized communication point means reliability and fault tolerance are extremely important. It also means that the communication backbone needs to be scalable, i.e., able to handle increased amounts of load. This is why Kafka operates as a cluster, and multiple machines, called *brokers*, are involved in the storage and retrieval of data.

Kafka clusters can be quite large, and can even span multiple data centers and geographic regions. However, in this book, we will usually work with a single-node Kafka cluster since that is all we need to start working with Kafka Streams and ksqlDB. In production, you'll likely want at least three brokers, and you will want to set the replication of your Kafka topic so that your data is replicated across multiple brokers (we'll see this later in this chapter's tutorial). This allows us to achieve high availability and to avoid data loss in case one machine goes down.

Now, when we talk about data being stored and replicated across brokers, we're really talking about individual partitions in a topic. For example, a topic may have three partitions that are spread across three brokers, as shown in Figure 1-9.

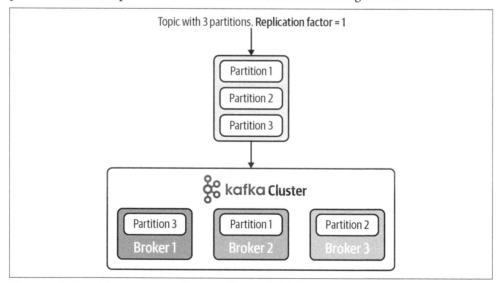

Figure 1-9. Partitions are spread across the available brokers, meaning that a topic can span multiple machines in the Kafka cluster

As you can see, this allows topics to be quite large, since they can grow beyond the capacity of a single machine. To achieve fault tolerance and high availability, you can set a replication factor when configuring the topic. For example, a replication factor of 2 will allow the partition to be stored on two different brokers. This is shown in Figure 1-10.

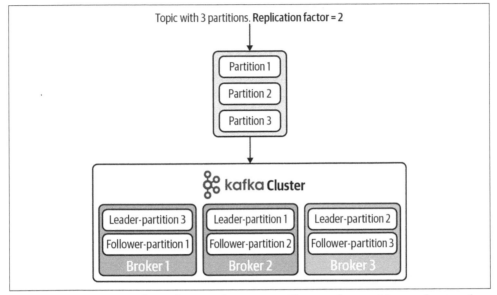

Figure 1-10. Increasing the replication factor to 2 will cause the partitions to be stored on two different brokers

Whenever a partition is replicated across multiple brokers, one broker will be designated as the *leader*, which means it will process all read/write requests from producers/consumers for the given partition. The other brokers that contain the replicated partitions are called *followers*, and they simply copy the data from the leader. If the leader fails, then one of the followers will be promoted as the new leader.

Furthermore, as the load on your cluster increases over time, you can expand your cluster by adding even more brokers, and triggering a partition reassignment. This will allow you to migrate data from the old machines to a fresh, new machine.

Finally, brokers also play an important role with maintaining the membership of consumer groups. We'll explore this in the next section.

Consumer Groups

Kafka is optimized for high throughput and low latency. To take advantage of this on the consumer side, we need to be able to parallelize work across multiple processes. This is accomplished with consumer groups.

Consumer groups are made up of multiple cooperating consumers, and the membership of these groups can change over time. For example, new consumers can come online to scale the processing load, and consumers can also go offline either for planned maintenance or due to unexpected failure. Therefore, Kafka needs some way of maintaining the membership of each group, and redistributing work when necessary.

To facilitate this, every consumer group is assigned to a special broker called the *group coordinator*, which is responsible for receiving heartbeats from the consumers, and triggering a *rebalance* of work whenever a consumer is marked as dead. A depiction of consumers heartbeating back to a group coordinator is shown in Figure 1-11.

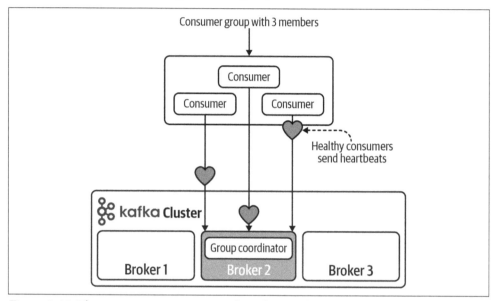

Figure 1-11. Three consumers in a group, heartbeating back to group coordinator

Every active member of the consumer group is eligible to receive a partition assignment. For example, the work distribution across three healthy consumers may look like the diagram in Figure 1-12.

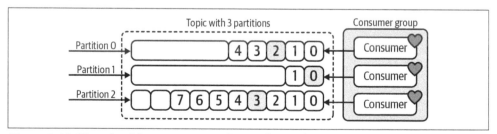

Figure 1-12. Three healthy consumers splitting the read/processing workload of a three-partition Kafka topic

However, if a consumer instance becomes unhealthy and cannot heartbeat back to the cluster, then work will automatically be reassigned to the healthy consumers. For example, in Figure 1-13, the middle consumer has been assigned the partition that was previously being handled by the unhealthy consumer.

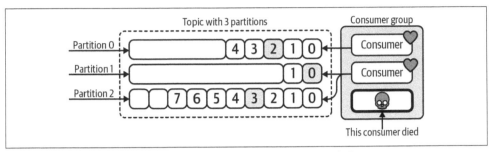

Figure 1-13. Work is redistributed when consumer processes fail

As you can see, consumer groups are extremely important in achieving high availability and fault tolerance at the data processing layer. With this, let's now commence our tutorial by learning how to install Kafka.

Installing Kafka

There are detailed instructions for installing Kafka manually in the official documentation (*https://oreil.ly/rU-j_*). However, to keep things as simple as possible, most of the tutorials in this book utilize Docker (*https://docker.com*), which allows us to deploy Kafka and our stream processing applications inside a containerized environment.

Therefore, we will be installing Kafka using Docker Compose, and we'll be using Docker images that are published by Confluent.[8] The first step is to download and install Docker from the Docker install page (*https://oreil.ly/1kS0h*).

Next, save the following configuration to a file called *docker-compose.yml*:

```
---
version: '2'

services:
  zookeeper: ❶
    image: confluentinc/cp-zookeeper:6.0.0
    hostname: zookeeper
    container_name: zookeeper
```

---

8 There are many Docker images to choose from for running Kafka. However, the Confluent images are a convenient choice since Confluent also provides Docker images for some of the other technologies we will use in this book, including ksqlDB and Confluent Schema Registry.

```
    ports:
      - "2181:2181"
    environment:
      ZOOKEEPER_CLIENT_PORT: 2181
      ZOOKEEPER_TICK_TIME: 2000

  kafka: ❷
    image: confluentinc/cp-enterprise-kafka:6.0.0
    hostname: kafka
    container_name: kafka
    depends_on:
      - zookeeper
    ports:
      - "29092:29092"
    environment:
      KAFKA_BROKER_ID: 1
      KAFKA_ZOOKEEPER_CONNECT: 'zookeeper:2181'
      KAFKA_LISTENER_SECURITY_PROTOCOL_MAP: |
        PLAINTEXT:PLAINTEXT,PLAINTEXT_HOST:PLAINTEXT
      KAFKA_ADVERTISED_LISTENERS: |
        PLAINTEXT://kafka:9092,PLAINTEXT_HOST://localhost:29092
      KAFKA_OFFSETS_TOPIC_REPLICATION_FACTOR: 1
      KAFKA_TRANSACTION_STATE_LOG_REPLICATION_FACTOR: 1
```

❶ The first container, which we've named zookeeper, will contain the ZooKeeper installation. We haven't talked about ZooKeeper in this introduction since, at the time of this writing, it is being actively removed from Kafka. However, it is a centralized service for storing metadata such as topic configuration. Soon, it will no longer be included in Kafka, but we are including it here since this book was published before ZooKeeper was fully removed.

❷ The second container, called kafka, will contain the Kafka installation. This is where our broker (which comprises our single-node cluster) will run and where we will execute some of Kafka's console scripts for interacting with the cluster.

Finally, run the following command to start a local Kafka cluster:

```
docker-compose up
```

With our Kafka cluster running, we are now ready to proceed with our tutorial.

Hello, Kafka

In this simple tutorial, we will demonstrate how to create a Kafka *topic*, write data to a topic using a *producer*, and finally, read data from a topic using a *consumer*. The first thing we need to do is log in to the container that has Kafka installed. We can do this by running the following command:

```
docker-compose exec kafka bash
```

Now, let's create a topic, called users. We'll use one of the console scripts (kafka-topics) that is included with Kafka. The following command shows how to do this:

```
kafka-topics \ ❶
    --bootstrap-server localhost:9092 \ ❷
    --create \ ❸
    --topic users \ ❹
    --partitions 4 \ ❺
    --replication-factor 1 ❻

# output
Created topic users.
```

❶ kafka-topics is a console script that is included with Kafka.

❷ A bootstrap server is the host/IP pair for one or more brokers.

❸ There are many flags for interacting with Kafka topics, including --list, --describe, and --delete. Here, we use the --create flag since we are creating a new topic.

❹ The topic name is users.

❺ Split our topic into four partitions.

❻ Since we're running a single-node cluster, we will set the replication factor to 1. In production, you will want to set this to a higher value (such as 3) to ensure high-availability.

The console scripts we use in this section are included in the Kafka source distribution. In a vanilla Kafka installation, these scripts include the *.sh* file extension (e.g., *kafka-topics.sh*, *kafka-console-producer.sh*, etc.). However, the file extension is dropped in Confluent Platform (which is why we ran *kafka-topics* instead of *kafka-topics.sh* in the previous code snippet).

Once the topic has been created, you can print a description of the topic, including its configuration, using the following command:

```
kafka-topics \
    --bootstrap-server localhost:9092 \
    --describe \ ❶
    --topic users

# output
Topic: users    PartitionCount: 4       ReplicationFactor: 1    Configs:
        Topic: users    Partition: 0    Leader: 1       Replicas: 1     Isr: 1
```

```
Topic: users    Partition: 1    Leader: 1    Replicas: 1    Isr: 1
Topic: users    Partition: 2    Leader: 1    Replicas: 1    Isr: 1
Topic: users    Partition: 3    Leader: 1    Replicas: 1    Isr: 1
```

❶ The `--describe` flag allows us to view configuration information for a given topic.

Now, let's produce some data using the built-in `kafka-console-producer` script:

```
kafka-console-producer \ ❶
    --bootstrap-server localhost:9092 \
    --property key.separator=, \ ❷
    --property parse.key=true \
    --topic users
```

❶ The `kafka-console-producer` script, which is included with Kafka, can be used to produce data to a topic. However, once we start working with Kafka Streams and ksqlDB, the producer processes will be embedded in the underlying Java library, so we won't need to use this script outside of testing and development purposes.

❷ We will be producing a set of key-value pairs to our `users` topic. This property states that our key and values will be separated using the `,` character.

The previous command will drop you in an interactive prompt. From here, we can input several key-value pairs to produce to the `users` topic. When you are finished, press Control-C on your keyboard to exit the prompt:

```
>1,mitch
>2,elyse
>3,isabelle
>4,sammy
```

After producing the data to our topic, we can use the `kafka-console-consumer` script to read the data. The following command shows how:

```
kafka-console-consumer \ ❶
    --bootstrap-server localhost:9092 \
    --topic users \
    --from-beginning ❷

# output
mitch
elyse
isabelle
sammy
```

❶ The `kafka-console-consumer` script is also included in the Kafka distribution. Similar to what we mentioned for the `kafka-console-producer` script, most of the tutorials in this book will leverage consumer processes that are built into Kafka Streams and ksqlDB, instead of using this standalone console script (which is useful for testing purposes).

❷ The `--from-beginning` flag indicates that we should start consuming from the beginning of the Kafka topic.

By default, the `kafka-console-consumer` will only print the message value. But as we learned earlier, events actually contain more information, including a key, a timestamp, and headers. Let's pass in some additional properties to the console consumer so that we can see the timestamp and key values as well:[9]

```
kafka-console-consumer \
    --bootstrap-server localhost:9092 \
    --topic users \
    --property print.timestamp=true \
    --property print.key=true \
    --property print.value=true \
    --from-beginning

# output
CreateTime:1598226962606        1        mitch
CreateTime:1598226964342        2        elyse
CreateTime:1598226966732        3        isabelle
CreateTime:1598226968731        4        sammy
```

That's it! You have now learned how to perform some very basic interactions with a Kafka cluster. The final step is to tear down our local cluster using the following command:

```
docker-compose down
```

Summary

Kafka's communication model makes it easy for multiple systems to communicate, and its fast, durable, and append-only storage layer makes it possible to work with fast-moving streams of data with ease. By using a clustered deployment, Kafka can achieve high availability and fault tolerance at the storage layer by replicating data across multiple machines, called brokers. Furthermore, the cluster's ability to receive heartbeats from consumer processes, and update the membership of consumer groups, allows for high availability, fault tolerance, and workload scalability at the

---

9 As of version 2.7, you can also use the `--property print.headers=true` flag to print the message headers.

stream processing and consumption layer. All of these features have made Kafka one of the most popular stream processing platforms in existence.

You now have enough background on Kafka to get started with Kafka Streams and ksqlDB. In the next section, we will begin our journey with Kafka Streams by seeing how it fits in the wider Kafka ecosystem, and by learning how we can use this library to work with data at the stream processing layer.

## PART II

Kafka Streams

## CHAPTER 2

Getting Started with Kafka Streams

Kafka Streams is a lightweight, yet powerful Java library for enriching, transforming, and processing real-time streams of data. In this chapter, you will be introduced to Kafka Streams at a high level. Think of it as a first date, where you will learn a little about Kafka Streams' background and get an initial glance at its features.

By the end of this date, er...I mean *chapter*, you will understand the following:

- Where Kafka Streams fits in the Kafka ecosystem
- Why Kafka Streams was built in the first place
- What kinds of features and operational characteristics are present in this library
- Who Kafka Streams is appropriate for
- How Kafka Streams compares to other stream processing solutions
- How to create and run a basic Kafka Streams application

So without further ado, let's get our metaphorical date started with a simple question for Kafka Streams: *where do you live* (…in the Kafka ecosystem)?

The Kafka Ecosystem

Kafka Streams lives among a group of technologies that are collectively referred to as the *Kafka ecosystem*. In Chapter 1, we learned that at the heart of Apache Kafka is a distributed, append-only log that we can produce messages to and read messages from. Furthermore, the core Kafka code base includes some important APIs for interacting with this log (which is separated into categories of messages called *topics*). Three APIs in the Kafka ecosystem, which are summarized in Table 2-1, are concerned with the *movement* of data to and from Kafka.

Table 2-1. APIs for moving data to and from Kafka

API	Topic interaction	Examples
Producer API	*Writing* messages to Kafka topics.	• Filebeat • rsyslog • Custom producers
Consumer API	*Reading* messages from Kafka topics.	• Logstash • kafkacat • Custom consumers
Connect API	*Connecting* external data stores, APIs, and filesystems to Kafka topics. Involves both *reading* from topics (sink connectors) and *writing* to topics (source connectors).	• JDBC source connector • Elasticsearch sink connector • Custom connectors

However, while moving data through Kafka is certainly important for creating data pipelines, some business problems require us to also *process* and *react* to data as it becomes available in Kafka. This is referred to as *stream processing*, and there are multiple ways of building stream processing applications with Kafka. Therefore, let's take a look at how stream processing applications were implemented before Kafka Streams was introduced, and how a dedicated stream processing library came to exist alongside the other APIs in the Kafka ecosystem.

Before Kafka Streams

Before Kafka Streams existed, there was a void in the Kafka ecosystem.[1] Not the kind of void you might encounter during your morning meditation that makes you feel refreshed and enlightened, but the kind of void that made building stream processing applications more difficult than it needed to be. I'm talking about the lack of library support for processing data in Kafka topics.

During these early days of the Kafka ecosystem, there were two main options for building Kafka-based stream processing applications:

* Use the Consumer and Producer APIs directly
* Use another stream processing framework (e.g., Apache Spark Streaming, Apache Flink)

With the Consumer and Producer APIs, you can read from and write to the event stream directly using a number of programming languages (Python, Java, Go, C/C++, Node.js, etc.) and perform any kind of data processing logic you'd like, as long

---

1 We are referring to the official ecosystem here, which includes all of the components that are maintained under the Apache Kafka project.

as you're willing to write a lot of code from scratch. These APIs are very basic and lack many of the primitives that would qualify them as a stream processing API, including:

- Local and fault-tolerant state[2]
- A rich set of operators for transforming streams of data
- More advanced representations of streams[3]
- Sophisticated handling of time[4]

Therefore, if you want to do anything nontrivial, like aggregate records, join separate streams of data, group events into windowed time buckets, or run ad hoc queries against your stream, you will hit a wall of complexity pretty quickly. The Producer and Consumer APIs do not contain any abstractions to help you with these kinds of use cases, so you will be left to your own devices as soon as it's time to do something more advanced with your event stream.

The second option, which involves adopting a full-blown streaming platform like Apache Spark or Apache Flink, introduces a lot of unneeded complexity. We talk about the downsides of this approach in "Comparison to Other Systems" on page 30, but the short version is that if we're optimizing for simplicity *and* power, then we need a solution that gives us the stream processing primitives without the overhead of a processing cluster. We also need better integration with Kafka, especially when it comes to working with intermediate representations of data outside of the source and sink topics.

Fortunately for us, the Kafka community recognized the need for a stream processing API in the Kafka ecosystem and decided to build it.[5]

Enter Kafka Streams

In 2016, the Kafka ecosystem was forever changed when the first version of Kafka Streams (also called the *Streams API*) was released. With its inception, the landscape of stream processing applications that relied so heavily on hand-rolled features gave way to more advanced applications, which leveraged community-developed patterns and abstractions for transforming and processing real-time event streams.

---

2 Jay Kreps, one of the original authors of Apache Kafka, discussed this in detail in an O'Reilly blog post back in 2014 (*https://oreil.ly/vzRH-*).

3 This includes aggregated streams/tables, which we'll discuss later in this chapter.

4 We have an entire chapter dedicated to time, but also see Matthias J. Sax's great presentation on the subject from Kafka Summit 2019 (*https://oreil.ly/wr123*).

5 Guozhang Wang, who has played a key role in the development of Kafka Streams, deserves much of the recognition for submitting the original KIP for what would later become Kafka Streams. See *https://oreil.ly/l2wbc*.

Unlike the Producer, Consumer, and Connect APIs, Kafka Streams is dedicated to helping you *process* real-time data streams, not just *move* data to and from Kafka.[6] It makes it easy to consume real-time streams of events as they move through our data pipeline, apply data transformation logic using a rich set of stream processing operators and primitives, and optionally write new representations of the data back to Kafka (i.e., if we want to make the transformed or enriched events available to downstream systems).

Figure 2-1 depicts the previously discussed APIs in the Kafka ecosystem, with Kafka Streams operating at the stream processing layer.

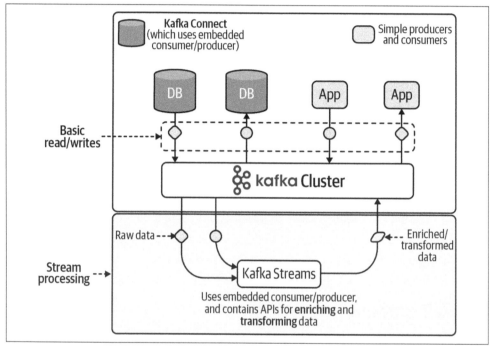

Figure 2-1. Kafka Streams is the "brain" of the Kafka ecosystem, consuming records from the event stream, processing the data, and optionally writing enriched or transformed records back to Kafka

As you can see from the diagram in Figure 2-1, Kafka Streams operates at an exciting layer of the Kafka ecosystem: the place where data from many sources converges. This is the layer where sophisticated data *enrichment*, *transformation*, and *processing* can happen. It's the same place where, in a pre–Kafka Streams world, we would have

---

6 Kafka Connect veered a little into event processing territory by adding support for something called *single message transforms*, but this is extremely limited compared to what Kafka Streams can do.

---

tediously written our own stream processing abstractions (using the Consumer/Producer API approach) or absorbed a complexity hit by using another framework. Now, let's get a first look at the features of Kafka Streams that allow us to operate at this layer in a fun and efficient way.

Features at a Glance

Kafka Streams offers many features that make it an excellent choice for modern stream processing applications. We'll be going over these in detail in the following chapters, but here are just a few of the features you can look forward to:

- A high-level DSL that looks and feels like Java's streaming API. The DSL provides a fluent and functional approach to processing data streams that is easy to learn and use.
- A low-level Processor API that gives developers fine-grained control when they need it.
- Convenient abstractions for modeling data as either streams or tables.
- The ability to join streams and tables, which is useful for data transformation and enrichment.
- Operators and utilities for building both stateless and stateful stream processing applications.
- Support for time-based operations, including windowing and periodic functions.
- Easy installation. It's just a library, so you can add Kafka Streams to any Java application.[7]
- Scalability, reliability, maintainability.

As you begin exploring these features in this book, you will quickly see why this library is so widely used and loved. Both the high-level DSL and low-level Processor API are not only easy to learn, but are also extremely powerful. Advanced stream processing tasks (such as joining live, moving streams of data) can be accomplished with very little code, which makes the development experience truly enjoyable.

Now, the last bullet point pertains to the long-term stability of our stream processing applications. After all, many technologies are exciting to learn in the beginning, but what really counts is whether or not Kafka Streams will continue to be a good choice as our relationship gets more complicated through real-world, long-term usage of this library. Therefore, it makes sense to evaluate the long-term viability of Kafka

---

7 Kafka Streams will work with other JVM-based languages as well, including Scala and Kotlin. However, we exclusively use Java in this book.

Streams before getting too far down the rabbit hole. So how should we go about doing this? Let's start by looking at Kafka Streams' operational characteristics.

Operational Characteristics

In Martin Kleppmann's excellent book, *Designing Data-Intensive Applications* (O'Reilly), the author highlights three important goals for data systems:

- Scalability
- Reliability
- Maintainability

These goals provide a useful framework for evaluating Kafka Streams, so in this section, we will define these terms and discover how Kafka Streams achieves each of them.

Scalability

Systems are considered *scalable* when they can cope and remain performant as load increases. In Chapter 1, we learned that scaling Kafka topics involves adding more partitions and, when needed, more Kafka brokers (the latter is only needed if the topic grows beyond the existing capacity of your Kafka cluster).

Similarly, in Kafka Streams, the unit of work is a single topic-partition, and Kafka automatically distributes work to groups of cooperating consumers called consumer groups.[8] This has two important implications:

- Since the unit of work in Kafka Streams is a single topic-partition, and since topics can be expanded by adding more partitions, the amount of work a Kafka Streams application can undertake can be scaled by increasing the number of partitions on the source topics.[9]
- By leveraging consumer groups, the total amount of work being handled by a Kafka Streams application can be distributed across multiple, cooperating instances of your application.

---

8 Multiple consumer groups can consume from a single topic, and each consumer group processes messages independently of other consumer groups.

9 While partitions can be added to an existing topic, the recommended pattern is to create a new source topic with the desired number of partitions, and to migrate all of the existing workloads to the new topic.

A quick note about the second point. When you deploy a Kafka Streams application, you will almost always deploy multiple application instances, each handling a subset of the work (e.g., if your source topic has 32 partitions, then you have 32 units of work that can be distributed across all cooperating consumers). For example, you could deploy four application instances, each handling eight partitions (4 * 8 = 32), or you could just as easily deploy sixteen instances of your application, each handling two partitions (16 * 2 = 32).

However, regardless of how many application instances you end up deploying, Kafka Streams' ability to cope with increased load by adding more partitions (units of work) and application instances (workers) makes Kafka Streams *scalable*.

On a similar note, Kafka Streams is also *elastic*, allowing you to seamlessly (albeit manually) scale the number of application instances in or out, with a limit on the scale-out path being the number of tasks that are created for your topology. We'll discuss tasks in more detail in "Tasks and Stream Threads" on page 41.

Reliability

Reliability is an important feature of data systems, not only from an engineering perspective (we don't want to be woken up at 3 a.m. due to some fault in the system), but also from our customers' perspective (we don't want the system to go offline in any noticeable way, and we certainly can't tolerate data loss or corruption). Kafka Streams comes with a few fault-tolerant features,[10] but the most obvious one is something we've already touched on in "Consumer Groups" on page 13: automatic failovers and partition rebalancing via consumer groups.

If you deploy multiple instances of your Kafka Streams application and one goes offline due to some fault in the system (e.g., a hardware failure), then Kafka will automatically redistribute the load to the other healthy instances. When the failure is resolved (or, in more modern architectures that leverage an orchestration system like Kubernetes, when the application is moved to a healthy node), then Kafka will rebalance the work again. This ability to gracefully handle faults makes Kafka Streams *reliable*.

---

10 Including some features that are specific to *stateful applications*, which we will discuss in Chapter 4.

Maintainability

> It is well known that the majority of the cost of software is not in its initial development, but in its ongoing maintenance—fixing bugs, keeping its systems operational, investigating failures…
>
> —Martin Kleppmann

Since Kafka Streams is a Java library, troubleshooting and fixing bugs is relatively straightforward since we're working with standalone applications, and patterns for both troubleshooting and monitoring Java applications are well established and may already be in use at your organization (collecting and analyzing application logs, capturing application and JVM metrics, profiling and tracing, etc.).

Furthermore, since the Kafka Streams API is succinct and intuitive, code-level maintenance is less time-consuming than one would expect with more complicated libraries, and is very easy to understand for beginners and experts alike. If you build a Kafka Streams application and then don't touch it for months, you likely won't suffer the usual project amnesia and require a lot of ramp-up time to understand the previous code you've written. For the same reasons, new project maintainers can typically get up to speed pretty quickly with a Kafka Streams application, which improves maintainability even further.

Comparison to Other Systems

By this point, you should be starting to feel comfortable about starting a long-term relationship with Kafka Streams. But before things get too serious, isn't it natural to see if there are other fish in the sea?

Actually, it is sometimes difficult to evaluate how good a technology is without knowing how it stacks up against its competitors. So let's take a look at how Kafka Streams compares to some other popular technologies in the stream processing space.[11] We'll start by comparing Kafka Streams' deployment model with other popular systems.

Deployment Model

Kafka Streams takes a different approach to stream processing than technologies like Apache Flink and Apache Spark Streaming. The latter systems require you to set up a dedicated processing cluster for submitting and running your stream processing program. This can introduce a lot of complexity and overhead. Even experienced engineers at well-established companies have conceded that the overhead of a processing

---

[11] The ever-growing nature of the stream processing space makes it difficult to compare every solution to Kafka Streams, so we have decided to focus on the most popular and mature stream processing solutions available at the time of this writing.

cluster is nontrivial. In an interview with Nitin Sharma at Netflix, I learned that it took around six months to adapt to the nuances of Apache Flink and build a highly reliable production Apache Flink application and cluster.

On the other hand, Kafka Streams is implemented as a Java *library*, so getting started is much easier since you don't need to worry about a cluster manager; you simply need to add the Kafka Streams dependency to your Java application. Being able to build a stream processing application as a standalone program also means you have a lot of freedom in terms of how you monitor, package, and deploy your code. For example, at Mailchimp, our Kafka Streams applications are deployed using the same patterns and tooling we use for other internal Java applications. This ability to immediately integrate into your company's systems is a huge advantage for Kafka Streams.

Next, let's explore how Kafka Streams' processing model compares to other systems in this space.

Processing Model

Another key differentiator between Kafka Streams and systems like Apache Spark Streaming or Trident is that Kafka Streams implements *event-at-a-time processing*, so events are processed immediately, one at a time, as they come in. This is considered true streaming and provides lower latency than the alternative approach, which is called *micro-batching*. Micro-batching involves grouping records into small groups (or *batches*), which are buffered in memory and later emitted at some interval (e.g., every 500 milliseconds). Figure 2-2 depicts the difference between event-at-a-time and micro-batch processing.

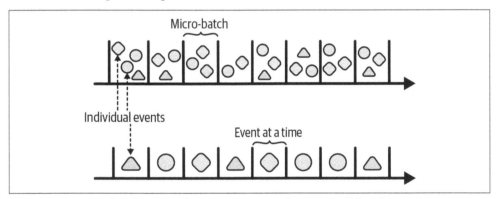

Figure 2-2. Micro-batching involves grouping records into small batches and emitting them to downstream processors at a fixed interval; event-at-a-time processing allows each event to be processed at soon as it comes in, instead of waiting for a batch to materialize

Frameworks that use micro-batching are often optimized for greater *throughput* at the cost of higher *latency*. In Kafka Streams, you can achieve extremely low latency while also maintaining high throughput by splitting data across many partitions.

Finally, let's take a look at Kafka Streams' data processing architecture, and see how its focus on streaming differs from other systems.

Kappa Architecture

Another important consideration when comparing Kafka Streams to other solutions is whether or not your use case requires support for both batch and stream processing. At the time of this writing, Kafka Streams focuses solely on streaming use cases[12] (this is called a *Kappa architecture*), while frameworks like Apache Flink and Apache Spark support both batch and stream processing (this is called a *Lambda architecture*). However, architectures that support both batch and streaming use cases aren't without their drawbacks. Jay Kreps discussed some of the disadvantages of a hybrid system (*https://oreil.ly/RwkNi*) nearly two years before Kafka Streams was introduced into the Kafka ecosystem:

> The operational burden of running and debugging two systems is going to be very high. And any new abstraction can only provide the features supported by the intersection of the two systems.

These challenges didn't stop projects like Apache Beam, which defines a unified programming model for batch and stream processing, from gaining popularity in recent years. But Apache Beam isn't comparable to Kafka Streams in the same way that Apache Flink is. Instead, Apache Beam is an API layer that relies on an execution engine to do most of the work. For example, both Apache Flink and Apache Spark can be used as execution engines (often referred to as *runners*) in Apache Beam. So when you compare Kafka Streams to Apache Beam, you must also consider the execution engine that you plan on using in addition to the Beam API itself.

Furthermore, Apache Beam–driven pipelines lack some important features that are offered in Kafka Streams. Robert Yokota, who created an experimental Kafka Streams Beam Runner (*https://oreil.ly/h0Hdz*) and who maintains several innovative projects in the Kafka ecosystem,[13] puts it this way in his comparison of different streaming frameworks (*https://oreil.ly/24zG9*):

---

12 Although there is an open, albeit dated, proposal to support batch processing in Kafka Streams (*https://oreil.ly/v3DbO*).

13 Including a Kafka-backed relational database called KarelDB, a graph analytics library built on Kafka Streams, and more. See *https://yokota.blog*.

One way to state the differences between the two systems is as follows:

- Kafka Streams is a *stream-relational* processing platform.
- Apache Beam is a *stream-only* processing platform.

A stream-relational processing platform has the following capabilities which are typically missing in a stream-only processing platform:

- Relations (or tables) are first-class citizens, i.e., each has an independent identity.
- Relations can be transformed into other relations.
- Relations can be queried in an ad-hoc manner.

We will demonstrate each of the bulleted features over the next several chapters, but for now, suffice it to say that many of Kafka Streams' most powerful features (including the ability to query the state of a stream) are not available in Apache Beam or other more generalized frameworks.[14] Furthermore, the Kappa architecture offers a simpler and more specialized approach for working with streams of data, which can improve the development experience and simplify the operation and maintenance of your software. So if your use case doesn't require batch processing, then hybrid systems will introduce unnecessary complexity.

Now that we've looked at the competition, let's look at some Kafka Streams use cases.

Use Cases

Kafka Streams is optimized for processing unbounded datasets quickly and efficiently, and is therefore a great solution for problems in low-latency, time-critical domains. A few example use cases include:

- Financial data processing (Flipkart (*https://oreil.ly/dAcbY*)), purchase monitoring, fraud detection
- Algorithmic trading
- Stock market/crypto exchange monitoring
- Real-time inventory tracking and replenishment (Walmart (*https://oreil.ly/VoF76*))

---

14 At the time of this writing, Apache Flink had recently released a beta version of queryable state, though the API itself was less mature and came with the following warning in the official Flink documentation: "The client APIs for queryable state are currently in an evolving state and there are no guarantees made about stability of the provided interfaces. It is likely that there will be breaking API changes on the client side in the upcoming Flink versions." Therefore, while the Apache Flink team is working to close this gap, Kafka Streams still has the more mature and production-ready API for querying state.

- Event booking, seat selection (Ticketmaster (*https://oreil.ly/V4t1h*))
- Email delivery tracking and monitoring (Mailchimp)
- Video game telemetry processing (Activision, the publisher of *Call of Duty* (*https://oreil.ly/Skan3*))
- Search indexing (Yelp (*https://oreil.ly/IhCnC*))
- Geospatial tracking/calculations (e.g., distance comparison, arrival projections)
- Smart Home/IoT sensor processing (sometimes called AIOT, or the Artificial Intelligence of Things)
- Change data capture (Redhat (*https://oreil.ly/INs3z*))
- Sports broadcasting/real-time widgets (Gracenote (*https://oreil.ly/YeX33*))
- Real-time ad platforms (Pinterest (*https://oreil.ly/cBgSG*))
- Predictive healthcare, vitals monitoring (Children's Healthcare of Atlanta (*https://oreil.ly/4MYLc*))
- Chat infrastructure (Slack (*https://oreil.ly/_n7sZ*)), chat bots, virtual assistants
- Machine learning pipelines (Twitter (*https://oreil.ly/RuPPV*)) and platforms (Kafka Graphs (*https://oreil.ly/8IHKT*))

The list goes on and on, but the common characteristic across all of these examples is that they require (or at least benefit from) *real-time decision making* or data processing. The spectrum of these use cases, and others you will encounter in the wild, is really quite fascinating. On one end of the spectrum, you may be processing streams at the hobbyist level by analyzing sensor output from a Smart Home device. However, you could also use Kafka Streams in a healthcare setting to monitor and react to changes in a trauma victim's condition, as Children's Healthcare of Atlanta has done.

Kafka Streams is also a great choice for building microservices on top of real-time event streams. It not only simplifies typical stream processing operations (filtering, joining, windowing, and transforming data), but as you will see in "Interactive Queries" on page 129, it is also capable of exposing the state of a stream using a feature called *interactive queries*. The state of a stream could be an aggregation of some kind (e.g., the total number of views for each video in a streaming platform) or even the latest representation for a rapidly changing entity in your event stream (e.g., the latest stock price for a given stock symbol).

Now that you have some idea of who is using Kafka Streams and what kinds of use cases it is well suited for, let's take a quick look at Kafka Streams' architecture before we start writing any code.

Processor Topologies

Kafka Streams leverages a programming paradigm called *dataflow programming* (DFP), which is a data-centric method of representing programs as a series of inputs, outputs, and processing stages. This leads to a very natural and intuitive way of creating stream processing programs and is one of the many reasons I think Kafka Streams is easy to pick up for beginners.

 This section will dive a little deeper into Kafka Streams architecture. If you prefer to get your feet wet with Kafka Streams and revisit this section later, feel free to proceed to "Introducing Our Tutorial: Hello, Streams" on page 45.

Instead of building a program as a sequence of steps, the stream processing logic in a Kafka Streams application is structured as a directed acyclic graph (DAG). Figure 2-3 shows an example DAG that depicts how data flows through a set of stream processors. The nodes (the rectangles in the diagram) represent a processing step, or processor, and the edges (the lines connecting the nodes in the diagram) represent input and output streams (where data flows from one processor to another).

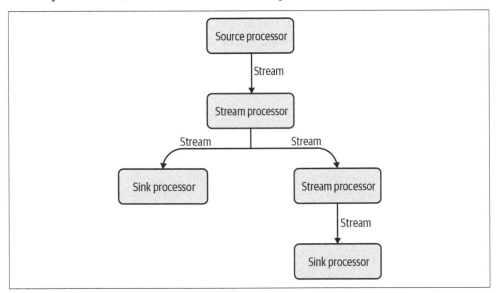

Figure 2-3. Kafka Streams borrows some of its design from dataflow programming, and structures stream processing programs as a graph of processors through which data flows

There are three basic kinds of processors in Kafka Streams:

Source processors
> Sources are where information flows into the Kafka Streams application. Data is read from a Kafka topic and sent to one or more *stream processors*.

Stream processors
> These processors are responsible for applying data processing/transformation logic on the input stream. In the high-level DSL, these processors are defined using a set of built-in *operators* that are exposed by the Kafka Streams library, which we will be going over in detail in the following chapters. Some example operators are `filter`, `map`, `flatMap`, and `join`.

Sink processors
> Sinks are where enriched, transformed, filtered, or otherwise processed records are written *back* to Kafka, either to be handled by another stream processing application or to be sent to a downstream data store via something like Kafka Connect. Like source processors, sink processors are connected to a Kafka topic.

A collection of processors forms a *processor topology*, which is often referred to as simply *the topology* in both this book and the wider Kafka Streams community. As we go through each tutorial in this part of the book, we will first design the topology by creating a DAG that connects the source, stream, and sink processors. Then, we will simply implement the topology by writing some Java code. To demonstrate this, let's go through the exercise of translating some project requirements into a processor topology (represented by a DAG). This will help you learn how to *think* like a Kafka Streams developer.

Scenario

Say we are building a chatbot with Kafka Streams, and we have a topic named `slack-mentions` that contains every Slack message that mentions our bot, `@StreamsBot`. We will design our bot so that it expects each mention to be followed by a command, like `@StreamsBot restart myservice`.

We want to implement a basic processor topology that does some preprocessing/validation of these Slack messages. First, we need to consume each message in the source topic, determine if the command is valid, and if so, write the Slack message to a topic called `valid-mentions`. If the command is not valid (e.g., someone makes a spelling error when mentioning our bot, such as `@StreamsBot restart serverrr`), then we will write to a topic named `invalid-mentions`).

In this case, we would translate these requirements to the topology shown in Figure 2-4.

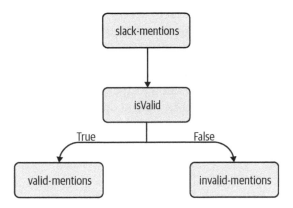

Figure 2-4. An example processor topology that contains a single source processor for reading Slack messages from Kafka (`slack-mentions`), a single stream processor that checks the validity of each message (`isValid`), and two sink processors that route the message to one of two output topics based on the previous check (`valid-mentions`, `invalid-mentions`)

Starting with the tutorial in the next chapter, we will then begin to implement any topology we design using the Kafka Streams API. But first, let's take a look at a related concept: sub-topologies.

Sub-Topologies

Kafka Streams also has the notion of sub-topologies. In the previous example, we designed a processor topology that consumes events from a single source topic (`slack-mentions`) and performs some preprocessing on a stream of raw chat messages. However, if our application needs to consume from multiple source topics, then Kafka Streams will (under most circumstances[15]) divide our topology into smaller sub-topologies to parallelize the work even further. This division of work is possible since operations on one input stream can be executed independently of operations on another input stream.

For example, let's keep building our chatbot by adding two new stream processors: one that consumes from the `valid-mentions` topic and performs whatever command

---

15 The exception to this is when topics are joined. In this case, a single topology will read from each source topic involved in the join without further dividing the step into sub-topologies. This is required for the join to work. See "Co-Partitioning" on page 114 for more information.

was issued to `StreamsBot` (e.g., `restart server`), and another processor that consumes from the `invalid-mentions` topic and posts an error response back to Slack.[16]

As you can see in Figure 2-5, our topology now has three Kafka topics it reads from: `slack-mentions`, `valid-mentions`, and `invalid-mentions`. Each time we read from a new source topic, Kafka Streams divides the topology into smaller sections that it can execute independently. In this example, we end up with three sub-topologies for our chatbot application, each denoted by a star in the figure.

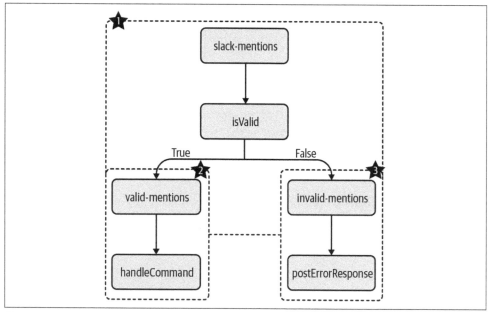

Figure 2-5. A processor topology, subdivided into sub-topologies (demarcated by dotted lines)

Notice that both the `valid-mentions` and `invalid-mentions` topics serve as a sink processor in the first sub-topology, but as a source processor in the second and third sub-topologies. When this occurs, there is no direct data exchange between sub-topologies. Records are produced to Kafka in the sink processor, and reread from Kafka by the source processors.

---

16 In this example, we write to two intermediate topics (`valid-mentions` and `invalid-mentions`) and then immediately consume data from each. Using intermediate topics like this is usually only required for certain operations (for example, repartitioning data). We do it here for discussion purposes only.

Now that we understand how to represent a stream processing program as a processor topology, let's take a look at how data actually flows through the interconnected processors in a Kafka Streams application.

Depth-First Processing

Kafka Streams uses a depth-first strategy when processing data. When a new record is received, it is routed through each stream processor in the topology before another record is processed. The flow of data through Kafka Streams looks something like what's shown in Figure 2-6.

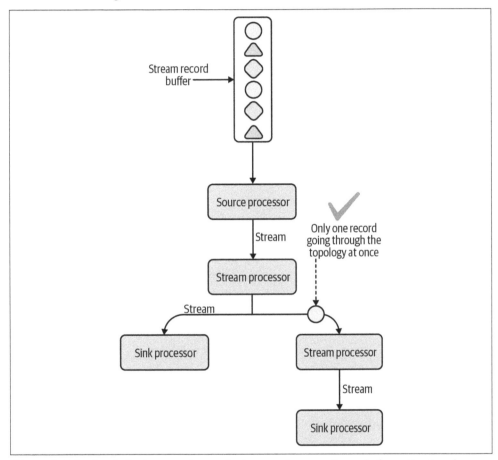

Figure 2-6. In depth-first processing, a single record moves through the entire topology before another record is processed

This depth-first strategy makes the dataflow much easier to reason about, but also means that slow stream processing operations can block other records from being processed in the same thread. Figure 2-7 demonstrates something you will never see happen in Kafka Streams: multiple records going through a topology at once.

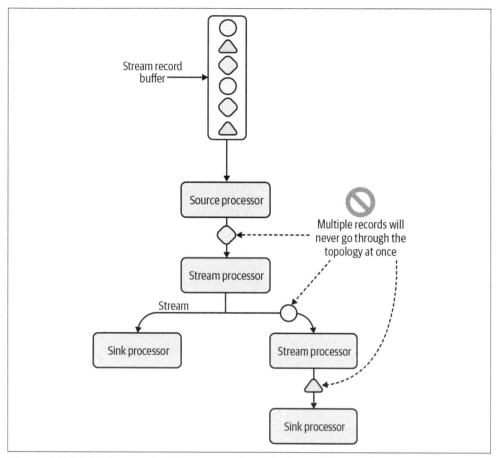

Figure 2-7. Multiple records will never go through the topology at the same time

 When multiple sub-topologies are in play, the single-event rule does not apply to the entire topology, but to each sub-topology.

Now that we know how to design processor topologies and how data flows through them, let's take a look at the advantages of this data-centric approach to building stream processing applications.

Benefits of Dataflow Programming

There are several advantages of using Kafka Streams and the dataflow programming model for building stream processing applications. First, representing the program as a directed graph makes it easy to reason about. You don't need to follow a bunch of conditionals and control logic to figure out how data is flowing through your application. Simply find the source and sink processors to determine where data enters and exits your program, and look at the stream processors in between to discover how the data is being processed, transformed, and enriched along the way.

Furthermore, expressing our stream processing program as a directed graph allows us to standardize the way we frame real-time data processing problems and, subsequently, the way we build our streaming solutions. A Kafka Streams application that I write will have some level of familiarity to anyone who has worked with Kafka Streams before in their own projects—not only due to the reusable abstractions available in the library itself, but also thanks to a common problem-solving approach: defining the flow of data using operators (nodes) and streams (edges). Again, this makes Kafka Streams applications easy to reason about and maintain.

Directed graphs are also an intuitive way of visualizing the flow of data for nontechnical stakeholders. There is often a disconnect about how a program works between engineering teams and nonengineering teams. Sometimes, this leads to nontechnical teams treating the software as a closed box. This can have dangerous side effects, especially in the age of data privacy laws and GDPR compliance, which requires close coordination between engineers, legal teams, and other stakeholders. Thus, being able to simply communicate how data is being processed in your application allows people who are focused on another aspect of a business problem to understand or even contribute to the design of your application.

Finally, the processor topology, which contains the source, sink, and stream processors, acts as a *template* that can be instantiated and parallelized very easily across multiple threads and application instances. Therefore, defining the dataflow in this way allows us to realize performance and scalability benefits since we can easily replicate our stream processing program when data volume demands it.

Now, to understand how this process of replicating topologies works, we first need to understand the relationship between tasks, stream threads, and partitions.

Tasks and Stream Threads

When we define a topology in Kafka Streams, we are not actually executing the program. Instead, we are building a template for how data should flow through our application. This template (our topology) can be instantiated multiple times in a single application instance, and parallelized across many *tasks* and *stream threads* (which we'll refer to as simply threads going forward.[17]) There is a close relationship between the number of tasks/threads and the amount of work your stream processing application can handle, so understanding the content in this section is especially important for achieving good performance with Kafka Streams.

Let's start by looking at tasks:

> A task is the smallest unit of work that can be performed in parallel in a Kafka Streams application…
>
> Slightly simplified, the maximum parallelism at which your application may run is bounded by the maximum number of stream tasks, which itself is determined by the maximum number of partitions of the input topic(s) the application is reading from.
>
> —Andy Bryant

Translating this quote into a formula, we can calculate the number of tasks that can be created for a given Kafka Streams sub-topology[18] with the following math:

```
max(source_topic_1_partitions, ... source_topic_n_partitions)
```

For example, if your topology reads from one source topic that contains 16 partitions, then Kafka Streams will create 16 tasks, each of which will instantiate its own copy of the underlying processor topology. Once Kafka Streams has created all of the tasks, it will assign the source partitions to be read from to each task.

As you can see, tasks are just logical units that are used to instantiate and run a processor topology. *Threads*, on the other hand, are what actually execute the task. In Kafka Streams, the stream threads are designed to be isolated and thread-safe.[19] Furthermore, unlike tasks, there isn't any formula that Kafka Streams applies to figure out how many threads your application should run. Instead, you are responsible for specifying the thread count using a configuration property named `num.stream.threads`. The upper bound for the number of threads you can utilize corresponds to the task count, and there are different strategies for deciding on the number of stream threads you should run with.[20]

---

17 A Java application may execute many different types of threads. Our discussion will simply focus on the stream threads that are created and managed by the Kafka Streams library for running a processor topology.

18 Remember, a Kafka Streams topology can be composed of multiple sub-topologies, so to get the number of tasks for the entire program, you should sum the task count across all sub-topologies.

19 This doesn't mean a poorly implemented stream processor is immune from concurrency issues. However, by default, the stream threads do not share any state.

20 For example, the number of cores that your application has access to could inform the number of threads you decide to run with. If your application instance is running on a 4-core machine and your topology supports 16 tasks, you may want to configure the thread count to 4, which will give you a thread for each core. On the other hand, if your 16-task application was running on a 48-core machine, you may want to run with 16 threads (you wouldn't run with 48 since the upper bound is the task count, or in this case: 16).

Now, let's improve our understanding of these concepts by visualizing how tasks and threads are created using two separate configs, each specifying a different number of threads. In each example, our Kafka Streams application is reading from a source topic that contains four partitions (denoted by p1 - p4 in Figure 2-8).

First, let's configure our application to run with two threads (num.stream.threads = 2). Since our source topic has four partitions, four tasks will be created and distributed across each thread. We end up with the task/thread layout depicted in Figure 2-8.

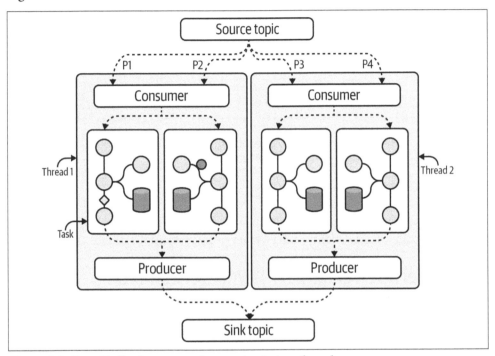

Figure 2-8. Four Kafka Streams tasks running in two threads

Running more than one task per thread is perfectly fine, but sometimes it is often desirable to run with a higher thread count to take full advantage of the available CPU resources. Increasing the number of threads doesn't change the number of tasks, but it does change the distribution of tasks among threads. For example, if we reconfigure the same Kafka Streams application to run with four threads instead of two (num.stream.threads = 4), we end up with the task/thread layout depicted in Figure 2-9.

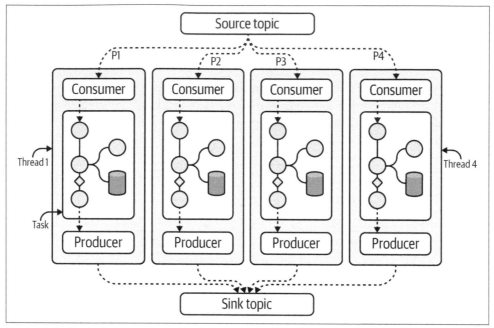

Figure 2-9. Four Kafka Streams tasks running in four threads

Now that we've learned about Kafka Streams' architecture, let's take a look at the APIs that Kafka Streams exposes for creating stream processing applications.

High-Level DSL Versus Low-Level Processor API

> Different solutions present themselves at different layers of abstraction.
>
> —James Clear[21]

A common notion in the software engineering field is that abstraction usually comes at a cost: the more you abstract the details away, the more the software feels like "magic," and the more control you give up. As you get started with Kafka Streams, you may wonder what kind of control you will be giving up by choosing to implement a stream processing application using a high-level library instead of designing your solution using the lower-level Consumer/Producer APIs directly.

Luckily for us, Kafka Streams allows developers to choose the abstraction level that works best for them, depending on the project and also the experience and preference of the developer.

---

21 From *First Principles: Elon Musk on the Power of Thinking for Yourself* (*https://oreil.ly/Ry4nI*).

The two APIs you can choose from are:

- The high-level DSL
- The low-level Processor API

The relative abstraction level for both the high-level DSL and low-level Processor API is shown in Figure 2-10.

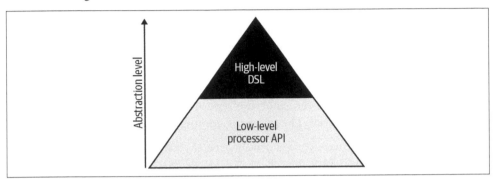

Figure 2-10. Abstraction levels of Kafka Streams APIs

The high-level DSL is built on top of the Processor API, but the interface each exposes is slightly different. If you would like to build your stream processing application using a functional style of programming, and would also like to leverage some higher-level abstractions for working with your data (streams and tables), then the DSL is for you.

On the other hand, if you need lower-level access to your data (e.g., access to record metadata), the ability to schedule periodic functions, more granular access to your application state, or more fine-grained control over the timing of certain operations, then the Processor API is a better choice. In the following tutorial, you will see examples of both the DSL and Processor API. In subsequent chapters, we will explore both the DSL and Processor API in further detail.

Now, the best way to see the difference between these two abstraction levels is with a code example. Let's move on to our first Kafka Streams tutorial: Hello Streams.

Introducing Our Tutorial: Hello, Streams

In this section, we will get our first hands-on experience with Kafka Streams. This is a variation of the "Hello, world" tutorial that has become the standard when learning new programming languages and libraries. There are two implementations of this tutorial: the first uses the high-level DSL, while the second uses the low-level Processor API. Both programs are functionally equivalent, and will print a simple greeting whenever they receive a message from the users topic in Kafka (e.g., upon receiving the message Mitch, each application will print Hello, Mitch).

Before we get started, let's take a look at how to set up the project.

Project Setup

All of the tutorials in this book will require a running Kafka cluster, and the source code for each chapter will include a *docker-compose.yml* file that will allow you to run a development cluster using Docker. Since Kafka Streams applications are meant to run outside of a Kafka cluster (e.g., on different machines than the brokers), it's best to view the Kafka cluster as a separate infrastructure piece that is required but distinct from your Kafka Streams application.

To start running the Kafka cluster, clone the repository and change to the directory containing this chapter's tutorial. The following commands will do the trick:

```
$ git clone git@github.com:mitch-seymour/mastering-kafka-streams-and-ksqldb.git
$ cd mastering-kafka-streams-and-ksqldb/chapter-02/hello-streams
```

Then, start the Kafka cluster by running:

```
docker-compose up
```

The broker will be listening on port 29092.[22] Furthermore, the preceding command will start a container that will precreate the users topic needed for this tutorial. Now, with our Kafka cluster running, we can start building our Kafka Streams application.

Creating a New Project

In this book, we will use a build tool called Gradle[23] to compile and run our Kafka Streams applications. Other build tools (e.g., Maven) are also supported, but we have chosen Gradle due to the improved readability of its build files.

In addition to being able to compile and run your code, Gradle can also be used to quickly bootstrap new Kafka Streams applications that you build outside of this book. This can be accomplished by creating a directory for your project to live in and then by running the gradle init command from within that directory. An example of this workflow is as follows:

```
$ mkdir my-project && cd my-project

$ gradle init \
```

---

22 If you want to verify and have telnet installed, you can run echo 'exit' | telnet localhost 29092. If the port is open, you should see "Connected to localhost" in the output.

23 Instructions for installing Gradle can be found at *https://gradle.org*. We used version 6.6.1 for the tutorials in this book.

```
--type java-application \
--dsl groovy \
--test-framework junit-jupiter \
--project-name my-project \
--package com.example
```

The source code for this book already contains the initialized project structure for each tutorial, so it's not necessary to run `gradle init` unless you are starting a new project for yourself. We simply mention it here with the assumption that you will be writing your own Kafka Streams applications at some point, and want a quick way to bootstrap your next project.

Here is the basic project structure for a Kafka Streams application:

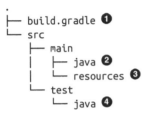

❶ This is the project's build file. It will specify all of the dependencies (including the Kafka Streams library) needed by our application.

❷ We will save our source code and topology definitions in *src/main/java*.

❸ *src/main/resources* is typically used for storing configuration files.

❹ Our unit and topology tests, which we will discuss in "Testing Kafka Streams" on page 352, will live in *src/test/java*.

Now that we've learned how to bootstrap new Kafka Streams projects and have had an initial look at the project structure, let's take a look at how to add Kafka Streams to our project.

Adding the Kafka Streams Dependency

To start working with Kafka Streams, we simply need to add the Kafka Streams library as a dependency in our build file. (In Gradle projects, our build file is called *build.gradle*.) An example build file is shown here:

```
plugins {
    id 'java'
    id 'application'
}

repositories {
```

```
        jcenter()
    }

    dependencies {
        implementation 'org.apache.kafka:kafka-streams:2.7.0' ❶
    }

    task runDSL(type: JavaExec) { ❷
        main = 'com.example.DslExample'
        classpath sourceSets.main.runtimeClasspath
    }

    task runProcessorAPI(type: JavaExec) { ❸
        main = 'com.example.ProcessorApiExample'
        classpath sourceSets.main.runtimeClasspath
    }
```

❶ Add the Kafka Streams dependency to our project.

❷ This tutorial is unique among others in this book since we will be creating two different versions of our topology. This line adds a Gradle task to execute the DSL version of our application.

❸ Similarly, this line adds a Gradle task to execute the Processor API version of our application.

Now, to build our project (which will actually pull the dependency from the remote repository into our project), we can run the following command:

```
./gradlew build
```

That's it! Kafka Streams is installed and ready to use. Now, let's continue with the tutorial.

DSL

The DSL example is exceptionally simple. We first need to use a Kafka Streams class called StreamsBuilder to build our processor topology:

```
StreamsBuilder builder = new StreamsBuilder();
```

Next, as we learned in "Processor Topologies" on page 35, we need to add a source processor in order to read data from a Kafka topic (in this case, our topic will be called users). There are a few different methods we could use here depending on how we decide to model our data (we will discuss different approaches in "Streams and Tables" on page 53), but for now, let's model our data as a stream. The following line adds the source processor:

```
KStream<Void, String> stream = builder.stream("users");❶
```

❶ We'll discuss this more in the next chapter, but the generics in KStream<Void, String> refer to the key and value types. In this case, the key is empty (Void) and the value is a String type.

Now, it's time to add a stream processor. Since we're just printing a simple greeting for each message, we can use the foreach operator with a simple lambda like so:

```
stream.foreach(
    (key, value) -> {
        System.out.println("(DSL) Hello, " + value);
    });
```

Finally, it's time to build our topology and start running our stream processing application:

```
KafkaStreams streams = new KafkaStreams(builder.build(), config);
streams.start();
```

The full code, including some boilerplate needed to run the program, is shown in Example 2-1.

Example 2-1. Hello, world—DSL example

```
class DslExample {

    public static void main(String[] args) {
        StreamsBuilder builder = new StreamsBuilder(); ❶

        KStream<Void, String> stream = builder.stream("users"); ❷

        stream.foreach( ❸
            (key, value) -> {
                System.out.println("(DSL) Hello, " + value);
            });

        // omitted for brevity
        Properties config = ...; ❹

        KafkaStreams streams = new KafkaStreams(builder.build(), config); ❺
        streams.start();

        // close Kafka Streams when the JVM shuts down (e.g., SIGTERM)
        Runtime.getRuntime().addShutdownHook(new Thread(streams::close)); ❻
    }
}
```

❶ The builder is used to construct the topology.

❷ Add a source processor that reads from the users topic.

❸ Use the DSL's `foreach` operator to print a simple message. The DSL includes many operators that we will be exploring in upcoming chapters.

❹ We have omitted the Kafka Streams configuration for brevity, but will discuss this in upcoming chapters. Among other things, this configuration allows us to specify which Kafka cluster our application should read from and what consumer group this application belongs to.

❺ Build the topology and start streaming.

❻ Close Kafka Streams when the JVM shuts down.

To run the application, simply execute the following command:

```
./gradlew runDSL --info
```

Now your Kafka Streams application is running and listening for incoming data. As you may recall from "Hello, Kafka" on page 16, we can produce some data to our Kafka cluster using the `kafka-console-producer` console script. To do this, run the following commands:

```
docker-compose exec kafka bash ❶

kafka-console-producer \ ❷
    --bootstrap-server localhost:9092 \
    --topic users
```

❶ The console scripts are available in the `kafka` container, which is running the broker in our development cluster. You can also download these scripts as part of the official Kafka distribution.

❷ Start a local producer that will write data to the `users` topic.

Once you are in the producer prompt, create one or more records by typing the name of the user, followed by the Enter key. When you are finished, press Control-C on your keyboard to exit the prompt:

```
>angie
>guy
>kate
>mark
```

Your Kafka Streams application should emit the following greetings:

```
(DSL) Hello, angie
(DSL) Hello, guy
(DSL) Hello, kate
(DSL) Hello, mark
```

We have now verified that our application is working as expected. We will explore some more interesting use cases over the next several chapters, but this process of defining a topology and running our application is a foundation we can build upon. Next, let's look at how to create the same Kafka Streams topology with the lower-level Processor API.

Processor API

The Processor API lacks some of the abstractions available in the high-level DSL, and its syntax is more of a direct reminder that we're building processor topologies, with methods like `Topology.addSource`, `Topology.addProcessor`, and `Topology.addSink` (the latter of which is not used in this example). The first step in using the processor topology is to instantiate a new `Topology` instance, like so:

```
Topology topology = new Topology();
```

Next, we will create a source processor to read data from the `users` topic, and a stream processor to print a simple greeting. The stream processor references a class called `SayHelloProcessor` that we'll implement shortly:

```
topology.addSource("UserSource", "users"); ❶
topology.addProcessor("SayHello", SayHelloProcessor::new, "UserSource"); ❷
```

❶ The first argument for the `addSource` method is an arbitrary name for this stream processor. In this case, we simply call this processor `UserSource`. We will refer to this name in the next line when we want to connect a child processor, which in turn defines how data should flow through our topology. The second argument is the topic name that this source processor should read from (in this case, `users`).

❷ This line creates a new downstream processor called `SayHello` whose processing logic is defined in the `SayHelloProcessor` class (we will create this in the next section). In the Processor API, we can connect one processor to another by specifying the name of the parent processor. In this case, we specify the `UserSource` processor as the parent of the `SayHello` processor, which means data will flow from the `UserSource` to `SayHello`.

As we saw before, in the DSL tutorial, we now need to build the topology and call `streams.start()` to run it:

```
KafkaStreams streams = new KafkaStreams(topology, config);
streams.start();
```

Before running the code, we need to implement the SayHelloProcessor class. Whenever you build a custom stream processor using the Processor API, you need to implement the Processor interface. The interface specifies methods for initializing the stream processor (init), applying the stream processing logic to a single record (process), and a cleanup function (close). The initialization and cleanup function aren't needed in this example.

The following is a simple implementation of SayHelloProcessor that we will use for this example. We will explore more complex examples, and all of the interface methods in the Processor interface (init, process, and close), in more detail in Chapter 7.

```
public class SayHelloProcessor implements Processor<Void, String, Void, Void> { ❶
  @Override
  public void init(ProcessorContext<Void, Void> context) {} ❷

  @Override
  public void process(Record<Void, String> record) { ❸
    System.out.println("(Processor API) Hello, " + record.value());
  }

  @Override
  public void close() {} ❹
}
```

❶ The first two generics in the Processor interface (in this example, Processor<Void, String, ..., ...>) refer to the *input* key and value types. Since our keys are null and our values are usernames (i.e., text strings), Void and String are the appropriate choices. The last two generics (Processor<..., ..., Void, Void>) refer to the *output* key and value types. In this example, our SayHelloProcessor simply prints a greeting. Since we aren't forwarding any output keys or values downstream, Void is the appropriate type for the final two generics.[24]

❷ No special initialization is needed in this example, so the method body is empty. The generics in the ProcessorContext interface (ProcessorContext<Void, Void>) refer to the output key and value types (again, as we're not forwarding any messages downstream in this example, both are Void).

---

24 This version of the Processor interface was introduced In Kafka Streams version 2.7 and deprecates an earlier version of the interface that was available in Kafka Streams 2.6 and earlier. In the earlier version of the Processor interface, only input types are specified. This presented some issues with type-safety checks, so the newer form of the Processor interface is recommended.

❸ The processing logic lives in the aptly named `process` method in the `Processor` interface. Here, we print a simple greeting. Note that the generics in the `Record` interface refer to the key and value type of the *input* records.

❹ No special cleanup needed in this example.

We can now run the code using the same command we used in the DSL example:

```
./gradlew runProcessorAPI --info
```

You should see the following output to indicate your Kafka Streams application is working as expected:

```
(Processor API) Hello, angie
(Processor API) Hello, guy
(Processor API) Hello, kate
(Processor API) Hello, mark
```

Now, despite the Processor API's power, which we will see in Chapter 7, using the DSL is often preferable because, among other benefits, it includes two very powerful abstractions: streams and tables. We will get our first look at these abstractions in the next section.

Streams and Tables

If you look closely at Example 2-1, you will notice that we used a DSL operator called `stream` to read a Kafka topic into a *stream*. The relevant line of code is:

```
KStream<Void, String> stream = builder.stream("users");
```

However, kafka streams also supports an additional way to view our data: as a *table*. in this section, we'll take a look at both options and learn when to use *streams* and when to use *tables*.

As discussed in "Processor Topologies" on page 35, designing a processor topology involves specifying a set of source and sink processors, which correspond to the topics your application will read from and write to. However, instead of working with Kafka topics *directly*, the Kafka Streams DSL allows you to work with different *representations* of a topic, each of which are suitable for different use cases. There are two ways to model the data in your Kafka topics: as a *stream* (also called a *record stream*) or a *table* (also known as a *changelog stream*). The easiest way to compare these two data models is through an example.

Say we have a topic containing ssh logs, where each record is keyed by a user ID as shown in Table 2-2.

Table 2-2. Keyed records in a single topic-partition

Key	Value	Offset

mitch	{
	  "action": "login"
	}
		0

mitch	{
	  "action": "logout"
	}
		1

elyse	{
	  "action": "login"
	}
		2

isabelle	{
	  "action": "login"
	}
		3

Before consuming this data, we need to decide which abstraction to use: a stream or a table. When making this decision, we need to consider whether or not we want to track only the latest state/representation of a given key, or the entire history of messages. Let's compare the two options side by side:

Streams

These can be thought of as inserts in database parlance. Each distinct record remains in this view of the log. The stream representation of our topic can be seen in Table 2-3.

Table 2-3. Stream view of ssh logs

Key	Value	Offset

mitch	{
	  "action": "login"
	}
		0

mitch	{
	  "action": "logout"
	}
		1

elyse	{
	  "action": "login"
	}
		2

isabelle	{
	  "action": "login"
	}
		3

Tables

Tables can be thought of as updates to a database. In this view of the logs, only the current state (either the latest record for a given key or some kind of aggregation) for each key is retained. Tables are usually built from *compacted topics* (i.e., topics that are configured with a `cleanup.policy` of `compact`, which tells Kafka that you only want to keep the latest representation of each key). The table representation of our topic can be seen in Table 2-4.

Table 2-4. Table view of ssh logs

Key	Value	Offset

mitch	{
	  "action": "logout"
	}
		1

elyse	{
	  "action": "login"
	}
		2

isabelle	{
	  "action": "login"
	}
		3

Tables, by nature, are *stateful*, and are often used for performing aggregations in Kafka Streams.[25] In Table 2-4, we didn't really perform a mathematical aggregation, we just kept the latest ssh event for each user ID. However, tables also support mathematical aggregations. For example, instead of tracking the latest record for each key, we could have just as easily calculated a rolling `count`. In this case, we would have ended up with a slightly different table, where the values contain the result of our count aggregation. You can see a count-aggregated table in Table 2-5.

Table 2-5. Aggregated table view of ssh logs

Key	Value	Offset
mitch	2	1
elyse	1	2
isabelle	1	3

Careful readers may have noticed a discrepancy between the design of Kafka's storage layer (a distributed, append-only log) and a table. Records that are written to Kafka are immutable, so how is it possible to model data as updates, using a *table* representation of a Kafka topic?

---

25 In fact, tables are sometimes referred to as *aggregated streams*. See "Of Streams and Tables in Kafka and Stream Processing, Part 1" by Michael Noll (*https://oreil.ly/dgSCn*), which explores this topic further.

The answer is simple: the table is materialized on the Kafka Streams side using a key-value store which, by default, is implemented using RocksDB.[26] By consuming an ordered stream of events and keeping only the latest record for each key in the client-side key-value store (more commonly called a *state store* in Kafka Streams terminology), we end up with a table or map-like representation of the data. In other words, the table isn't something we *consume* from Kafka, but something we *build* on the client side.

You can actually write a few lines of Java code to implement this basic idea. In the following code snippet, the `List` represents a stream since it contains an ordered collection of records,[27] and the table is constructed by iterating through the list (`stream.forEach`) and only retaining the latest record for a given key using a `Map`. The following Java code demonstrates this basic idea:

```java
import java.util.Map.Entry;

var stream = List.of(
    Map.entry("a", 1),
    Map.entry("b", 1),
    Map.entry("a", 2));

var table = new HashMap<>();

stream.forEach((record) -> table.put(record.getKey(), record.getValue()));
```

If you were to print the stream and table after running this code, you would see the following output:

```
stream ==> [a=1, b=1, a=2]

table ==> {a=2, b=1}
```

Of course, the Kafka Streams implementation of this is more sophisticated, and can leverage fault-tolerant data structures as opposed to an in-memory `Map`. But this ability to construct a table representation of an unbounded stream is only one side of a more complex relationship between streams and tables, which we will explore next.

---

26 RocksDB is a fast, embedded key-value store that was originally developed at Facebook. We will talk more about RocksDB and key-value stores in Chapters 4–6.

27 To go even deeper with the analogy, the index position for each item in the list would represent the offset of the record in the underlying Kafka topic.

Stream/Table Duality

The *duality* of tables and streams comes from the fact that tables can be represented as streams, and streams can be used to reconstruct tables. We saw the latter transformation of a stream into a table in the previous section, when discussing the discrepancy between Kafka's append-only, immutable log and the notion of a mutable table structure that accepts updates to its data.

This ability to reconstruct tables from streams isn't unique to Kafka Streams, and is in fact pretty common in various types of storage. For example, MySQL's replication process relies on the same notion of taking a stream of events (i.e., row changes) to reconstruct a source table on a downstream replica. Similarly, Redis has the notion of an append-only file (AOF) that captures every command that is written to the in-memory key-value store. If a Redis server goes offline, then the stream of commands in the AOF can be replayed to reconstruct the dataset.

What about the other side of the coin (representing a table as a stream)? When viewing a table, you are viewing a single point-in-time representation of a stream. As we saw earlier, tables can be updated when a new record arrives. By changing our view of the table to a stream, we can simply process the update as an insert, and append the new record to the end of the log instead of updating the key. Again, the intuition behind this can be seen using a few lines of Java code:

```
var stream = table.entrySet().stream().collect(Collectors.toList());

stream.add(Map.entry("a", 3));
```

This time, if you print the contents of the stream, you'll see we're no longer using update semantics, but instead insert semantics:

```
stream ==> [a=2, b=1, a=3]
```

So far, we've been working with the standard libraries in Java to build intuition around streams and tables. However, when working with streams and tables in Kafka Streams, you'll use a set of more specialized abstractions. We'll take a look at these abstractions next.

KStream, KTable, GlobalKTable

One of the benefits of using the high-level DSL over the lower-level Processor API in Kafka Streams is that the former includes a set of abstractions that make working with streams and tables extremely easy.

The following list includes a high-level overview of each:

KStream

A KStream is an abstraction of a partitioned *record stream*, in which data is represented using insert semantics (i.e., each event is considered to be *independent* of other events).

KTable

A KTable is an abstraction of a partitioned table (i.e., *changelog stream*), in which data is represented using update semantics (the latest representation of a given key is tracked by the application). Since KTables are partitioned, each Kafka Streams task contains only a subset of the full table.[28]

GlobalKTable

This is similar to a KTable, except each GlobalKTable contains a complete (i.e., unpartitioned) copy of the underlying data. We'll learn when to use KTables and when to use GlobalKTables in Chapter 4.

Kafka Streams applications can make use of multiple stream/table abstractions, or just one. It's entirely dependent on your use case, and as we work through the next few chapters, you will learn when to use each one. This completes our initial discussion of streams and tables, so let's move on to the next chapter and explore Kafka Streams in more depth.

Summary

Congratulations, you made it through the end of your first date with Kafka Streams. Here's what you learned:

- Kafka Streams lives in the stream processing layer of the Kafka ecosystem. This is where sophisticated data processing, transformation, and enrichment happen.

- Kafka Streams was built to simplify the development of stream processing applications with a simple, functional API and a set of stream processing primitives that can be reused across projects. When more control is needed, a lower-level Processor API can also be used to define your topology.

- Kafka Streams has a friendlier learning curve and a simpler deployment model than cluster-based solutions like Apache Flink and Apache Spark Streaming. It also supports event-at-a-time processing, which is considered true streaming.

---

28 Assuming your source topic contains more than one partition.

- Kafka Streams is great for solving problems that require or benefit from real-time decision making and data processing. Furthermore, it is reliable, maintainable, scalable, and elastic.

- Installing and running Kafka Streams is simple, and the code examples in this chapter can be found at *https://github.com/mitch-seymour/mastering-kafka-streams-and-ksqldb*.

In the next chapter, we'll learn about stateless processing in Kafka Streams. We will also get some hands-on experience with several new DSL operators, which will help us build more advanced and powerful stream processing applications.

## CHAPTER 3

Stateless Processing

The simplest form of stream processing requires no memory of previously seen events. Each event is consumed, processed,[1] and subsequently forgotten. This paradigm is called *stateless processing*, and Kafka Streams includes a rich set of operators for working with data in a stateless way.

In this chapter, we will explore the *stateless operators* that are included in Kafka Streams, and in doing so, we'll see how some of the most common stream processing tasks can be tackled with ease. The topics we will explore include:

- Filtering records
- Adding and removing fields
- Rekeying records
- Branching streams
- Merging streams
- Transforming records into one or more outputs
- Enriching records, one at a time

We'll take a tutorial-based approach for introducing these concepts. Specifically, we'll be streaming data about cryptocurrencies from Twitter and applying some stateless operators to convert the raw data into something more meaningful: investment signals. By the end of this chapter, you will understand how to use stateless operators in Kafka Streams to enrich and transform raw data, which will prepare you for the more advanced concepts that we will explore in later chapters.

---

1 Processed is a loaded word. Here, we use the word in its broadest sense, and refer to the process of *enriching*, *transforming*, *reacting* to, and optionally *writing* the processed data to an output topic.

Before we jump into the tutorial, let's get a better frame of reference for what stateless processing is by comparing it to the other form of stream processing: *stateful processing*.

Stateless Versus Stateful Processing

One of the most important things you should consider when building a Kafka Streams application is whether or not your application requires stateful processing. The following describes the distinction between stateless and stateful stream processing:

- In *stateless applications*, each event handled by your Kafka Streams application is processed independently of other events, and only *stream* views are needed by your application (see "Streams and Tables" on page 53). In other words, your application treats each event as a self-contained insert and requires no memory of previously seen events.

- *Stateful applications*, on the other hand, need to remember information about previously seen events *in one or more steps* of your processor topology, usually for the purpose of aggregating, windowing, or joining event streams. These applications are more complex under the hood since they need to track additional data, or *state*.

In the high-level DSL, the type of stream processing application you ultimately build boils down to the individual *operators* that are used in your topology.[2] Operators are stream processing functions (e.g., `filter`, `map`, `flatMap`, `join`, etc.) that are applied to events as they flow through your topology. Some operators, like `filter`, are considered *stateless* because they only need to look at the current record to perform an action (in this case, `filter` looks at each record individually to determine whether or not the record should be forwarded to downstream processors). Other operators, like `count`, are *stateful* since they require knowledge of previous events (`count` needs to know how many events it has seen so far in order to track the number of messages).

If your Kafka Streams application requires *only* stateless operators (and therefore does not need to maintain any memory of previously seen events), then your application is considered *stateless*. However, if you introduce one or more stateful operators (which we will learn about in the next chapter), regardless of whether or not your application also uses stateless operators, then your application is considered *stateful*. The added complexity of stateful applications warrants additional considerations with

---

2 We'll focus on the DSL in this chapter, but we will also cover stateless and stateful processing via the Processor API in Chapter 7.

regards to maintenance, scalability, and fault tolerance, so we will cover this form of stream processing separately in the next chapter.

If all of this sounds a little abstract, don't worry. We'll demonstrate these concepts by building a stateless Kafka Streams application in the following sections, and getting some first-hand experience with stateless operators. So without further ado, let's introduce this chapter's tutorial.

Introducing Our Tutorial: Processing a Twitter Stream

In this tutorial, we will explore the use case of algorithmic trading. Sometimes called *high-frequency trading* (HFT), this lucrative practice involves building software to evaluate and purchase securities automatically, by processing and responding to many types of market signals with minimal latency.

To assist our fictional trading software, we will build a stream processing application that will help us gauge market sentiment around different types of cryptocurrencies (Bitcoin, Ethereum, Ripple, etc.), and use these sentiment scores as investment/ divestment signals in a custom trading algorithm.[3] Since millions of people use Twitter to share their thoughts on cryptocurrencies and other topics, we will use Twitter as the data source for our application.

Before we get started, let's look at the steps required to build our stream processing application. We will then use these requirements to design a processor topology, which will be a helpful guide as we build our stateless Kafka Streams application. The key concepts in each step are italicized:

1. Tweets that mention certain digital currencies (#bitcoin, #ethereum) should be consumed from a source topic called `tweets`:

   - Since each record is JSON-encoded, we need to figure out how to properly *deserialize* these records into higher-level data classes.

   - Unneeded fields should be removed during the deserialization process to simplify our code. Selecting only a subset of fields to work with is referred to as *projection*, and is one of the most common tasks in stream processing.

2. Retweets should be excluded from processing. This will involve some form of data *filtering*.

3. Tweets that aren't written in English should be *branched* into a separate stream for translating.

---

3 We won't develop the full trading algorithm in this tutorial since, ideally, our trading algorithm would include many types of signals, not just market sentiment (unless we wanted to lose a bunch of money).

4. Non-English tweets need to be translated to English. This involves *mapping* one input value (the non-English tweet) to a new output value (an English-translated tweet).

5. The newly translated tweets should be *merged* with the English tweets stream to create one unified stream.

6. Each tweet should be enriched with a sentiment score, which indicates whether Twitter users are conveying positive or negative emotion when discussing certain digital currencies. Since a single tweet could mention multiple cryptocurrencies, we will demonstrate how to convert each input (tweet) into a variable number of outputs using a `flatMap` operator.

7. The enriched tweets should be serialized using Avro, and written to an output topic called `crypto-sentiment`. Our fictional trading algorithm will read from this topic and make investment decisions based on the signals it sees.

Now that the requirements have been captured, we can design our processor topology. Figure 3-1 shows what we'll be building in this chapter and how data will flow through our Kafka Streams application.

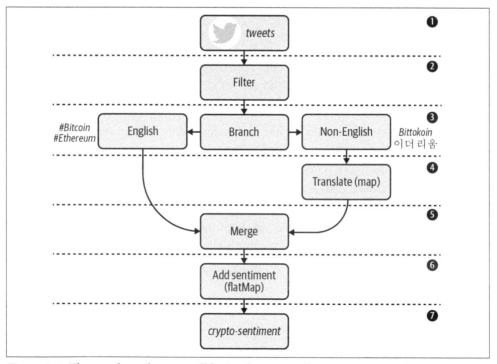

Figure 3-1. The topology that we will be implementing for our tweet enrichment application

With our topology design in hand, we can now start implementing our Kafka Streams application by working our way through each of the processing steps (labeled 1–7) in Figure 3-1. We will start by setting up our project, and then move on to the first step in our topology: streaming tweets from the source topic.

Project Setup

The code for this chapter is located at *https://github.com/mitch-seymour/mastering-kafka-streams-and-ksqldb.git*.

If you would like to reference the code as we work our way through each topology step, clone the repository and change to the directory containing this chapter's tutorial. The following command will do the trick:

```
$ git clone git@github.com:mitch-seymour/mastering-kafka-streams-and-ksqldb.git
$ cd mastering-kafka-streams-and-ksqldb/chapter-03/crypto-sentiment
```

You can build the project anytime by running the following command:

```
$ ./gradlew build --info
```

 We have omitted the implementation details of tweet translation and sentiment analysis (steps 4 and 6 in Figure 3-1) since they aren't necessary to demonstrate the stateless operators in Kafka Streams. However, the source code in GitHub does include a full working example, so please consult the project's *README.md* file if you are interested in these implementation details.

Now that our project is set up, let's start creating our Kafka Streams application.

Adding a KStream Source Processor

All Kafka Streams applications have one thing in common: they consume data from one or more source topics. In this tutorial, we only have one source topic: `tweets`. This topic is populated with tweets from the Twitter source connector (*https://oreil.ly/yvEoX*), which streams tweets from Twitter's streaming API and writes JSON-encoded tweet records to Kafka. An example tweet value[4] is shown in Example 3-1.

---

4 We won't worry about the record keys in this chapter since our application doesn't perform any key-level operations.

Example 3-1. Example record value in the `tweets` source topic

```json
{
    "CreatedAt": 1602545767000,
    "Id": 1206079394583924736,
    "Text": "Anyone else buying the Bitcoin dip?",
    "Source": "",
    "User": {
        "Id": "123",
        "Name": "Mitch",
        "Description": "",
        "ScreenName": "timeflown",
        "URL": "https://twitter.com/timeflown",
        "FollowersCount": "1128",
        "FriendsCount": "1128"
    }
}
```

Now that we know what the data looks like, the first step we need to tackle is getting the data from our source topic into our Kafka Streams application. In the previous chapter, we learned that we can use the KStream abstraction to represent a stateless record stream. As you can see in the following code block, adding a KStream source processor in Kafka Streams is simple and requires just a couple of lines of code:

```java
StreamsBuilder builder = new StreamsBuilder(); ❶

KStream<byte[], byte[]> stream = builder.stream("tweets"); ❷
```

❶ When using the high-level DSL, processor topologies are built using a StreamsBuilder instance.

❷ KStream instances are created by passing the topic name to the StreamsBuilder.stream method. The stream method can optionally accept additional parameters, which we will explore in later sections.

One thing you may notice is that the KStream we just created is parameterized with byte[] types:

```java
KStream<byte[], byte[]>
```

We briefly touched on this in the previous chapter, but the KStream interface leverages two generics: one for specifying the type of keys (K) in our Kafka topic and the other for specifying the type of values (V). If we were to peel back the floorboards in the Kafka Streams library, we would see an interface that looks like this:

```java
public interface KStream<K, V> {
  // omitted for brevity
}
```

Therefore, our KStream instance, which is parameterized as KStream<byte[], byte[]>, indicates that the record keys and values coming out of the tweets topic are being encoded as byte arrays. However, we just mentioned that the tweet records are actually encoded as JSON objects by the source connector (see Example 3-1), so what gives?

Kafka Streams, *by default*, represents data flowing through our application as byte arrays. This is due to the fact that Kafka itself stores and transmits data as raw byte sequences, so representing the data as a byte array will always work (and is therefore a sensible default). Storing and transmitting raw bytes makes Kafka flexible because it doesn't impose any particular data format on its clients, and also fast, since it requires less memory and CPU cycles on the brokers to transfer a raw byte stream over the network.[5] However, this means that Kafka clients, including Kafka Streams applications, are responsible for serializing and deserializing these byte streams in order to work with higher-level objects and formats, including strings (delimited or non-delimited), JSON, Avro, Protobuf, etc.[6]

Before we address the issue of deserializing our tweet records into higher-level objects, let's add the additional boilerplate code needed to run our Kafka Streams application. For testability purposes, it's often beneficial to separate the logic for building a Kafka Streams topology from the code that actually runs the application. So the boilerplate code will include two classes. First, we'll define a class for building our Kafka Streams topology, as shown in Example 3-2.

Example 3-2. A Java class that defines our Kafka Streams topology

```
class CryptoTopology {

  public static Topology build() {
    StreamsBuilder builder = new StreamsBuilder();

    KStream<byte[], byte[]> stream = builder.stream("tweets");
    stream.print(Printed.<byte[], byte[]>toSysOut().withLabel("tweets-stream")); ❶

    return builder.build();
  }
}
```

---

5 Storing and transmitting data as a byte array allows Kafka to leverage something called zero-copy, which means the data doesn't need to cross the user-kernel space boundary for serialization/deserialization purposes, since this is handled on the client side. This is a major performance benefit.

6 So when we say that the Twitter connector encodes tweets as JSON, we don't mean the tweet records in Kafka are stored as raw JSON. We simply mean the bytes representing these tweets in the underlying Kafka topic should, *when deserialized*, be formatted as JSON.

❶ The print operator allows us to easily view data as it flows through our application. It is generally recommended for development use only.

The second class, which we'll call App, will simply instantiate and run the topology, as shown in Example 3-3.

Example 3-3. A separate Java class used to run our Kafka Streams application

```java
class App {
  public static void main(String[] args) {
    Topology topology = CryptoTopology.build();

    Properties config = new Properties(); ❶
    config.put(StreamsConfig.APPLICATION_ID_CONFIG, "dev");
    config.put(StreamsConfig.BOOTSTRAP_SERVERS_CONFIG, "localhost:29092");

    KafkaStreams streams = new KafkaStreams(topology, config); ❷

    Runtime.getRuntime().addShutdownHook(new Thread(streams::close)); ❸

    System.out.println("Starting Twitter streams");
    streams.start(); ❹
  }
}
```

❶ Kafka Streams requires us to set some basic configuration, including an application ID (which corresponds to a consumer group) and the Kafka bootstrap servers. We set these configs using a Properties object.

❷ Instantiate a KafkaStreams object with the processor topology and streams config.

❸ Add a shutdown hook to gracefully stop the Kafka Streams application when a global shutdown signal is received.

❹ Start the Kafka Streams application. Note that streams.start() does not block, and the topology is executed via background processing threads. This is the reason why a shutdown hook is required.

Our application is now ready to run. If we were to start our Kafka Streams application and then produce some data to our tweets topic, we would see the raw byte arrays (the cryptic values that appear after the comma in each output row) being printed to the screen:

```
[tweets-stream]: null, [B@c52d992
[tweets-stream]: null, [B@a4ec036
[tweets-stream]: null, [B@3812c614
```

As you might expect, the low-level nature of byte arrays makes them a little difficult to work with. In fact, additional stream processing steps will be much easier to implement if we find a different method of representing the data in our source topic. This is where the concepts of data serialization and deserialization come into play.

Serialization/Deserialization

Kafka is a bytes-in, bytes-out stream processing platform. This means that clients, like Kafka Streams, are responsible for converting the byte streams they consume into higher-level objects. This process is called *deserialization*. Similarly, clients must also convert any data they want to write back to Kafka back into byte arrays. This process is called *serialization*. These processes are depicted in Figure 3-2.

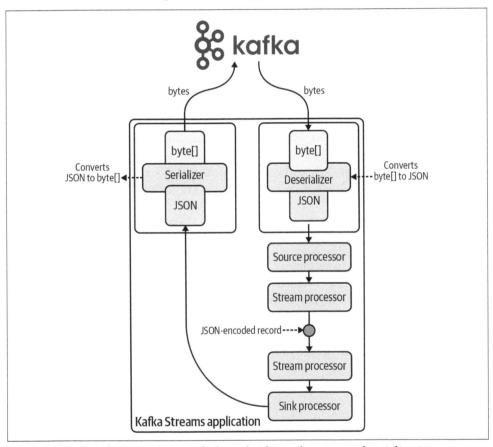

Figure 3-2. An architectural view of where the deserialization and serialization processes occur in a Kafka Streams application

In Kafka Streams, serializer and deserializer classes are often combined into a single class called a *Serdes*, and the library ships with several implementations, shown in Table 3-1.[7] For example, the String Serdes (accessible via the `Serdes.String()` method) includes both the String serializer *and* deserializer class.

Table 3-1. Default Serdes implementations that are available in Kafka Streams

Data type	Serdes class
byte[]	`Serdes.ByteArray()`, `Serdes.Bytes()`
ByteBuffer	`Serdes.ByteBuffer()`
Double	`Serdes.Double()`
Integer	`Serdes.Integer()`
Long	`Serdes.Long()`
String	`Serdes.String()`
UUID	`Serdes.UUID()`
Void	`Serdes.Void()`

Whenever you need to deserialize/serialize data in Kafka Streams, you should first check to see whether or not one of the built-in Serdes classes fits your needs. However, as you may have noticed, Kafka Streams doesn't ship with Serdes classes for some common formats, including JSON,[8] Avro, and Protobuf. However, we can implement our own Serdes when the need arises, and since tweets are represented as JSON objects, we will learn how to build our own custom Serdes to handle this format next.

Building a Custom Serdes

As mentioned earlier, the tweets in our source topic are encoded as JSON objects, but only the raw bytes are stored in Kafka. So, the first thing we will do is write some code for deserializing tweets as higher-level JSON objects, which will ensure the data is easy to work with in our stream processing application. We could just use the built-in String Serdes, `Serdes.String()`, instead of implementing our own, but that would make working with the Twitter data difficult, since we couldn't easily access each field in the tweet object.[9]

---

7 More Serdes classes are likely to be introduced in future releases. Please refer to the official documentation for a complete list of the available Serdes classes (*https://oreil.ly/GIsuV*).

8 An example JSON Serdes is included in the Kafka source code, but was not exposed via the `Serdes` factory class like the official Serdes at the time of this writing.

9 This would require a nasty use of regex, and even then, still wouldn't work very well.

If your data is in a common format, like JSON or Avro, then you won't need to reinvent the wheel by implementing your own low-level JSON serialization/deserialization logic. There are many Java libraries for serializing and deserializing JSON, but the one we will be using in this tutorial is Gson (*https://oreil.ly/C2_5K*). Gson was developed by Google and has an intuitive API for converting JSON bytes to Java objects. The following code block demonstrates the basic method for deserializing byte arrays with Gson, which will come in handy whenever we need to read JSON records from Kafka:

```
Gson gson = new Gson();
byte[] bytes = ...; ❶
Type type = ...; ❷
gson.fromJson(new String(bytes), type); ❸
```

❶   The raw bytes that we need to deserialize.

❷   `type` is a Java class that will be used to represent the deserialized record.

❸   The `fromJson` method actually converts the raw bytes into a Java class.

Furthermore, Gson also supports the inverse of this process, which is to say it allows us to convert (i.e., serialize) Java objects into raw byte arrays. The following code block shows how serialization works in Gson:

```
Gson gson = new Gson();
gson.toJson(instance).getBytes(StandardCharsets.UTF_8);
```

Since the Gson library takes care of the more complex task of serializing/deserializing JSON at a low level, we just need to leverage Gson's capabilities when implementing a custom Serdes. The first step is to define a data class, which is what the raw byte arrays will be deserialized into.

Defining Data Classes

One feature of Gson (and some other JSON serialization libraries, like Jackson) is that it allows us to convert JSON byte arrays into Java objects. In order to do this, we simply need to define a data class, or POJO (Plain Old Java Object), that contains the fields that we want to deserialize from the source object.

As you can see in Example 3-4, our data class for representing raw tweet records in our Kafka Streams application is pretty simple. We simply define a class property for each field we want to capture from the raw tweet (e.g., `createdAt`), and a corresponding getter/setter method for accessing each property (e.g., `getCreatedAt`).

Example 3-4. A data class to use for deserializing tweet records

```java
public class Tweet {
  private Long createdAt;
  private Long id;
  private String lang;
  private Boolean retweet;
  private String text;

  // getters and setters omitted for brevity
}
```

If we don't want to capture certain fields in the source record, then we can just omit the field from the data class, and Gson will drop it automatically. Whenever you create your own deserializer, you should consider dropping any fields in the source record that aren't needed by your application or downstream applications during the deserialization process. This process of reducing the available fields to a smaller subset is called *projection* and is similar to using a SELECT statement in the SQL world to only select the columns of interest.

Now that we have created our data class, we can implement a Kafka Streams deserializer for converting the raw byte arrays from the tweets topic to higher-level Tweet Java objects (which will be much easier to work with).

Implementing a Custom Deserializer

The code required for implementing a custom deserializer is pretty minimal, especially when you leverage a library that hides most of the complexity of deserializing byte arrays (as we're doing with Gson). We simply need to implement the Deserializer interface in the Kafka client library, and invoke the deserialization logic whenever deserialize is invoked. The following code block shows how to implement the Tweet deserializer:

```java
public class TweetDeserializer implements Deserializer<Tweet> {
  private Gson gson =
      new GsonBuilder()
          .setFieldNamingPolicy(FieldNamingPolicy.UPPER_CAMEL_CASE) ❶
          .create();

  @Override
  public Tweet deserialize(String topic, byte[] bytes) { ❷
    if (bytes == null) return null; ❸
    return gson.fromJson(
      new String(bytes, StandardCharsets.UTF_8), Tweet.class); ❹
  }
}
```

❶ Gson supports several different formats for JSON field names. Since the Twitter Kafka connector uses upper camel case for field names, we set the appropriate field naming policy to ensure the JSON objects are deserialized correctly. This is pretty implementation-specific, but when you write your own deserializer, feel free to leverage third-party libraries and custom configurations like we're doing here to help with the heavy lifting of byte array deserialization.

❷ We override the deserialize method with our own logic for deserializing records in the tweets topic. This method returns an instance of our data class (Tweet).

❸ Don't try to deserialize the byte array if it's null.

❹ Use the Gson library to deserialize the byte array into a Tweet object.

Now, we are ready to implement our serializer.

Implementing a Custom Serializer

The code for implementing a custom serializer is also very straightforward. This time, we need to implement the serialize method of the Serializer interface that is included in the Kafka client library. Again, we will leverage Gson's serialization capabilities to do most of the heavy lifting. The following code block shows the Tweet serializer we will be using in this chapter:

```
class TweetSerializer implements Serializer<Tweet> {
  private Gson gson = new Gson();

  @Override
  public byte[] serialize(String topic, Tweet tweet) {
    if (tweet == null) return null; ❶
    return gson.toJson(tweet).getBytes(StandardCharsets.UTF_8); ❷
  }
}
```

❶ Don't try to deserialize a null Tweet object.

❷ If the Tweet object is not null, use Gson to convert the object into a byte array.

With both a Tweet deserializer *and* serializer in place, we can now combine these two classes into a Serdes.

Building the Tweet Serdes

So far, the deserializer and serializer implementations have been very light on code. Similarly, our custom Serdes class, whose sole purpose is to combine the deserializer and serializer in a convenient wrapper class for Kafka Streams to use, is also pretty minimal. The following code block shows how easy it is to implement a custom Serdes class:

```
public class TweetSerdes implements Serde<Tweet> {

  @Override
  public Serializer<Tweet> serializer() {
    return new TweetSerializer();
  }

  @Override
  public Deserializer<Tweet> deserializer() {
    return new TweetDeserializer();
  }
}
```

Now that our custom Serdes is in place, we can make a slight modification to the code in Example 3-2. Let's change:

```
KStream<byte[], byte[]> stream = builder.stream("tweets");
stream.print(Printed.<byte[], byte[]>toSysOut().withLabel("tweets-stream"));
```

to:

```
KStream<byte[], Tweet> stream = ❶
  builder.stream(
    "tweets",
    Consumed.with(Serdes.ByteArray(), new TweetSerdes())); ❷

stream.print(Printed.<byte[], Tweet>toSysOut().withLabel("tweets-stream"));
```

❶ Notice that our value type has changed from byte[] to Tweet. Working with Tweet instances will make our life much easier, as you will see in upcoming sections.

❷ Explicitly set the key and value Serdes to use for this KStream using Kafka Stream's Consumed helper. By setting the value Serdes to new TweetSerdes(), our stream will now be populated with Tweet objects instead of byte arrays. The key Serdes remains unchanged.

Note, the keys are still being serialized as byte arrays. This is because our topology doesn't require us to do anything with the record keys, so there is no point in deserializing these.[10] Now, if we were to run our Kafka Streams application and produce some data to the source topic, you would see that we are now working with Tweet objects, which include the helpful getter methods for accessing the original JSON fields that we will leverage in later stream processing steps:

```
[tweets-stream]: null, Tweet@182040a6
[tweets-stream]: null, Tweet@46efe0cb
[tweets-stream]: null, Tweet@176ef3db
```

Now that we have created a KStream that leverages our Tweet data class, we can start implementing the rest of the topology. The next step is to filter out any retweets from our Twitter stream.

Handling Deserialization Errors in Kafka Streams

You should always be explicit with how your application handles deserialization errors, otherwise you may get an unwelcome surprise if a malformed record ends up in your source topic. Kafka Streams has a special config, DEFAULT_DESERIALIZATION_EXCEP TION_HANDLER_CLASS_CONFIG, that can be used to specify a deserialization exception handler. You can implement your own exception handler, or use one of the built-in defaults, including LogAndFailExceptionHandler (which logs an error and then sends a shutdown signal to Kafka Streams) or LogAndContinueException Handler (which logs an error and continues processing).

Filtering Data

One of the most common stateless tasks in a stream processing application is filtering data. Filtering involves selecting only a subset of records to be processed, and ignoring the rest. Figure 3-3 shows the basic idea of filtering.

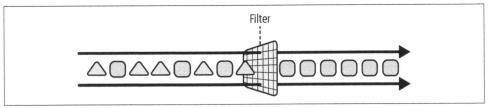

Figure 3-3. Filtering data allows us to process only a subset of data in our event stream

---

10 Unnecessary serialization/deserialization can negatively impact performance in some applications.

In Kafka Streams, the two primary operators[11] that are used for filtering are:

- `filter`
- `filterNot`

We'll start by exploring the `filter` operator. `filter` simply requires us to pass in a Boolean expression, called a `Predicate`, in order to determine if a message should be kept. If the predicate returns `true`, the event will be forwarded to downstream processors. If it returns `false`, then the record will be excluded from further processing. Our use case requires us to filter out retweets, so our predicate will leverage the `Tweet.isRetweet()` method.

Since `Predicate` is a functional interface,[12] we can use a lambda with the `filter` operator. Example 3-5 shows how to filter out retweets using this method.

Example 3-5. An example of how to use the DSL's `filter` operator

```
KStream<byte[], Tweet> filtered =
  stream.filter(
      (key, tweet) -> {
        return !tweet.isRetweet();
      });
```

The `filterNot` operator is very similar to `filter`, except the Boolean logic is inverted (i.e., returning `true` will result in the record being dropped, which is the opposite of `filter`). As you can see in Example 3-5, our filtering condition is negated: `! tweet.isRetweet()`. We could have just as easily negated at the operator level instead, using the code in Example 3-6.

Example 3-6. An example of how to use the DSL's `filterNot` operator

```
KStream<byte[], Tweet> filtered =
  stream.filterNot(
      (key, tweet) -> {
        return tweet.isRetweet();
      });
```

These two approaches are functionally equivalent. However, when the filtering logic contains a negation, I prefer to use `filterNot` to improve readability. For this

---

11 As you'll see later, `flatMap` and `flatMapValues` can also be used for filtering. But for clarity, it's advisable to use `filter` or `filterNot` unless the filtering step sometimes needs to produce more than one record.

12 In Java, functional interfaces have a single abstract method. The `Predicate` class only contains one abstract method, called `test`.

tutorial, we will use the `filterNot` implementation shown in Example 3-6 to exclude retweets from further processing.

 If your application requires a filtering condition, you should filter as early as possible. There's no point in transforming or enriching data that will simply be thrown away in a subsequent step, especially if the logic for processing the unneeded event is computationally expensive.

We have now implemented steps 1 and 2 in our processor topology (Figure 3-1). We are ready to move on to the third step: separating our filtered stream into substreams based on the source language of the tweet.

Branching Data

In the previous section, we learned how to use Boolean conditions called predicates to filter streams. Kafka Streams also allows us to use predicates to separate (or *branch*) streams. Branching is typically required when events need to be routed to different stream processing steps or output topics based on some attribute of the event itself.

Revisiting our requirements list, we see that tweets can appear in multiple languages in our source topic. This is a great use case for branching, since a subset of records in our stream (non-English tweets) require an extra processing step: they need to be translated to English. The diagram in Figure 3-4 depicts the branching behavior we need to implement in our application.

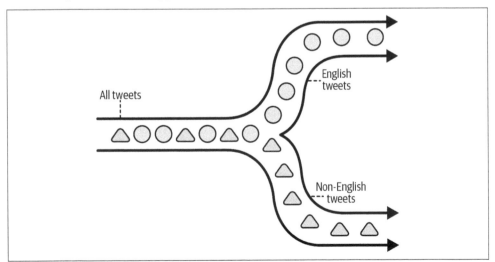

Figure 3-4. Branching operations split a single stream into multiple output streams

Let's create two lambda functions: one for capturing English tweets, and another for capturing everything else. Thanks to our earlier deserialization efforts, we can leverage another getter method in our data class to implement our branching logic: Tweet.getLang(). The following code block shows the predicates we will use for branching our stream:

```
Predicate<byte[], Tweet> englishTweets =
  (key, tweet) -> tweet.getLang().equals("en"); ❶

Predicate<byte[], Tweet> nonEnglishTweets =
  (key, tweet) -> !tweet.getLang().equals("en"); ❷
```

❶ This predicate matches all English tweets.

❷ This predicate is the inverse of the first, and captures all non-English tweets.

Now that we have defined our branching conditions, we can leverage Kafka Streams' branch operator, which accepts one or more predicates and returns a list of output streams that correspond to each predicate. Note that each predicate is evaluated in order, and a record can only be added to a single branch. If a record doesn't match any predicate, then it will be dropped:

```
KStream<byte[], Tweet>[] branches =
  filtered.branch(englishTweets, nonEnglishTweets); ❶

KStream<byte[], Tweet> englishStream = branches[0]; ❷

KStream<byte[], Tweet> nonEnglishStream = branches[1]; ❸
```

❶ We create two branches of our stream by evaluating the source language of a tweet.

❷ Since we passed the englishTweets predicate first, the first KStream in our list (at the 0 index) contains the English output stream.

❸ Since the nonEnglishTweets predicate was used as the final branching condition, the tweets that need translating will be the last KStream in our list (at index position 1).

 The method of branching streams may be changing in an upcoming Kafka Streams release. If you are using a Kafka Streams version greater than 2.7.0, you may want to check "KIP-418: A method-chaining way to branch KStream" (*https://oreil.ly/h_GvU*) for potential API changes. Some backward compatibility is expected, and the current implementation does work on the latest version of Kafka Streams at the time of writing (version 2.7.0).

Now that we have created two substreams (`englishStream` and `nonEnglishStream`), we can apply different processing logic to each. This takes care of the third step of our processor topology (see Figure 3-1), so we're now ready to move on to the next step: translating non-English tweets into English.

Translating Tweets

At this point, we have two record streams: tweets that are written in English (`english Stream`), and tweets that are written in another language (`nonEnglishStream`). We would like to perform sentiment analysis on each tweet, but the API we will be using to perform this sentiment analysis only supports a few languages (English being one of them). Therefore, we need to translate each tweet in the `nonEnglishStream` to English.

We're talking about this as a business problem, though. Let's look at the requirement from a stream processing perspective. What we really need is a way of transforming one input record into exactly one new output record (whose key or value may or may not be the same type as the input record). Luckily for us, Kafka Streams has two operators that fit the bill:

- `map`
- `mapValues`

A visualization of a mapping operation is shown in Figure 3-5.

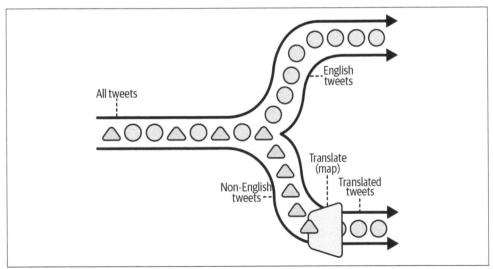

Figure 3-5. Mapping operations allow us to perform a 1:1 transformation of records

The map and mapValues operators are very similar (they both have a 1:1 mapping between input and output records), and both could work for this use case. The only difference is that map requires us to specify a new record value *and* record key, while mapValues requires us to just set a new value.

Let's first take a look at how we might implement this with map. Assume that we not only want to translate the tweet text, but also rekey each record by the Twitter username associated with a given tweet. We could implement the tweet translation step as shown in the following code block:

```
KStream<byte[], Tweet> translatedStream =
  nonEnglishStream.map(
      (key, tweet) -> { ❶
        byte[] newKey = tweet.getUsername().getBytes();
        Tweet translatedTweet = languageClient.translate(tweet, "en");
        return KeyValue.pair(newKey, translatedTweet); ❷
      });
```

❶ Our mapping function is invoked with the current record key and record value (called tweet).

❷ Our mapping function is required to return a new record key *and* value, represented using Kafka Streams' KeyValue class. Here, the new key is set to the Twitter username, and the new value is set to the translated tweet. The actual logic for translating text is out of scope for this tutorial, but you can check the source code for implementation details.

However, the requirements we outlined don't require us to rekey any records. As we'll see in the next chapter, rekeying records is often used when stateful operations will be performed in a latter stream processing step.[13] So while the preceding code works, we can simplify our implementation by using the mapValues operator instead, which is only concerned with transforming record values.

An example of how to use the mapValues operator is shown in the following code block:

```
KStream<byte[], Tweet> translatedStream =
  nonEnglishStream.mapValues(
      (tweet) -> { ❶
        return languageClient.translate(tweet, "en"); ❷
      });
```

---

13 Rekeying helps ensure related data is colocated to the same streams task, which is important when aggregating and joining data. We will discuss this in detail in the next chapter

❶ Our `mapValues` function is invoked with *only* the record value.

❷ We are only required to return the new record value when using the `mapValues` operator. In this case, the value is a translated `Tweet`.

We will stick with the `mapValues` implementation since we don't need to rekey any records.

 It is recommended to use `mapValues` instead of `map` whenever possible, as it allows Kafka Streams to potentially execute the program more efficiently.

After translating all non-English tweets, we now have two `KStreams` that contain English tweets:

- `englishStream`, the original stream of English tweets
- `translatedStream`, the newly translated tweets, which are now in English

This wraps up step 4 in our processor topology (see Figure 3-1). However, the goal of our application is to perform sentiment analysis on *all* English tweets. We *could* duplicate this logic across both of these streams: `englishStream` and `translated Stream`. However, instead of introducing unnecessary code duplication, it would be better to *merge* these two streams. We'll explore how to merge streams in the next section.

Merging Streams

Kafka Streams provides an easy method for combining multiple streams into a single stream. Merging streams can be thought of as the opposite of a branching operation, and is typically used when the same processing logic can be applied to more than one stream in your application.

 The equivalent of a `merge` operator in the SQL world is a union query. For example:
```
SELECT column_name(s) FROM table1
UNION
SELECT column_name(s) FROM table2;
```

Now that we have translated all tweets in the non-English stream, we have two separate streams that we need to perform sentiment analysis on: `englishStream` and `translatedStream`. Furthermore, all tweets that we enrich with sentiment scores will need to be written to a single output topic: `crypto-sentiment`. This is an ideal use case for merging since we can reuse the same stream/sink processors for both of these separate streams of data.

The diagram in Figure 3-6 depicts what we are trying to accomplish.

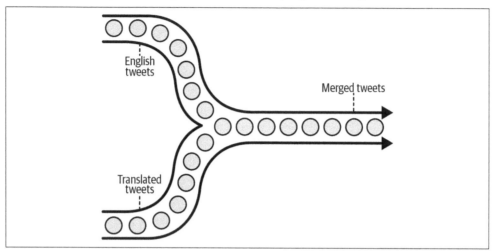

Figure 3-6. Merging operations combine multiple streams into a single stream

The code for merging streams is very simple. We only need to pass the streams we want to combine to the `merge` operator, as shown here:

```
KStream<byte[], Tweet> merged = englishStream.merge(translatedStream);
```

Now that our streams are combined, we are ready to move to the next step.

Enriching Tweets

We are nearing the goal of being able to enrich each tweet with a sentiment score. However, as you may have noticed, our current data class, `Tweet`, represents the structure of the raw tweets in our *source topic*. We need a new data class for representing the enriched records that we will be writing to our *output topic* (`crypto-sentiment`). This time, instead of serializing our data using JSON, we will be using a data serialization format called Avro (*https://oreil.ly/eFV8s*). Let's take a deeper look at Avro and learn how to create an Avro data class for representing the enriched records in our Kafka Streams application.

Avro Data Class

Avro is a popular format in the Kafka community, largely due to its compact byte representation (which is advantageous for high throughput applications), native support for record schemas,[14] and a schema management tool called Schema Registry, which works well with Kafka Streams and has had strong support for Avro since its inception.[15] There are other advantages as well. For example, some Kafka Connectors can use Avro schemas to automatically infer the table structure of downstream data stores, so encoding our output records in this format can help with data integration downstream.

When working with Avro, you can use either *generic records* or *specific records*. Generic records are suitable when the record schema isn't known at runtime. They allow you to access field names using generic getters and setters. For example: `GenericRecord.get(String key)` and `GenericRecord.put(String key, Object value)`.

Specific records, on the other hand, are Java classes that are generated from Avro schema files. They provide a much nicer interface for accessing record data. For example, if you generate a specific record class named `EntitySentiment`, then you can access fields using dedicated getters/setters for each field name. For example: `entitySentiment.getSentimentScore()`.[16]

Since our application defines the format of its output records (and therefore, the schema is known at build time), we'll use Avro to generate a specific record (which we'll refer to as a data class from here on out). A good place to add a schema definition for Avro data is in the *src/main/avro* directory of your Kafka Streams project. Example 3-7 shows the Avro schema definition we will be using for our sentiment-enriched output records. Save this schema in a file named *entity_sentiment.avsc* in the *src/main/avro/* directory.

Example 3-7. An Avro schema for our enriched tweets

```
{
  "namespace": "com.magicalpipelines.model", ❶
  "name": "EntitySentiment", ❷
  "type": "record",
  "fields": [
    {
      "name": "created_at",
```

---

14 Record schemas define the field names and types for a given record. They allow us to provide strong contracts about the data format between different applications and services.

15 Both Protobuf and JSON schemas are supported since Confluent Platform 5.5. See *https://oreil.ly/4hsQh*.

16 `entitySentiment` here is an instance of the Avro-generated `EntitySentiment` class, which we will be creating later in this section.

```
      "type": "long"
    },
    {
      "name": "id",
      "type:" "long"
    },
    {
      "name": "entity",
      "type": "string"
    },
    {
      "name": "text",
      "type": "string"
    },
    {
      "name": "sentiment_score",
      "type": "double"
    },
    {
      "name": "sentiment_magnitude",
      "type": "double"
    },
    {
      "name": "salience",
      "type": "double"
    }
  ]
}
```

❶ The desired package name for your data class.

❷ The name of the Java class that will contain the Avro-based data model. This class will be used in subsequent stream processing steps.

Now that we have defined our schema, we need to generate a data class from this definition. In order to do that, we need to add some dependencies to our project. This can be accomplished by adding the following lines in the project's *build.gradle* file:

```
plugins {
  id 'com.commercehub.gradle.plugin.avro' version '0.9.1' ❶
}

dependencies {
  implementation 'org.apache.avro:avro:1.8.2' ❷
}
```

❶ This Gradle plug-in is used to autogenerate Java classes from Avro schema definitions, like the one we created in Example 3-7.

❷ This dependency contains the core classes for working with Avro.

Now, when we build our project (see "Project Setup" on page 65), a new data class named `EntitySentiment` will be automatically generated for us.[17] This generated data class contains a new set of fields for storing tweet sentiment (`sentiment_score`, `sentiment_magnitude`, and `salience`) and corresponding getter/setter methods. With our data class in hand, we can now proceed with adding sentiment scores to our tweets. This will introduce us to a new set of DSL operators that are extremely useful for transforming data.

Sentiment Analysis

We have already seen how to transform records during the tweet translation step by using `map` and `mapValues`. However, both `map` and `mapValues` produce exactly one output record for each input record they receive. In some cases, we may want to produce zero, one, or even multiple output records for a single input record.

Consider the example of a tweet that mentions multiple cryptocurrencies:

> #bitcoin is looking super strong. #ethereum has me worried though

This fictional tweet explicitly mentions two cryptocurrencies, or *entities* (Bitcoin and Ethereum) and includes two separate sentiments (positive sentiment for Bitcoin, and negative for Ethereum). Modern Natural Language Processing (NLP) libraries and services are often smart enough to calculate the sentiment for each entity within the text, so a single input string, like the one just shown, could lead to multiple output records. For example:

```
{"entity": "bitcoin", "sentiment_score": 0.80}
{"entity": "ethereum", "sentiment_score": -0.20}
```

Once again, let's consider this requirement outside of the business problem itself. Here, we have a very common stream processing task: we need to convert a single input record into a variable number of output records. Luckily for us, Kafka Streams includes two operators that can help with this use case:

- `flatMap`
- `flatMapValues`

Both `flatMap` and `flatMapValues` are capable of producing zero, one, or multiple output records every time they are invoked. Figure 3-7 visualizes this 1:N mapping of input to output records.

---

17 The Gradle Avro plug-in will automatically scan the *src/main/avro* directory and pass any schema files it finds to the Avro compiler.

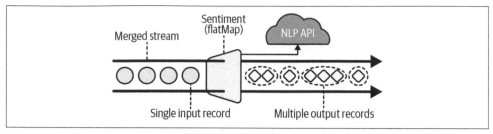

Figure 3-7. flatMap operations allow us to transform one input record into zero or more output records

Similar to the map operation we saw earlier, flatMap requires us to set a new record key and value. On the other hand, flatMapValues only requires us to specify a new value. Since we don't need to process the record key in this example, we will use flatMapValues to perform entity-level sentiment analysis for our tweets, as shown in the following code block (notice that we are using our new Avro-based data class, EntitySentiment):

```
KStream<byte[], EntitySentiment> enriched =
  merged.flatMapValues(
      (tweet) -> {
        List<EntitySentiment> results =
          languageClient.getEntitySentiment(tweet); ❶

        results.removeIf(
            entitySentiment -> !currencies.contains(
              entitySentiment.getEntity())); ❷

        return results; ❸
      });
```

❶ Get a list of sentiment scores for each entity in the tweet.

❷ Remove all entities that don't match one of the cryptocurrencies we are tracking. The final list size after all of these removals is variable (a key characteristic of flatMap and flatMapValues return values), and could have zero or more items.

❸ Since the flatMap and flatMapValues operators can return any number of records, we will return a list that contains every record that should be added to the output stream. Kafka Streams will handle the "flattening" of the collection we return (i.e., it will break out each element in the list into a distinct record in the stream).

Similar to our recommendation about using `mapValues`, it is also recommended to use `flatMapValues` instead of `flatMap` whenever possible, as it allows Kafka Streams to potentially execute the program more efficiently.

We are now ready to tackle the final step: writing the enriched data (the sentiment scores) to a new output topic. In order to do this, we need to build an Avro Serdes that can be used for serializing the Avro-encoded `EntitySentiment` records that we created.

Serializing Avro Data

As mentioned earlier, Kafka is a bytes-in, bytes-out stream processing platform. Therefore, in order to write the `EntitySentiment` records to our output topic, we need to serialize these Avro records into byte arrays.

When we serialize data using Avro, we have two choices:

- Include the Avro schema in each record.
- Use an even more compact format, by saving the Avro schema in Confluent Schema Registry, and only including a much smaller schema ID in each record instead of the entire schema.

As shown in Figure 3-8, the benefit of the first approach is you don't have to set up and run a separate service alongside your Kafka Streams application. Since Confluent Schema Registry is a REST service for creating and retrieving Avro, Protobuf, and JSON schemas, it requires a separate deployment and therefore introduces a maintenance cost and an additional point of failure. However, with the first approach, you do end up with larger message sizes since the schema is included.

However, if you are trying to eke every ounce of performance out of your Kafka Streams application, the smaller payload sizes that Confluent Schema Registry enables may be necessary. Furthermore, if you anticipate ongoing evolution of your record schemas and data model, the schema compatibility checks that are included in Schema Registry help ensure that future schema changes are made in safe, non-breaking ways.[18]

---

18 For more information about schema compatibility, check out Gwen Shapira's 2019 Confluent article on the subject (*https://oreil.ly/kVwHQ*).

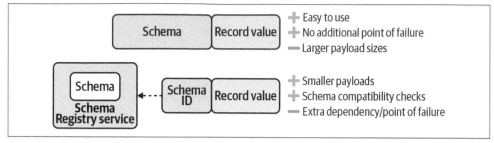

Figure 3-8. Advantages and disadvantages of including an Avro schema in each record

Since Avro Serdes classes are available for both approaches, the amount of code you need to introduce to your application for serializing Avro data is minimal. The following sections show how to configure both a registryless and Schema Registry-aware Avro Serdes.

Registryless Avro Serdes

While a registryless Avro Serdes can be implemented very simply by yourself, I have open sourced a version under the `com.mitchseymour:kafka-registryless-avro-serdes` package.[19] You can use this package by updating your *build.gradle* file with the following code:

```
dependencies {
    implementation 'com.mitchseymour:kafka-registryless-avro-serdes:1.0.0'
}
```

Whenever you need to use this Serdes in your Kafka Streams application, just provide an Avro-generated class to the `AvroSerdes.get` method, as shown here:

```
AvroSerdes.get(EntitySentiment.class)
```

The resulting Serdes can be used anywhere you would normally use one of Kafka's built-in Serdes.

Schema Registry–Aware Avro Serdes

Confluent has also published a package for distributing its Schema Registry–aware Avro Serdes. If you want to leverage the Confluent Schema Registry, update your *build.gradle* file as follows:

```
repositories {
    mavenCentral()

    maven {
```

---

19 The code repository for the registryless Avro Serdes can be found at *https://oreil.ly/m1kk7*.

```
      url "https://packages.confluent.io/maven/" ❶
  }
}

dependencies {
  implementation ('io.confluent:kafka-streams-avro-serde:6.0.1') { ❷
    exclude group: 'org.apache.kafka', module: 'kafka-clients' ❸
  }
}
```

❶ Add the Confluent Maven repository since this is where the artifact for the Schema Registry–aware Avro Serdes lives.

❷ Add the required dependency for using a Schema Registry–aware Avro Serdes.

❸ Exclude an incompatible transitive dependency included in the kafka-streams-avro-serde at the time of writing.[20]

The Schema Registry–aware Avro Serdes requires some additional configuration, so you can improve the readability of your code by creating a factory class for instantiating Serdes instances for each of the data classes in your project. For example, the following code block shows how to create a registry-aware Avro Serdes for the TweetSentiment class:

```
public class AvroSerdes {
  public static Serde<EntitySentiment> EntitySentiment(
    String url, boolean isKey) {

      Map<String, String> serdeConfig =
        Collections.singletonMap("schema.registry.url", url); ❶
      Serde<EntitySentiment> serde = new SpecificAvroSerde<>();
      serde.configure(serdeConfig, isKey);
      return serde;
  }
}
```

❶ The register-aware Avro Serdes requires us to configure the Schema Registry endpoint.

Now, you can instantiate the Serdes wherever you need it in your Kafka Streams application with the following code:

```
AvroSerdes.EntitySentiment("http://localhost:8081", false) ❶
```

---

20 This may not be needed when using future versions of the kafka-streams-avro-serde library, but at the time of writing, the latest version of kafka-streams-avro-serde (6.0.1) conflicts with a dependency in Kafka Streams 2.7.0.

❶ Update the Schema Registry endpoint to the appropriate value.

 You can interact with Schema Registry directly for registering, deleting, modifying, or listing schemas (*https://oreil.ly/GXBgi*). However, when using a registry-aware Avro Serdes from Kafka Streams, your schema will automatically be registered for you. Furthermore, to improve performance, the registry-aware Avro Serdes minimizes the number of schema lookups by caching schema IDs and schemas locally.

Now that we have our Avro Serdes in place, we can create our sink processor.

Adding a Sink Processor

The last step is to write the enriched data to our output topic: `crypto-sentiment`. There are a few operators for doing this:

- `to`
- `through`
- `repartition`

If you want to return a new `KStream` instance for appending additional operators/stream processing logic, then you should use the `repartition` or `through` operator (the latter was deprecated right before this book was published, but is still widely used and backward compatibility is expected). Internally, these operators call `builder.stream` again, so using them will result in additional sub-topologies (see "Sub-Topologies" on page 37) being created by Kafka Streams. However, if you have reached a terminal step in your stream, as we have, then you should use the `to` operator, which returns `void` since no other stream processors need to be added to the underlying `KStream`.

In this example, we will use the `to` operator since we have reached the last step of our processor topology, and we will also use the Schema Registry–aware Avro Serdes since we want better support for schema evolution and also smaller message sizes. The following code shows how to add the sink processor:

```
enriched.to(
  "crypto-sentiment",
  Produced.with(
    Serdes.ByteArray(),
    AvroSerdes.EntitySentiment("http://localhost:8081", false)));
```

We have now implemented each of the steps in our processor topology (see Figure 3-1). The final step is to run our code and verify that it works as expected.

Running the Code

In order to run the application, you'll need to stand up a Kafka cluster and Schema Registry instance. The source code for this tutorial includes a Docker Compose environment to help you accomplish this.[21] Once the Kafka cluster and Schema Registry service are running, you can start your Kafka Streams application with the following command:

```
./gradlew run --info
```

Now we're ready to test. The next section shows how to verify that our application works as expected.

Empirical Verification

As mentioned in Chapter 2, one of the easiest ways to verify that your application is working as expected is through empirical verification. This involves generating data in a local Kafka cluster and subsequently observing the data that gets written to the output topic. The easiest way to do this is to save some example tweet records in a text file, and use the kafka-console-producer to write these records to our source topic: tweets.

The source code includes a file called *test.json*, with two records that we will use for testing. Note: the actual example records are flattened in *test.json*, but we have shown the pretty version of each record in Example 3-8 to improve readability.

Example 3-8. Two example tweets used for testing our Kafka Streams application

```
{
  "CreatedAt": 1577933872630,
  "Id": 10005,
  "Text": "Bitcoin has a lot of promise. I'm not too sure about #ethereum",
  "Lang": "en",
  "Retweet": false, ❶
  "Source": "",
  "User": {
    "Id": "14377871",
    "Name": "MagicalPipelines",
    "Description": "Learn something magical today.",
    "ScreenName": "MagicalPipelines",
    "URL": "http://www.magicalpipelines.com",
    "FollowersCount": "248247",
    "FriendsCount": "16417"
```

---

21 Instructions for running the Kafka cluster and Schema Registry instance can be found at *https://oreil.ly/ DEoaJ*.

```
    }
  }
  {
    "CreatedAt": 1577933871912,
    "Id": 10006,
    "Text": "RT Bitcoin has a lot of promise. I'm not too sure about #ethereum",
    "Lang": "en",
    "Retweet": true, ❷
    "Source": "",
    "User": {
      "Id": "14377870",
      "Name": "Mitch",
      "Description": "",
      "ScreenName": "Mitch",
      "URL": "http://mitchseymour.com",
      "FollowersCount": "120",
      "FriendsCount": "120"
    }
  }
```

❶ This first tweet (ID 10005) is *not* a retweet. We expect this tweet to be enriched
with sentiment scores.

❷ The second tweet (ID 10006) *is* a retweet, and we expect this record to be
ignored.

Now, let's produce these example records to our local Kafka cluster using the following command:

```
kafka-console-producer \
  --bootstrap-server kafka:9092 \
  --topic tweets < test.json
```

In another tab, let's use `kafka-console-consumer` to consume the enriched records.
Run the following command:

```
kafka-console-consumer \
  --bootstrap-server kafka:9092 \
  --topic crypto-sentiment \
  --from-beginning
```

You should see some cryptic-looking output with lots of strange symbols:

```
◆◆◆◆[◆◆|Bitcoin has a lot of promise.
I'm not too sure about #ethereumbitcoin`ff◆?`ff◆? -◆◆?
◆◆◆◆[◆◆|Bitcoin has a lot of promise.
I'm not too sure about #ethereumethereum◆◆◆1◆◆◆1◆◆◆?
```

This is because Avro is a binary format. If you're using Schema Registry, as we are, then you can use a special console script developed by Confluent that improves the readability of Avro data. Simply change `kafka-console-consumer` to `kafka-avro-console-consumer` as shown here:

```
kafka-avro-console-consumer \
  --bootstrap-server kafka:9092 \
  --topic crypto-sentiment \
  --from-beginning
```

Finally, you should see output similar to the following:

```
{
  "created_at": 1577933872630,
  "id": 10005,
  "text": "Bitcoin has a lot of promise. I'm not too sure about #ethereum",
  "entity": "bitcoin",
  "sentiment_score": 0.699999988079071,
  "sentiment_magnitude": 0.699999988079071,
  "salience": 0.47968605160713196
}
{
  "created_at": 1577933872630,
  "id": 10005,
  "text": "Bitcoin has a lot of promise. I'm not too sure about #ethereum",
  "entity": "ethereum",
  "sentiment_score": -0.20000000298023224,
  "sentiment_magnitude": -0.20000000298023224,
  "salience": 0.030233483761548996
}
```

Notice that tweet ID `10006` does not appear in the output. This was a retweet, and therefore was filtered in the second topology step in Figure 3-1. Also notice that tweet ID `10005` resulted in two output records. This is expected since this tweet mentioned two separate cryptocurrencies (each with a separate sentiment), and verifies that our `flatMapValues` operator worked as expected (the sixth topology step in Figure 3-1).

If you would like to verify the language translation step, feel free to update the example records in *test.json* with a foreign language tweet.[22] We will leave this as an exercise for the reader.

---

22 Additional setup steps may be required. See the README for this chapter's tutorial (*https://oreil.ly/o6Ofk*).

Summary

You have now learned a new set of capabilities for building stateless stream processing applications with Kafka Streams, including:

- Filtering data with `filter` and `filterNot`
- Creating substreams using the `branch` operator
- Combining streams with the `merge` operator
- Performing 1:1 record transformations using `map` and `mapValues`
- Performing 1:N record transformations using `flatMap` and `flatMapValues`
- Writing records to output topics using `to`, `through`, and `repartition`
- Serializing, deserializing, and reserializing data using custom serializers, deserializers, and Serdes implementations

In the next chapter, we will explore more complex stream processing operations by introducing stateful tasks, including joining, windowing, and aggregating streams.

## CHAPTER 4

Stateful Processing

In the previous chapter, we learned how to perform stateless transformations of record streams using the `KStream` abstraction and a rich set of stateless operators that are available in Kafka Streams. Since stateless transformations don't require any memory of previously seen events, they are easy to reason about and use. We treat every event as an immutable *fact* and process it independently of other events.

However, Kafka Streams also gives us the ability to capture and remember information about the events we consume. The captured information, or *state*, allows us to perform more advanced stream processing operations, including joining and aggregating data. In this chapter, we will explore stateful stream processing in detail. Some of the topics we will cover include:

- The benefits of stateful stream processing
- The differences between facts and behaviors
- What kinds of stateful operators are available in Kafka Streams
- How state is captured and queried in Kafka Streams
- How the `KTable` abstraction can be used to represent local, partitioned state
- How the `GlobalKTable` abstraction can be used to represent global, replicated state
- How to perform stateful operations, including joining and aggregating data
- How to use interactive queries to expose state

As with the previous chapter, we will explore these concepts using a tutorial-based approach. This chapter's tutorial is inspired by the video game industry, and we'll be building a real-time leaderboard that will require us to use many of Kafka Streams' stateful operators. Furthermore, we'll spend a lot of time discussing joins since this is one of the most common forms of data enrichment in stateful applications. But before we get to the tutorial, let's start by looking at some of the benefits of stateful processing.

Benefits of Stateful Processing

Stateful processing helps us understand the *relationships between events* and leverage these relationships for more advanced stream processing use cases. When we are able to understand how an event relates to other events, we can:

- Recognize patterns and behaviors in our event streams
- Perform aggregations
- Enrich data in more sophisticated ways using joins

Another benefit of stateful stream processing is that it gives us an additional abstraction for representing data. By replaying an event stream one event at a time, and saving the latest state of each key in an embedded key-value store, we can build a point-in-time representation of continuous and unbounded record streams. These point-in-time representations, or snapshots, are referred to as *tables*, and Kafka Streams includes different types of table abstractions that we'll learn about in this chapter.

Tables are not only at the heart of stateful stream processing, but when they are materialized, they can also be queried. This ability to query a real-time snapshot of a fast-moving event stream is what makes Kafka Streams a *stream-relational* processing platform,[1] and enables us to not only build stream processing applications, but also low-latency, event-driven microservices as well.

Finally, stateful stream processing allows us to understand our data using more sophisticated mental models. One particularly interesting view comes from Neil Avery, who discusses the differences between facts and behaviors in his discussion of event-first thinking (*https://oreil.ly/Q-hop*):

> An event represents a fact, something happened; it is immutable…

Stateless applications, like the ones we discussed in the previous chapter, are fact-driven. Each event is treated as an independent and atomic fact, which can be processed using immutable semantics (think of inserts in a never-ending stream), and then subsequently forgotten.

---

1 For more information about stream-relational processing platforms, please see Robert Yokota's 2018 blog post on the subject (*https://oreil.ly/7u71d*).

However, in addition to leveraging stateless operators to filter, branch, merge, and transform facts, we can ask even more advanced questions of our data if we learn how to model *behaviors* using stateful operators. So what are behaviors? According to Neil:

> The accumulation of facts captures behavior.

You see, events (or facts) rarely occur in isolation in the real world. Everything is interconnected, and by capturing and remembering facts, we can begin to understand their meaning. This is possible by understanding events in their larger historical context, or by looking at other, related events that have been captured and stored by our application.

A popular example is shopping cart abandonment, which is a behavior comprised of multiple facts: a user adds one or more items to a shopping cart, and then a session is terminated either manually (e.g., the user logs off) or automatically (e.g., due to a long period of inactivity). Processing either fact independently tells us very little about where the user is in the checkout process. However, collecting, remembering, and analyzing each of the facts (which is what stateful processing enables) allows us to recognize and react to the *behavior*, and provides much greater business value than viewing the world as a series of unrelated events.

Now that we understand the benefits of stateful stream processing, and the differences between facts and behaviors, let's get a preview of the stateful operators in Kafka Streams.

Preview of Stateful Operators

Kafka Streams includes several stateful operators that we can use in our processor topologies. Table 4-1 includes an overview of several operators that we will be working with in this book.

Table 4-1. Stateful operators and their purpose

Use case	Purpose	Operators
Joining data	Enrich an event with additional information or context that was captured in a separate stream or table	• `join` (inner join) • `leftJoin` • `outerJoin`
Aggregating data	Compute a continuously updating mathematical or combinatorial transformation of related events	• `aggregate` • `count` • `reduce`
Windowing data	Group events that have close temporal proximity	• `windowedBy`

Furthermore, we can *combine* stateful operators in Kafka Streams to understand even more complex relationships/behaviors between events. For example, performing a *windowed join* allows us to understand how discrete event streams relate during a certain period of time. As we'll see in the next chapter, *windowed aggregations* are another useful way of combining stateful operators.

Now, compared to the stateless operators we encountered in the previous chapter, stateful operators are more complex under the hood and have additional compute and storage[2] requirements. For this reason, we will spend some time learning about the inner workings of stateful processing in Kafka Streams before we start using the stateful operators listed in Table 4-1.

Perhaps the most important place to begin is by looking at how state is stored and queried in Kafka Streams.

State Stores

We have already established that stateful operations require our application to maintain some memory of previously seen events. For example, an application that counts the number of error logs it sees needs to keep track of a single number for each key: a rolling count that gets updated whenever a new error log is consumed. This count represents the historical context of a record and, along with the record key, becomes part of the application's state.

To support stateful operations, we need a way of storing and retrieving the remembered data, or state, required by each stateful operator in our application (e.g., count, aggregate, join, etc.). The storage abstraction that addresses these needs in Kafka Streams is called a *state store*, and since a single Kafka Streams application can leverage *many* stateful operators, a single application may contain several state stores.

 This section provides some lower-level information about how state is captured and stored in Kafka Streams. If you are eager to get started with the tutorial, feel free to skip ahead to "Introducing Our Tutorial: Video Game Leaderboard" on page 102 and revisit this section later.

There are many state store implementations and configuration possibilities available in Kafka Streams, each with specific advantages, trade-offs, and use cases. Whenever you use a stateful operator in your Kafka Streams application, it's helpful to consider which type of state store is needed by the operator, and also how to configure the state store based on your optimization criteria (e.g., are you optimizing for high

---

2 In memory, on disk, or some combination of both.

throughput, operational simplicity, fast recovery times in the event of failure, etc.). In most cases, Kafka Streams will choose a sensible default if you don't explicitly specify a state store type or override a state store's configuration properties.

Since the variation in state store types and configurations makes this quite a deep topic, we will initially focus our discussion on the common characteristics of all of the default state store implementations, and then take a look at the two broad categories of state stores: persistent and in-memory stores. More in-depth discussions of state stores will be covered in Chapter 6, and as we encounter specific topics in our tutorial.

Common Characteristics

The default state store implementations included in Kafka Streams share some common properties. We will discuss these commonalities in this section to get a better idea of how state stores work.

Embedded

The default state store implementations that are included in Kafka Streams are *embedded* within your Kafka Streams application at the task level (we first discussed tasks in "Tasks and Stream Threads" on page 41). The advantage of embedded state stores, as opposed to using an external storage engine, is that the latter would require a network call whenever state needed to be accessed, and would therefore introduce unnecessary latency and processing bottlenecks. Furthermore, since state stores are embedded at the task level, a whole class of concurrency issues for accessing shared state are eliminated.

Additionally, if state stores were remote, you'd have to worry about the availability of the remote system separately from your Kafka Streams application. Allowing Kafka Streams to manage a local state store ensures it will always be available and reduces the error surface quite a bit. A *centralized* remote store would be even worse, since it would become a single point of failure for all of your application instances. Therefore, Kafka Streams' strategy of colocating an application's state alongside the application itself not only improves performance (as discussed in the previous paragraph), but also availability.

All of the default state stores leverage RocksDB under the hood. RocksDB is a fast, embedded key-value store that was originally developed at Facebook. Since it supports arbitrary byte streams for storing key-value pairs, it works well with Kafka, which also decouples serialization from storage. Furthermore, both reads and writes are extremely fast, thanks to a rich set of optimizations that were made to the forked LevelDB code.[3]

Multiple access modes

State stores support multiple access modes and query patterns. Processor topologies require read and write access to state stores. However, when building microservices using Kafka Streams' *interactive queries* feature, which we will discuss later in "Interactive Queries" on page 129, clients require only *read* access to the underlying state. This ensures that state is never mutable outside of the processor topology, and is accomplished through a dedicated read-only wrapper that clients can use to safely query the state of a Kafka Streams application.

Fault tolerant

By default, state stores are backed by changelog topics in Kafka.[4] In the event of failure, state stores can be restored by replaying the individual events from the underlying changelog topic to reconstruct the state of an application. Furthermore, Kafka Streams allows users to enable standby replicas for reducing the amount of time it takes to rebuild an application's state. These standby replicas (sometimes called *shadow copies*) make state stores *redundant*, which is an important characteristic of highly available systems. In addition, applications that allow their state to be queried can rely on standby replicas to serve query traffic when other application instances go down, which also contributes to high availability.

Key-based

Operations that leverage state stores are key-based. A record's key defines the relationship between the current event and other events. The underlying data structure will vary depending on the type of state store you decide to use,[5] but each implementation can be conceptualized as some form of key-value store, where keys may be simple, or even compounded (i.e., multidimensional) in some cases.[6]

---

3 LevelDB was written at Google, but when Facebook engineers started using it, they found it to be too slow for their embedded workflows. By changing the single-threaded compaction process in LevelDB to a multi-threaded compaction process, and by leveraging bloom filters for reads, both read and write performance were drastically improved.

4 We mentioned that state stores are highly configurable, and even fault tolerance can be turned off by disabling the change logging behavior.

5 For example, inMemoryKeyValueStore uses a Java TreeMap, which is based on a red-black tree, while all persistent key-value stores use RocksDB.

6 For example, window stores are key-value stores, but the keys also include the window time in addition to the record key.

To complicate things slightly, Kafka Streams explicitly refers to certain types of state stores as key-value stores, even though all of the default state stores are key-based. When we refer to key-value stores in this chapter and elsewhere in this book, we are referring to nonwindowed state stores (windowed state stores will be discussed in the next chapter).

Now that we understand the commonalities between the default state stores in Kafka Streams, let's look at two broad categories of state stores to understand the differences between certain implementations.

Persistent Versus In-Memory Stores

One of the most important differentiators between various state store implementations is whether or not the state store is *persistent*, or if it simply stores remembered information *in-memory* (RAM). Persistent state stores flush state to disk asynchronously (to a configurable *state directory*), which has two primary benefits:

- State can exceed the size of available memory.
- In the event of failure, persistent stores can be restored quicker than in-memory stores.

To clarify the first point, a persistent state store may keep some of its state in-memory, while writing to disk when the size of the state gets too big (this is called *spilling to disk*) or when the write buffer exceeds a configured value. Second, since the application state is persisted to disk, Kafka Streams does not need to replay the entire topic to rebuild the state store whenever the state is lost (e.g., due to system failure, instance migration, etc.). It just needs to replay whatever data is missing between the time the application went down and when it came back up.

 The state store directory used for persistent stores can be set using the `StreamsConfig.STATE_DIR_CONFIG` property. The default location is */tmp/kafka-streams*, but it is highly recommended that you override this to a directory outside of */tmp*.

The downside is that persistent state stores are operationally more complex and can be slower than a pure in-memory store, which always pulls data from RAM. The additional operational complexity comes from the secondary storage requirement (i.e., disk-based storage) and, if you need to tune the state store, understanding RocksDB and its configurations (the latter may not be an issue for most applications).

Regarding the performance gains of an in-memory state store, these may not be drastic enough to warrant their use (since failure recovery takes longer). Adding more partitions to parallelize work is always an option if you need to squeeze more performance out of your application. Therefore, my recommendation is to start with persistent stores and only switch to in-memory stores if you have measured a noticeable performance improvement and, when quick recovery is concerned (e.g., in the event your application state is lost), you are using standby replicas to reduce recovery time.

Now that we have some understanding of what state stores are, and how they enable stateful/behavior-driven processing, let's take a look at this chapter's tutorial and see some of these ideas in action.

Introducing Our Tutorial: Video Game Leaderboard

In this chapter, we will learn about *stateful processing* by implementing a video game leaderboard with Kafka Streams. The video game industry is a prime example of where stream processing excels, since both gamers and game systems require low-latency processing and immediate feedback. This is one reason why companies like Activision (the company behind games like *Call of Duty* and remasters of *Crash Bandicoot* and *Spyro*) use Kafka Streams for processing video game telemetry.[7]

The leaderboard we will be building will require us to model data in ways that we haven't explored yet. Specifically, we'll be looking at how to use Kafka Streams' table abstractions to model data as a sequence of updates. Then, we'll dive into the topics of joining and aggregating data, which are useful whenever you need to understand or compute the relationship between multiple events. This knowledge will help you solve more complicated business problems with Kafka Streams.

Once we've created our real-time leaderboard using a new set of stateful operators, we will demonstrate how to query Kafka Streams for the latest leaderboard information using *interactive queries*. Our discussion of this feature will teach you how to build event-driven microservices with Kafka Streams, which in turn will broaden the type of clients we can share data with from our stream processing applications.[8]

Without further ado, let's take a look at the architecture of our video game leaderboard. Figure 4-1 shows the topology design we'll be implementing in this chapter. Additional information about each step is included after the diagram.

---

7 Tim Berglund and Yaroslav Tkachenko talk about Activision's use case in the *Streaming Audio* podcast (*https://oreil.ly/gNYZZ*).

8 We've already seen how Kafka Streams can write directly to output topics, which allows us to *push* processed/enriched data to downstream applications. However, interactive queries can be used by clients who want to issue ad hoc queries against a Kafka Streams application instead.

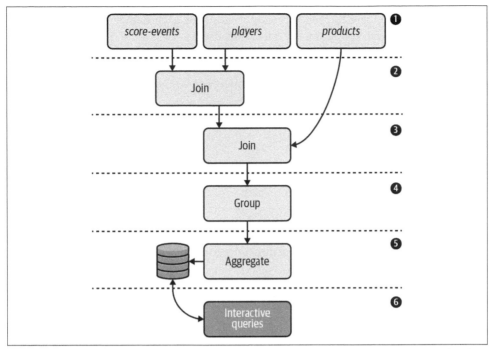

Figure 4-1. The topology that we will be implementing in our stateful video game leader-board application

❶ Our Kafka cluster contains three topics:

- The `score-events` topic contains game scores. The records are unkeyed and are therefore distributed in a round-robin fashion across the topic's partitions.

- The `players` topic contains player profiles. Each record is keyed by a player ID.

- The `products` topic contains product information for various video games. Each record is keyed by a product ID.

❷ We need to enrich our score events data with detailed player information. We can accomplish this using a join.

❸ Once we've enriched the `score-events` data with player data, we need to add detailed product information to the resulting stream. This can also be accomplished using a join.

❹ Since grouping data is a prerequisite for aggregating, we need to group the enriched stream.

❺ We need to calculate the top three high scores for each game. We can use Kafka Streams' aggregation operators for this purpose.

❻ Finally, we need to expose the high scores for each game externally. We will accomplish this by building a RESTful microservice using the *interactive queries* feature in Kafka Streams.

With our topology design in hand, we can now move on to the project setup.

Project Setup

The code for this chapter is located at *https://github.com/mitch-seymour/mastering-kafka-streams-and-ksqldb.git*.

If you would like to reference the code as we work our way through each topology step, clone the repo and change to the directory containing this chapter's tutorial. The following command will do the trick:

```
$ git clone git@github.com:mitch-seymour/mastering-kafka-streams-and-ksqldb.git
$ cd mastering-kafka-streams-and-ksqldb/chapter-04/video-game-leaderboard
```

You can build the project anytime by running the following command:

```
$ ./gradlew build --info
```

Now that our project is set up, let's start implementing our video game leaderboard.

Data Models

As always, we'll start by defining our data models. Since the source topics contain JSON data, we will define our data models using POJO data classes, which we will serialize and deserialize using our JSON serialization library of choice (throughout this book, we use Gson, but you could easily use Jackson or another library).[9]

I like to group my data models in a dedicated package in my project, for example, com.magicalpipelines.model. A filesystem view of where the data classes for this tutorial are located is shown here:

```
src/
└── main
    └── java
        └── com
            └── magicalpipelines
                └── model
```

---

9 As mentioned in Chapter 3, if our topics contained Avro data, we could define our data model in an Avro schema file instead.

```
├── ScoreEvent.java ❶
├── Player.java ❷
└── Product.java ❸
```

❶ The `ScoreEvent.java` data class will be used to represent records in the `score-events` topic.

❷ The `Player.java` data class will be used to represent records in the `players` topic.

❸ The `Product.java` data class will be used to represent records in the `products` topic.

Now that we know which data classes we need to implement, let's create a data class for each topic. Table 4-2 shows the resulting POJOs that we have implemented for this tutorial.

Table 4-2. Example records and data classes for each topic

Kafka topic	Example record	Data class

score-events	`{`
	`    "score": 422,`
	`    "product_id": 6,`
	`    "player_id": 1`
	`}`
		`public class ScoreEvent {`
		`    private Long playerId;`
		`    private Long productId;`
		`    private Double score;`
		`}`

players	`{`
	`    "id": 2,`
	`    "name": "Mitch"`
	`}`
		`public class Player {`
		`    private Long id;`
		`    private String name;`
		`}`

products	`{`
	`    "id": 1,`
	`    "name": "Super Smash Bros"`
	`}`
		`public class Product {`
		`    private Long id;`
		`    private String name;`
		`}`

We have already discussed serialization and deserialization in detail in "Serialization/Deserialization" on page 69. In that chapter's tutorial, we implemented our own custom serializer, deserializer, and Serdes. We won't spend more time on that here, but you can check out the code for this tutorial to see how we've implemented the Serdes for each of the data classes shown in Table 4-2.

Adding the Source Processors

Once we've defined our data classes, we can set up our source processors. In this topology, we need three of them since we will be reading from three source topics. The first thing we need to do when adding a source processor is determine which Kafka Streams abstraction we should use for representing the data in the underlying topic.

Up until now, we have only worked with the KStream abstraction, which is used to represent stateless record streams. However, our topology requires us to use both the products and players topics as lookups, so this is a good indication that a table-like abstraction may be appropriate for these topics.[10] Before we start mapping our topics to Kafka Streams abstractions, let's first review the difference between KStream, KTable, and GlobalKTable representations of a Kafka topic. As we review each abstraction, we'll fill in the appropriate abstraction for each topic in Table 4-3.

Table 4-3. The topic-abstraction mapping that we'll update in the following sections

Kafka topic	Abstraction
score-events	???
players	???
products	???

KStream

When deciding which abstraction to use, it helps to determine the nature of the topic, the topic configuration, and the keyspace of records in the underlying source topic. Even though stateful Kafka Streams applications use one or more table abstractions, it is also very common to use stateless KStreams alongside a KTable or GlobalKTable when the mutable table semantics aren't needed for one or more data sources.

In this tutorial, our score-events topic contains raw score events, which are unkeyed (and therefore, distributed in a round-robin fashion) in an uncompacted topic. Since tables are key-based, this is a strong indication that we should be using a KStream for our unkeyed score-events topic. We could change our keying strategy upstream (i.e., in whatever application is producing to our source topic), but that's not always possible. Furthermore, our application cares about the *highest score* for each player, not the *latest score*, so table semantics (i.e., retain only the most recent record for a given key) don't translate well for how we intend to use the score-events topic, even if it were keyed.

---

10 We can also use KStreams for lookup/join operations, but this is always a windowed operation, so we have reserved discussion of this topic until the next chapter.

Therefore, we will use a KStream for the score-events topic, so let's update the table in Table 4-3 to reflect this decision as follows:

Kafka topic	Abstraction
score-events	KStream
players	???
products	???

The remaining two topics, players and products, are keyed, and we only care about the latest record for each unique key in the topic. Hence, the KStream abstraction isn't ideal for these topics. So, let's move on and see if the KTable abstraction is appropriate for either of these topics.

KTable

The players topic is a compacted topic that contains player profiles, and each record is keyed by the player ID. Since we only care about the latest state of a player, it makes sense to represent this topic using a table-based abstraction (either KTable or GlobalKTable).

One important thing to look at when deciding between using a KTable or GlobalKTable is the keyspace. If the keyspace is very large (i.e., has high cardinality/lots of unique keys), or is expected to grow into a very large keyspace, then it makes more sense to use a KTable so that you can distribute fragments of the entire state across all of your running application instances. By partitioning the state in this way, we can lower the local storage overhead for each individual Kafka Streams instance.

Perhaps a more important consideration when choosing between a KTable or GlobalKTable is whether or not you need time synchronized processing. A KTable is time synchronized, so when Kafka Streams is reading from multiple sources (e.g., in the case of a join), it will look at the timestamp to determine which record to process next. This means a join will reflect what the combined record would have been at a certain time, and this makes the join behavior more predictable. On the other hand, GlobalKTables are *not* time synchronized, and are "completely populated before any processing is done."[11] Therefore, joins are always made against the most up-to-date version of a GlobalKTable, which changes the semantics of the program.

In this case, we're not going to focus too much on the second consideration since we've reserved the next chapter for our discussion of time and the role it plays in

---

11 Florian Trossbach and Matthias J. Sax go much deeper on this subject in their "Crossing the Streams: Joins in Apache Kafka" article (*https://oreil.ly/dUo3a*).

Kafka Streams. With regards to the keyspace, players contains a record for each unique player in our system. While this may be small depending on where we are in the life cycle of our company or product, it is a number we expect to grow significantly over time, so we'll use a KTable abstraction for this topic.

Figure 4-2 shows how using a KTable leads to the underlying state being distributed across multiple running application instances.

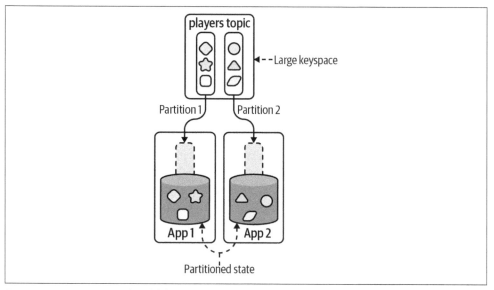

Figure 4-2. A KTable should be used when you want to partition state across multiple application instances and need time synchronized processing

Our updated abstraction table now looks like this:

Kafka topic	Abstraction
score-events	KStream
players	KTable
products	???

We have one topic left: the products topic. This topic is relatively small, so we should be able to replicate the state in full across all of our application instances. Let's take a look at the abstraction that allows us to do this: GlobalKTable.

GlobalKTable

The products topic is similar to the players topic in terms of configuration (it's compacted) and its bounded keyspace (we maintain the latest record for each unique product ID, and there are only a fixed number of products that we track). However, the products topic has much lower cardinality (i.e., fewer unique keys) than the players topic, and even if our leaderboard tracked high scores for several hundred games, this still translates to a state space small enough to fit entirely in-memory.

In addition to being smaller, the data in the products topic is also relatively static. Video games take a long time to build, so we don't expect a lot of updates to our products topic.

These two characteristics (small and static data) are what GlobalKTables were designed for. Therefore, we will use a GlobalKTable for our products topic. As a result, each of our Kafka Streams instances will store a full copy of the product information, which, as we'll see later, makes performing joins much easier.

Figure 4-3 shows how each Kafka Streams instance maintains a full copy of the products table.

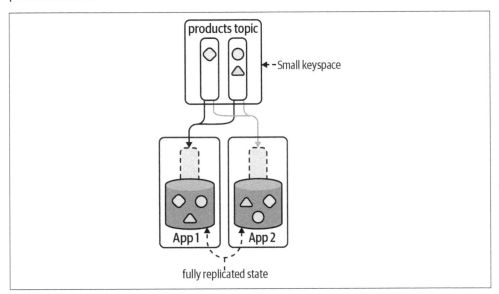

Figure 4-3. A GlobalKTable should be used when your keyspace is small, you want to avoid the co-partitioning requirements of a join (we will discuss co-partitioning in "Co-Partitioning" on page 114), and when time synchronization is not needed

We can now make the final update to our topic-abstraction mapping:

Kafka topic	Abstraction
score-events	KStream
players	KTable
products	GlobalKTable

Now that we've decided which abstraction to use for each of our source topics, we can register the streams and tables.

Registering Streams and Tables

Registering streams and tables is simple. The following code block shows how to use the high-level DSL to create a KStream, KTable, and GlobalKTable using the appropriate builder methods:

```
StreamsBuilder builder = new StreamsBuilder();

KStream<byte[], ScoreEvent> scoreEvents =
    builder.stream(
        "score-events",
        Consumed.with(Serdes.ByteArray(), JsonSerdes.ScoreEvent())); ❶

KTable<String, Player> players =
    builder.table(
        "players",
        Consumed.with(Serdes.String(), JsonSerdes.Player())); ❷

GlobalKTable<String, Product> products =
    builder.globalTable(
        "products",
        Consumed.with(Serdes.String(), JsonSerdes.Product())); ❸
```

❶ Use a KStream to represent data in the score-events topic, which is currently unkeyed.

❷ Create a partitioned (or sharded) table for the players topic, using the KTable abstraction.

❸ Create a GlobalKTable for the products topic, which will be replicated in full to each application instance.

By registering the source topics, we have now implemented the first step of our leaderboard topology (see Figure 4-1). Let's move on to the next step: joining streams and tables.

Joins

The most common method for combining datasets in the relational world is through joins.[12] In relational systems, data is often highly dimensional and scattered across many different tables. It is common to see these same patterns in Kafka as well, either because events are sourced from multiple locations, developers are comfortable or used to relational data models, or because certain Kafka integrations (e.g., the JDBC Kafka Connector, Debezium, Maxwell, etc.) bring both the raw data and the data models of the source systems with them.

Regardless of how data becomes scattered in Kafka, being able to combine data in separate streams and tables based on *relationships* opens the door for more advanced data enrichment opportunities in Kafka Streams. Furthermore, the join method for combining datasets is very different from simply merging streams, as we saw in Figure 3-6. When we use the `merge` operator in Kafka Streams, records on both sides of the merge are unconditionally combined into a single stream. Simple merge operations are therefore stateless since they do not need additional context about the events being merged.

Joins, however, can be thought of as a special kind of *conditional merge* that cares about the relationship between events, and where the records are not copied verbatim into the output stream but rather combined. Furthermore, these relationships must be captured, stored, and referenced at merge time to facilitate joining, which makes joining a stateful operation. Figure 4-4 shows a simplified depiction of how one type of join works (there are several types of joins, as we'll see in Table 4-5).

As with relational systems, Kafka Streams includes support for multiple kinds of joins. So, before we learn how to join our `score-events` stream with our `players` table, let's first familiarize ourselves with the various join operators that are available to us so that we can select the best option for our particular use case.

---

12 `UNION` queries are another method for combining datasets in the relational world. The behavior of the `merge` operator in Kafka Streams is more closely related to how a `UNION` query works.

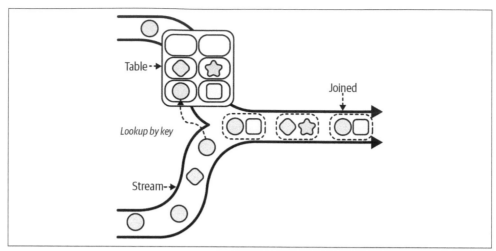

Figure 4-4. Joining messages

Join Operators

Kafka Streams includes three different join operators for joining streams and tables. Each operator is detailed in Table 4-4.

Table 4-4. Join operators

Operator	Description
join	Inner join. The join is triggered when the input records on both sides of the join share the same key.
leftJoin	Left join. The join semantics are different depending on the type of join: • For stream-table joins: a join is triggered when a record on the *left side* of the join is received. If there is no record with the same key on the right side of the join, then the right value is set to null. • For stream-stream and table-table joins: same semantics as a stream-stream left join, except an input on the right side of the join can also trigger a lookup. If the right side triggers the join and there is no matching key on the left side, then the join will not produce a result.
outerJoin	Outer join. The join is triggered when a record on *either side* of the join is received. If there is no matching record with the same key on the opposite side of the join, then the corresponding value is set to null.

When discussing the differences between join operators, we refer to different *sides of the join*. Just remember, the *right side* of the join is always passed as a parameter to the relevant join operator. For example:

```
KStream<String, ScoreEvent> scoreEvents = ...;
KTable<String, Player> players = ...;

scoreEvents.join(players, ...); ❶
```

❶ scoreEvents is the *left side* of the join. players is the *right side* of the join.

Now, let's look at the type of joins we can create with these operators.

Join Types

Kafka Streams supports many different types of joins, as shown in Table 4-5. The co-partitioning column refers to something we will discuss in "Co-Partitioning" on page 114. For now, it's sufficient to understand that co-partitioning is simply an extra set of requirements that are needed to actually perform the join.

Table 4-5. Join types

Type	Windowed	Operators	Co-partitioning required
KStream-KStream	Yes[a]	• join • leftJoin • outerJoin	Yes
KTable-KTable	No	• join • leftJoin • outerJoin	Yes
KStream-KTable	No	• join • leftJoin	Yes
KStream-GlobalKTable	No	• join • leftJoin	No

[a] One key thing to note is that KStream-KStream joins are windowed. We will discuss this in detail in the next chapter.

The two types of joins we need to perform in this chapter are:

- KStream-KTable to join the score-events KStream and the players KTable
- KStream-GlobalKTable to join the output of the previous join with the products GlobalKTable

We will use an inner join, using the `join` operator for each of the joins since we only want the join to be triggered when there's a match on both sides. However, before we do that, we can see that the first join we'll be creating (`KStream-KTable`) shows that co-partitioning is required. Let's take a look at what that means before we write any more code.

Co-Partitioning

> If a tree falls in a forest and no one is around to hear it, does it make a sound?
>
> —Aphorism

This famous thought experiment raises a question about what role an observer has in the occurrence of an event (in this case, sound being made in a forest). Similarly, in Kafka Streams, we must always be aware of the effect an observer has on the *processing of an event*.

In "Tasks and Stream Threads" on page 41, we learned that each partition is assigned to a single Kafka Streams task, and these tasks will act as the observers in our analogy since they are responsible for actually consuming and processing events. Because there's no guarantee that events on different partitions will be handled by the same Kafka Streams task, we have a potential observability problem.

Figure 4-5 shows the basic observability issue. If related events are processed by different tasks, then we cannot accurately determine the relationship between events because we have two separate observers. Since the whole purpose of joining data is to combine related events, an observability problem will make our joins fail when they should otherwise succeed.

In order to understand the relationship between events (through joins) or compute aggregations on a sequence of events, we need to ensure that related events are routed to the same partition, and so are handled by the same task.

To ensure related events are routed to the same partition, we must ensure the following *co-partitioning requirements* are met:

- Records on both sides must be keyed by the same field, and must be partitioned on that key using the same partitioning strategy.
- The input topics on both sides of the join must contain the same number of partitions. (This is the one requirement that is checked at startup. If this requirement is not met, then a `TopologyBuilderException` will be thrown.)

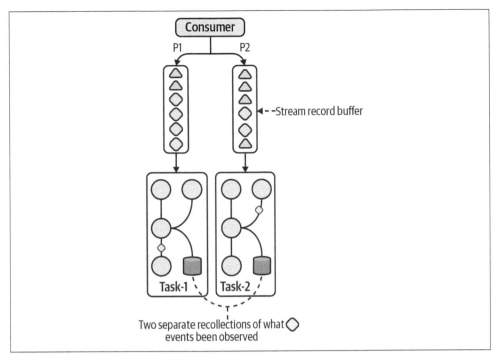

Figure 4-5. If we want to join related records but these records aren't always processed by the same task, then we have an observability problem

In this tutorial, we meet all of the requirements to perform a `KTable-KTable` join except the first one. Recall that records in the `score-events` topic are unkeyed, but we'll be joining with the `players` KTable, which is keyed by player ID. Therefore, we need to rekey the data in `score-events` by player ID as well, *prior to performing the join*. This can be accomplished using the `selectKey` operator, as shown in Example 4-1.

Example 4-1. The `selectKey` operator allows us to rekey records; this is often needed to meet the co-partitioning requirements for performing certain types of joins

```
KStream<String, ScoreEvent> scoreEvents =
  builder
    .stream(
      "score-events",
      Consumed.with(Serdes.ByteArray(), JsonSerdes.ScoreEvent()))
    .selectKey((k, v) -> v.getPlayerId().toString()); ❶
```

❶ `selectKey` is used to rekey records. In this case, it helps us meet the first co-partitioning requirement of ensuring records on both sides of the join (the `score-events` data and `players` data) are keyed by the same field.

A visualization of how records are rekeyed is shown in Figure 4-6.

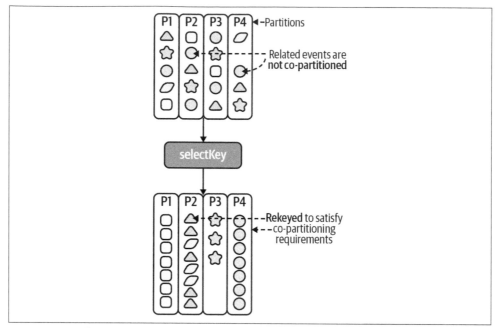

Figure 4-6. Rekeying messages ensures related records appear on the same partition

 When we add a key-changing operator to our topology, the underlying data will be *marked for repartitioning*. This means that as soon as we add a downstream operator that reads the new key, Kafka Streams will:

- Send the rekeyed data to an internal repartition topic
- Reread the newly rekeyed data back into Kafka Streams

This process ensures related records (i.e., records that share the same key) will be processed by the same task in subsequent topology steps. However, the network trip required for rerouting data to a special repartition topic means that rekey operations can be expensive.

What about our `KStream-GlobalKTable` for joining the `products` topic? As shown in Table 4-5, co-partitioning is not required for `GlobalKTable` joins since the state is fully replicated across each instance of our Kafka Streams app. Therefore, we will never encounter this kind of observability problem with a `GlobalKTable` join.

We're almost ready to join our streams and tables. But first, let's take a look at how records are actually combined during a join operation.

Value Joiners

When performing a join using traditional SQL, we simply need to use the join opera-tor in conjunction with a SELECT clause to specify the shape (or *projection*) of the combined join record. For example:

```
SELECT a.customer_name, b.purchase_amount ❶
FROM customers a
LEFT JOIN purchases b
ON a.customer_id = b.customer_id
```

❶ The projection of the combined join record includes two columns.

However, in Kafka Streams, we need to use a ValueJoiner to specify how different records should be combined. A ValueJoiner simply takes each record that is involved in the join, and produces a new, combined record. Looking at the first join, in which we need to join the score-events KStream with the players KTable, the behavior of the value joiner could be expressed using the following pseudocode:

```
(scoreEvent, player) -> combine(scoreEvent, player);
```

But we can do much better than that. It's more typical to have a dedicated data class that does one of the following:

- Wraps each of the values involved in the join
- Extracts the relevant fields from each side of the join, and saves the extracted val-ues in class properties

We will explore both approaches next. First, let's start with a simple wrapper class for the score-events -> players join. Example 4-2 shows a simple implementation of a data class that wraps the record on each side of the join.

Example 4-2. The data class that we'll use to construct the joined score-events -> players record

```
public class ScoreWithPlayer {
  private ScoreEvent scoreEvent;
  private Player player;

  public ScoreWithPlayer(ScoreEvent scoreEvent, Player player) {❶
    this.scoreEvent = scoreEvent; ❷
    this.player = player;
  }

  // accessors omitted from brevity
}
```

❶ The constructor contains a parameter for each side of the join. The left side of the join contains `ScoreEvent`, and the right side contains a `Player`.

❷ We simply save a reference to each record involved in the join inside of our wrapper class.

We can use our new wrapper class as the return type in our `ValueJoiner`. Example 4-3 shows an example implementation of a `ValueJoiner` that combines a `ScoreEvent` (from the `score-events` KStream) and a `Player` (from the `players` KTable) into a `ScoreWithPlayer` instance.

Example 4-3. The ValueJoiner for combining score-events and players

```
ValueJoiner<ScoreEvent, Player, ScoreWithPlayer> scorePlayerJoiner =
    (score, player) -> new ScoreWithPlayer(score, player); ❶
```

❶ We could also simply use a static method reference here, such as `ScoreWithPlayer::new`.

Let's move on to the second join. This join needs to combine a `ScoreWithPlayer` (from the output of the first join) with a `Product` (from the `products` GlobalKTable). We could reuse the wrapper pattern again, but we could also simply extract the properties we need from each side of the join, and discard the rest.

The following code block shows an implementation of a data class that follows the second pattern. We simply extract the values we want and save them to the appropriate class properties:

```
public class Enriched {
  private Long playerId;
  private Long productId;
  private String playerName;
  private String gameName;
  private Double score;

  public Enriched(ScoreWithPlayer scoreEventWithPlayer, Product product) {
    this.playerId = scoreEventWithPlayer.getPlayer().getId();
    this.productId = product.getId();
    this.playerName = scoreEventWithPlayer.getPlayer().getName();
    this.gameName = product.getName();
    this.score = scoreEventWithPlayer.getScoreEvent().getScore();
  }

  // accessors omitted from brevity
}
```

With this new data class in place, we can build our `ValueJoiner` for the KStream-GlobalKTable join using the code shown in Example 4-4.

Example 4-4. A ValueJoiner, expressed as a lambda, that we will use for the join

```
ValueJoiner<ScoreWithPlayer, Product, Enriched> productJoiner =
    (scoreWithPlayer, product) -> new Enriched(scoreWithPlayer, product);
```

Now that we've told Kafka Streams *how* to combine our join records, we can actually perform the joins.

KStream to KTable Join (players Join)

It's time to join our `score-events` KStream with our `players` KTable. Since we only want to trigger the join when the `ScoreEvent` record can be matched to a `Player` record (using the record key), we'll perform an inner join using the `join` operator, as shown here:

```
Joined<String, ScoreEvent, Player> playerJoinParams =
  Joined.with( ❶
    Serdes.String(),
    JsonSerdes.ScoreEvent(),
    JsonSerdes.Player()
  );

KStream<String, ScoreWithPlayer> withPlayers =
  scoreEvents.join( ❷
    players,
    scorePlayerJoiner, ❸
    playerJoinParams
  );
```

❶ The join parameters define how the keys and values for the join records should be serialized.

❷ The join operator performs an inner join.

❸ This is the ValueJoiner we created in Example 4-3. A new ScoreWithPlayer value is created from the two join records. Check out the ScoreWithPlayer data class in Example 4-2 to see how the left and right side of the join values are passed to the constructor.

It's that simple. Furthermore, if you were to run the code at this point and then list all of the topics that are available in your Kafka cluster, you would see that Kafka Streams created two new internal topics for us.

These topics are:

- A repartition topic to handle the rekey operation that we performed in Example 4-1.
- A changelog topic for backing the state store, which is used by the join operator. This is part of the fault-tolerance behavior that we initially discussed in "Fault tolerant" on page 100.

You can verify with the `kafka-topics` console script:[13]

```
$ kafka-topics --bootstrap-server kafka:9092 --list

players
products
score-events
dev-KSTREAM-KEY-SELECT-0000000001-repartition ❶
dev-players-STATE-STORE-0000000002-changelog ❷
```

❶ An internal repartition topic that was created by Kafka Streams. It is prefixed with the application ID of our Kafka Streams application (`dev`).

❷ An internal changelog topic that was created by Kafka Streams. As with the repartition topic, this changelog topic is also prefixed with the application ID of our Kafka Streams application.

OK, we're ready to move on to the second join.

KStream to GlobalKTable Join (products Join)

As we discussed in the co-partitioning requirements, records on either side of a `GlobalKTable` join do not need to share the same key. Since the local task has a full copy of the table, we can actually perform a join using some attribute of the record value itself on the stream side of the join,[14] which is more efficient than having to rekey records through a repartition topic just to ensure related records are handled by the same task.

To perform a `KStream-GlobalKTable` join, we need to create something called a `KeyValueMapper`, whose purpose is to specify how to map a `KStream` record to a `GlobalKTable` record.For this tutorial, we can simply extract the product ID from the `ScoreWithPlayer` value to map these records to a `Product`, as shown here:

---

13 If you're not using Confluent Platform, the script is *kafka-topics.sh*.

14 The `GlobalKTable` side of the join will still use the record key for the lookup.

```
KeyValueMapper<String, ScoreWithPlayer, String> keyMapper =
  (leftKey, scoreWithPlayer) -> {
    return String.valueOf(scoreWithPlayer.getScoreEvent().getProductId());
  };
```

With our `KeyValueMapper` in place, and also the `ValueJoiner` that we created in Example 4-4, we can now perform the join:

```
KStream<String, Enriched> withProducts =
  withPlayers.join(products, keyMapper, productJoiner);
```

This completes the second and third steps of our leaderboard topology (see Figure 4-1). The next thing we need to tackle is grouping the enriched records so that we can perform an aggregation.

Grouping Records

Before you perform any stream or table aggregations in Kafka Streams, you must first group the `KStream` or `KTable` that you plan to aggregate. The purpose of grouping is the same as rekeying records prior to joining: to ensure the related records are processed by the same observer, or Kafka Streams task.

There are some slight differences between grouping streams and tables, so we will take a look at each.

Grouping Streams

There are two operators that can be used for grouping a `KStream`:

- `groupBy`
- `groupByKey`

Using `groupBy` is similar to the process of rekeying a stream using `selectKey`, since this operator is a key-changing operator and causes Kafka Streams to mark the stream for repartitioning. If a downstream operator is added that reads the new key, Kafka Streams will automatically create a repartition topic and route the data back to Kafka to complete the rekeying process.

Example 4-5 shows how to use the `groupBy` operator to group a `KStream`.

Example 4-5. Use the groupBy operator to rekey and group a KStream at the same time

```
KGroupedStream<String, Enriched> grouped =
  withProducts.groupBy(
      (key, value) -> value.getProductId().toString(), ❶
      Grouped.with(Serdes.String(), JsonSerdes.Enriched())); ❷
```

❶ We can use a lambda to select the new key, since the groupBy operator expects a KeyValueMapper, which happens to be a functional interface.

❷ Grouped allows us to pass in some additional options for grouping, including the key and value Serdes to use when serializing the records.

However, if your records don't need to be rekeyed, then it is preferable to use the groupByKey operator instead. groupByKey will *not* mark the stream for repartitioning, and will therefore be more performant since it avoids the additional network calls associated with sending data back to Kafka for repartitioning. The groupByKey implementation is shown here:

```
KGroupedStream<String, Enriched> grouped =
    withProducts.groupByKey(
      Grouped.with(Serdes.String(),
      JsonSerdes.Enriched()));
```

Since we want to calculate the high scores for each *product ID*, and since our enriched stream is currently keyed by *player ID*, we will use the groupBy variation shown in Example 4-5 in the leaderboard topology.

Regardless of which operator you use for grouping a stream, Kafka Streams will return a new type that we haven't discussed before: KGroupedStream. KGroupedStream is just an intermediate representation of a stream that allows us to perform aggregations. We will look at aggregations shortly, but first, let's take a look at how to group KTables.

Grouping Tables

Unlike grouping streams, there is only one operator available for grouping tables: groupBy. Furthermore, instead of returning a KGroupedStream, invoking groupBy on a KTable returns a different intermediate representation: KGroupedTable. Otherwise, the process of grouping KTables is identical to grouping a KStream. For example, if we wanted to group the players KTable so that we could later perform some aggregation (e.g., count the number of players), then we could use the following code:

```
KGroupedTable<String, Player> groupedPlayers =
    players.groupBy(
        (key, value) -> KeyValue.pair(key, value),
        Grouped.with(Serdes.String(), JsonSerdes.Player()));
```

The preceding code block isn't needed for this tutorial since we don't need to group the players table, but we are showing it here to demonstrate the concept. We now know how to group streams and tables, and have completed step 4 of our processor topology (see Figure 4-1). Next, we'll learn how to perform aggregations in Kafka Streams.

Aggregations

One of the final steps required for our leaderboard topology is to calculate the high scores for each game. Kafka Streams gives us a set of operators that makes performing these kinds of aggregations very easy:

- `aggregate`
- `reduce`
- `count`

At a high level, aggregations are just a way of combining multiple input values into a single output value. We tend to think of aggregations as mathematical operations, but they don't have to be. While `count` is a mathematical operation that computes the number of events per key, both the `aggregate` and `reduce` operators are more generic, and can combine values using any combinational logic you specify.

reduce is very similar to `aggregate`. The difference lies in the return type. The `reduce` operator requires the output of an aggregation to be of the same type as the input, while the `aggregate` operator can specify a different type for the output record.

Furthermore, aggregations can be applied to both streams and tables. The semantics are a little different across each, since streams are immutable while tables are mutable. This translates into slightly different versions of the `aggregate` and `reduce` operators, with the streams version accepting two parameters: an *initializer* and an *adder*, and the table version accepting three parameters: an *initializer*, *adder*, and *subtractor*.[15]

Let's take a look at how to aggregate streams by creating our high scores aggregation.

Aggregating Streams

In this section, we'll learn how to apply aggregations to record streams, which involves creating a function for initializing a new aggregate value (called an *initializer*) and a function for performing subsequent aggregations as new records come in for a given key (called an *adder* function). First, we'll learn about initializers.

---

15 Streams are append-only, so do not need a subtractor.

Initializer

When a new key is seen by our Kafka Streams topology, we need some way of initializing the aggregation. The interface that helps us with this is `Initializer`, and like many of the classes in the Kafka Streams API, `Initializer` is a functional interface (i.e., contains a single method), and therefore can be defined as a lambda.

For example, if you were to look at the internals of the `count` aggregation, you'd see an initializer that sets the initial value of the aggregation to 0:

```
Initializer<Long> countInitializer = () -> 0L; ❶
```

❶ The initializer is defined as a lambda, since the `Initializer` interface is a functional interface.

For more complex aggregations, you can provide your own custom initializer instead. For example, to implement a video game leaderboard, we need some way to compute the top three high scores for a given game. To do this, we can create a separate class that will include the logic for tracking the top three scores, and provide a new instance of this class whenever an aggregation needs to be initialized.

In this tutorial, we will create a custom class called `HighScores` to act as our aggregation class. This class will need some underlying data structure to hold the top three scores for a given video game. One approach is to use a `TreeSet`, which is an ordered set included in the Java standard library, and is therefore pretty convenient for holding high scores (which are inherently ordered).

An initial implementation of our data class that we'll use for the high scores aggregation is shown here:

```
public class HighScores {

    private final TreeSet<Enriched> highScores = new TreeSet<>();

}
```

Now we need to tell Kafka Streams how to initialize our new data class. Initializing a class is simple; we just need to instantiate it:

```
Initializer<HighScores> highScoresInitializer = HighScores::new;
```

Once we have an initializer for our aggregation, we need to implement the logic for actually performing the aggregation (in this case, keeping track of the top three high scores for each video game).

Adder

The next thing we need to do in order to build a stream aggregator is to define the logic for combining two aggregates. This is accomplished using the Aggregator interface, which, like Initializer, is a functional interface that can be implemented using a lambda. The implementing function needs to accept three parameters:

- The record key
- The record value
- The current aggregate value

We can create our high scores aggregator with the following code:

```
Aggregator<String, Enriched, HighScores> highScoresAdder =
    (key, value, aggregate) -> aggregate.add(value);
```

Note that aggregate is a HighScores instance, and since our aggregator invokes the HighScores.add method, we simply need to implement that in our HighScores class. As you can see in the following code block, the code is extremely simple, with the add method simply appending a new high score to the internal TreeSet, and then removing the lowest score if we have more than three high scores:

```
public class HighScores {
  private final TreeSet<Enriched> highScores = new TreeSet<>();

  public HighScores add(final Enriched enriched) {
    highScores.add(enriched); ❶

    if (highScores.size() > 3) { ❷
      highScores.remove(highScores.last());
    }

    return this;
  }
}
```

❶ Whenever our adder method (HighScores.add) is called by Kafka Streams, we simply add the new record to the underlying TreeSet, which will sort each entry automatically.

❷ If we have more than three high scores in our TreeSet, remove the lowest score.

In order for the TreeSet to know how to sort Enriched objects (and therefore, be able to identify the Enriched record with the lowest score to remove when our high Scores aggregate exceeds three values), we will implement the Comparable interface, as shown in Example 4-6.

Example 4-6. The updated Enriched class, which implements the Comparable interface

```
public class Enriched implements Comparable<Enriched> { ❶

  @Override
  public int compareTo(Enriched o) { ❷
    return Double.compare(o.score, score);
  }

  // omitted for brevity
}
```

❶ We will update our Enriched class so that it implements Comparable, since determining the top three high scores will involve comparing one Enriched object to
another.

❷ Our implementation of the compareTo method uses the score property as a
method of comparing two different Enriched objects.

Now that we have both our initializer and adder function, we can perform the aggregation using the code in Example 4-7.

*Example 4-7. Use Kafka Streams' aggregate operator to perform our high scores
aggregation*

```
KTable<String, HighScores> highScores =
    grouped.aggregate(highScoresInitializer, highScoresAdder);
```

Aggregating Tables

The process of aggregating tables is pretty similar to aggregating streams. We need an
initializer and an *adder* function. However, tables are mutable, and need to be able to
update an aggregate value whenever a key is deleted.[16] We also need a third parameter, called a *subtractor* function.

Subtractor

While this isn't necessary for the leaderboard example, let's assume we want to count
the number of players in our players KTable. We could use the count operator, but
to demonstrate how to build a subtractor function, we'll build our own aggregate
function that is essentially equivalent to the count operator. A basic implementation
of an aggregate that uses a subtractor function (as well as an initializer and adder

---

16 We haven't talked about deleting keys yet, but we will cover this topic in Chapter 6, when we discuss cleaning
up state stores.

function, which is required for both `KStream` and `KTable` aggregations), is shown here:

```
KGroupedTable<String, Player> groupedPlayers =
  players.groupBy(
      (key, value) -> KeyValue.pair(key, value),
      Grouped.with(Serdes.String(), JsonSerdes.Player()));

groupedPlayers.aggregate(
    () -> 0L, ❶
    (key, value, aggregate) -> aggregate + 1L, ❷
    (key, value, aggregate) -> aggregate - 1L); ❸
```

❶ The initializer function initializes the aggregate to 0.

❷ The adder function increments the current count when a new key is seen.

❸ The subtractor function decrements the current count when a key is removed.

We have now completed step 5 of our leaderboard topology (Figure 4-1). We've written a decent amount of code, so let's see how the individual code fragments fit together in the next section.

Putting It All Together

Now that we've constructed the individual processing steps on our leaderboard topology, let's put it all together. Example 4-8 shows how the topology steps we've created so far come together.

Example 4-8. The processor topology for our video game leaderboard application

```
// the builder is used to construct the topology
StreamsBuilder builder = new StreamsBuilder();

// register the score events stream
KStream<String, ScoreEvent> scoreEvents = ❶
    builder
        .stream(
          "score-events",
          Consumed.with(Serdes.ByteArray(), JsonSerdes.ScoreEvent()))
        .selectKey((k, v) -> v.getPlayerId().toString()); ❷

// create the partitioned players table
KTable<String, Player> players = ❸
    builder.table("players", Consumed.with(Serdes.String(), JsonSerdes.Player()));

// create the global product table
GlobalKTable<String, Product> products = ❹
    builder.globalTable(
```

```
    "products",
    Consumed.with(Serdes.String(), JsonSerdes.Product()));

// join params for scoreEvents - players join
Joined<String, ScoreEvent, Player> playerJoinParams =
    Joined.with(Serdes.String(), JsonSerdes.ScoreEvent(), JsonSerdes.Player());

// join scoreEvents - players
ValueJoiner<ScoreEvent, Player, ScoreWithPlayer> scorePlayerJoiner =
    (score, player) -> new ScoreWithPlayer(score, player);
KStream<String, ScoreWithPlayer> withPlayers =
    scoreEvents.join(players, scorePlayerJoiner, playerJoinParams); ❺

// map score-with-player records to products
KeyValueMapper<String, ScoreWithPlayer, String> keyMapper =
  (leftKey, scoreWithPlayer) -> {
    return String.valueOf(scoreWithPlayer.getScoreEvent().getProductId());
  };

// join the withPlayers stream to the product global ktable
ValueJoiner<ScoreWithPlayer, Product, Enriched> productJoiner =
  (scoreWithPlayer, product) -> new Enriched(scoreWithPlayer, product);
KStream<String, Enriched> withProducts =
  withPlayers.join(products, keyMapper, productJoiner); ❻

// Group the enriched product stream
KGroupedStream<String, Enriched> grouped =
  withProducts.groupBy( ❼
      (key, value) -> value.getProductId().toString(),
      Grouped.with(Serdes.String(), JsonSerdes.Enriched()));

// The initial value of our aggregation will be a new HighScores instance
Initializer<HighScores> highScoresInitializer = HighScores::new;

// The logic for aggregating high scores is implemented in the HighScores.add method
Aggregator<String, Enriched, HighScores> highScoresAdder =
  (key, value, aggregate) -> aggregate.add(value);

// Perform the aggregation, and materialize the underlying state store for querying
KTable<String, HighScores> highScores =
    grouped.aggregate( ❽
        highScoresInitializer,
        highScoresAdder);
```

❶ Read the score-events into a KStream.

❷ Rekey the messages to meet the co-partitioning requirements needed for the join.

❸ Read the `players` topic into a `KTable` since the keyspace is large (allowing us to shard the state across multiple application instances) and since we want time synchronized processing for the `score-events -> players` join.

❹ Read the `products` topic as a `GlobalKTable`, since the keyspace is small and we don't need time synchronized processing.

❺ Join the `score-events` stream and the `players` table.

❻ Join the enriched `score-events` with the `products` table.

❼ Group the enriched stream. This is a prerequisite for aggregating.

❽ Aggregate the grouped stream. The aggregation logic lives in the `HighScores` class.

Let's add the necessary configuration for our application and start streaming:

```
Properties props = new Properties();
props.put(StreamsConfig.APPLICATION_ID_CONFIG, "dev");
props.put(StreamsConfig.BOOTSTRAP_SERVERS_CONFIG, "localhost:9092");

KafkaStreams streams = new KafkaStreams(builder.build(), props);
streams.start();
```

At this point, our application is ready to start receiving records and calculating high scores for our leaderboard. However, we still have one final step to tackle in order to expose the leaderboard results to external clients. Let's move on to the final step of our processor topology, and learn how to expose the state of our Kafka Streams application using interactive queries.

Interactive Queries

One of the defining features of Kafka Streams is its ability to expose application state, both locally and to the outside world. The latter makes it easy to build event-driven microservices with extremely low latency. In this tutorial, we can use interactive queries to expose our high score aggregations.

In order to do this, we need to *materialize* the state store. We'll learn how to do this in the next section.

Materialized Stores

We already know that stateful operators like `aggregate`, `count`, `reduce`, etc., leverage state stores to manage internal state. However, if you look closely at our method for aggregating high scores in Example 4-7, you won't see any mention of a state store.

This variant of the `aggregate` method uses an *internal state store* that is only accessed by the processor topology.

If we want to enable read-only access of the underlying state store for ad hoc queries, we can use one of the overloaded methods to force the materialization of the state store locally. *Materialized state stores* differ from internal state stores in that they are explicitly named and are queryable outside of the processor topology. This is where the `Materialized` class comes in handy. Example 4-9 shows how to materialize a persistent key-value store using the `Materialized` class, which will allow us to query the store using interactive queries.

Example 4-9. Materialized state store with minimal configuration

```
KTable<String, HighScores> highScores =
    grouped.aggregate(
        highScoresInitializer,
        highScoresAdder,
        Materialized.<String, HighScores, KeyValueStore<Bytes, byte[]>> ❶
            as("leader-boards") ❷
            .withKeySerde(Serdes.String()) ❸
            .withValueSerde(JsonSerdes.HighScores()));
```

❶ This variation of the `Materialized.as` method includes three generics:

- The key type of the store (in this case, `String`)

- The value type of the store (in this case, `HighScores`)

- The type of state store (in this case, we'll use a simple key-value store, represented by `KeyValueStore<Bytes, byte[]>`)

❷ Provide an explicit name for the store to make it available for querying outside of the processor topology.

❸ We can customize the materialized state store using a variety of parameters, including the key and value Serdes, as well as other options that we will explore in Chapter 6.

Once we've materialized our `leader-boards` state store, we are almost ready to expose this data via ad hoc queries. The first thing we need to do, however, is to retrieve the store from Kafka Streams.

Accessing Read-Only State Stores

When we need to access a state store in read-only mode, we need two pieces of information:

- The name of the state store
- The type of state store

As we saw in Example 4-9, the name of our state store is leader-boards. We need to retrieve the appropriate read-only wrapper for our underlying state store using the QueryableStoreTypes factory class. There are multiple state stores supported, including:

- QueryableStoreTypes.keyValueStore()
- QueryableStoreTypes.timestampedKeyValueStore()
- QueryableStoreTypes.windowStore()
- QueryableStoreTypes.timestampedWindowStore()
- QueryableStoreTypes.sessionStore()

In our case, we're using a simple key-value store, so we need the QueryableStore Type.keyValueStore() method. With both the state store name and the state store type, we can instantiate an instance of a queryable state store to be used in interactive queries, by using the KafkaStreams.store() method, as shown in Example 4-10.

Example 4-10. Instantiate a key-value store that can be used for performing interactive queries

```
ReadOnlyKeyValueStore<String, HighScores> stateStore =
    streams.store(
        StoreQueryParameters.fromNameAndType(
            "leader-boards",
            QueryableStoreTypes.keyValueStore()));
```

When we have our state store instance, we can query it. The next section discusses the different query types available in key-value stores.

Querying Nonwindowed Key-Value Stores

Each state store type supports different kinds of queries. For example, windowed stores (e.g., ReadOnlyWindowStore) support key lookups using time ranges, while simple key-value stores (ReadOnlyKeyValueStore) support point lookups, range scans, and count queries.

We will discuss windowed state stores in the next chapter, so for now, let's demonstrate the kinds of queries we can make to our `leader-boards` store.

The easiest way to determine which query types are available for your state store type is to check the underlying interface. As we can see from the interface definition in the following snippet, simple key-value stores support several different types of queries:

```
public interface ReadOnlyKeyValueStore<K, V> {

    V get(K key);

    KeyValueIterator<K, V> range(K from, K to);

    KeyValueIterator<K, V> all();

    long approximateNumEntries();
}
```

Let's take a look at each of these query types, starting with the first: point lookups (`get()`).

Point lookups

Perhaps the most common query type, point lookups simply involve querying the state store for an individual key. To perform this type of query, we can use the `get` method to retrieve the value for a given key. For example:

```
HighScores highScores = stateStore.get(key);
```

Note that a point lookup will return either a deserialized instance of the value (in this case, a `HighScores` object, since that is what we're storing in our state store) or `null` if the key is not found.

Range scans

Simple key-value stores also support range scan queries. Range scans return an iterator for an inclusive range of keys. It's very important to close the iterator once you are finished with it to avoid memory leaks.

The following code block shows how to execute a range query, iterate over each result, and close the iterator:

```
KeyValueIterator<String, HighScores> range = stateStore.range(1, 7); ❶

while (range.hasNext()) {
    KeyValue<String, HighScores> next = range.next(); ❷

    String key = next.key;
    HighScores highScores = next.value; ❸

    // do something with high scores object
```

```
    }
    range.close(); ❹
```

❶ Returns an iterator that can be used for iterating through each key in the selected range.

❷ Get the next element in the iteration.

❸ The HighScores value is available in the next.value property.

❹ It's very important to close the iterator to avoid memory leaks. Another way of closing is to use a try-with-resources statement when getting the iterator.

All entries

Similar to a range scan, the all() query returns an iterator of key-value pairs, and is similar to an unfiltered SELECT * query. However, this query type will return an iterator for all of the entries in our state store, instead of those within a specific key range only. As with range queries, it's important to close the iterator once you're finished with it to avoid memory leaks. The following code shows how to execute an all() query. Iterating through the results and closing the iterator is the same as the range scan query, so we have omitted that logic for brevity:

```
    KeyValueIterator<String, HighScores> range = stateStore.all();
```

Number of entries

Finally, the last query type is similar to a COUNT(*) query, and returns the approximate number of entries in the underlying state store.

 When using RocksDB persistent stores, the returned value is approximate since calculating a precise count can be expensive and, when it comes to RocksDB-backed stores, challenging as well. Taken from the RocksDB FAQ (*https://oreil.ly/1r9GD*):

> Obtaining an accurate number of keys [in] LSM databases like RocksDB is a challenging problem as they have duplicate keys and deletion entries (i.e., tombstones) that will require a full compaction in order to get an accurate number of keys. In addition, if the RocksDB database contains merge operators, it will also make the estimated number of keys less accurate.

On the other hand, if using an in-memory store, the count will be exact.

To execute this type of query against a simple key-value store, we could run the following code:

```
long approxNumEntries = stateStore.approximateNumEntries();
```

Now that we know how to query simple key-value stores, let's see where we can actually execute these queries from.

Local Queries

Each instance of a Kafka Streams application can query its own local state. However, it's important to remember that unless you are materializing a GlobalKTable or running a single instance of your Kafka Streams app,[17] the local state will only represent a partial view of the entire application state (this is the nature of a KTable, as discussed in "KTable" on page 107).

Luckily for us, Kafka Streams provides some additional methods that make it easy to connect distributed state stores, and to execute *remote queries*, which allow us to query the entire state of our application. We'll learn about remote queries next.

Remote Queries

In order to query the full state of our application, we need to:

- Discover which instances contain the various fragments of our application state
- Add a remote procedure call (RPC) or REST *service* to expose the local state to other running application instances[18]
- Add an RPC or REST *client* for querying remote state stores from a running application instance

Regarding the last two points, you have a lot of flexibility in choosing which server and client components you want to use for inter-instance communication. In this tutorial, we'll use Javalin (*https://javalin.io*) to implement a REST service due to its simple API. We will also use OkHttp (*https://oreil.ly/okhttp*), developed by Square, for our REST client for its ease of use. Let's add these dependencies to our application by updating our *build.gradle* file with the following:

```
dependencies {

  // required for interactive queries (server)
```

---

17 The latter of these is not advisable. Running a single Kafka Streams application would consolidate the entire application state to a single instance, but Kafka Streams is meant to be run in a distributed fashion for maximizing performance and fault tolerance.

18 And other clients if desired, e.g., humans.

```
    implementation 'io.javalin:javalin:3.12.0'

    // required for interactive queries (client)
    implementation 'com.squareup.okhttp3:okhttp:4.9.0'

    // other dependencies
}
```

Now let's tackle the issue of instance discovery. We need some way of broadcasting which instances are running at any given point in time and where they are running. The latter can be accomplished using the APPLICATION_SERVER_CONFIG parameter to specify a host and port pair in Kafka Streams, as shown here:

```
Properties props = new Properties();

props.put(StreamsConfig.APPLICATION_SERVER_CONFIG, "myapp:8080"); ❶

// other Kafka Streams properties omitted for brevity

KafkaStreams streams = new KafkaStreams(builder.build(), props);
```

❶ Configure an endpoint. This will be communicated to other running application instances through Kafka's consumer group protocol. It's important to use an IP and port pair that other instances can use to communicate with your application (i.e., localhost would not work since it would resolve to different IPs depending on the instance).

Note that setting the APPLICATION_SERVER_CONFIG parameter config doesn't actually tell Kafka Streams to start listening on whatever port you configure. In fact, Kafka Streams does not include a built-in RPC service. However, this host/port information is transmitted to other running instances of your Kafka Streams application and is made available through dedicated API methods, which we will discuss later. But first, let's set up our REST service to start listening on the appropriate port (8080 in this example).

In terms of code maintainability, it makes sense to define our leaderboard REST service in a dedicated file, separate from the topology definition. The following code block shows a simple implementation of the leaderboard service:

```
class LeaderboardService {
  private final HostInfo hostInfo; ❶
  private final KafkaStreams streams; ❷

  LeaderboardService(HostInfo hostInfo, KafkaStreams streams) {
    this.hostInfo = hostInfo;
    this.streams = streams;
  }

  ReadOnlyKeyValueStore<String, HighScores> getStore() { ❸
    return streams.store(
```

```
        StoreQueryParameters.fromNameAndType(
            "leader-boards",
            QueryableStoreTypes.keyValueStore()));
  }

  void start() {
    Javalin app = Javalin.create().start(hostInfo.port()); ❹

    app.get("/leaderboard/:key", this::getKey); ❺
  }
}
```

❶ HostInfo is a simple wrapper class in Kafka Streams that contains a hostname and port. We'll see how to instantiate this shortly.

❷ We need to keep track of the local Kafka Streams instance. We will use some API methods on this instance in the next code block.

❸ Add a dedicated method for retrieving the state store that contains the leader-board aggregations. This follows the same method for retrieving a read-only state store wrapper that we saw in Example 4-10.

❹ Start the Javalin-based web service on the configured port.

❺ Adding endpoints with Javalin is easy. We simply map a URL path to a method, which we will implement shortly. Path parameters, which are specified with a leading colon (e.g., :key), allow us to create dynamic endpoints. This is ideal for a point lookup query.

Now, let's implement the /leaderboard/:key endpoint, which will show the high scores for a given key (which in this case is a product ID). As we recently learned, we can use a point lookup to retrieve a single value from our state store. A naive implementation is shown in the following:

```
void getKey(Context ctx) {
    String productId = ctx.pathParam("key");
    HighScores highScores = getStore().get(productId); ❶
    ctx.json(highScores.toList()); ❷
}
```

❶ Use a point lookup to retrieve a value from the local state store.

❷ Note: the toList() method is available in the source code.

Unfortunately, this isn't sufficient. Consider the example where we have two running instances of our Kafka Streams application. Depending on *which* instance we query and *when* we issue the query (state can move around whenever there is a consumer rebalance), we may not be able to retrieve the requested value. Figure 4-7 shows this conundrum.

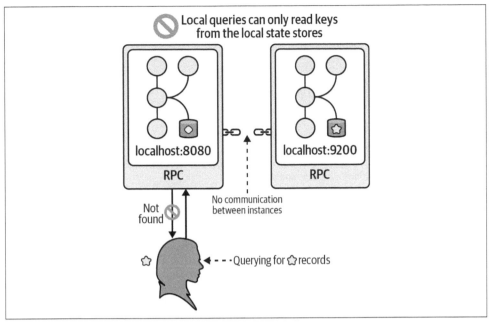

Figure 4-7. When state is partitioned across multiple application instances, local queries are not sufficient

Fortunately, Kafka Streams provides a method called queryMetadataForKey,[19] which allows us to discover the application instance (local or remote) that a specific key lives on. An improved implementation of our getKey method is shown in Example 4-11.

Example 4-11. An updated implementation of the getKey method, which leverages remote queries to pull data from different application instances

```
void getKey(Context ctx) {

  String productId = ctx.pathParam("key");

  KeyQueryMetadata metadata =
      streams.queryMetadataForKey(
          "leader-boards", productId, Serdes.String().serializer()); ❶

  if (hostInfo.equals(metadata.activeHost())) {
```

---

19 Which replaces the metadataForKey method that was widely used in versions < 2.5, but officially deprecated in that release.

```
HighScores highScores = getStore().get(productId); ❷

if (highScores == null) { ❸
  // game was not found
  ctx.status(404);
  return;
}

// game was found, so return the high scores
ctx.json(highScores.toList()); ❹
  return;
}

// a remote instance has the key
String remoteHost = metadata.activeHost().host();
int remotePort = metadata.activeHost().port();
String url =
  String.format(
      "http://%s:%d/leaderboard/%s",
      remoteHost, remotePort, productId); ❺

OkHttpClient client = new OkHttpClient();
Request request = new Request.Builder().url(url).build();

try (Response response = client.newCall(request).execute()) { ❻
  ctx.result(response.body().string());
} catch (Exception e) {
  ctx.status(500);
}
}
```

❶ queryMetadataForKey allows us to find which host a specific key should live on.

❷ If the local instance has the key, just query the local state store.

❸ The queryMetadataForKey method doesn't actually check to see if the key exists. It uses the default stream partitioner[20] to determine where the key *would exist, if it existed.* Therefore, we check for null (which is returned if the key isn't found) and return a 404 response if it doesn't exist.

❹ Return a formatted response containing the high scores.

---

20 There is an overloaded version of the queryMetadataForKey method that accepts a custom StreamParti tioner as well.

❺ If we made it this far, then the key exists on a remote host, if it exists at all. There-fore, construct a URL using the metadata, which includes the host and port of the Kafka Streams instance that would contain the specified key.

❻ Invoke the request, and return the result if successful.

To help visualize what is happening here, Figure 4-8 shows how distributed state stores can be connected using a combination of instance discovery and an RPC/REST service.

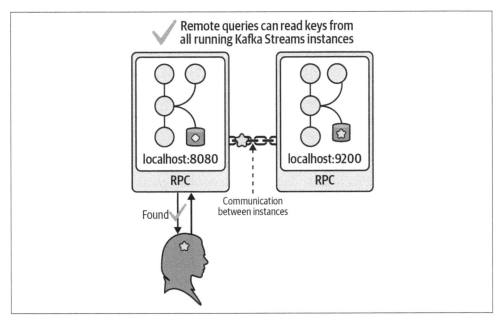

Figure 4-8. Remote queries allow us to query the state of other running application instances

But what if you need to execute a query that doesn't operate on a single key? For example, what if you need to count the number of entries across all of your dis-tributed state stores? The queryMetadataForKey wouldn't work well in this case, since it requires us to specify a single key. Instead, we would leverage another Kafka Streams method, called allMetadataForStore, which returns the endpoint for every running Kafka Streams application that shares the same application ID *and* has at least one active partition for the provided store name.

Let's add a new endpoint to our leaderboard service that surfaces the number of high score records across all of the running application instances:

```
app.get("/leaderboard/count", this::getCount);
```

Now, we'll implement the `getCount` method referenced in the preceding code, which leverages the `allMetadataForStore` method to get the total number of records in each remote state store:

```
void getCount(Context ctx) {
  long count = getStore().approximateNumEntries(); ❶
                                                    ❷
  for (StreamsMetadata metadata : streams.allMetadataForStore("leader-boards")) {
    if (!hostInfo.equals(metadata.hostInfo())) {
      continue; ❸
    }
    count += fetchCountFromRemoteInstance( ❹
      metadata.hostInfo().host(),
      metadata.hostInfo().port());
  }

  ctx.json(count);
}
```

❶ Initialize the count with the number of entries in the local state store.

❷ On the following line, we use the `allMetadataForStore` method to retrieve the host/port pairs for each Kafka Streams instance that contains a fragment of the state we want to query.

❸ If the metadata is for the current host, then continue through the loop since we've already pulled the entry count from the local state store.

❹ If the metadata does not pertain to the local instance, then retrieve the count from the remote instance. We've omitted the implementation details of `fetch CountFromRemoteInstance` from this text since it is similar to what we saw in Example 4-11, where we instantiated a REST client and issued a request against a remove application instance. If you're interested in the implementation details, please check the source code for this chapter.

This completes the last step of our leaderboard topology (see Figure 4-1). We can now run our application, generate some dummy data, and query our leaderboard service.

The dummy data for each of the source topics is shown in Example 4-12.

> For the keyed topics (`players` and `products`), the record key is formatted as `<key>|<value>`. For the `score-events` topic, the dummy records are simply formatted as `<value>`.

Example 4-12. Dummy records that we will be producing to our source topics

```
# players
1|{"id": 1, "name": "Elyse"}
2|{"id": 2, "name": "Mitch"}
3|{"id": 3, "name": "Isabelle"}
4|{"id": 4, "name": "Sammy"}

# products
1|{"id": 1, "name": "Super Smash Bros"}
6|{"id": 6, "name": "Mario Kart"}

# score-events
{"score": 1000, "product_id": 1, "player_id": 1}
{"score": 2000, "product_id": 1, "player_id": 2}
{"score": 4000, "product_id": 1, "player_id": 3}
{"score": 500, "product_id": 1, "player_id": 4}
{"score": 800, "product_id": 6, "player_id": 1}
{"score": 2500, "product_id": 6, "player_id": 2}
{"score": 9000.0, "product_id": 6, "player_id": 3}
{"score": 1200.0, "product_id": 6, "player_id": 4}
```

If we produce this dummy data into the appropriate topics and then query our leaderboard service, we will see that our Kafka Streams application not only processed the high scores, but is now exposing the results of our stateful operations. An example response to an interactive query is shown in the following code block:

```
$ curl -s localhost:7000/leaderboard/1 | jq '.'

[
  {
    "playerId": 3,
    "productId": 1,
    "playerName": "Isabelle",
    "gameName": "Super Smash Bros",
    "score": 4000
  },
  {
    "playerId": 2,
    "productId": 1,
    "playerName": "Mitch",
    "gameName": "Super Smash Bros",
    "score": 2000
  },
  {
    "playerId": 1,
    "productId": 1,
    "playerName": "Elyse",
    "gameName": "Super Smash Bros",
    "score": 1000
  }
]
```

Summary

In this chapter, you learned how Kafka Streams captures information about the events it consumes, and how to leverage the remembered information (state) to perform more advanced stream processing tasks, including:

- Performing a `KStream-KTable` join
- Rekeying messages to meet the co-partitioning requirements for certain join types
- Performing a `KStream-GlobalKTable` join
- Grouping records into intermediate representations (`KGroupedStream`, `KGroupedTable`) to prepare our data for aggregating
- Aggregating streams and tables
- Using the interactive queries to expose the state of our application using both local and remote queries

In the next chapter, we will discuss another aspect of stateful programming that is concerned with not only *what* events our application has seen, but *when* they occurred. Time plays a key role in stateful processing, so understanding the different notions of time and also the several time-based abstractions in the Kafka Streams library will help us expand our knowledge of stateful processing even further.

## CHAPTER 5

Windows and Time

Time is such an important concept that we measure our lives by the passing of it. Each year, half a dozen people stand around me, singing happy birthday, and as the last flat note dissipates from the air, a cake is offered at the feet of this mysterious force. I like to think the cake is for me, but it's for time.

Not only is time so intricately woven into the physical world, but it also permeates our event streams. In order to unlock the full power of Kafka Streams, we must understand the relationship between events and time. This chapter explores this relationship in detail, and will give us hands-on experience with something called *windows*. Windows allow us to group events into explicit time buckets, and can be used for creating more advanced joins and aggregations (which we first explored in the previous chapter).

By the end of this chapter, you will understand the following:

- The differences between event time, ingestion time, and processing time
- How to build a custom timestamp extractor for associating events with a particular timestamp and time semantic
- How time controls the flow of data through Kafka Streams
- What types of windows are supported in Kafka Streams
- How to perform windowed joins
- How to perform windowed aggregations
- What strategies are available for dealing with late and out-of-order events
- How to use the `suppress` operator to process the final results of windows
- How to query windowed key-value stores

As with previous chapters, we will introduce these concepts through a tutorial. So without further ado, let's take a look at the application we will be building in this chapter.

Introducing Our Tutorial: Patient Monitoring Application

Some of the most important use cases for time-centric stream processing are in the medical field. Patient monitoring systems are capable of producing hundreds of measurements per second, and processing/responding to this data quickly is important for treating certain types of medical conditions. This is why Children's Healthcare of Atlanta uses Kafka Streams and ksqlDB to make real-time predictions about whether or not children with head trauma will need surgical intervention in the near future.[1]

Inspired by this use case, we will demonstrate several time-centric streaming concepts by building an application to monitor patient vitals. Instead of monitoring for head trauma, we will try to detect the presence of a medical condition called *systemic inflammatory response syndrome*, or SIRS. According to Bridgette Kadri, a physician's assistant at the Medical University of South Carolina, there are several vital signs, including body temperature, blood pressure, and heart rate, that can be used as indicators of SIRS. In this tutorial, we will look at two of these measurements: body temperature and heart rate. When both of these vitals reach predefined thresholds (heart rate >= 100 beats per minute, body temperature >= 100.4°F), we will send a record to an *alerts* topic to notify the appropriate medical personnel.[2]

Let's look at the architecture of our patient monitoring application. Figure 5-1 shows the topology design we'll be implementing in this chapter. Additional information about each step is included after the diagram.

---

[1] This is accomplished by measuring intracranial pressure, aggregating the measurements, and sending the aggregations to a predictive model. When the model predicts that the pressure will reach dangerous levels in the next 30 minutes, then healthcare professionals will be notified so they can take the appropriate action. All of this is made possible through time-aware stream processing. Check out Tim Berglund's interview with Ramesh Sringeri (*https://oreil.ly/GHbVd*) for an in-depth look at this use case.

[2] We won't actually implement the monitoring application in this tutorial since it isn't necessary to demonstrate the time-centric features of Kafka Streams.

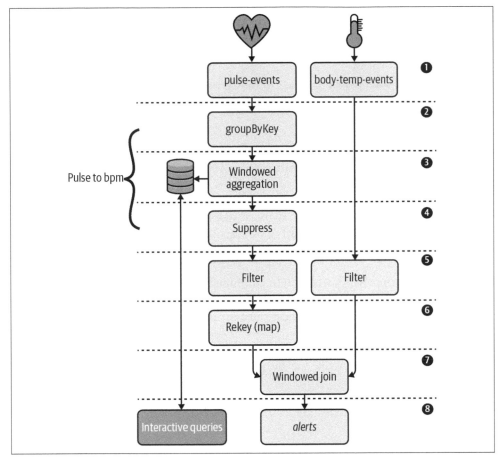

Figure 5-1. The topology that we will be implementing for our patient monitoring application

❶ Our Kafka cluster contains two topics that capture patient vitals measurements:

- The `pulse-events` topic is populated by a heartbeat sensor. Every time the sensor picks up a patient's heartbeat, it appends a record to this topic. Records are keyed by patient ID.

- The `body-temp-events` topic is populated by a wireless body temperature sensor. Every time the patient's core body temperature is taken, a record is appended to this topic. These records are also keyed by patient ID.

❷ In order to detect elevated heart rates, we need to convert the raw pulse events into a heart rate (measured using *beats per minute*, or bpm). As we learned in the previous chapter, we must first group the records to satisfy Kafka Streams' prerequisite for performing aggregations.

③ We will use a windowed aggregation to convert the pulse events into a heart rate. Since our unit of measurement is beats per minute, our window size will be 60 seconds.

④ We will use the `suppress` operator to only emit the final computation of the bpm window. We'll see why this is needed once we discuss this operator later in the chapter.

⑤ In order to detect an infection, we will filter all vitals measurements that breach a set of predefined thresholds (heart rate >= 100 beats per minute, body temperature >= 100.4°F).

⑥ As we'll see shortly, windowed aggregations change the record key. Therefore, we'll need to rekey the heart rate records by patient ID to meet the co-partitioning requirements for joining records.

⑦ We will perform a windowed join to combine the two vitals streams. Since we are performing the join *after* filtering for elevated bpm and body temperature measures, each joined record will indicate an alerting condition for SIRS.

⑧ Finally, we will expose the results of our heart rate aggregation via interactive queries. We will also write the output of our joined stream to a topic called `alerts`.

Let's now quickly run through the project setup so you can follow along with this tutorial.

Project Setup

The code for this chapter is located at *https://github.com/mitch-seymour/mastering-kafka-streams-and-ksqldb.git*.

If you would like to reference the code as we work our way through each topology step, clone the repo and change to the directory containing this chapter's tutorial. The following command will do the trick:

```
$ git clone git@github.com:mitch-seymour/mastering-kafka-streams-and-ksqldb.git
$ cd mastering-kafka-streams-and-ksqldb/chapter-05/patient-monitoring
```

You can build the project anytime by running the following command:

```
$ ./gradlew build --info
```

Now that our project is set up, let's start implementing our patient monitoring application.

Data Models

As usual, we'll start by defining our data models. Since each vitals measurement is associated with a timestamp, we will first create a simple interface for each data class to implement. This interface allows us to extract the timestamp from a given record in a consistent manner, and will come in handy when we implement a timestamp extractor later in this chapter. The following code block shows the interface each data class will implement:

```java
public interface Vital {
  public String getTimestamp();
}
```

Here are the data classes we'll be working with. Note: the accessor methods (including the interface method, `getTimestamp`) have been omitted for brevity:

Kafka topic	Example record	Data class
pulse-events	```{ "timestamp": "2020-11-05T09:02:00.000Z" }```	```public class Pulse implements Vital { private String timestamp; }```
body-temp-events	```{ "timestamp": "2020-11-04T09:02:06.500Z", "temperature": 101.2, "unit": "F" }```	```public class BodyTemp implements Vital { private String timestamp; private Double temperature; private String unit; }```

Now that we have a good understanding of what the source data looks like, we're almost ready to register the input streams. However, this application requires special attention to time, and so far in this book, we haven't put much thought into how records are associated with timestamps. So, before we register the input streams, let's look at the various time semantics in Kafka Streams.

Time Semantics

There are several different notions of time in Kafka Streams, and choosing the correct semantic is important when performing time-based operations, including windowed joins and aggregations. In this section, we will take some time to understand the different notions of time in Kafka Streams, starting with some simple definitions:

Event time
> When an event was created at the source. This timestamp can be embedded in the payload of an event, or set directly using the Kafka producer client as of version 0.10.0.

Ingestion time

When the event is appended to a topic on a Kafka broker. This always occurs after event time.

Processing time

When the event is processed by your Kafka Streams application. This always occurs after event time *and* ingestion time. It is less static than event time, and reprocessing the same data (i.e., for bug fixes) will lead to new processing time-stamps, and therefore nondeterministic windowing behavior.

To illustrate where these notions of time are physically manifested in an event stream, see Figure 5-2.

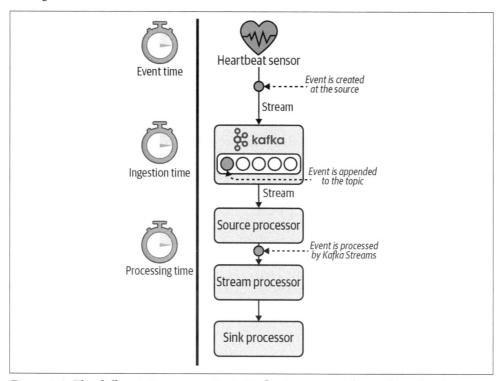

Figure 5-2. The different time semantics in Kafka Streams, as shown through a heart-beat sensor

Event time is probably the most intuitive notion of time since it describes when the event actually occurred. For example, if a heartbeat sensor records a pulse at 9:02 a.m., then the event time is 9:02 a.m.

The event time is typically embedded in the payload, as shown in the following code example:

```
{
  "timestamp": "2020-11-12T09:02:00.000Z", ❶
  "sensor": "smart-pulse"
}
```

❶ An embedded event timestamp that must be extracted.

Alternatively, Kafka producers allow the default timestamp that gets set for each record to be overridden, which can also be used to achieve event-time semantics. However, for systems that use this method for associating timestamps with events, it's important to be aware of two Kafka configurations (one at the broker level and one at the topic level) to ensure you don't accidentally end up with ingestion-time semantics. The relevant configurations are:

- `log.message.timestamp.type` (broker level)
- `message.timestamp.type` (topic level)

There are two possible values for these configs: `CreateTime` or `LogAppendTime`. Furthermore, the topic-level config takes precedence over the broker-level config. If the topic is configured with the `LogAppendTime` timestamp type,[3] the timestamp that the producer appends to the message will be overwritten with the local system time of the broker whenever a record is appended to the topic (therefore, you'll be working with ingestion-time semantics, even if that wasn't your intent). If you want to achieve event-time semantics and you're relying on the producer timestamp, be sure that you are using `CreateTime` as the message timestamp type.

The benefit of using event-time semantics is that this timestamp is more meaningful to the event itself, and is therefore more intuitive for users. Event time also allows time-dependent operations to be deterministic (e.g., when reprocessing data). This is not the case when using processing time. Processing time is usually used if you aren't leveraging time-based operations, if the time at which the event is processed is more meaningful to the semantics of the application than when the event initially occurred, or if you can't associate an event with a timestamp for some reason. Interestingly enough, the latter issue, which occurs when an event time can't be associated with a record, is sometimes addressed by using ingestion time. In systems where there isn't a lot of lag between the time an event is created and when the event is subsequently

---

3 Either directly via the topic-level config or indirectly using the broker-level config and no override for the topic-level config.

appended to a topic, ingestion time can be used to approximate event time, so it can be a viable alternative when event time can't be used.[4]

Now that we've learned about the different notions of time in Kafka Streams, how do we actually leverage the time semantic of our choice? We'll learn about this in the next section.

Timestamp Extractors

In Kafka Streams, *timestamp extractors* are responsible for associating a given record with a timestamp, and these timestamps are used in time-dependent operations like windowed joins and windowed aggregations. Each timestamp extractor implementation must adhere to the following interface:

```
public interface TimestampExtractor {
    long extract(
        ConsumerRecord<Object, Object> record, ❶
        long partitionTime ❷
    );
}
```

❶ The current consumer record being processed.

❷ Kafka Streams keeps track of the most recent timestamp it has seen for each partition it consumes from, and passes this timestamp to the extract method using the partitionTime parameter.

The second parameter, partitionTime, is particularly interesting since it can be used as a fallback if a timestamp cannot be extracted. We'll dig into that shortly, but first, let's look at the timestamp extractors that are included in Kafka Streams.

Included Timestamp Extractors

FailOnInvalidTimestamp, which is the default timestamp extractor in Kafka Streams, extracts the timestamp from the consumer record, which is either the event time (when message.timestamp.type is set to CreateTime) or ingestion time (when message.timestamp.type is set to LogAppendTime). This extractor will throw a StreamsException if the timestamp is invalid. A timestamp is considered invalid if it is negative (which can happen if the record was produced using a message format older than 0.10.0). At the time of this writing, it's been over four years since version 0.10.0 was released, so negative/invalid timestamps are becoming more of a corner case at this point.

---

4 Matthias J. Sax has a great presentation (*https://oreil.ly/MRiCu*) that talks about this, as well as some of the other topics discussed in this chapter.

The LogAndSkipOnInvalidTimestamp extractor can also be used to achieve event-time semantics, but unlike the FailOnInvalidTimestamp extractor, it simply logs a warning when an invalid timestamp is encountered. This will result in the record being skipped, allowing Kafka Streams to continue processing when it encounters invalid timestamps.

There is another built-in extractor that we can use if we want processing-time semantics. As you can see in the code that follows, the WallclockTimestampExtractor simply returns the local system time of your stream processing application:

```
public class WallclockTimestampExtractor implements TimestampExtractor {

    @Override
    public long extract(
      final ConsumerRecord<Object, Object> record,
      final long partitionTime
    ) {
        return System.currentTimeMillis(); ❶
    }
}
```

❶ The WallclockTimestampExtractor, which is one of the included timestamp extractors in Kafka Streams, simply returns the current system time.

Regardless of which timestamp extractor you use, you can override the default timestamp extractor by setting the DEFAULT_TIMESTAMP_EXTRACTOR_CLASS_CONFIG property as shown in Example 5-1.

Example 5-1. An example of how to override the default timestamp extractor in Kafka Streams

```
Properties props = new Properties();
props.put( ❶
  StreamsConfig.DEFAULT_TIMESTAMP_EXTRACTOR_CLASS_CONFIG,
  WallclockTimestampExtractor.class
);

// ... other configs

KafkaStreams streams = new KafkaStreams(builder.build(), props);
```

❶ Override the default timestamp extractor.

When your Kafka Streams application leverages windows, as our patient monitoring application does, using processing-time semantics can have unintended side effects. For example, we want to capture the number of heartbeats within a one-minute window. If we use processing-time semantics (e.g., via WallclockTimestampExtractor) for our windowed aggregation, then our window boundaries won't represent the pulse time at all, but will instead represent the time our Kafka Streams application observed the pulse event. If our application experiences even a few seconds of lag, an event may fall outside of the intended window and therefore could impact our expectations in certain ways (i.e., our ability to detect an elevated heart rate).

 When a timestamp is extracted and subsequently associated with a record, the record is said to be *stamped*.

After reviewing the built-in timestamp extractors, it's clear that we need a custom timestamp extractor since the event time is embedded in the payloads of each of our vitals data (pulse and body temperature events). We'll discuss how to build a custom timestamp extractor in the next section.

Custom Timestamp Extractors

It's very common to build a custom timestamp extractor whenever you need event-time semantics and the event timestamp is embedded in the record payload. The following code block shows a custom timestamp extractor that we will use to extract the timestamp of a patient vitals measurement. As mentioned before, our custom timestamp extractor implements the `TimestampExtractor` interface included in Kafka Streams:

```
public class VitalTimestampExtractor implements TimestampExtractor {

  @Override
  public long extract(ConsumerRecord<Object, Object> record, long partitionTime) {
    Vital measurement = (Vital) record.value();         ❶
    if (measurement != null && measurement.getTimestamp() != null) {   ❷
      String timestamp = measurement.getTimestamp();    ❸
      return Instant.parse(timestamp).toEpochMilli();   ❹
    }
    return partitionTime;                               ❺
  }
}
```

❶ Cast the record value to a `Vital` object. This is where our interface comes in handy, since it allows us to extract the timestamp from `Pulse` and `BodyTemp` records in a consistent way.

❷ Make sure the record contains a timestamp before we attempt to parse it.

❸ Extract the timestamp from the record.

❹ The `TimestampExtractor.extract` method expects us to return the record's timestamp in milliseconds. So we perform the timestamp-to-milliseconds conversion here.

❺ If we cannot extract a timestamp for some reason, we can fall back to the partition time in order to approximate when the event occurred.

One thing you should consider when using timestamp extractors is how records without valid timestamps should be handled. The three most common options are to:

- Throw an exception and stop processing (giving the developers an opportunity to resolve the bug)
- Fallback to the partition time
- Return a negative timestamp, which will allow Kafka Streams to skip over the record and continue processing

In our implementation of the `VitalTimestampExtractor` we've decided to fallback to the partition time, which will resolve to the highest timestamp that has already been observed for the current partition.

Now that we have created our timestamp extractor, let's register our input streams.

Registering Streams with a Timestamp Extractor

Registering a set of input streams should be familiar by now, but this time, we'll pass in an extra `Consumed` parameter that will explicitly set the timestamp extractor to our custom timestamp extractor implementation (`VitalTimestampExtractor`). Example 5-2 shows how to register our two source streams using a custom timestamp extractor, which is the first step of our processor topology (see Figure 5-1).

Example 5-2. An example of how to override the timestamp extractor for source streams

```
StreamsBuilder builder = new StreamsBuilder(); ❶

Consumed<String, Pulse> pulseConsumerOptions =
    Consumed.with(Serdes.String(), JsonSerdes.Pulse())
        .withTimestampExtractor(new VitalTimestampExtractor()); ❷

KStream<String, Pulse> pulseEvents =
    builder.stream("pulse-events", pulseConsumerOptions); ❸

Consumed<String, BodyTemp> bodyTempConsumerOptions =
    Consumed.with(Serdes.String(), JsonSerdes.BodyTemp())
        .withTimestampExtractor(new VitalTimestampExtractor()); ❹
```

```
KStream<String, BodyTemp> tempEvents =
        builder.stream("body-temp-events", bodyTempConsumerOptions); ❺
```

❶ As always with the DSL, use a `StreamsBuilder` to construct our processor topology.

❷ Use `Consumed.withTimestampExtractor` to tell Kafka Streams to use our custom timestamp extractor (`VitalTimestampExtractor`) for extracting vitals timestamps.

❸ Register the stream for capturing pulse events.

❹ Use our custom timestamp extractor in the body temperature options as well.

❺ Register the stream for capturing body temperature events.

Alternatively, we could override the default timestamp extractor using the method shown in Example 5-1. Either method is fine, but for now, we'll stick with setting the extractor for each input stream directly. Now that we've registered our source streams, let's move on to the second and third steps of our processor topology (see Figure 5-1): grouping and windowing the `pulse-events` stream.

Windowing Streams

The `pulse-events` topic receives data whenever a patient's heartbeat is recorded. However, for our purposes, we're interested in the patient's heart rate, which is measured by the number of beats per minute (bpm). We know that the `count` operator can be used to count the number of heartbeats, but we need some way of only counting the records that fall within each 60-second window. This is where *windowed aggregations* come into play. Windowing is a method for grouping records into different time-based subgroups for the purpose of aggregating and joining. Kafka Streams supports a few different types of windows, so let's take a look at each type to determine which implementation we will need for our patient monitoring system.

Window Types

Windows are used to group records with close *temporal proximity*. Temporal proximity can mean different things depending on which time semantic you are using. For example, when using event-time semantics, it can mean "records that *occurred* around the same time," whereas with processing-time semantics, it means "records that were *processed* around the same time." For most cases, "around the same time" is defined by the window size (e.g., five minutes, one hour, etc.), though session windows (which we'll discuss shortly) utilize an activity period.

There are four different types of windows in Kafka Streams. We will discuss the characteristics of each window type next, and then use these properties to create a decision tree for deciding which window to use in our tutorial (you can also use the resulting decision tree in your own applications).

Tumbling windows

Tumbling windows are fixed-sized windows that never overlap. They are defined using a single property, the *window size* (in milliseconds), and have predictable time ranges since they are aligned with the epoch.[5] The following code shows how to create a tumbling window in Kafka Streams:

```
TimeWindows tumblingWindow =
    TimeWindows.of(Duration.ofSeconds(5)); ❶
```

❶ The size of the window is five seconds.

As you can see in Figure 5-3, a tumbling window is very simple to reason about, visually. You don't have to worry about overlapping window boundaries or records appearing in more than one time bucket.

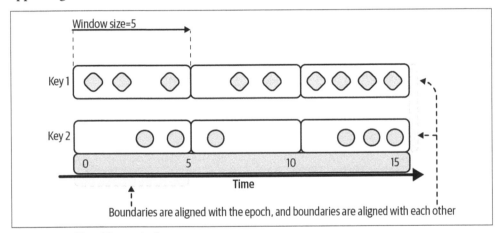

Figure 5-3. Tumbling window

---

5 Taken from the Java docs (*https://oreil.ly/osqwA*): "Aligned to the epoch means that the first window starts at timestamp zero." In other words, a window size of 5,000 would have boundaries of 0–5,000, 5,000–10,000, etc. Note that the start time is inclusive but the end time is exclusive.

Hopping windows

Hopping windows are fixed-sized windows that may overlap.[6] When configuring a hopping window, you must specify both the *window size* and the *advance interval* (how much the window moves forward). When the advance interval is less than the window size, as shown in Figure 5-4, then windows will overlap, allowing some records to appear in multiple windows. Furthermore, hopping windows have predictable time ranges since they are aligned with the epoch, and the start time is inclusive while the end time is exclusive. The following code depicts how to create a simple hopping window with Kafka Streams:

```
TimeWindows hoppingWindow = TimeWindows
  .of(Duration.ofSeconds(5))    ❶
  .advanceBy(Duration.ofSeconds(4));    ❷
```

❶ The size of the window is five seconds.

❷ The window has a four-second advance interval (or *hop*).

A visualization of this hopping window is shown in Figure 5-4.

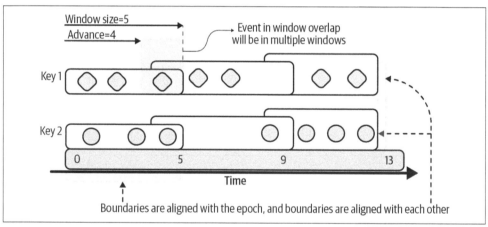

Figure 5-4. Hopping window

Session windows

Session windows are variable-sized windows that are determined by periods of activity followed by gaps of inactivity. A single parameter called the *inactivity gap* is used to define a session window. If the inactivity gap is five seconds, then each record that has a timestamp within five seconds of the previous record with the same key will be

---

6 In some systems, the term "sliding window" is used to refer to hopping windows. However, in Kafka Streams, hopping windows are distinct from sliding windows, which we will discuss shortly.

merged into the same window. Otherwise, if the timestamp of a new record is greater than the inactivity gap (in this case, five seconds), then a new window will be created. Unlike tumbling and hopping windows, both the lower and upper boundaries are inclusive. The following code snippet shows how to define a session window:

```
SessionWindows sessionWindow = SessionWindows
    .with(Duration.ofSeconds(5)); ❶
```

❶ A session window with an inactivity gap of five seconds.

As you can see in Figure 5-5, session windows are unaligned (the range is specific to each key) and variable in length. The range is completely dependent on the record timestamps, with hot keys leading to long window ranges, and less active keys leading to shorter windows.

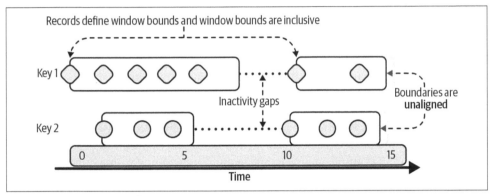

Figure 5-5. Session window

Sliding join windows

Sliding join windows are fixed-sized windows that are used for joins and created using the `JoinWindows` class. Two records fall within the same window if the difference between their timestamps is less than or equal to the window size. Thus, similar to session windows, both the lower and upper window boundaries are inclusive. Here is an example of how to create a join window with a duration of five seconds:

```
JoinWindows joinWindow = JoinWindows
    .of(Duration.ofSeconds(5)); ❶
```

❶ Timestamps must be less than or equal to five seconds apart to fall within the same window.

Visually, join windows look a little different than other types of windows since their use in joins allows them to span multiple input streams. Figure 5-6 illustrates this, and shows how a five-second window is used to determine which records are combined in a windowed join.

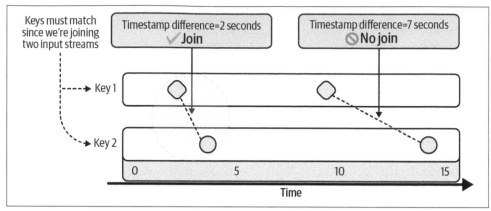

Figure 5-6. Join window

Sliding aggregation windows

In the previous section, we discussed a special type of sliding window that is used for joins. Since Kafka Streams 2.7.0, sliding windows can also be used with aggregations. Like sliding join windows, the window boundaries in a sliding aggregation window are aligned to the record timestamps (as opposed to the epoch) and the lower *and* upper window boundaries are both inclusive. Additionally, records will fall within the same window if the difference between their timestamps is within the specified window size. Here is an example of how to create a sliding window with a duration of five seconds and a grace period of zero seconds:[7]

```
SlidingWindows slidingWindow =
  SlidingWindows.withTimeDifferenceAndGrace(
    Duration.ofSeconds(5),
    Duration.ofSeconds(0));
```

Selecting a Window

Now that we've learned which window types are supported in Kafka Streams, we need to decide which type is appropriate for converting raw pulse events into a heart rate using a windowed aggregation.

Session windows aren't a good fit for measuring the heart rate, because the window size could extend indefinitely as long as there is activity on the stream. This doesn't meet our requirement of having fixed-size windows of 60 seconds. Furthermore, a sliding join window is used for joins only, so we can rule that choice out, as well (though we will use a sliding join window later in this tutorial).

---

[7] Sliding aggregation windows are the only window type that require us to explicitly set a grace period. We'll discuss grace periods later in this chapter.

You could arguably use any of the other window types for our aggregation, but to keep things simple, let's align our window boundaries with the epoch (which rules out sliding aggregation windows) and avoid overlapping windows (which means we don't need a hopping window). This leaves us with a tumbling window for our heart rate aggregation. With our window type selected, we are ready to perform a windowed aggregation.

Windowed Aggregation

Since we've decided to use a tumbling window for the heart rate aggregation, we can build our windowed aggregation. First, we'll construct the window using the `TimeWindows.of` method, and then we'll window our stream with the `windowedBy` operator before performing the aggregation. The following code shows how to accomplish both of these steps:

```
TimeWindows tumblingWindow =
  TimeWindows.of(Duration.ofSeconds(60));

KTable<Windowed<String>, Long> pulseCounts =
  pulseEvents
      .groupByKey() ❶
      .windowedBy(tumblingWindow) ❷
      .count(Materialized.as("pulse-counts")); ❸

pulseCounts
  .toStream() ❹
  .print(Printed.<Windowed<String>, Long>toSysOut().withLabel("pulse-counts")); ❺
```

❶ Grouping records is a prerequisite for performing an aggregation. However, the records in the `pulse-events` topic are already keyed using the desired scheme (i.e., by patient ID), so we can use the `groupByKey` operator instead of `groupBy` to avoid an unnecessary repartition of our data.

❷ Window the stream using a 60-second tumbling window. This will allow us to turn the raw pulse events into a heart rate (measured by beats per minute).

❸ Materialize the heart rate for interactive queries (this will be needed by step 8 in our processor topology—see Figure 5-1.

❹ For debugging purposes only, convert the `KTable` to a stream so we can print the contents to the console.

❺ Print the contents of our windowed stream to the console. Print statements are useful for local development purposes, but should be removed before deploying our application to production.

One interesting thing to highlight in this code example is that the key of the KTable changed from String to Windowed<String>. This is because the windowedBy operator converts KTables into *windowed KTables*, which have multidimensional keys that contain not only the original record key, but also the time range of the window. This makes sense because we need some way of grouping keys into subgroups (windows), and simply using the original key would cause all of the pulse events to be included in the same subgroup. We can see this multidimensional key transformation in action by producing some records to the pulse-events topic and viewing the printed output of the windowed stream. The records we will produce are shown here (the record key and value are demarcated by the | character):

```
1|{"timestamp": "2020-11-12T09:02:00.000Z"}
1|{"timestamp": "2020-11-12T09:02:00.500Z"}
1|{"timestamp": "2020-11-12T09:02:01.000Z"}
```

Producing these records leads to the output in Example 5-3. Note that the old key for each of these records, 1, has been changed to the following format:

```
[<oldkey>@<window_start_ms>/<window_end_ms>]
```

Example 5-3. The output of the print operator, which shows the multidimensional keys in our windowed pulseCounts table

```
[pulse-counts]: [1@1605171720000/1605171780000], 1  ❶
[pulse-counts]: [1@1605171720000/1605171780000], 2
[pulse-counts]: [1@1605171720000/1605171780000], 3
```

❶ The multidimensional record key, which contains not only the original key, but also the window boundaries.

Apart from the key transformation logic, the preceding output highlights a peculiar behavior of Kafka Streams. The heart rate count, which we compute in our windowed aggregation, gets updated each time a new heartbeat is recorded. We can see this in Example 5-3, since the first heart rate that is emitted is 1, followed by 2, 3, etc. Therefore, downstream operators will see not just the final results of a window (the beats per minute), but also the intermediate results of the window (the number of *heartbeats* in this 60-second window *so far*). In applications that are highly tuned for low latency, these intermediate or incomplete window results are useful. However, in our case, we can't truly know the patient's heart rate until a window has been closed, so it is misleading at best. Let's look at why Kafka Streams emits each intermediate result and see if we can tune this behavior.

Emitting Window Results

The decision of *when* to emit a window's computation is a surprisingly complex one for stream processing systems. The complexity is caused by two facts:

- Unbounded event streams may not always be in *timestamp order*, especially when using event-time semantics.[8]

 Kafka does guarantee events will always be in *offset order* at the partition level. This means that every consumer will always read the events in the same sequence that they were appended to the topic (by ascending offset value).

- Events are sometimes *delayed*.

The lack of timestamp order means that we can't just assume that if we've seen a record containing a certain timestamp, we've seen all records that should have arrived before that timestamp, and therefore can emit what we think is the final window result. Furthermore, delayed and out-of-order data requires us to make a choice: do we wait a certain amount of time for all of the data to arrive, or do we output the window result whenever it is updated (as seen in Example 5-3)? This is a trade-off between completeness and latency. Since waiting for data is more likely to produce a complete result, this approach optimizes for completeness. On the other hand, propagating updates downstream immediately (even though they may be incomplete) reduces latency. It's up to you and potentially any service-level agreements (SLAs) you've established to decide what to optimize for.

Figure 5-7 demonstrates how both of these issues could occur. Patient #1 is attached to a vitals monitoring machine that is having intermittent networking issues. This leads to producer retries, causing some vitals measurements to have a delayed arrival into our Kafka cluster. Furthermore, since we have multiple producers writing to the `pulse-events` topic (one for each vitals monitoring machine), this also causes some events to be unordered with respect to their event timestamp.

---

8 Of course, if you use ingestion-time semantics by setting `message.timestamp.type` to `LogAppendTime`, then the record timestamps will always appear in order. This is because the timestamp is overwritten at topic append time. However, the ingestion time is somewhat arbitrary in relation to the event itself, and in the best-case scenario is just a close approximation of the event time (assuming the event is written right after it's created).

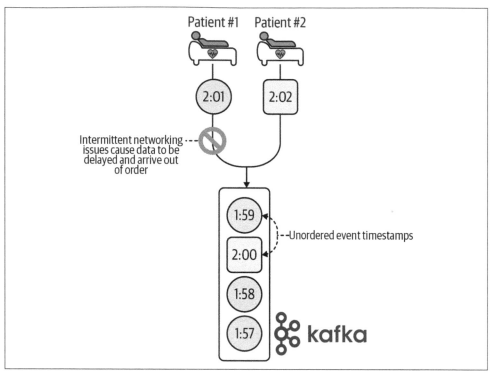

Figure 5-7. Data can arrive out of timestamp order for many reasons; one common example is a topic having multiple producers, which introduces a race condition

One important thing to note is that there doesn't need to be some failure scenario to result in out-of-order data. This could happen even in normal operating conditions, such as when multiple producers are writing to the same topic.

As mentioned previously, to overcome these issues, we need to optimize for either latency or completeness. By default, Kafka Streams optimizes for latency, using an approach called *continuous refinement* (*https://oreil.ly/-tii3*). Continuous refinement means that whenever a new event is added to the window, Kafka Streams will emit the new computation immediately. This is why we saw each intermediate window result when we produced some records to our patient monitoring application (see Example 5-3). However, with continuous refinement, each result should be seen as potentially incomplete, and an emitted event does *not* mean we have processed every record that will eventually fall into the window. Furthermore, delayed data can continue causing events to be emitted at unexpected times.

The next two sections discuss how to address each of these issues in our patient monitoring application. First, let's look at a strategy for handling delayed data in Kafka Streams. After that, we will learn how to suppress intermediate window calculations using Kafka Streams' `suppress` operator.

Grace Period

One of the biggest challenges faced by stream processing systems is how to handle delayed data. Many frameworks, including those that adhere to the influential Dataflow model (*https://oreil.ly/wAhJZ*) (e.g., Apache Flink), leverage *watermarks*. Watermarks are used to estimate when all of the data for a given window should have arrived (usually by configuring the *window size* and the *allowed lateness* of events). Users can then specify how late events (as determined by the watermark) should be handled, with a popular default (in Dataflow, Flink, and others) being to discard late events.

Similar to the watermark approach, Kafka Streams allows us to configure the *allowed lateness* of events using a *grace period*. Setting a grace period will keep the window open for a specific amount of time, in order to admit delayed/unordered events to the window. For example, we initially configured our tumbling window using the following code:

```
TimeWindows tumblingWindow =
  TimeWindows.of(Duration.ofSeconds(60));
```

However, if we want to be able to tolerate five seconds of lag for pulse events (which we will use to calculate a heart rate), we could define our tumbling window with a grace period as well:

```
TimeWindows tumblingWindow =
  TimeWindows
    .of(Duration.ofSeconds(60))
    .grace(Duration.ofSeconds(5));
```

We could increase the grace period further, but just remember the trade-off: higher grace periods optimize for completeness, because they keep the window open longer (allowing for data to be delayed), but they do this at the expense of higher latency (windows won't be closed until the grace period ends).

Now, let's see how to solve the problem of intermediate results being emitted in our windowed heart rate aggregation.

Suppression

As we learned in the previous section, Kafka Streams' strategy of continuous refinement, which involves emitting the results of a window whenever new data arrives, is ideal when we are optimizing for low latency and can tolerate incomplete (i.e., intermediate) results being emitted from the window.[9]

---

9 This is different than how many other streaming systems work, in which processing occurs only when a window is closed.

However, in our patient monitoring application, this is undesirable. We cannot calculate a heart rate using less than 60 seconds of data, so we need to only emit the final result of a window. This is where the `suppress` operator comes into play. The `suppress` operator can be used to only emit the final computation of a window, and to suppress (i.e., temporarily hold intermediate computations in memory) all other events. In order to use the `suppress` operator, we need to decide three things:

- Which suppression strategy should be used for suppressing intermediate window computations

- How much memory should be used for buffering the suppressed events (this is set using a *Buffer Config*)

- What to do when this memory limit is exceeded (this is controlled using a *Buffer Full Strategy*)

Let's first look at the two suppression strategies. Table 5-1 describes each strategy available in Kafka Streams. Note that each strategy is available as a method on the `Suppressed` class.

Table 5-1. Window suppression strategies

Strategy	Description
`Suppressed.untilWindowCloses`	Only emit the final results of a window.
`Suppressed.untilTimeLimit`	Emit the results of a window after a configurable amount of time has elapsed since the last event was received. If another event with the same key arrives before the time limit is up, it replaces the first event in the buffer (note, the timer is not restarted when this happens). This has the effect of *rate-limiting* updates.

In our patient monitoring application, we only want to emit the results of our heart rate window once a full 60 seconds has elapsed. Therefore, we will use the `Suppressed.untilWindowCloses` suppression strategy. However, before we can use this strategy in our processor topology, we need to tell Kafka Streams how to buffer the unemitted results in memory. After all, suppressed records aren't *discarded*; instead, the latest unemitted record for each key in a given window is kept in memory until it's time to emit the result. Memory is a limited resource, so Kafka Streams requires us to be explicit with how it is used for this potentially memory-intensive task of suppressing updates.[10] In order to define our buffering strategy, we need to use Buffer

---

10 Since Kafka Streams holds the latest record for each key when using the `suppress` operator, the required amount of memory is a function of your keyspace, with smaller keyspaces for a given input stream requiring less memory than large keyspaces. The grace period can also impact memory usage.

Configs. Table 5-2 contains a description of each Buffer Config available in Kafka Streams.

Table 5-2. Buffer Configs

Buffer Config	Description
`BufferConfig.maxBytes()`	The in-memory buffer for storing suppressed events will be constrained by a configured number of bytes.
`BufferConfig.maxRecords()`	The in-memory buffer for storing suppressed events will be constrained by a configured number of keys.
`BufferConfig.unbounded()`	The in-memory buffer for storing suppressed events will use as much heap space as needed to hold the suppressed records in the window. If the application runs out of heap, an `OutOfMemoryError` (OOM) exception will be thrown.

Finally, the last requirement for suppressing records is to tell Kafka Streams what to do when the buffer is full. Kafka Streams exposes a couple of Buffer Full Strategies, each of which is described in Table 5-3.

Table 5-3. Buffer Full Strategies

Buffer Full Strategy	Description
`shutDownWhenFull`	Gracefully shut down the application when the buffer is full. You will never see intermediate window computations when using this strategy.
`emitEarlyWhenFull`	Emit the oldest results when the buffer is full instead of shutting down the application. You may still see intermediate window computations using this strategy.

Now that we understand which suppression strategies, Buffer Configs, and Buffer Full Strategies are available, let's make a decision about which combination of the three works for us. We don't want to rate-limit updates, so we won't use `untilTimeLimit`. Instead, we want to only emit the final results of the heart rate window, so `untilWindowCloses` is a better fit here. Second, we expect our keyspace to be relatively small, so we'll choose the `unbounded` Buffer Config. Finally, we never want to emit results early since that would lead to an inaccurate heart rate calculation (e.g., if we were to emit the number of heartbeats after only 20 seconds elapsed). Therefore, we will use `shutDownWhenFull` as our Buffer Config strategy.

Putting this all together, we can update our patient monitoring topology to use the `suppress` operator as shown in Example 5-4.

Example 5-4. Use the `suppress` operator to only emit the final results of the heart rate window (`tumblingWindow`)

```
TimeWindows tumblingWindow =
  TimeWindows
    .of(Duration.ofSeconds(60))
    .grace(Duration.ofSeconds(5));

KTable<Windowed<String>, Long> pulseCounts =
  pulseEvents
   .groupByKey()
   .windowedBy(tumblingWindow)
   .count(Materialized.as("pulse-counts"))
   .suppress(
     Suppressed.untilWindowCloses(BufferConfig.unbounded().shutDownWhenFull()));  ❶
```

❶ Suppress the results of the window so that only the final computation is emitted.

Now that we've completed step 4 in our processor topology (see Figure 5-1), let's move on to steps 5 and 6: filtering and rekeying the pulse-events and body-temp-events data.

Filtering and Rekeying Windowed KTables

If you look closely at the KTable in Example 5-4, you'll see that windowing caused our key to change from a String type to a Windowed<String>. As mentioned before, this is because windowing causes our records to be grouped by an extra dimension: the window range. So, in order to join the body-temp-events stream, we need to rekey the pulse-events stream. We also need to filter both streams of data since we are only interested in records that exceed our predefined thresholds.

It may seem like we should perform the filter and rekeying operation in any order, and that's true. However, one piece of advice is to perform filtering as early as you can. We know that rekeying records requires a repartition topic, so if we filter first, then we will reduce the number of reads/writes to this topic, making our application more performant.

Since both filtering and rekeying were discussed in previous chapters, we won't do another deep dive into these concepts. But you can see the filtering and rekeying code for our patient monitoring application in the following code block:

```
KStream<String, Long> highPulse =
  pulseCounts
      .toStream()  ❶
      .filter((key, value) -> value >= 100)  ❷
      .map(
```

```
        (windowedKey, value) -> {
            return KeyValue.pair(windowedKey.key(), value); ❸
    });

KStream<String, BodyTemp> highTemp =
    tempEvents.filter((key, value) -> value.getTemperature() > 100.4); ❹
```

❶ Convert to a stream so we can use the map operator to rekey the records.

❷ Filter for only heart rates that exceed our predefined threshold of 100 bpm.

❸ Rekey the stream using the original key, which is available in windowed
   Key.key(). Note that windowedKey is an instance of org.apache.kaf
   ka.streams.kstream.Windowed. This class contains methods for accessing the
   original key (as we saw with windowedKey.key()) and also the underlying time
   window (using windowedKey.window()).

❹ Filter for only core body temperature readings that exceed our predefined threshold of 100.4°F.

We have completed steps 5 and 6 in our processor topology, so we are ready to perform a windowed join.

Windowed Joins

As discussed in "Sliding join windows" on page 157, windowed joins require a sliding
join window. Sliding join windows compare the timestamps of events on both sides of
the join to determine which records should be joined together. Windowed joins are
required for KStream-KStream joins since streams are unbounded. Therefore, the
data needs to be materialized into a local state store for performing quick lookups of
related values.

We can build a sliding join window and join the pulse rate and body temperature
streams like so:

```
StreamJoined<String, Long, BodyTemp> joinParams =
    StreamJoined.with(Serdes.String(), Serdes.Long(), JsonSerdes.BodyTemp()); ❶

JoinWindows joinWindows =
    JoinWindows
        .of(Duration.ofSeconds(60)) ❷
        .grace(Duration.ofSeconds(10)); ❸

ValueJoiner<Long, BodyTemp, CombinedVitals> valueJoiner = ❹
    (pulseRate, bodyTemp) -> new CombinedVitals(pulseRate.intValue(), bodyTemp);

KStream<String, CombinedVitals> vitalsJoined =
    highPulse.join(highTemp, valueJoiner, joinWindows, joinParams); ❺
```

❶ Specify the Serdes to be used in the join.

❷ Records with timestamps one minute apart or less will fall into the same window, and will therefore be joined.

❸ Tolerate a delay of up to 10 seconds.

❹ Combine the heart rate and body temp into a `CombinedVitals` object.

❺ Perform the join.

Joins are particularly interesting with regard to time because each side of the join could receive records at different rates, and so some additional synchronization is required to ensure events are joined at the appropriate time. Luckily for us, Kafka Streams is able to handle this scenario by allowing the timestamps on each side of the join to determine how data flows (and is subsequently joined) through our processor topology. We'll explore these ideas in more detail in the next section.

Time-Driven Dataflow

We've already seen how time can impact the behavior of certain operations, including windowed joins and windowed aggregations. However, time also controls the flow of data through our streams. It's important for stream processing applications to synchronize the input streams to ensure correctness, especially when processing historical data from multiple sources.

To facilitate this synchronization, Kafka Streams creates a single *partition group* for each stream task. A partition group buffers the queued records for each partition being handled by the given task using a priority queue, and includes the algorithm for selecting the next record (across all input partitions) for processing. The record with the lowest timestamp is selected for processing.

 Stream time is the highest timestamp observed for a particular topic-partition. It is initially unknown and can only increase or stay the same. It advances only when new data is seen. This is different from the other notions of time we discussed since it is internal to Kafka Streams itself.

When a single Kafka Streams task consumes data from more than one partition (e.g., in the case of a join), Kafka Streams will compare the timestamps for the next unprocessed records (called *head records*) in each partition (record queue) and will choose the record with the lowest timestamp for processing. The selected record is forwarded to the appropriate source processor in the topology. Figure 5-8 shows how this works.

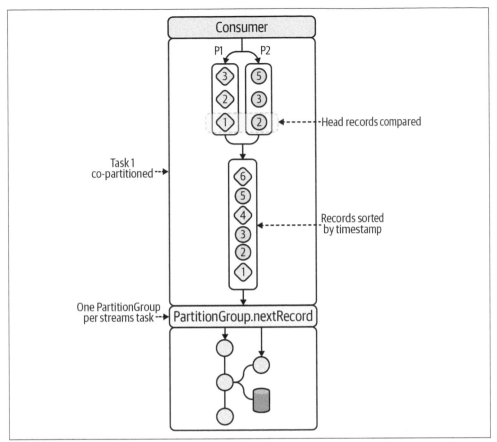

Figure 5-8. Record timestamps are compared to determine how data flows through your Kafka Streams application

With our join in place, and some reassurances that Kafka Streams will attempt to process our records in timestamp order using time-based flow-control mechanisms,[11] we are now ready to tackle the final steps of our patient monitoring topology. We'll briefly recap how to add a sink processor to our topology, and then we'll learn how to query windowed key-value stores.

---

11 It's important to note that this is best-effort when one of the input streams becomes empty. However, you can use the `max.task.idle.ms` configuration, which controls how long you are willing to wait for new records to arrive in the drained input stream, to help avoid this. The default value is 0, but increasing this will allow you to improve time synchronization by waiting longer.

Alerts Sink

In order to make our join results available to downstream consumers, we need to write the enriched data back to Kafka. As we've seen in previous chapters, adding a sink is extremely easy in Kafka Streams. The following code shows how to add the alerts sink. This sink will be written to whenever our application determines that a patient is at risk for SIRS, as determined by our thresholds and windowed join:

```
vitalsJoined.to(
  "alerts",
  Produced.with(Serdes.String(), JsonSerdes.CombinedVitals())
);
```

One benefit of using a timestamp extractor when registering our source streams (see Example 5-2) is that our output records will also be associated with the extracted timestamp. For unjoined streams/tables, the timestamp is propagated from the initial timestamp extraction that occurred when you registered the source processors. However, if you perform a join, like we've done with our patient monitoring application, then Kafka Streams will look at the timestamps for each record involved in the join and choose the maximum value for the output record.[12]

Registering the alerts sink exposes our patient monitoring data to real-time consumers of the alerts topic. Now, let's learn how to query windowed key-value stores by exposing the results of our windowed aggregation (which calculates a patient's heart rate).

Querying Windowed Key-Value Stores

In "Querying Nonwindowed Key-Value Stores" on page 131, we saw how to query nonwindowed key-value stores. However, *windowed key-value stores* support a different set of queries because the record keys are multidimensional, and consist of both the original key *and* the window range, as opposed to just the original record key (which is what we see in nonwindowed key-value stores). We'll start by looking at key and window range scans.

Key + window range scans

There are two different types of range scans that can be used for windowed key-value stores. The first type searches for a specific key in a given window range, and therefore requires three parameters:

---

12 Prior to version 2.3, the timestamp on the output record was set to the timestamp of whatever record triggered the join. Using the maximum value in newer versions of Kafka Streams is an improvement over the old behavior, since it ensures the result timestamp is the same whether data is out of order or not.

- The key to search for (in the case of our patient monitoring application, this would correspond to the patient ID, e.g., 1)
- The lower boundary of the window range, represented as milliseconds from the epoch[13] (e.g., 1605171720000, which translates to 2020-11-12T09:02:00.00Z)
- The upper boundary of the window range, represented as milliseconds from the epoch (e.g., 1605171780000, which translates to 2020-11-12T09:03:00Z)

An example of how to execute this type of range scan, and how to extract the relevant properties from the result, is shown here:

```
String key = 1;
Instant fromTime = Instant.parse("2020-11-12T09:02:00.00Z");
Instant toTime = Instant.parse("2020-11-12T09:03:00Z");

WindowStoreIterator<Long> range = getBpmStore().fetch(key, fromTime, toTime); ❶
while (range.hasNext()) {
  KeyValue<Long, Long> next = range.next(); ❷
  Long timestamp = next.key; ❸
  Long count = next.value; ❹
  // do something with the extracted values
}

range.close(); ❺
```

❶ Returns an iterator that can be used for iterating through each key in the selected time range.

❷ Get the next element in the iteration.

❸ The timestamp of the record is available in the key property.

❹ The value can be extracted using the value property.

❺ Close the iterator to avoid memory leaks.

Window range scans

The second type of range scan that can be performed on windowed key-value stores searches for *all keys* within a given time range. This type of query requires two parameters:

---

13 1970-01-01T00:00:00Z (UTC)

- The lower boundary of the window range, represented as milliseconds from the epoch[14] (e.g., 1605171720000, which translates to 2020-11-12T09:02:00.00Z)
- The upper boundary of the window range, represented as milliseconds from the epoch (e.g., 1605171780000, which translates to 2020-11-12T09:03:00Z)

The following code block shows how to execute this type of range scan, and how to extract the relevant properties from the result:

```
Instant fromTime = Instant.parse("2020-11-12T09:02:00.00Z");
Instant toTime = Instant.parse("2020-11-12T09:03:00Z");

KeyValueIterator<Windowed<String>, Long> range =
  getBpmStore().fetchAll(fromTime, toTime);

while (range.hasNext()) {
  KeyValue<Windowed<String>, Long> next = range.next();
  String key = next.key.key();
  Window window = next.key.window();
  Long start = window.start();
  Long end = window.end();
  Long count = next.value;
    // do something with the extracted values
}

range.close();
```

All entries

Similar to range scan queries, the `all()` query returns an iterator for all windowed key-value pairs that are available in the local state store.[15] The following code snippet shows how to execute an `all()` query against a local windowed key-value store. Iterating through the results is the same as the range scan query, so we have omitted that logic for brevity:

```
KeyValueIterator<Windowed<String>, Long> range = getBpmStore().all();
```

 It's very important to close the iterator once you are finished with it to avoid memory leaks. For example, looking at the preceding code snippet, we would call `range.close()` when we are finished with the iterator.

---

14 1970-01-01T00:00:00Z (UTC)

15 Depending on the number of keys in your state store, this could be a heavyweight call.

Using these query types, you can build an interactive query service in the same way that we discussed in the previous chapter. We just need to add an RPC service and client to our application, leverage the Kafka Streams instance discovery logic for discovering remote application instances, and wire up the preceding windowed key-value store queries to the RPC or RESTful endpoints (see "Remote Queries" on page 134 for more information).

Summary

In this chapter, we learned how time can be used for more advanced stream processing use cases. By being deliberate with the time semantics we use in our topology definitions, we can achieve more deterministic processing in Kafka Streams. Time not only drives the behavior of windowed aggregations, windowed joins, and other time-based operations, but since Kafka Streams tries to synchronize input streams based on time, it even controls how and when data flows through our application.

Windowing data allows us to derive temporal relationships between events. Whether we want to leverage these relationships for aggregating data (as we did by converting raw pulse events into a time-based heart rate aggregation) or joining data (e.g., when we joined the heart rate stream with the body temperature stream), time opens the door for more meaningful data enrichment.

Finally, learning how to query windowed key-value stores taught us something important about windowed state stores: keys are multidimensional (containing both the original key and the time range of the window), and therefore support a different set of queries, including windowed range scans.

In the next chapter, we will wrap up our discussion of stateful Kafka Streams applications by looking at advanced state management tasks.

## CHAPTER 6

Advanced State Management

In the past two chapters, we discussed stateful processing in Kafka Streams. As we learned how to perform aggregations, joins, and windowed operations, it became apparent that stateful processing is pretty easy to get started with.

However, as I alluded to previously, state stores come with additional operational complexity. As you scale your application, experience failures, and perform routine maintenance, you will learn that stateful processing requires a deeper understanding of the underlying mechanics to ensure your application continues to operate smoothly over time.

The goal of this chapter is to dig deeper into state stores so that you can achieve a higher level of reliability when building stateful stream processing applications. A large portion of this chapter is dedicated to the topic of *rebalancing*, which occurs when work needs to be redistributed across your consumer group. Rebalancing can be especially impactful for stateful applications, so we'll develop our understanding so that you are equipped to deal with this in your own applications.

Some of the questions we will answer include:

- How are persistent state stores represented on disk?
- How do stateful applications achieve fault tolerance?
- How can we configure built-in state stores?
- What kinds of events are the most impactful for stateful applications?
- What measures can be taken to minimize recovery time of stateful tasks?
- How do you ensure that state stores don't grow indefinitely?
- How can the DSL cache be used to rate limit downstream updates?

- How do you track progress of state restoration using a State Restore Listener?
- How can State Listeners be used to detect rebalances?

Let's start by looking at the on-disk layout of persistent state stores.

Persistent Store Disk Layout

Kafka Streams includes both in-memory and persistent state stores. The latter category of state stores are generally preferred because they can help reduce the recovery time of an application whenever state needs to be reinitialized (e.g., in the event of failure or task migration).

By default, persistent state stores live in the */tmp/kafka-streams* directory. You can override this by setting the StreamsConfig.STATE_DIR_CONFIG property, and given the ephemeral nature of a */tmp* directory (the contents of this directory are deleted during system reboots/crashes), you should choose another location for persisting your application state.

Since persistent state stores live on disk, we can inspect the files very easily.[1] Doing so allows us to glean a surprising amount of information from the directory and file-names alone. The file tree in Example 6-1 was taken from the patient monitoring application that we created in the previous chapter. The annotations provide additional detail about the important directories and files.

Example 6-1. An example of how a persistent state store is represented on disk

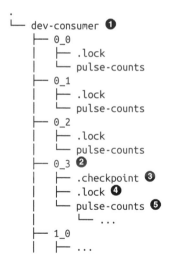

---

1 Note: you should never attempt to modify the files.

❶ The top-level directory contains the application ID. This is helpful to understand which applications are running on the server, especially in a shared environment where workloads can be scheduled on any number of nodes (e.g., in a Kubernetes cluster).

❷ Each of the second-level directories corresponds to a single Kafka Streams task. The directory name is formatted as a task ID. Task IDs are composed of two parts: `<sub-topology-id>_<partition>`. Note that, as we discussed in "Sub-Topologies" on page 37, a sub-topology might process data from one or multiple topics, depending on the logic of your program.

❸ Checkpoint files store offsets from changelog topics (see "Changelog Topics" on page 178). They indicate to Kafka Streams what data has been read into the local state store and, as you'll see shortly, play an important role in state store recovery.

❹ The lock file is used by Kafka Streams to acquire a lock on the state directory. This helps prevent concurrency issues.

❺ The actual data is stored in named state directories. Here, `pulse-counts` corresponds to an explicit name that we set when materializing the state store.

The main benefit of knowing what state stores look like on disk is to simply remove some of the mystery around how they work. Furthermore, the lock file and checkpoint files are especially important, and are referenced in certain error logs (for example, permissions issues could surface as a failure to write to a checkpoint file, while a concurrency issue could lead to an error about Kafka Streams failing to acquire a lock), so understanding their location and utility is helpful.

The checkpoint file plays an important role in state store recovery. Let's dig into this further by first looking at the fault-tolerant features of stateful applications, and then seeing how offset checkpoints are used to reduce recovery time.

Fault Tolerance

Kafka Streams owes much of its fault-tolerant characteristics to Kafka's storage layer and group management protocol. For example, data replication at the partition level means if a broker goes offline, data can still be consumed from one of the replicated partitions on another broker. Furthermore, by using consumer groups, if a single instance of your application goes down, work will be redistributed to one of the healthy instances.

However, when it comes to stateful applications, Kafka Streams takes additional measures to ensure applications are resilient to failure. This includes using changelog topics to back state stores, and standby replicas to minimize reinitialization time in the event that state is lost. We'll discuss these Kafka Streams–specific fault-tolerant features in further detail in the following sections.

Changelog Topics

Unless explicitly disabled, state stores are backed by changelog topics, which are created and managed by Kafka Streams. These topics capture state updates for every key in the store, and can be replayed in the event of failure to rebuild the application state.[2] In the event of a total state loss (or when spinning up a new instance), the changelog topic is replayed from the beginning. However, if a checkpoint file exists (see Example 6-1), then the state can be replayed from the checkpointed offset found in that file, since this offset indicates what data has already been read into the state store. The latter is much quicker because recovering only part of the state takes less time than recovering the full state.

Changelog topics are configurable using the `Materialized` class in the DSL. For example, in the previous chapter, we materialized a state store named `pulse-counts` using the following code:

```
pulseEvents
  .groupByKey()
  .windowedBy(tumblingWindow)
  .count(Materialized.as("pulse-counts"));
```

There are some additional methods on the `Materialized` class that allow us to customize the changelog topics even further. For example, to disable change logging completely, we could use the following code to create what is sometimes called an *ephemeral store* (i.e., state stores that cannot be restored on failure):

```
Materialized.as("pulse-counts").withLoggingDisabled();
```

However, disabling change logging isn't usually a good idea since it means your state store will no longer be fault tolerant, and it prevents you from using standby replicas. When it comes to configuring changelog topics, you will more commonly either override the retention of windowed or session stores using the `withRetention` method (this is covered a little later in "Window retention" on page 190) or pass in certain topic configs for the changelog topic. For example, if we wanted to bump the number of `insync` replicas to two, we could use the following code:

```
Map<String, String> topicConfigs =
  Collections.singletonMap("min.insync.replicas", "2"); ❶

KTable<Windowed<String>, Long> pulseCounts =
  pulseEvents
```

---

2 A dedicated consumer called the *restore consumer* is used to replay the changelog topic when a state store needs to be reinitialized.

```
        .groupByKey()
        .windowedBy(tumblingWindow)
        .count(
            Materialized.<String, Long, WindowStore<Bytes, byte[]>>
                as("pulse-counts")
                .withValueSerde(Serdes.Long())
                .withLoggingEnabled(topicConfigs)); ❷
```

❶ Create a map for saving our topic configs. The entries can include any valid topic config (*https://oreil.ly/L_WOj*) and value.

❷ Configure the changelog topic by passing the topic configs to the `Material ized.withLoggingEnabled` method.

Now, if you describe the topic, you'll see the topic was configured accordingly:

```
$ kafka-topics \
    --bootstrap-server localhost:9092 \
    --topic dev-consumer-pulse-counts-changelog \ ❶
    --describe

# output
Topic: dev-consumer-pulse-counts-changelog
PartitionCount: 4
ReplicationFactor:1
Configs: min.insync.replicas=2
...
```

❶ Note that changelog topics have the following naming scheme: `<application_id>-<internal_store_name>-changelog`.

One thing to note is that, at the time of this writing, you cannot reconfigure a changelog topic using this method after it has been created.[3] If you need to update a topic configuration on an existing changelog topic, then you'll need to do so using the Kafka console scripts. An example of how to manually update a changelog topic after it has been created is shown here:

```
$ kafka-configs \ ❶
    --bootstrap-server localhost:9092 \
    --entity-type topics \
    --entity-name dev-consumer-pulse-counts-changelog \
    --alter \
    --add-config min.insync.replicas=1 ❷

# output
Completed updating config for topic dev-consumer-pulse-counts-changelog
```

---

3 There is a ticket for allowing internal topics to be reconfigured, which you can track at *https://oreil.ly/OoKBV*.

❶ You can also use the `kafka-topics` console script. Remember to append the file extension (*.sh*) if you are running vanilla Kafka outside of Confluent Platform.

❷ Update the topic configurations.

Now that we understand the purpose of the state store–backing changelog topics, as well as how to override the default topic configurations, let's take a look at a feature that makes Kafka Streams highly available: standby replicas.

Standby Replicas

One method for reducing the downtime of stateful application failure is to create and maintain copies of task state across multiple application instances.

Kafka Streams handles this automatically, as long as we set a positive value for the `NUM_STANDBY_REPLICAS_CONFIG` property. For example, to create two standby replicas, we can configure our application like so:

```
props.put(StreamsConfig.NUM_STANDBY_REPLICAS_CONFIG, 2);
```

When standby replicas are configured, Kafka Streams will attempt to reassign any failed stateful tasks to an instance with a hot standby. This will drastically reduce downtime for applications with large state by removing the need to reinitialize the underlying state store from scratch.

Furthermore, as we'll see toward the end of the chapter, newer versions of Kafka Streams allow us to fall back to standby replicas when querying state stores during a rebalance. But before we get to that, let's discuss what rebalancing is, and why it is the biggest enemy of stateful Kafka Streams applications.

Rebalancing: Enemy of the State (Store)

We've learned that changelog topics and standby replicas help reduce the impact of stateful application failure. The former allows Kafka Streams to reconstruct state whenever it's lost, and the latter allows us to minimize the time it takes to reinitialize state stores.

However, while Kafka Streams handles failure transparently, it doesn't change the fact that losing a state store, even temporarily, can be incredibly disruptive (especially for heavily stateful applications). Why? Because the change-logging technique for backing up state still requires us to replay each message in the underlying topic, and if that topic is huge, then rereading each record could take several minutes or, in extreme cases, even hours.

The biggest culprit that leads to reinitializing state is *rebalancing*. We first encountered this term when we discussed consumer groups in "Consumer Groups" on page 13. A simplified explanation is that Kafka automatically distributes work across the active members of a consumer group, but occasionally the work needs to be redistributed in response to certain events—most notably group membership changes.[4] We won't cover the entire rebalance protocol in depth, but the level of detail we will cover requires a quick vocabulary review:

- The *group coordinator* is a designated broker that is responsible for maintaining the membership of a consumer group (e.g., by receiving heartbeats and triggering a rebalance when a membership change is detected).

- The *group leader* is a designated consumer in each consumer group that is responsible for determining the partition assignments.

We will encounter these terms as we discuss rebalancing more in the following sections. But for now, the important takeaway is that rebalances are expensive when they cause a stateful task to be migrated to another instance that does not have a standby replica. There are a couple of strategies for dealing with the issues that rebalancing can introduce:

- Prevent state from being moved when possible

- If state does need to be moved or replayed, make recovery time as quick as possible

With both strategies, there are measures that Kafka Streams takes automatically, as well as actions we can take ourselves, to minimize the impact of rebalances. We'll explore this in more detail, starting with the first strategy: preventing state migration.

Preventing State Migration

When stateful tasks are reassigned to another running instance, the underlying state is migrated as well. For applications with large state, it could take a long time to rebuild the state store on the destination node, and therefore should be avoided if possible.

Since the group leader (one of the consumers) is responsible for determining how work is distributed among the active consumers, there is some onus on the Kafka Streams library (which implements the load balancing logic) to prevent unnecessary state store migration. One way it achieves this is through something called a *sticky*

---

4 Adding or removing partitions from the source topics could also trigger a rebalance.

assignor, and it's something we get for free when we use Kafka Streams. We'll explore this in the next section.

Sticky Assignment

To help prevent stateful tasks from being reassigned, Kafka Streams uses a custom partition assignment strategy[5] that attempts to reassign tasks to instances that previously owned the task (and therefore, should still have a copy of the underlying state store). This strategy is called *sticky assignment*.

To understand the problem Kafka Streams is solving with its sticky assignor, consider the default rebalancing strategy for other types of Kafka clients. Figure 6-1 shows that when a rebalance occurs, a stateful task could potentially be migrated to another application instance, which would be extremely expensive.

The sticky partition assignor that is included in Kafka Streams addresses this issue by keeping track of which task owned each partition (and the associated state stores) and reassigning the stateful task to its previous owner. As you can see in Figure 6-2, this drastically improves the availability of our application since it helps us avoid unnecessary reinitialization of potentially large state stores.

While the sticky assignor helps reassign tasks to their previous owners, state stores can still be migrated if Kafka Streams clients are temporarily offline. Now, let's discuss something we, as Kafka Streams developers, can enable to help avoid rebalances during transient downtime.

---

5 The internal class is called `StickyTaskAssignor`. Note that it is not possible to override the default partitioner in Kafka Streams.

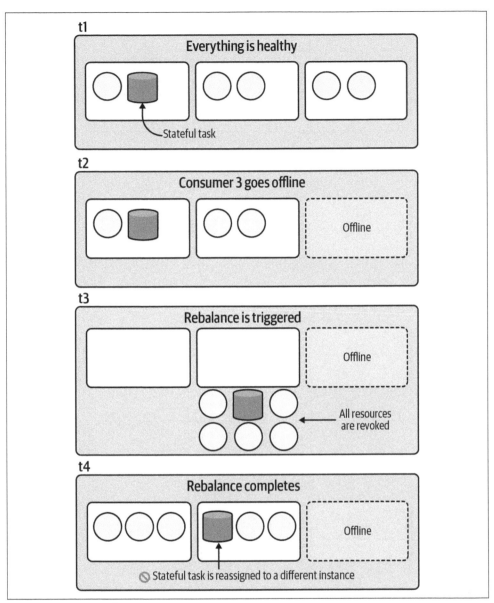

Figure 6-1. Nonsticky partition assignment

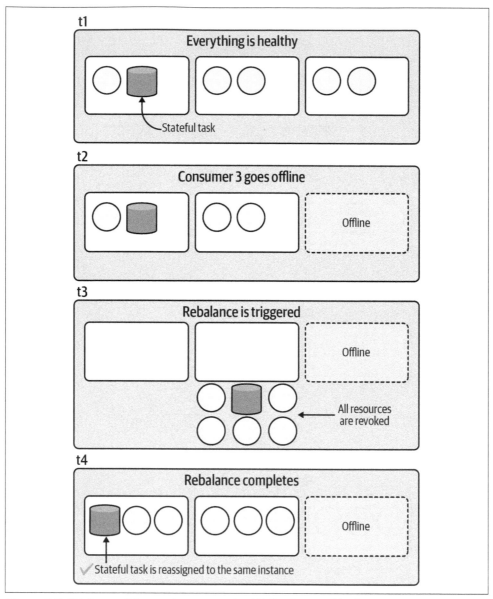

Figure 6-2. *Sticky partition assignment using Kafka Streams' built-in partition assignor*

Static Membership

One of the issues that can cause state to be moved around is *unnecessary rebalances*. Sometimes, even a healthy event, like a rolling bounce, can lead to several rebalances. If the group coordinator detects membership changes during these brief periods of unavailability, it will trigger a rebalance and immediately reassign the work to the remaining application instances.

When an instance comes back online after a brief period of being down, the coordinator won't recognize it because its member ID (a unique identifier assigned by the coordinator whenever a consumer is registered) is erased, so the instance is treated as a new member and work may be reassigned.

To prevent this, you can use *static membership* (*https://oreil.ly/Psghk*). Static membership aims to reduce the number of rebalances due to transient downtime. It achieves this by using a hardcoded instance ID for identifying each unique application instance. The following configuration property allows you to set the ID:

```
group.instance.id = app-1 ❶
```

❶ In this case, we set the ID to `app-1`. If we spin up another instance, we would assign it a unique ID as well (e.g., `app-2`). This ID must be unique across the entire cluster (even among different Kafka Streams applications, independent of `application.id`, and other consumers, independent of `group.id`).

The hardcoded instance ID is typically used in conjunction with higher session timeouts,[6] which buys the application even more time for restarting so that the coordinator doesn't think the consumer instance is dead when it goes offline for a short period of time.

Static membership is only available for Kafka versions >= 2.3, so if your client or brokers are on an older version, you'll need to upgrade first. Be aware that increasing the session timeout is a double-edged sword. While it can prevent the coordinator from assuming an instance is dead during a brief period of downtime, the trade-off is that it can lead to slower detection of actual failure.

Now that we've learned how we can use static membership to help avoid unnecessary rebalances, let's look at how to reduce the impact of rebalances when they do happen. Once again, there are measures that Kafka Streams takes for us and actions we can take ourselves to reduce this impact. We will discuss both in the upcoming sections.

---

6 See the `session.timeout.ms` consumer configuration.

Reducing the Impact of Rebalances

While static membership can be used to avoid unnecessary rebalances, sometimes a rebalance cannot be avoided. After all, failure is expected in distributed systems. Historically, rebalancing has been very costly. This is because at the start of each rebalancing round, each client gives up all of its resources. We saw this in Figure 6-2, and a detailed view of this rebalancing step is shown in Figure 6-3.

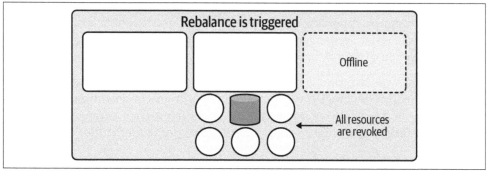

Figure 6-3. Revoking all resources during an eager rebalance is extremely inefficient

This rebalancing strategy is called *eager rebalancing*, and is impactful for two reasons:

- A so-called stop-the-world effect occurs when all clients give up their resources, which means an application can fall behind on its work very quickly since processing is halted.

- If a stateful task gets reassigned to a new instance, then the state will need to be replayed/rebuilt before processing starts. This leads to additional downtime.

Remember, Kafka Streams tries to mitigate the second issue (stateful task migration) for us by using a custom sticky partition assignor. However, it has historically relied on its own implementation to achieve task stickiness instead of the rebalance protocol itself. As of version 2.4, however, an update to the rebalance protocol introduces additional measures that help reduce the impact of rebalances. We will discuss this new protocol, called *incremental cooperative rebalancing*, in the next section.

Incremental Cooperative Rebalancing

Incremental cooperative rebalancing is a more efficient rebalancing protocol than eager rebalancing, and is enabled by default in versions >= 2.4. If you are using an older Kafka Streams version, you will want to upgrade in order to take advantage of this feature, since it provides the following advantages over the older eager rebalancing protocol:

- One global round of rebalancing is replaced with several smaller rounds (*incremental*).
- Clients hold on to resources (tasks) that do not need to change ownership, and they only stop processing the tasks that are being migrated (*cooperative*).

Figure 6-4 shows how incremental cooperative rebalancing works at a high level when an application instance goes offline for a long period of time (i.e., any period of time that exceeds the `session.timeout.ms` config, which is the timeout that the coordinator uses to detect consumer failures).

As you can see, the healthy application instances (including the one with the stateful task) did not need to give up their resources when a rebalance was initiated. This is a huge improvement over the eager rebalancing strategy since it allows the application to continue processing during a rebalance.

There's a lot of detailed information about incremental cooperative rebalancing that we won't cover here, but it's important to know that newer versions of Kafka Streams implement this protocol under the hood, so we just need to make sure we're running with a supported version of Kafka Streams.[7]

We've seen how incremental cooperative rebalancing can help reduce the impact of rebalances, so let's look at a more active role application developers can take to ensure rebalances are less painful.

---

7 Versions >= 2.4 use the improved rebalancing strategy. More information about incremental cooperative rebalancing can be found at *https://oreil.ly/P3iVG*.

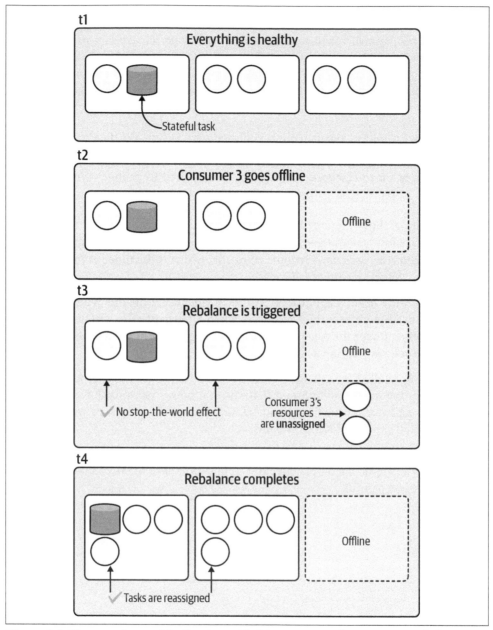

Figure 6-4. The stop-the-world effect is avoided in incremental cooperative rebalancing

Controlling State Size

If you're not careful, your state stores could grow unbounded and cause operational issues. For example, imagine the keyspace in your compacted changelog topic is very large (let's say one billion keys), and the application state is evenly distributed across 10 physical nodes.[8] If one of the nodes goes offline, then you'll need to replay a minimum of 100 million records to rebuild the state. This takes a lot of time and could lead to availability issues. It's also not a great use of computational or storage resources to retain more data than you need.

Depending on your use case, you may not need to retain the entire application state indefinitely. Perhaps the value of each record has a fixed lifetime. For example, at Mailchimp, we track the number of active email messages that haven't yet been delivered, and perform per-key aggregations to expose various stats about these messages. Eventually, however, these email messages become inactive (i.e., they are delivered, or they bounce), and we no longer need to track them. Use cases like these necessitate active cleanup of our state stores. Removing unneeded data to keep your state store small greatly reduces the impact of rebalancing. If a stateful task needs to be migrated, it's a lot easier to rebuild a small state store than an unnecessarily large one. So how do we remove unneeded state in Kafka Streams? We use *tombstones*.

Tombstones

Tombstones are special records that indicate that some state needs to be deleted. They are sometimes referred to as delete markers, and they always have a key and a null value. As mentioned previously, state stores are key-based, so the key in a tombstone record indicates which record from the state store needs to be deleted.

An example of how to generate a tombstone is shown in the following code block. In this hypothetical scenario, we are performing some aggregation for a hospital patient, but once we see a patient checkout event, we no longer expect any additional events for this patient, so we remove their data from the underlying state store:

```
StreamsBuilder builder = new StreamsBuilder();
KStream<byte[], String> stream = builder.stream("patient-events");

stream
    .groupByKey()
    .reduce(
        (value1, value2) -> {
          if (value2.equals(PATIENT_CHECKED_OUT)) {
            // create a tombstone
            return null; ❶
```

---

8 It's unlikely the keyspace would be exactly evenly split in a real-world scenario, but it's convenient for this discussion and the point remains the same.

```
        }
        return doSomething(value1, value2);  ❷
    });
```

❶ Return `null` to generate a tombstone (i.e., a delete marker) whenever a patient checks out. This will cause the related key to be removed from the underlying state store.

❷ If a patient has not checked out, then perform the aggregation logic.

While tombstones are useful for keeping key-value stores small, there is another method we can use to remove unneeded data from windowed key-value stores. We'll discuss this in the next section.

Window retention

Windowed stores have a configurable retention period to keep the state stores small. For example, in the previous chapter, we created a windowed store in our patient monitoring application to convert raw pulse events into a heart rate. The relevant code is shown here:

```
TimeWindows tumblingWindow =
    TimeWindows.of(Duration.ofSeconds(60)).grace(Duration.ofSeconds(5));

KTable<Windowed<String>, Long> pulseCounts =
    pulseEvents
        .groupByKey()
        .windowedBy(tumblingWindow)
        .count(Materialized.<String, Long, WindowStore<Bytes, byte[]>>
            as("pulse-counts"))  ❶
        .suppress(
            Suppressed.untilWindowCloses(BufferConfig.unbounded().shutDownWhenFull()));
```

❶ Materialize a windowed store with the default retention period (one day) since this value is not explicitly overridden.

However, the `Materialized` class has an additional method, called `withRetention`, that we can use to specify how long Kafka Streams should keep records in a windowed store. The following code demonstrates how to specify the retention of a windowed store:

```
TimeWindows tumblingWindow =
    TimeWindows.of(Duration.ofSeconds(60)).grace(Duration.ofSeconds(5));

KTable<Windowed<String>, Long> pulseCounts =
    pulseEvents
        .groupByKey()
        .windowedBy(tumblingWindow)
        .count(
            Materialized.<String, Long, WindowStore<Bytes, byte[]>>
```

```
        as("pulse-counts")
        .withRetention(Duration.ofHours(6))) ❶
    .suppress(
        Suppressed.untilWindowCloses(BufferConfig.unbounded().shutDownWhenFull()));
```

❶ Materialize a windowed store with a retention period of six hours.

Note that the retention period should always be larger than the window size *and* the grace period combined. In the preceding example, the retention period must be larger than 65 seconds (60 seconds for the tumbling window size + 5 seconds for the grace period). The default window retention period is one day, so lowering this value can reduce the size of your windowed state stores (and their underlying changelog topics) and therefore speed up recovery time.

So far, we've discussed two methods we can employ in our application code for keeping our state stores small (namely, generating tombstones and setting the retention period for windowed stores). Let's look at another method for keeping the underlying changelog topics small: aggressive topic compaction.

Aggressive topic compaction

By default, changelog topics are compacted. This means that only the latest value for each key is retained and, when tombstones are used, the value for the related key is deleted entirely. However, while the state store will reflect the compacted or deleted value immediately, the underlying topic may remain larger than it needs to be, by retaining the uncompacted/deleted values for a longer period of time.

The reason for this behavior is related to how Kafka represents topics on disk. We've already talked about how topics are split into partitions, and these partitions translate to a single unit of work in Kafka Streams. However, while partitions are the lowest-level topic abstraction we typically deal with on the application side (we generally think about partitions when we consider how many threads we need, and also when figuring out how data should be routed or co-partitioned with related data), there is an even lower-level abstraction on the Kafka broker side: *segments*.

Segments are files that contain a subset of messages for a given topic partition. At any given point in time, there is always an *active segment*, which is the file that is currently being written to for the underlying partition. Over time, the active segments will reach their size threshold and become inactive. Only once a segment is inactive will it be eligible for cleaning.

 Uncompacted records are sometimes referred to as *dirty*. The log cleaner is a process that performs compaction on dirty logs, which benefits both the brokers, by increasing available disk space, and the Kafka Streams clients, by reducing the number of records that need to be replayed in order to rebuild a state store.

Since the active segment isn't eligible for cleaning, and could therefore include a large number of uncompacted records and tombstones that would need to be replayed when initializing a state store, it is sometimes beneficial to reduce the segment size in order to enable more aggressive topic compaction.[9] Furthermore, the log cleaner will also avoid cleaning a log if more than 50% of the log has already been cleaned/compacted. This is also configurable and can be adjusted to increase the frequency at which log cleaning occurs.

The topic configurations listed in Table 6-1 are useful for enabling more aggressive compaction, leading to fewer records that need to be replayed in the event of a state store needing to be reinitialized.[10]

Table 6-1. Topic configurations that can be used for triggering more frequent log cleaning/compaction

Configuration	Default	Definition
segment.bytes	1073741824 (1 GB)	This configuration controls the segment file size for the log. Cleaning is always done a file at a time, so a larger segment size means fewer files but less granular control over retention.
segment.ms	604800000 (7 days)	This configuration controls the period of time after which Kafka will force the log to roll, even if the segment file isn't full, to ensure older data can be compacted or deleted.
min.cleanable.dirty.ratio	0.5	This configuration controls how frequently the log compactor will attempt to clean the log (assuming log compaction is enabled). By default we will avoid cleaning a log where more than 50% of the log has been compacted. This ratio bounds the maximum space wasted in the log by duplicates (with the default setting, at most, 50% of the log could contain duplicates). A higher ratio will mean fewer, more efficient cleanings but will mean more wasted space in the log. If the max.compaction.lag.ms or the min.compaction.lag.ms configurations are also specified, then the log compactor considers the log to be eligible for compaction as soon as either: (i) the dirty ratio threshold has been met and the log has had dirty (uncompacted) records for at least the min.compaction.lag.ms duration, or (ii) the log has had dirty (uncompacted) records for at most the max.compaction.lag.ms period.

---

9 For more on this, see "Achieving High Availability with Stateful Kafka Streams Applications" by Levani Kokhreidze (*https://oreil.ly/ZR4A6*).

10 Configuration definitions come from the official Kafka documentation.

Configuration	Default	Definition
max.compaction.lag.ms	Long.MAX_VALUE - 1	The maximum time a message will remain ineligible for compaction in the log. Only applicable for logs that are being compacted.
min.compaction.lag.ms	0	The minimum time a message will remain uncompacted in the log. Only applicable for logs that are being compacted.

An example of how to change two of these configs in a materialized store is shown in the following code. These topic configurations could help trigger more frequent log cleaning by reducing the segment size and also the minimum cleanable dirty ratio:

```
Map<String, String> topicConfigs = new HashMap<>();
topicConfigs.put("segment.bytes", "536870912"); ❶
topicConfigs.put("min.cleanable.dirty.ratio", "0.3"); ❷

StreamsBuilder builder = new StreamsBuilder();
KStream<byte[], String> stream = builder.stream("patient-events");

KTable<byte[], Long> counts =
    stream
        .groupByKey()
        .count(
            Materialized.<byte[], Long, KeyValueStore<Bytes, byte[]>>as("counts")
                .withKeySerde(Serdes.ByteArray())
                .withValueSerde(Serdes.Long())
                .withLoggingEnabled(topicConfigs));
```

❶ Reduce the segment size to 512 MB.

❷ Reduce the minimum cleanable dirty ratio to 30%.

Now, topic compaction is needed because the underlying storage medium is theoretically unbounded. Another approach to the problem of minimizing state store size is to instead use a fixed-size data structure. While there are some drawbacks to this approach, Kafka Streams does include a state store that tackles the problem from this angle. We'll discuss this next.

Fixed-size LRU cache

A less common method for ensuring state stores don't grow indefinitely is to use an in-memory LRU cache. This is a simple key-value store that has a configurable, fixed capacity (specified by the max number of entries) that automatically deletes the least-recently used entry when the state exceeds the configured size. Furthermore, whenever an entry is removed from the in-memory store, a tombstone is automatically sent to the underlying changelog topic as well.

An example of how to use an in-memory LRU map is shown here:

```
KeyValueBytesStoreSupplier storeSupplier = Stores.lruMap("counts", 10); ❶

StreamsBuilder builder = new StreamsBuilder();
KStream<String, String> stream = builder.stream("patient-events");

stream
    .groupByKey()
    .count(
        Materialized.<String, Long>as(storeSupplier) ❷
            .withKeySerde(Serdes.String())
            .withValueSerde(Serdes.Long())));

return builder.build();
```

❶ Create an in-memory LRU store named *counts* with a max size of 10 entries.

❷ Materialize the in-memory LRU store using a store supplier.

To achieve this in the Processor API, you could use a store builder as follows:

```
StreamsBuilder builder = new StreamsBuilder();

KeyValueBytesStoreSupplier storeSupplier = Stores.lruMap("counts", 10);

StoreBuilder<KeyValueStore<String, Long>> lruStoreBuilder =
  Stores.keyValueStoreBuilder(storeSupplier, Serdes.String(), Serdes.Long());

builder.addStateStore(lruStoreBuilder);
```

As mentioned in "Aggressive topic compaction" on page 191, compaction and deletion will not happen immediately in the underlying changelog topic that backs the LRU cache, so in the event of failure, the restore time could be higher than a persistent state store since the entire topic will need to be replayed in order to reinitialize the state store (even if it resolves to only 10 records in the LRU map!). This is a major downside to using in-memory stores that we initially discussed in "Persistent Versus In-Memory Stores" on page 101, so this option should be used with a full understanding of the trade-offs.

This wraps up our discussion for keeping state stores and their underlying changelog topics free of unneeded records. Now, let's look at a strategy you can pursue if it appears that your state stores are bottlenecked by either read latency or write volume.

Deduplicating Writes with Record Caches

As we discussed in "Suppression" on page 163, there are some DSL methods (namely, suppress, in combination with a buffer config; see Table 5-2) for rate-limiting updates in a windowed store. We also have an operational parameter[11] for controlling the frequency with which state updates are written to both the underlying state stores and downstream processors. These parameters are shown in Table 6-2.

Table 6-2. Topic configurations that can be used to reduce writes to state stores and downstream processors

Raw config	StreamsConfig property	Default	Definition
cache.max.bytes.buffering	CACHE_MAX_BYTES_BUFFERING_CONFIG	1048576 (10 MB)	The maximum amount of memory, in bytes, to be used for buffering across all threads
commit.interval.ms	COMMIT_INTERVAL_MS_CONFIG	30000 (30 seconds)	The frequency with which to save the position of the processor

A larger cache size and higher commit interval can help deduplicate consecutive updates to the same key. This has a few benefits, including:

- Reducing read latency
- Reducing write volume to:
  — State stores
  — Their underlying changelog topics (if enabled)
  — Downstream stream processors

Therefore, if your bottleneck appears to be with reading/writing to the state store, or with network I/O (which can be a byproduct of frequent updates to the changelog topic), you should consider adjusting these parameters. Of course, larger record caches do come with a couple of trade-offs:

- Higher memory usage
- Higher latency (records are emitted less frequently)

---

11 The distinction between this operational parameter and a business logic type of approach that suppress offers is discussed in "Watermarks, Tables, Event Time, and the Dataflow Model" by Eno Thereska et al. on the Confluent blog (*https://oreil.ly/MTN-R*).

Regarding the first point, the total memory that is allocated for the record caches (controlled by the `cache.max.bytes.buffering` parameter) is shared across all of the streaming threads. The memory pool will be subdivided evenly, so threads that are processing "hot partitions" (i.e., partitions with relatively high data volume compared to others) will flush their cache more frequently. Regardless of the cache size or commit interval, the final stateful computation will be the same.

There is also a trade-off with using larger commit intervals. Namely, the amount of work that needs to be redone after a failure will increase as you increase the value of this configuration.

Finally, sometimes it may be desirable to see each intermediate state change without any caching at all. In fact, sometimes people who are new to Kafka Streams will observe the deduplication or the delay in flushing the cache and think something is wrong with their topology, because they produced a certain number of records to their source topic and only saw a subset of the state changes get flushed (possibly after a delay of several seconds, instead of immediately). Therefore, sometimes people will disable the cache entirely and have a smaller commit interval in their development environments. Just be careful of doing this in production because it could impact performance.

State Store Monitoring

Before deploying your application to production, it's important to ensure you have sufficient visibility into your application to properly support it. In this section, we will discuss the common approaches for monitoring stateful applications so that you can reduce operational toil and have enough info to debug it when an error occurs.

Adding State Listeners

A Kafka Streams application can be in one of many states (not to be confused with state stores). Figure 6-5 shows each of these states and their valid transitions.

As mentioned before, the rebalancing state can be especially impactful for stateful Kafka Streams applications, so being able to track when your applications transition to a rebalancing state, and how often this happens, can be useful for monitoring purposes. Luckily for us, Kafka Streams makes it extremely easy to monitor when the application state changes, using something called a *State Listener*. A State Listener is simply a callback method that is invoked whenever the application state changes.

Depending on your application, you may want to take a certain action when a rebalance occurs. For example, at Mailchimp, we create a special metric in our Kafka Streams applications that gets incremented whenever a rebalance is triggered. The metric is sent to our monitoring system (Prometheus), where it can be queried or even used for creating alerts.

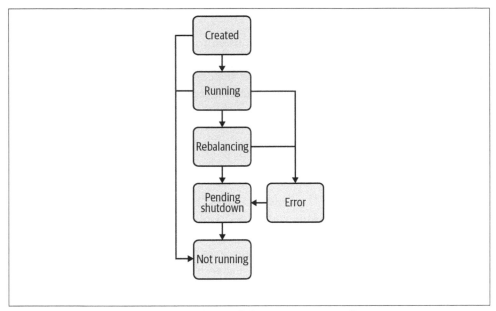

Figure 6-5. Application states and their valid transitions in Kafka Streams

The following code shows an example of how to add a State Listener to a Kafka Streams topology, which listens specifically for transitions to the rebalancing state:

```
KafkaStreams streams = new KafkaStreams(...);

streams.setStateListener( ❶
    (oldState, newState) -> { ❷
      if (newState.equals(State.REBALANCING)) {❸
        // do something
      }
    });
```

❶ Use the `KafkaStreams.setStateListener` method to invoke a method whenever the application state changes.

❷ The method signature for the `StateListener` class includes both the old state and new state.

❸ Conditionally perform some action whenever the application enters a rebalancing state.

While State Listeners are very useful, they are not the only listeners we can leverage in our Kafka Streams applications. The next section will discuss another method that can be used for improving visibility of our stateful applications.

Adding State Restore Listeners

In the previous section, we learned how to listen to rebalance triggers in our Kafka Streams application. However, rebalances are primarily of interest when they cause a state store to be reinitialized. Kafka Streams includes another listener, called a *State Restore Listener*, that can be invoked whenever a state store is reinitialized. The following code shows how to add a State Restore Listener to your Kafka Streams application:

```
KafkaStreams streams = new KafkaStreams(...);

streams.setGlobalStateRestoreListener(new MyRestoreListener());
```

The class `MyRestoreListener` is an instance of a `StateRestoreListener`, which we have implemented in the following code block. Unlike the State Listener we built in the previous section, a State Restore Listener requires us to implement three methods, each of which is hooked into part of the life cycle of the state restoration process. The annotations of the following code describe what each method is used for:

```
class MyRestoreListener implements StateRestoreListener {

    private static final Logger log =
        LoggerFactory.getLogger(MyRestoreListener.class);

    @Override
    public void onRestoreStart(        ❶
        TopicPartition topicPartition,
        String storeName,
        long startingOffset,
        long endingOffset) {

      log.info("The following state store is being restored: {}", storeName);

    }

    @Override
    public void onRestoreEnd(        ❷
        TopicPartition topicPartition,
        String storeName,
        long totalRestored) {

      log.info("Restore complete for the following state store: {}", storeName);

    }

    @Override
    public void onBatchRestored(        ❸
        TopicPartition topicPartition,
        String storeName,
        long batchEndOffset,
        long numRestored) {
```

```
      // this is very noisy. don't log anything
   }
}
```

❶ The onRestoreStart method is invoked at the beginning of a state reinitialization. The startingOffset parameter is of particular interest, since it indicates whether or not the entire state needs to be replayed (this is the most impactful type of reinitialization, and occurs when using in-memory stores, or when using persistent stores and the previous state is lost). If the startingOffset is set to 0, a full reinitialization is required. If it is set to a value greater than 0, then only a partial restore is necessary.

❷ The onRestoreEnd method is invoked whenever a restore is completed.

❸ The onBatchRestored method is invoked whenever a single batch of records is restored. The maximum size of a batch is the same as the MAX_POLL_RECORDS config. This method could potentially be called a lot of times, so be careful when doing any synchronous processing in this method because it can slow down the restore process. I typically don't do anything in this method (even logging can be extremely noisy).

Built-in Metrics

We'll defer most of our discussion of monitoring Kafka Streams applications to Chapter 12 (see "Monitoring" on page 366). However, it's important to note that Kafka Streams includes a set of built-in JMX metrics, many of which relate to state stores.

For example, you can access the rate of certain state store operations and queries (e.g., get, put, delete, all, range), the average and maximum execution time for these operations, and the size of the suppression buffer. There are a number of metrics for RocksDB-backed stores as well, with bytes-written-rate and bytes-read-rate being especially useful when looking at I/O traffic at the byte level.

A detailed breakdown of these metrics can be found in Confluent's monitoring documentation (*https://oreil.ly/vpBn0*). In practice, I typically use higher-level measures of the application's health (e.g., consumer lag) for alerting purposes, but it's nice to have these detailed state store metrics for certain troubleshooting scenarios.

Interactive Queries

Prior to Kafka Streams 2.5, rebalances were especially painful for applications that exposed their state using interactive queries. In these older versions of the library, offline or rebalancing partitions would cause interactive queries to your state stores to fail. Since even healthy rebalances (e.g., a rolling update) could introduce an availability issue, it was a deal breaker for microservices that require high availability.

However, starting in Kafka Streams 2.5 (*https://oreil.ly/1nY9t*), standby replicas can be used to serve stale results while the newly migrated state store is being initialized. This keeps your API highly available even when your application enters a rebalancing state. Recall that in Example 4-11, we learned how to retrieve the metadata for a given key in our state store. In our initial example, we extracted the *active Kafka Streams* instance:

```
KeyQueryMetadata metadata =
  streams.queryMetadataForKey(storeName, key, Serdes.String().serializer());  ❶

String remoteHost = metadata.activeHost().host();  ❷
int remotePort = metadata.activeHost().port();  ❸
```

❶ Get the metadata for the specified key, which includes the host and port pair that a specific key should live on if it exists.

❷ Extract the hostname of the active Kafka Streams instance.

❸ Extract the port of the active Kafka Streams instance.

As of version 2.5, we can retrieve the standby hosts using the following code:

```
KeyQueryMetadata metadata =
    streams.queryMetadataForKey(storeName, key, Serdes.String().serializer());  ❶

if (isAlive(metadata.activeHost())) {  ❷
  // route the query to the active host
} else {
  // route the query to the standby hosts
  Set<HostInfo> standbys = metadata.standbyHosts();  ❸
}
```

❶ Use the `KafkaStreams.queryMetadataForKey` method to get both the active and standby hosts for a given key.

❷ Check to see if the active host is alive. You will need to implement this yourself, but you could potentially add a State Listener (see "Adding State Listeners" on page 196) and a corresponding API endpoint in your RPC server to surface the current state of your application. `isAlive` should resolve to true whenever your application is in the *Running* state.

❸ If the active host is not alive, retrieve the standby hosts so you can query one of the replicated state stores. Note: if no standbys are configured, then this method will return an empty set.

As you can see, this ability to query standby replicas ensures our application is highly available, even when the active instance is down or unable to serve queries. This wraps up our discussion of how to mitigate the impact of rebalances. Next, we'll discuss custom state stores.

Custom State Stores

It's also possible to implement your own state store. In order to do this, you need to implement the `StateStore` interface. You can either implement this directly or, more likely, use one of the higher-level interfaces like `KeyValueStore`, `WindowStore`, or `SessionStore`, which add additional interface methods specific to how the store is intended to be used.[12]

In addition to the `StateStore` interface, you will also want to implement the `StoreSupplier` interface, which will contain the logic for creating new instances of your custom state store. Since the performance characteristics of the built-in RocksDB-based state stores are hard to match, it's typically not necessary to go through the very tedious and error-prone task of implementing your own custom store. For this reason, and given the sheer amount of code that would be needed just to implement a very basic custom store, we will instead point you to one of the few examples of a custom store on GitHub (*https://oreil.ly/pZf9g*).

Finally, if you do decide to implement a custom store, be aware that any storage solution that requires a network call could potentially greatly impact performance. One of the reasons RocksDB or a local, in-memory store is a good choice is because they are colocated with the streams task. Of course, your mileage will vary based on your project's requirements, so ultimately, just be sure to define your performance targets up front and choose your state store accordingly.

---

12 For example, the `KeyValueStore` interface adds the `void put(K key, V value)` method, among others, since it knows the underlying store will need to write key-value pairs to the underlying storage engine.

Summary

You should now have a deeper understanding of how state stores are internally managed by Kafka Streams, and what options are available to you, as the developer, for ensuring your stateful applications run smoothly over time. This includes using tombstones, aggressive topic compaction, and other techniques for removing old data from state stores (and therefore reducing state reinitialization time). Also, by using standby replicas, you can reduce failover time for stateful tasks and also keep your application highly available when a rebalance occurs. Finally, rebalancing, while impactful, can be avoided to some extent using static membership, and the impact can be minimized by using a version of Kafka Streams that supports an improved rebalance protocol called incremental cooperative rebalancing.

## CHAPTER 7

Processor API

Just a few chapters ago, we embarked on our journey to learn about Kafka Streams. We started with Kafka Streams' high-level DSL, which allows us to build stream processing applications using a functional and fluent interface. This involves composing and chaining stream processing functions using the library's built-in operators (e.g., `filter`, `flatMap`, `groupBy`, etc.) and abstractions (`KStream`, `KTable`, `GlobalKTable`).

In this chapter, we will explore a lower-level API that is available in Kafka Streams: the Processor API (sometimes called PAPI). The Processor API has fewer abstractions than the high-level DSL and uses an imperative style of programming. While the code is generally more verbose, it is also more powerful, giving us fine-grained control over the following: how data flows through our topologies, how stream processors relate to each other, how state is created and maintained, and even the timing of certain operations.

Some of the questions we will answer in this chapter include:

- When should you use the Processor API?
- How do you add source, sink, and stream processors using the Processor API?
- How can you schedule periodic functions?
- Is it possible to mix the Processor API with the higher-level DSL?
- What is the difference between processors and transformers?

As usual, we will demonstrate the fundamentals of the API through a tutorial, answering the preceding questions along the way. However, before we show you *how* to use the Processor API, let's first discuss *when* to use it.

When to Use the Processor API

Deciding which abstraction level to use for your stream processing application is important. In general, whenever you introduce complexity into a project, you should have a good reason for doing so. While the Processor API isn't unnecessarily complex, its low-level nature (compared to the DSL and ksqlDB) and fewer abstractions can lead to more code and, if you're not careful, more mistakes.

In general, you may want to utilize the Processor API if you need to take advantage of any of the following:

- Access to record metadata (topic, partition, offset information, record headers, and so on)
- Ability to schedule periodic functions
- More fine-grained control over when records get forwarded to downstream processors
- More granular access to state stores
- Ability to circumvent any limitations you come across in the DSL (we'll see an example of this later)

On the other hand, using the Processor API can come with some disadvantages, including:

- More verbose code, which can lead to higher maintenance costs and impair readability
- A higher barrier to entry for other project maintainers
- More footguns, including accidental reinvention of DSL features or abstractions, exotic problem-framing,[1] and performance traps[2]

Fortunately, Kafka Streams allows us to mix both the DSL and Processor API in an application, so you don't need to go all in on either choice. You can use the DSL for simpler and more standard operations, and the Processor API for more complex or unique functions that require lower-level access to the processing context, state, or record metadata. We will discuss how to combine the DSL and Processor API at the end of this chapter, but initially, we will see how to implement an application using

---

1 The DSL is expressive and problem-framing is easy when we take advantage of its built-in operators. Losing some of this expressiveness and the operators themselves can make our problem-framing less standardized, and our solutions harder to communicate.

2 For example, committing too aggressively or accessing state stores in a way that could impact performance.

only the Processor API. So without further ado, let's take a look at the application we'll be building in this chapter.

Introducing Our Tutorial: IoT Digital Twin Service

In this tutorial, we will use the Processor API to build a *digital twin* service for an offshore wind farm. Digital twins (sometimes called device shadows) are popular in both IoT (Internet of Things) and IIoT (industrial IoT) use cases,[3] in which the state of a physical object is mirrored in a digital copy. This is a great use case for Kafka Streams, which can easily ingest and process high-volume sensor data, capture the state of a physical object using state stores, and subsequently expose this state using interactive queries.

To give you a quick example of what a digital twin is (this will make our tutorial a little clearer), consider the following. We have a wind farm with 40 wind turbines. Whenever one of the turbines reports its current state (wind speed, temperature, power status, etc.), we save that information in a key-value store. An example of a *reported state* record value is shown here:

```
{
  "timestamp": "2020-11-23T09:02:00.000Z",
  "wind_speed_mph": 40,
  "temperature_fahrenheit": 60,
  "power": "ON"
}
```

Note that a device ID is communicated via the record key (e.g., the preceding value may correspond to a device with an ID of `abc123`). This will allow us to distinguish the reported/desired state events of one device from another.

Now, if we want to interact with a particular wind turbine,[4] we don't do so directly. IoT devices can and do frequently go offline, so we can achieve higher availability and reduce errors if we instead only interact with the digital copy (twin) of a physical device.

---

3 In this chapter, we use the broader term IoT, even when we're talking about use cases that have industrial applications. Also, a notable example of where digital twins are used is Tesla Motors. "Tesla creates a digital twin of every car it sells. Tesla then updates software based on individual vehicles' sensor data and uploads updates to its products." See the following link for more information: *https://oreil.ly/j6_mj*.

4 Usually, an interaction means either getting the latest state of a device, or changing the state of a device by updating one of the mutable state properties, like the power status.

For example, if we want to set the power state from ON to OFF, instead of sending that signal to the turbine directly, we would set the so-called *desired state* on the digital copy. The physical turbine would subsequently synchronize its state (i.e., disable power to the blades) whenever it comes online, and usually at set intervals, thereafter. Therefore, a digital twin record will include both a *reported* and *desired* state, and we will create and expose digital twin records like the following using Kafka Streams' Processor API:

```
{
  "desired": {
    "timestamp": "2020-11-23T09:02:01.000Z",
    "power": "OFF"
  },
  "reported": {
    "timestamp": "2020-11-23T09:00:01.000Z",
    "windSpeedMph": 68,
    "power": "ON"
  }
}
```

With this in mind, our application needs to ingest a stream of sensor data from a set of wind turbines,[5] perform some minor processing on the data, and maintain the latest state of each wind turbine in a persistent key-value state store. We will then expose the data via Kafka Streams' interactive queries feature.

Though we will avoid much of the technical detail around interactive queries since this has already been covered in previous chapters, we will present some additional value statements of interactive queries that IoT use cases afford.

Figure 7-1 shows the topology we will be building in this chapter. Each step is detailed after the diagram.

---

[5] In IoT use cases, sensor data is often sent over a protocol called MQTT. One method for getting this data into Kafka would be to use Confluent's MQTT Kafka connector (*https://oreil.ly/pTRmb*).

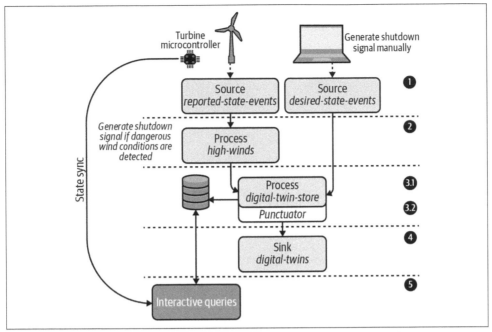

Figure 7-1. The topology that we will be implementing for our IoT digital twin service

❶ Our Kafka cluster contains two topics, and therefore we need to learn how to add source processors using the Processor API. Here is a description of these topics:

- Each wind turbine (edge node) is outfitted with a set of environmental sensors, and this data (e.g., wind speed), along with some metadata about the turbine itself (e.g., power state), is sent to the `reported-state-events` topic periodically.

- The `desired-state-events` topic is written to whenever a user or process wants to change the power state of a turbine (i.e., turn it off or on).

❷ Since the environmental sensor data is reported in the `reported-state-events` topic, we will add a stream processor that determines whether or not the reported wind speed for a given turbine exceeds safe operating levels,[6] and if it does, we will automatically generate a shutdown signal. This will teach you how to add a stateless stream processor using the Processor API.

---

6 In practice, the wind speed threshold could be two-sided. While higher wind speeds introduce dangerous operating conditions, low wind speeds may not justify the cost of running the turbine.

❸ The third step is broken into two parts:

- First, both types of events (reported and desired) will be combined into a so-called digital twin record. These records will be processed and then written to a persistent key-value store called `digital-twin-store`. In this step, you will learn how to connect to and interact with state stores using the Processor API, and also how to access certain record metadata that isn't accessible via the DSL.

- The second part of this step involves scheduling a periodic function, called a *punctuator*, to clean out old digital twin records that haven't seen an update in more than seven days. This will introduce you to the Processor API's punctuation interface, and also demonstrate an alternative method for removing keys from state stores.[7]

❹ Each digital twin record will be written to an output topic called `digital-twins` for analytical purposes. In this step, you will learn how to add sink processors using the Processor API.

❺ We will expose the digital twin records via Kafka Streams' interactive queries feature. Every few seconds, the microcontroller on the wind turbine will attempt to synchronize its own state with the desired state exposed by Kafka Streams. For example, if we generate a shutdown signal in step 2 (which would set the desired power state to `OFF`), then the turbine would see this desired state when it queries our Kafka Streams app, and kill power to the blades.

Now that we understand what we'll be building (and what we'll learn at each step), let's set up our project.

Project Setup

The code for this chapter is located at *https://github.com/mitch-seymour/mastering-kafka-streams-and-ksqldb.git*.

If you would like to reference the code as we work our way through each topology step, clone the repo and change to the directory containing this chapter's tutorial. The following command will do the trick:

```
$ git clone git@github.com:mitch-seymour/mastering-kafka-streams-and-ksqldb.git
$ cd mastering-kafka-streams-and-ksqldb/chapter-07/digital-twin
```

---

7 For another method, see our discussion of tombstones in "Tombstones" on page 189.

You can build the project anytime by running the following command:

```
$ ./gradlew build --info
```

With our project set up, let's start implementing our digital twin application.

Data Models

As usual, before we start creating our topology, we'll first define our data models. The example records and class definition shown in Table 7-1 correspond to the data in our input topics (see step 1 in our processor topology: Figure 7-1).

Note that the data coming through both of the input topics is formatted as JSON for simplicity, and both types of records are represented using a common class: TurbineState. We have omitted the accessor functions in the TurbineState class for brevity's sake.

Table 7-1. Example records and data classes for each source topic

Kafka topic	Example record	Data class

reported-state-events	`{`
	  `"timestamp": "...",`
	  `"wind_speed_mph": 40,`
	  `"power": "ON"`
	`}`
		`public class TurbineState {`
		  `private String timestamp;`
		  `private Double windSpeedMph;`
		
		  `public enum Power { ON, OFF }`
		
		  `public enum Type { DESIRED, REPORTED }`
		
		  `private Power power;`
		  `private Type type;`
		`}`

desired-state-events	`{`
	  `"timestamp": "...",`
	  `"power": "OFF"`
	`}`
		Same as the data class for reported-state

As mentioned in the tutorial overview, we need to combine the reported and desired state records to create a digital twin record. Therefore, we also need a data class for the combined record. The following table shows the JSON structure of the combined digital twin record, as well as the corresponding data class:

Example record	Data class
``` { "desired": { "timestamp": "2020-11-23T09:02:01.000Z", "power": "OFF" }, "reported": { "timestamp": "2020-11-23T09:00:01.000Z", "windSpeedMph": 68, "power": "ON" } } ```	``` public class DigitalTwin { private TurbineState desired; private TurbineState reported; // getters and setters omitted for // brevity } ```

As you can see from the example record, the desired state shows the turbine powered off, but the last reported state shows that the power is on. The turbine will eventually synchronize its state with the digital twin and power the blades off.

Now, at this point, you may be wondering how record serialization and deserialization work in the Processor API compared to the high-level DSL. In other words, how do we actually convert the raw record bytes in our Kafka topics into the data classes shown in Table 7-1? In "Serialization/Deserialization" on page 69, we talked about using Serdes classes in the DSL, which are wrapper classes that contain both a serializer and deserializer. Many DSL operators, like stream, table, join, etc., allow you to specify a Serdes instance, so they are commonplace in applications that use the DSL.

In the Processor API, the various API methods only require the underlying serializer or deserializer that a Serdes instance would typically contain. However, it is still often convenient to define a Serdes for your data classes, since 1) you can always extract the underlying serializer/deserializer to satisfy a Processor API method signature, and 2) Serdes are often useful for testing purposes.

With that said, for this tutorial, we will leverage the Serdes classes shown in Example 7-1.

Example 7-1. Serdes for our digital twin and turbine state records

```
public class JsonSerdes {

  public static Serde<DigitalTwin> DigitalTwin() { ❶
    JsonSerializer<DigitalTwin> serializer = new JsonSerializer<>();
    JsonDeserializer<DigitalTwin> deserializer =
      new JsonDeserializer<>(DigitalTwin.class);

    return Serdes.serdeFrom(serializer, deserializer);
  }

  public static Serde<TurbineState> TurbineState() { ❷
    JsonSerializer<TurbineState> serializer = new JsonSerializer<>();
    JsonDeserializer<TurbineState> deserializer =
```

```
    new JsonDeserializer<>(TurbineState.class);

    return Serdes.serdeFrom(serializer, deserializer); ❸
  }
}
```

❶ A method for retrieving a `DigitalTwin` Serdes.

❷ A method for retrieving a `TurbineState` Serdes.

❸ In previous tutorials, we implemented the `Serde` interface directly (see "Building the Tweet Serdes" on page 74 for an example). This shows an alternative approach, which is to use the `Serdes.serdeFrom` method in Kafka Streams to construct a Serdes from a serializer and deserializer instance.

In the next section, we'll learn how to add source processors and deserialize input records using the Processor API.

Adding Source Processors

Now that we have defined our data classes, we are ready to tackle step 1 of our processor topology (see Figure 7-1). This involves adding two source processors, which will allow us to stream data from our input topics into our Kafka Streams application. Example 7-2 shows how we can accomplish this using the Processor API.

Example 7-2. The initial topology with both of our source processors added

```
Topology builder = new Topology(); ❶

builder.addSource(❷
    "Desired State Events", ❸
    Serdes.String().deserializer(), ❹
    JsonSerdes.TurbineState().deserializer(), ❺
    "desired-state-events"); ❻

builder.addSource(❼
    "Reported State Events",
    Serdes.String().deserializer(),
    JsonSerdes.TurbineState().deserializer(),
    "reported-state-events");
```

❶ Instantiate a `Topology` instance directly. This is what we will use to add and connect source, sink, and stream processors. Note: instantiating a `Topology` directly is different than how we work with the DSL, which requires us to instantiate a `StreamsBuilder` object, add our DSL operators (e.g., `map`, `flatMap`, `merge`, branch, etc.) to the `StreamsBuilder` instance, and ultimately build a `Topology` instance using the `StreamsBuilder#build` method.

❷ Use the `addSource` method to create a source processor. There are many overloaded versions of this method, including variations that support offset reset strategies, topic patterns, and more. So check out the Kafka Streams Javadocs or navigate to the Topology class using your IDE and choose the `addSource` variation that best fits your needs.

❸ The name of the source processor. Each processor must have a unique name, since under the hood, Kafka Streams stores these names in a topologically sorted map (and therefore, each key must be unique). As we'll see shortly, names are important in the Processor API since they are used to connect child processors. Again, this is very different from how the DSL makes connections, which doesn't need an explicit name to define the relationship between processors (by default, the DSL generates an internal name for you). It's advisable to use a descriptive name here to improve the readability of your code.

❹ The key deserializer. Here, we use the built-in `String` deserializer since our keys are formatted as strings. This is another difference between the Processor API and the DSL. The latter requires us to pass in a Serdes (an object that contains both a record serializer and deserializer), while the Processor API only requires the underlying deserializer (which can be extracted directly from the Serdes, as we have done here).

❺ The value deserializer. Here, we use a custom Serdes (found in the source code of this tutorial) to convert the record values into a `TurbineState` object. The additional notes about the key deserializer also apply here.

❻ The name of the topic this source processor consumes from.

❼ Add a second source processor for the `reported-state-events` topic. We won't go through each parameter again since the parameter types match the previous source processor.

One thing to note about the preceding example is that you will see no mention of a stream or table. These abstractions do not exist in the Processor API. However, conceptually speaking, both source processors we have added in the preceding code represent a stream. This is because the processors are not stateful (i.e., they are not connected to a state store) and therefore have no way of remembering the latest state/ representation of a given key.

We will see a table-like representation of our stream when we get to step 3 of our processor topology, but this section completes step 1 of our topology. Now, let's see how to add a stream processor for generating shutdown signals when our wind turbine is reporting dangerous wind speeds.

Adding Stateless Stream Processors

The next step in our processor topology requires us to automatically generate a shutdown signal whenever the wind speed recorded by a given turbine exceeds safe operating levels (65 mph). In order to do this, we need to learn how to add a stream processor using the Processor API. The API method we can use for this purpose is called addProcessor, and an example of how to use this method is shown here:

```
builder.addProcessor(
    "High Winds Flatmap Processor", ❶
    HighWindsFlatmapProcessor::new, ❷
    "Reported State Events"); ❸
```

❶ The name of this stream processor.

❷ The second argument expects us to provide a ProcessSupplier, which is a functional interface that returns a Processor instance. Processor instances contain all of the data processing/transformation logic for a given stream processor. In the next section, we will define a class called HighWindsFlatmapProcessor, which will implement the Processor interface. Therefore, we can simply use a method reference for that class's constructor.

❸ Names of the parent processors. In this case, we only have one parent processor, which is the Reported State Events processor that we created in Example 7-2. Stream processors can be connected to one or more parent nodes.

Whenever you add a stream processor, you need to implement the Processor interface. This isn't a functional interface (unlike ProcessSupplier, which we just discussed), so you can't just pass in a lambda expression to the addProcessor method, like we often do with DSL operators. It's a little more involved and requires more code than we may be accustomed to, but we'll walk through how to do this in the next section.

Creating Stateless Processors

Whenever we use the `addProcessor` method in the Processor API, we need to implement the `Processor` interface, which will contain the logic for processing and transforming records in a stream. The interface has three methods, as shown here:

```
public interface Processor<K, V> { ❶

    void init(ProcessorContext context); ❷

    void process(K key, V value); ❸

    void close(); ❹
}
```

❶ Notice that the `Processor` interface specifies two generics: one for the key type (K) and one for the value type (V). We will see how to leverage these generics when we implement our own processor later in this section.

❷ The `init` method is called when the `Processor` is first instantiated. If your processor needs to perform any initialization tasks, you can specify the initialization logic in this method. The `ProcessorContext` that is passed to the `init` method is extremely useful, and contains many methods that we will explore in this chapter.

❸ The `process` method is called whenever this processor receives a new record. It contains the per-record data transformation/processing logic. In our example, this is where we will add the logic for detecting whether or not wind speeds exceed safe operating levels for our turbine.

❹ The `close` method is invoked by Kafka Streams whenever it is finished with this operator (e.g., during shutdown). This method typically encapsulates any clean up logic you need for your processor and its local resources. However, you should not attempt to cleanup any Kafka Streams–managed resources, like state stores, in this method, since that is handled by the library itself.

With this interface in mind, let's implement a `Processor` that will generate a shutdown signal when wind speeds reach dangerous levels. The code in Example 7-3 shows what our high winds processor looks like.

Example 7-3. A `Processor` implementation that detects dangerous wind speeds

```
public class HighWindsFlatmapProcessor
    implements Processor<String, TurbineState, String, TurbineState> { ❶
  private ProcessorContext<String, TurbineState> context;

  @Override
```

```
  public void init(ProcessorContext<String, TurbineState> context) { ❷
    this.context = context; ❸
  }

  @Override
  public void process(Record<String, TurbineState> record) {
    TurbineState reported = record.value();
    context.forward(record); ❹

    if (reported.getWindSpeedMph() > 65 && reported.getPower() == Power.ON) { ❺
      TurbineState desired = TurbineState.clone(reported); ❻
      desired.setPower(Power.OFF);
      desired.setType(Type.DESIRED);

      Record<String, TurbineState> newRecord = ❼
        new Record<>(record.key(), desired, record.timestamp());
      context.forward(newRecord); ❽
    }
  }

  @Override
  public void close() {
    // nothing to do ❾
  }
}
```

❶ Recall that the Processor interface is parameterized with four generics. The first two generics (in this case, Processor<String, TurbineState, ..., ...>) refer to the *input* key and value types. The last two generics (in this case, Processor<..., ..., String, TurbineState>) refer to the *output* key and value types.

❷ The generics in the ProcessorContext interface refer to the output key and value types (in this case, ProcessorContext<String, TurbineState>).

❸ It is typical to save the processor context as an instance property, as we do here, so that we can access it later (e.g., from the process and/or close methods).

❹ Whenever you want to send a record to downstream processors, you can call the forward method on the ProcessorContext instance (we have saved this in the context property). This method accepts the record that you would like to forward. In our processor implementation, we always want to forward the reported state records, which is why we call context.forward using an unmodified record in this line.

❺ Check to see if our turbine meets the conditions for sending a shutdown signal. In this case, we check that wind speeds exceed a safe threshold (65 mph), and that our turbine is currently powered on.

❻ If the previous conditions are met, generate a new record containing a desired power state of `OFF`. Since we have already sent the original reported state record downstream, and we are now generating a desired state record, this is effectively a type of `flatMap` operation (our processor has created two output records from one input record).

❼ Create an output record that includes the desired state that we saved to the state store. The record key and timestamp are inherited from the input record.

❽ Call the `context.forward` method in order to send the new record (the shutdown signal) to downstream processors.

❾ In this processor, there's no special logic that we need to execute when our processor is closed.

As you can see, implementing a `Processor` is pretty straightforward. One interesting thing to call out is that when you build processors like this, you usually don't need to concern yourself with *where* the output records will be forwarded to from the `Processor` implementation itself (you can define the dataflow by setting the parent name of a downstream processor). The exception to this is if you use a variation of `ProcessorContext#forward` that accepts a list of downstream processor names, which tells Kafka Streams which *child processors* to forward the output to. An example of this is shown here:

```
context.forward(newRecord, "some-child-node");
```

Whether or not you use this variation of the `forward` method depends on if you want to broadcast the output to all of the downstream processors or to a specific downstream processor. For example, the DSL's branch method uses the above variation since it only needs to broadcast its output to a subset of the available downstream processors.

This completes step 2 of our processor topology (see Figure 7-1). Next, we need to implement a stateful stream processor that creates and saves digital twin records in a key-value store.

Creating Stateful Processors

In "State Stores" on page 98, we learned that stateful operations in Kafka Streams require so-called state stores for maintaining some memory of previously seen data. In order to create our digital twin records, we need to combine desired state and recorded state events into a single record. Since these records will arrive at different times for a given wind turbine, we have a stateful requirement of remembering the last recorded and desired state record for each turbine.

So far in this book, we have mostly focused on using state stores in the DSL. Furthermore, the DSL gives us a couple of different options for using state stores. We can use a default internal state store by simply using a stateful operator without specifying a state store, like so:

```
grouped.aggregate(initializer, adder);
```

Or we can use the `Stores` factory class to create a *store supplier*, and materialize the state store using the `Materialized` class in conjunction with a stateful operator, as shown in the following code:

```
KeyValueBytesStoreSupplier storeSupplier =
    Stores.persistentTimestampedKeyValueStore("my-store");

grouped.aggregate(
    initializer,
    adder,
    Materialized.<String, String>as(storeSupplier));
```

Using state stores in the Processor API is a little different. Unlike the DSL, the Processor API won't create an internal state store for you. Therefore, you must always create *and* connect state stores to the appropriate stream processors yourself when you need to perform stateful operations. Furthermore, while we can still use the `Stores` factory class, we will use a different set of methods that are available in this class for creating state stores. Instead of using one of the methods that returns a *store supplier*, we will use the methods for creating *store builders*.

For example, to store the digital twin records, we need a simple key-value store. The factory method for retrieving a key-value store *builder* is called `keyValueStoreBuilder`, and the following code demonstrates how we can use this method for creating our digital twin store:

```
StoreBuilder<KeyValueStore<String, DigitalTwin>> storeBuilder =
    Stores.keyValueStoreBuilder(
        Stores.persistentKeyValueStore("digital-twin-store"),
        Serdes.String(), ❶
        JsonSerdes.DigitalTwin()); ❷
```

❶ We'll use the built-in String Serdes for serializing/deserializing keys.

❷ Use the Serdes we defined in Example 7-1 for serializing/deserializing values.

Once you've created a store builder for your stateful processor, it's time to implement the `Processor` interface. This process is very similar to what we saw when we added a stateless processor in "Creating Stateless Processors" on page 214. We simply need to use the `addProcessor` method in the Processor API, as shown in the following code:

```
builder.addProcessor(
  "Digital Twin Processor", ❶
  DigitalTwinProcessor::new, ❷
  "High Winds Flatmap Processor", "Desired State Events"); ❸
```

❶ The name of this stream processor.

❷ A `ProcessSupplier`, which is a method that can be used to retrieve a `Processor` instance. We will implement the `DigitalTwinProcessor` referenced in this line shortly.

❸ Names of the parent processors. By specifying multiple parents, we are effectively performing what would be a `merge` operation in the DSL.

Before we implement the `DigitalTwinProcessor`, let's go ahead and add our new state store to the topology. We can do this using the `Topology#addStateStore` method, and a demonstration of its usage is shown in Example 7-4.

Example 7-4. Example usage of the `addStateStore` method

```
builder.addStateStore(
  storeBuilder, ❶
  "Digital Twin Processor" ❷
);
```

❶ A store builder that can be used to obtain the state store.

❷ We can *optionally* pass in the name of the processors that should have access to this store. In this case, the `DigitalTwinProcessor` that we created in the previous code block should have access. We could also have passed in more processor names here if we had multiple processors with shared state. Finally, if we omit this optional argument, we could instead use the `Topology#connectProcessor AndState` to connect a state store to a processor *after* the store was added to the topology (instead of at the same time, which is what we're doing here).

The last step is to implement our new stateful processor: `DigitalTwinProcessor`. Like stateless stream processors, we will need to implement the `Processor` interface. However, this time, our implementation will be slightly more involved since this processor needs to interact with a state store. The code in Example 7-5, and the annotations that follow it, will describe how to implement a stateful processor.

Example 7-5. A stateful processor for creating digital twin records

```java
public class DigitalTwinProcessor
    implements Processor<String, TurbineState, String, DigitalTwin> { ❶
  private ProcessorContext<String, DigitalTwin> context;
  private KeyValueStore<String, DigitalTwin> kvStore;

  @Override
  public void init(ProcessorContext<String, DigitalTwin> context) { ❷
    this.context = context; ❸
    this.kvStore = (KeyValueStore) context.getStateStore("digital-twin-store"); ❹
  }

  @Override
  public void process(Record<String, TurbineState> record) {
    String key = record.key(); ❺
    TurbineState value = record.value();
    DigitalTwin digitalTwin = kvStore.get(key); ❻
    if (digitalTwin == null) { ❼
      digitalTwin = new DigitalTwin();
    }

    if (value.getType() == Type.DESIRED) { ❽
      digitalTwin.setDesired(value);
    } else if (value.getType() == Type.REPORTED) {
      digitalTwin.setReported(value);
    }

    kvStore.put(key, digitalTwin); ❾

    Record<String, DigitalTwin> newRecord =
      new Record<>(record.key(), digitalTwin, record.timestamp()); ❿
    context.forward(newRecord); ⓫
  }

  @Override
  public void close() {
    // nothing to do
  }
}
```

❶ The first two generics in the Processor interface (in this case, Processor<String, TurbineState, ..., ...>) refer to the *input* key and value types, and the last two generics (Processor<..., ..., String, DigitalTwin>) refer to the *output* key and value types.

❷ The generics in the ProcessorContext interface (ProcessorContext<String, DigitalTwin>) refer to the output key and value types

❸ We'll save the ProcessorContext (referenced by the context property) so that we can access it later on.

❹ The getStateStore method on the ProcessorContext allows us to retrieve the state store we previously attached to our stream processor. We will interact with this state store directly whenever a record is processed, so we will save it to an instance property named kvStore.

❺ This line and the one that follows it show how to extract the key and value of the input record

❻ Use our key-value store to perform a point lookup for the current record's key. If we have seen this key before, then this will return the previously saved digital twin record.

❼ If the point lookup didn't return any results, then we will create a new digital twin record.

❽ In this code block, we set the appropriate value in the digital twin record depending on the current record's type (reported state or desired state).

❾ Store the digital twin record in the state store directly, using the key-value store's put method.

❿ Create an output record that includes the digital twin instance that we saved to the state store. The record key and timestamp are inherited from the input record.

⓫ Forward the output record to downstream processors.

We've now implemented the first part of step 3 in our processor topology. The next step (step 3.2 in Figure 7-1) will introduce you to a very important feature in the Processor API that has no DSL equivalent. Let's take a look at how to schedule periodic functions in the DSL.

Periodic Functions with Punctuate

Depending on your use case, you may need to perform some periodic task in your Kafka Streams application. This is one area where the Processor API really shines, since it allows you to easily schedule a task using the `ProcessorContext#schedule` method. Recall that in "Tombstones" on page 189, we discussed how to keep our state store size to a minimum by removing unneeded records. In this tutorial, we will present another method for cleaning out state stores that leverages this task scheduling capability. Here, we will remove all digital twin records that haven't seen any state updates in the last seven days. We will assume these turbines are no longer active or are under long-term maintenance, and therefore we'll delete these records from our key-value store.

In Chapter 5, we showed that when it comes to stream processing, *time* is a complex subject. When we think about *when* a periodic function will execute in Kafka Streams, we are reminded of this complexity. There are two *punctuation types* (i.e., timing strategies) that you can select from, as shown in Table 7-2.

Table 7-2. The types of punctuations that are available in Kafka Streams

Punctuation type	Enum	Description
Stream time	`PunctuationType.STREAM_TIME`	Stream time is the highest timestamp observed for a particular topic-partition. It is initially unknown and can only increase or stay the same. It advances only when new data is seen, so if you use this punctuation type, then your function will not execute unless data arrives on a continuous basis.
Wall clock time	`PunctuationType.WALL_CLOCK_TIME`	The local system time, which is advanced during each iteration of the consumer poll method. The upper bound for how often this gets updated is defined by the `StreamsConfig#POLL_MS_CONFIG` configuration, which is the maximum amount of time (in milliseconds) the underlying poll method will block as it waits for new data. This means periodic functions will continue to execute regardless of whether or not new messages arrive.

Since we don't want our periodic function to be tied to new data arriving (in fact, the very presence of this TTL ("time to live") function is based on the assumption that data may stop arriving), then we will use wall clock time as our punctuation type. Now that we've decided which abstraction to use, the rest of the work is simply a matter of scheduling and implementing our TTL function.

The following code shows our implementation:

```java
public class DigitalTwinProcessor
    implements Processor<String, TurbineState, String, DigitalTwin> {

  private Cancellable punctuator; ❶

  // other omitted for brevity

  @Override
  public void init(ProcessorContext<String, DigitalTwin> context) {

    punctuator = this.context.schedule(
        Duration.ofMinutes(5),
        PunctuationType.WALL_CLOCK_TIME, this::enforceTtl); ❷

    // ...
  }

  @Override
  public void close() {
    punctuator.cancel(); ❸
  }

  public void enforceTtl(Long timestamp) {
    try (KeyValueIterator<String, DigitalTwin> iter = kvStore.all()) { ❹

      while (iter.hasNext()) {
        KeyValue<String, DigitalTwin> entry = iter.next();
        TurbineState lastReportedState = entry.value.getReported(); ❺
        if (lastReportedState == null) {
          continue;
        }

        Instant lastUpdated = Instant.parse(lastReportedState.getTimestamp());
        long daysSinceLastUpdate =
          Duration.between(lastUpdated, Instant.now()).toDays(); ❻
        if (daysSinceLastUpdate >= 7) {
          kvStore.delete(entry.key); ❼
        }
      }
    }
  }

  // ...
}
```

❶ When we schedule the punctuator function, it will return a `Cancellable` object that we can use to stop the scheduled function later on. We'll use an object variable named `punctuator` to keep track of this object.

❷ Schedule our periodic function to execute every five minutes based on wall clock time, and save the returned `Cancellable` under the `punctuator` property (see the preceding callout).

❸ Cancel the punctuator when our processor is closed (e.g., during a clean shutdown of our Kafka Streams application).

❹ During each invocation of our function, retrieve each value in our state store. Note that we use a try-with-resources statement to ensure the iterator is closed properly, which will prevent resource leaks.

❺ Extract the last reported state of the current record (which corresponds to a physical wind turbine).

❻ Determine how long it's been (in days) since this turbine last reported its state.

❼ Delete the record from the state store if it's stale (hasn't been updated in at least seven days).

 The `process` function and any punctuations we schedule will be executed in the same thread (i.e., there's no background thread for punctuations) so you don't need to worry about concurrency issues.

As you can see, scheduling periodic functions is extremely easy. Next, let's look at another area where the Processor API shines: accessing record metadata.

Accessing Record Metadata

When we use the DSL, we typically only have access to a record's key and value. However, there's a lot of additional information associated with a given record that is not exposed by the DSL, but that we can access using the Processor API. Some of the more prominent examples of record metadata that you might want to access are shown in Table 7-3. Note that the `context` variable in the following table refers to an instance of `ProcessorContext`, which is made available in the `init` method, as we first showed in Example 7-3.

Table 7-3. Methods for accessing additional record metadata

Metadata	Example
Record headers	context.headers()
Offset	context.offset()
Partition	context.partition()
Timestamp	context.timestamp()
Topic	context.topic()

 The methods shown in Table 7-3 pull metadata about the current record, and can be used within the process() function. However, there isn't a current record when the init() or close() functions are invoked *or* when a punctuation is executing, so there's no metadata to extract.

So what could you do with this metadata? One use case is to decorate the record values with additional context before they are written to some downstream system. You can also decorate application logs with this information to help with debugging purposes. For example, if you encounter a malformed record, you could log an error containing the partition and offset of the record in question, and use that as a basis for further troubleshooting.

Record headers are also interesting, because they can be used to inject additional metadata (for example, tracing context that can be used for distributed tracing (*https://oreil.ly/ZshyG*)). Some examples of how to interact with record headers are shown here:

```
Headers headers = context.headers();
headers.add("hello", "world".getBytes(StandardCharsets.UTF_8)); ❶
headers.remove("goodbye"); ❷
headers.toArray(); ❸
```

❶ Add a header named hello. This header will be propagated to downstream processors.

❷ Remove a header named goodbye.

❸ Get an array of all of the available headers. You could iterate over this and do something with each.

Finally, if you'd like to trace the origin of a record, the topic() method could be useful for this purpose. In this tutorial, we don't need to do this, or really access any metadata at all, but you should now have a good understanding of how to access additional metadata in case you encounter a use case that requires it in the future.

We're ready to move to the next step of our processor topology and learn how to add a sink processor using the Processor API.

Adding Sink Processors

Tackling step 4 of our processor topology (see Figure 7-1). involves adding a sink processor that will write all digital twin records to an output topic called `digital-twins`. This is very simple with the Processor API, so this section will be short. We simply need to use the `addSink` method and specify a few additional parameters, which are detailed in the following code:

```
builder.addSink(
    "Digital Twin Sink", ❶
    "digital-twins", ❷
    Serdes.String().serializer(), ❸
    JsonSerdes.DigitalTwin().serializer(), ❹
    "Digital Twin Processor"); ❺
```

❶ The name of this sink node.

❷ The name of the output topic.

❸ The key serializer.

❹ The value serializer.

❺ The name of one or more parent nodes to connect to this sink.

That's all there is to adding a sink processor. Of course, as with most methods in Kafka Streams, there are some additional variations of this method you may want to utilize. For example, one variation allows you to specify a custom `StreamParti tioner` to map the output record to a partition number. Another variation allows you to exclude the key and value serializers and, instead, use the default serializers that are derived from the `DEFAULT_KEY_SERDE_CLASS_CONFIG` property. But no matter which overloaded method you use, adding a sink processor is a pretty simple operation.

Let's move on to the final step of exposing digital twin records to external services (including the wind turbines themselves, which will synchronize their state to the digital twin records in our state store).

Interactive Queries

We've completed steps 1–4 of our topology (see Figure 7-1). The fifth step simply involves exposing the digital twin records using Kafka Streams' interactive queries feature. We already covered this topic in detail in "Interactive Queries" on page 129, so we won't go into too much detail or show the entire implementation. However, Example 7-6 shows a very simple REST service that uses interactive queries to pull the latest digital twin record. Note that in this example, remote queries aren't shown, but you can view this example's source code for a more complete example.

The important thing to note is that from an interactive query perspective, using the Processor API is exactly the same as using the DSL.

Example 7-6. An example REST service to expose digital twin records

```
class RestService {
  private final HostInfo hostInfo;
  private final KafkaStreams streams;

  RestService(HostInfo hostInfo, KafkaStreams streams) {
    this.hostInfo = hostInfo;
    this.streams = streams;
  }

  ReadOnlyKeyValueStore<String, DigitalTwin> getStore() {
    return streams.store(
        StoreQueryParameters.fromNameAndType(
            "digital-twin-store", QueryableStoreTypes.keyValueStore()));
  }

  void start() {
    Javalin app = Javalin.create().start(hostInfo.port());
    app.get("/devices/:id", this::getDevice);
  }

  void getDevice(Context ctx) {
    String deviceId = ctx.pathParam("id");
    DigitalTwin latestState = getStore().get(deviceId);
    ctx.json(latestState);
  }
}
```

This completes step 5 of our processor topology (see Figure 7-1). Let's put the various pieces that we've constructed together.

Putting It All Together

The following code block shows what our full processor topology looks like at this point:

```
Topology builder = new Topology();

builder.addSource( ❶
    "Desired State Events",
```

```
        Serdes.String().deserializer(),
        JsonSerdes.TurbineState().deserializer(),
        "desired-state-events");

builder.addSource( ❷
    "Reported State Events",
    Serdes.String().deserializer(),
    JsonSerdes.TurbineState().deserializer(),
    "reported-state-events");

builder.addProcessor( ❸
    "High Winds Flatmap Processor",
    HighWindsFlatmapProcessor::new,
    "Reported State Events");

builder.addProcessor( ❹
    "Digital Twin Processor",
    DigitalTwinProcessor::new,
    "High Winds Flatmap Processor",
    "Desired State Events");

StoreBuilder<KeyValueStore<String, DigitalTwin>> storeBuilder =
    Stores.keyValueStoreBuilder( ❺
        Stores.persistentKeyValueStore("digital-twin-store"),
        Serdes.String(),
        JsonSerdes.DigitalTwin());

builder.addStateStore(storeBuilder, "Digital Twin Processor"); ❻

builder.addSink( ❼
    "Digital Twin Sink",
    "digital-twins",
    Serdes.String().serializer(),
    JsonSerdes.DigitalTwin().serializer(),
    "Digital Twin Processor");
```

❶ Create a *source processor* named Desired State Events that consumes data from the desired-state-events topic. This is the equivalent of a *stream* in the DSL.

❷ Create a *source processor* named Reported State Events that consumes data from the reported-state-events topic. This is also the equivalent of a *stream* in the DSL.

❸ Add a *stream processor* named High Winds Flatmap Processor that generates a shutdown signal if high winds are detected. This processor receives events from the Reported State Events processor. This would be a flatMap operation in the DSL since there is a 1:N relationship between the number of input and output records for this stream processor. Example 7-3 shows the implementation of this processor.

❹ Add a *stream processor* named `Digital Twin Processor` that creates digital twin records using data emitted from both the `High Winds Flatmap Processor` and `Desired State Events`. This would be a *merge* operation in the DSL since multiple sources are involved. Furthermore, since this is a stateful processor, this would be the equivalent of an aggregated *table* in the DSL. Example 7-5 shows the implementation of this processor.

❺ Use the `Stores` factory class to create a *store builder*, which can be used by Kafka Streams to build persistent key-value stores that are accessible from the `Digital Twin Processor` node.

❻ Add the state store to the topology and connect it to the `Digital Twin Processor` node.

❼ Create a *sink processor* named `Digital Twin Sink` that writes all digital twin records that get emitted from the `Digital Twin Processor` node to an output topic named `digital-twins`.

We can now run our application, write some test data to our Kafka cluster, and query our digital twin service. Running our application is no different than what we've seen in previous chapters, as you can see from the following code block:

```
Properties props = new Properties();
props.put(StreamsConfig.APPLICATION_ID_CONFIG, "dev-consumer"); ❶
// ...

KafkaStreams streams = new KafkaStreams(builder, props); ❷
streams.start(); ❸

Runtime.getRuntime().addShutdownHook(new Thread(streams::close)); ❹

RestService service = new RestService(hostInfo, streams); ❺
service.start();
```

❶ Configure the Kafka Streams application. This works the same way as we saw when building applications with the DSL. Most of the configs are omitted for brevity's sake.

❷ Instantiate a new `KafkaStreams` instance that can be used to execute our topology.

❸ Start the Kafka Streams application.

❹ Add a shutdown hook to gracefully stop the Kafka Streams application when a global shutdown signal is received.

❺ Instantiate and (on the following line) start the REST service, which we implemented in Example 7-6.

Our application now reads from multiple source topics, but we will only produce test data to the `reported-state-events` topic in this book (see the source code (*https://oreil.ly/LySHt*) for a more complete example). To test that our application generates a shutdown signal, we will include one record that contains a wind speed that exceeds our safe operating threshold of 65 mph. The following code shows the test data we will produce, with record keys and values separated by | and timestamps omitted for brevity:

```
1|{"timestamp": "...", "wind_speed_mph": 40, "power": "ON", "type": "REPORTED"}
1|{"timestamp": "...", "wind_speed_mph": 42, "power": "ON", "type": "REPORTED"}
1|{"timestamp": "...", "wind_speed_mph": 44, "power": "ON", "type": "REPORTED"}
1|{"timestamp": "...", "wind_speed_mph": 68, "power": "ON", "type": "REPORTED"} ❶
```

❶ This sensor data shows a wind speed of 68 mph. When our application sees this record, it should generate a shutdown signal by creating a new `TurbineState` record, with a desired power state of OFF.

If we produce this test data into the `reported-state-events` topic and then query our digital twin service, we will see that our Kafka Streams application not only processed the reported states of our windmill, but also produced a desired state record where the power is set to `OFF`. The following code block shows an example request and response to our REST service:

```
$ curl localhost:7000/devices/1 | jq '.'

{
  "desired": {
    "timestamp": "2020-11-23T09:02:01.000Z",
    "windSpeedMph": 68,
    "power": "OFF",
    "type": "DESIRED"
  },
  "reported": {
    "timestamp": "2020-11-23T09:02:01.000Z",
    "windSpeedMph": 68,
    "power": "ON",
    "type": "REPORTED"
  }
}
```

Now, our wind turbines can query our REST service and synchronize their own state with the desired state that was either captured (via the `desired-state-events` topic) or enforced (using the high winds processor to send a shutdown signal) by Kafka Streams.

Combining the Processor API with the DSL

We've verified that our application works. However, if you look closely at our code, you'll see that only one of the topology steps requires the low-level access that the Processor API offers. The step I'm referring to is the `Digital Twin Processor` step (see step 3 in Figure 7-1), which leverages an important feature of the Processor API: the ability to schedule periodic functions.

Since Kafka Streams allows us to combine the Processor API and the DSL, we can easily refactor our application to *only* use the Processor API for the `Digital Twin Processor` step, and to use the DSL for everything else. The biggest benefit of performing this kind of refactoring is that other stream processing steps can be simplified. In this tutorial, the `High Winds Flatmap Processor` offers the biggest opportunity of simplification, but in larger applications, this kind of refactoring reduces complexity on an even greater scale.

The first two steps in our processor topology (registering the source processors and generating a shutdown signal using a `flatMap`-like operation) can be refactored using operators we've already discussed in this book. Specifically, we can make the following changes:

Processor API	DSL
`Topology builder = new Topology();`	`StreamsBuilder builder = new StreamsBuilder();`

`builder.addSource(`
`  "Desired State Events",`
`  Serdes.String().deserializer(),`
`  JsonSerdes.TurbineState().deserializer(),`
`  "desired-state-events");`
	`KStream<String, TurbineState> desiredStateEvents =`
	`  builder.stream("desired-state-events",`
	`    Consumed.with(`
	`      Serdes.String(),`
	`      JsonSerdes.TurbineState()));`

`builder.addSource(`
`  "Reported State Events",`
`  Serdes.String().deserializer(),`
`  JsonSerdes.TurbineState().deserializer(),`
`  "reported-state-events");`
	`KStream<String, TurbineState> highWinds =`
	`  builder.stream("reported-state-events",`
	`    Consumed.with(`
	`      Serdes.String(),`
	`      JsonSerdes.TurbineState()))`
	`    .flatMapValues((key, reported) -> ... )`
	`    .merge(desiredStateEvents);`

`builder.addProcessor(`
`  "High Winds Flatmap Processor",`
`  HighWindsFlatmapProcessor::new,`
`  "Reported State Events");`	

As you can see, these changes are pretty straightforward. However, step 3 in our topology actually does require the Processor API, so how do we go about combining the

DSL and Processor API in this step? The answer lies in a special set of DSL operators, which we will explore next.

Processors and Transformers

The DSL includes a special set of operators that allow us to use the Processor API whenever we need lower-level access to state stores, record metadata, and processor context (which can be used for scheduling periodic functions, among other things). These special operators are broken into two categories: *processors* and *transformers*. The following outlines the distinction between these two groups:

- A *processor* is a *terminal operation* (meaning it returns void and downstream operators cannot be chained), and the computational logic must be implemented using the `Processor` interface (which we first discussed in "Adding Stateless Stream Processors" on page 213). Processors should be used whenever you need to leverage the Processor API from the DSL, but don't need to chain any downstream operators. There is currently only one variation of this type of operator, as shown in the following table:

DSL operator	Interface to implement	Description
process	Processor	Apply a Processor to each record at a time

- *Transformers* are a more diverse set of operators and can return one or more records (depending on which variation you use), and are therefore more optimal if you need to chain a downstream operator. The variations of the transform operator are shown in Table 7-4.

Table 7-4. Various transform operators that are available in Kafka Streams

DSL operator	Interface to implement	Description	Input/output ratio
transform	Transformer	Apply a Transformer to each record, generating one or more output records. Single records can be returned from the Transformer#transform method, and multiple values can be emitted using ProcessorContext#forward.[a] The transformer has access to the record key, value, metadata, processor context (which can be used for scheduling periodic functions), and connected state stores.	1:N

DSL operator	Interface to implement	Description	Input/output ratio
transform Values	ValueTransformer	Similar to transform, but *does not* have access to the record key and *cannot* forward multiple records using ProcessorContext#forward (if you try to forward multiple records, you will get a StreamsException). Since state store operations are key-based, this operator is not ideal if you need to perform lookups against a state store. Furthermore, output records will have the same key as the input records, and downstream auto-repartitioning will not be triggered since the key cannot be modified (which is advantageous since it can help avoid network trips).	1:1
transform Values	ValueTransformerWithKey	Similar to transform, but the record key is *read-only* and *should not be modified*. Also, you cannot forward multiple records using ProcessorContext#forward (if you try to forward multiple records, you will get a StreamsException).	1:1
flatTrans form	Transformer (with an iterable return value)	Similar to transform, but instead of relying on ProcessorContext#forward to return multiple records, you can simply return a collection of values. For this reason, it's recommended to use flatTransform over transform if you need to emit multiple records, since this method is type-safe while the latter is not (since it relies on ProcessorContext#forward).	1:N
flatTrans formValues	ValueTransformer (with an iterable return value)	Apply a Transformer to each record, returning one or more output records directly from the ValueTransformer#trans form method.	1:N
flatTrans formValues	ValueTransformerWithKey (with an iterable return value)	A stateful variation of flatTransformVal ues in which a read-only key is passed to the transform method, which can be used for state lookups. One or more output records are returned directly from the ValueTransfor merWithKey#transform method.	1:N

[a] Though 1:N transformations are technically supported, transform is better for 1:1 or 1:0 transformations in which a single record is returned directly, since the ProcessorContext#forward approach is not type-safe. Therefore, if you need to forward multiple records from your transform, flatTransform is recommended instead, since it is type-safe.

No matter which variation you choose, if your operator is stateful, you will need to connect the state store to your topology builder before adding your new operator.

Since we are refactoring our stateful `Digital Twin Processor` step, let's go ahead and do that:

```
StoreBuilder<KeyValueStore<String, DigitalTwin>> storeBuilder =
  Stores.keyValueStoreBuilder(
      Stores.persistentKeyValueStore("digital-twin-store"),
      Serdes.String(),
      JsonSerdes.DigitalTwin());

builder.addStateStore(storeBuilder); ❶
```

❶ In Example 7-4, we discussed an optional second parameter to the `Topology#add StateStore` method, which specifies the processor names that should be connected with the state store. Here, we omit the second parameter, so this state store is *dangling* (though we will connect it in the next code block).

Now, we need to make a decision. Do we use a processor or transformer for refactoring the `Digital Twin Processor` step? Looking at the definitions in the preceding tables, you may be tempted to use the `process` operator since we already implemented the `Processor` interface in the pure Processor API version of our app (see Example 7-5). If we were to take this approach (which is problematic for reasons we'll discuss shortly), we'd end up with the following implementation:

```
highWinds.process(
    DigitalTwinProcessor::new, ❶
    "digital-twin-store"); ❷
```

❶ A `ProcessSupplier`, which is used to retrieve an instance of our `DigitalTwinPro cessor`.

❷ The name of the state store that our processor will interact with.

Unfortunately, this isn't ideal because we need to connect a sink processor to this node, and the `process` operator is a terminal operation. Instead, one of the transformer operators would work better here since it allows us to easily connect a sink processor (as we'll see shortly). Now, looking at Table 7-4, let's find an operator that meets our requirements:

- Each input record will always produce one output record (1:1 mapping)
- We need read-only access to the record key since we're performing point lookups in our state store, but do not need to modify the key in any way

The operator that best fits these requirements is `transformValues` (the variation that uses a `ValueTransformerWithKey`). We've already implemented the computational logic for this step using a `Processor` (see Example 7-5), so we just need to implement the `ValueTransformerWithKey` interface and copy the logic from the `process` method in Example 7-5 to the `transform` method, shown in the following. Most of the code has been omitted because it's the same as the processor implementation. The changes are highlighted in the annotations following this example:

```java
public class DigitalTwinValueTransformerWithKey
    implements ValueTransformerWithKey<String, TurbineState, DigitalTwin> { ❶

  @Override
  public void init(ProcessorContext context) {
    // ...
  }

  @Override
  public DigitalTwin transform(String key, TurbineState value) {
    // ...
    return digitalTwin; ❷
  }

  @Override
  public void close() {
    // ...
  }

  public void enforceTtl(Long timestamp) {
    // ...
  }
}
```

❶ Implement the `ValueTransformerWithKey` interface. `String` refers to the key type, `TurbineState` refers to the value type of the input record, and `DigitalTwin` refers to the value type of the output record.

❷ Instead of using `context.forward` to send records to downstream processors, we can return the record directly from the `transform` method. As you can see, this is already feeling much more DSL-like.

With our transformer implementation in place, we can add the following line to our application:

```java
highWinds
  .transformValues(DigitalTwinValueTransformerWithKey::new, "digital-twin-store")
  .to("digital-twins", Produced.with(Serdes.String(), JsonSerdes.DigitalTwin()));
```

Putting It All Together: Refactor

Now that we've discussed the individual steps in our DSL refactor, let's take a look at the two implementations of our application side by side, as seen in Table 7-5.

Table 7-5. Two different implementations of our digital twin topology

Processor API only	DSL + Processor API
```Topology builder = new Topology();```	```StreamsBuilder builder = new StreamsBuilder();```
```builder.addSource(``   `` "Desired State Events",``   `` Serdes.String().deserializer(),``   `` JsonSerdes.TurbineState().deserializer(),``   `` "desired-state-events");```	```KStream<String, TurbineState> desiredStateEvents =``   `` builder.stream("desired-state-events",``   `` Consumed.with(``   `` Serdes.String(),``   `` JsonSerdes.TurbineState()));```
```builder.addSource(``   `` "Reported State Events",``   `` Serdes.String().deserializer(),``   `` JsonSerdes.TurbineState().deserializer(),``   `` "reported-state-events");```	```KStream<String, TurbineState> highWinds =``   `` builder.stream("reported-state-events",``   `` Consumed.with(``   `` Serdes.String(),``   `` JsonSerdes.TurbineState()))``   `` .flatMapValues((key, reported) -> ...)``   `` .merge(desiredStateEvents);```
```builder.addProcessor(``   `` "High Winds Flatmap Processor",``   `` HighWindsFlatmapProcessor::new,``   `` "Reported State Events");```	
```builder.addProcessor(``   `` "Digital Twin Processor",``   `` DigitalTwinProcessor::new,``   `` "High Winds Flatmap Processor",``   `` "Desired State Events");```	```// empty space to align next topology step```
```StoreBuilder<KeyValueStore<String, DigitalTwin>>``   `` storeBuilder =``   `` Stores.keyValueStoreBuilder(``   `` Stores.persistentKeyValueStore(``   `` "digital-twin-store"),``   `` Serdes.String(),``   `` JsonSerdes.DigitalTwin());```	```StoreBuilder<KeyValueStore<String, DigitalTwin>>``   `` storeBuilder =``   `` Stores.keyValueStoreBuilder(``   `` Stores.persistentKeyValueStore(``   `` "digital-twin-store"),``   `` Serdes.String(),``   `` JsonSerdes.DigitalTwin());```
```builder.addStateStore(storeBuilder,``   `` "Digital Twin Processor");```	```builder.addStateStore(storeBuilder);```
```builder.addSink(``   `` "Digital Twin Sink",``   `` "digital-twins",``   `` Serdes.String().serializer(),``   `` JsonSerdes.DigitalTwin().serializer(),``   `` "Digital Twin Processor");```	```highWinds``   `` .transformValues(``   `` DigitalTwinValueTransformerWithKey::new,``   `` "digital-twin-store")``   `` .to("digital-twins",``   `` Produced.with(``   `` Serdes.String(),``   `` JsonSerdes.DigitalTwin()));```

Either implementation is perfectly fine. But going back to something I mentioned earlier, you don't want to introduce additional complexity unless you have a good reason for doing so.

The benefits of the hybrid DSL + Processor API implementation are:

- It's easier to construct a mental map of your dataflow by chaining operators instead of having to define the relationship between processors using node names and parent names.

- The DSL has lambda support for most operators, which can be beneficial for succinct transformations (the Processor API requires you to implement the Processor interface, even for simple operations, which can be tedious).

- Although we didn't need to rekey any records in this tutorial, the method for doing this in the Processor API is much more tedious. You not only need to implement the Processor interface for a simple rekey operation, but you also have to handle the rewrite to an intermediate repartition topic (this involves adding an additional sink and source processor explicitly, which can lead to unnecessarily complex code).

- The DSL operators give us a standard vocabulary for defining what happens at a given stream processing step. For example, we can infer that a flatMap operator may produce a different number of records than the input, without knowing anything else about the computational logic. On the other hand, the Processor API makes it easy to disguise the nature of a given Processor implementation, which hurts code readability and can have a negative impact on maintenance.

- The DSL also gives us a common vocabulary for different types of streams. These include pure record streams, local aggregated streams (which we usually refer to as tables), and global aggregated streams (which we refer to as global tables).

Therefore, I usually recommend leveraging the DSL's special set of operators for using the Processor API whenever you need lower-level access, as opposed to implementing an application purely in the Processor API.

Summary

In this chapter, we learned how to use the Processor API to gain lower-level access to Kafka records and Kafka Streams' processor context. We also discussed a useful feature of the Processor API that allows us to schedule periodic functions, and the various notions of time that can be used when defining a punctuator for these scheduled functions. Finally, we showed that combining the Processor API and high-level DSL is a great way to leverage the benefits of both APIs. In the next chapter, we will start exploring ksqlDB, which will take us to the opposite side of the spectrum in terms of simplicity (it is the simplest option for building stream processing applications that we will discuss in this book, and arguably the simplest option, period).

ksqlDB

SQL Syntax Notation

The chapters in this part of the book will include several syntax references that we will use to describe how certain SQL statements can be constructed in ksqlDB. For example, the syntax reference for listing the running queries on a ksqlDB server is as follows:

```
{ SHOW | LIST } QUERIES [EXTENDED];
```

The notation we will use for all SQL syntax references in this part is as follows:

- Square brackets [ ] enclose optional elements or clauses.
- Curly braces { } enclose a set of alternative choices.
- Parentheses ( ) are literal parentheses.
- A vertical bar | represents a logical OR.
- An ellipsis preceded by a comma within square brackets [, ...] indicates that the preceding item can be repeated in a comma-separated list.

For example, using the syntax reference, we can see that our statement can begin with either SHOW or LIST, and we can optionally append the EXTENDED keyword to the end of our example statement. Thus, the following is a valid ksqlDB statement:

```
SHOW QUERIES ;
```

Note that we will follow this pattern whenever we introduce a new ksqlDB statement.

## CHAPTER 8

Getting Started with ksqlDB

The story of ksqlDB is one of simplification and evolution. It was built with the same goal as Kafka Streams: simplify the process of building stream processing applications. However, as ksqlDB evolved, it became clear that its goals were much more ambitious than even Kafka Streams. That's because it not only simplifies how we build stream processing applications, but also how we integrate these applications with other systems (including those external to Kafka). It does all of this with a SQL interface, making it easy for beginners and experts alike to leverage the power of Kafka.

Now, I know what you're thinking: why would you need to know both Kafka Streams and ksqlDB, and can you rip out one of the sections of this book and sell it on Craigslist to recover some of your investment? Actually, both Kafka Streams and ksqlDB are excellent tools to have in your stream processing toolbelt, and complement each other quite well. You can use ksqlDB for stream processing applications that can be expressed in SQL, and for easily setting up data sources and sinks to create end-to-end data processing pipelines using a single tool. On the other hand, you can use Kafka Streams for more complex applications, and your knowledge of that library will only deepen your understanding of ksqlDB since it's actually built on top of Kafka Streams.

I was going to save the part about ksqlDB being built on top of Kafka Streams as a big reveal later in this chapter, which hopefully would have caught you in the middle of drinking a large sip of water. But I couldn't make it two paragraphs in before I shared that. This is such a huge selling point and one of the reasons I think you'll love working with ksqlDB. Most databases get really complicated as you start peeling back the floorboards, making it difficult to establish expertise in the technology without dedicating months to the tedious study of its internals. However, having Kafka Streams at its core means ksqlDB is built on well-designed and easily understood layers of abstraction, allowing you to dive deeper into the internals and learn how to fully leverage the power of this technology in a fun and accessible way. In fact, you could even view the Kafka Streams part of this book as an initial look at the internals of ksqlDB.

There are so many great features in ksqlDB that we have dedicated a few chapters to its study. In this first chapter, we'll get our first look at this technology and answer some important questions, including:

- What exactly is ksqlDB?
- When should you use ksqlDB?
- How have ksqlDB's features evolved over time?
- Which areas does ksqlDB offer simplification in?
- What are the key components of ksqlDB's architecture?
- How can we install and run ksqlDB?

So without further ado, let's start by providing more context about what ksqlDB actually is and what it's capable of.

What Is ksqlDB?

ksqlDB is an open source *event streaming database* that was released by Confluent in 2017 (a little more than a year after Kafka Streams was introduced into the Kafka ecosystem). It simplifies the way stream processing applications are built, deployed, and maintained, by integrating two specialized components in the Kafka ecosystem (Kafka Connect and Kafka Streams) into a single system, and by giving us a high-level SQL interface for interacting with these components. Some of the things we can do with ksqlDB include:

- Model data as either streams or tables (each of which is considered a *collection* in ksqlDB) using SQL.
- Apply a wide number of SQL constructs (e.g., for joining, aggregating, transforming, filtering, and windowing data) to create new derived representations of data without touching a line of Java code.
- Query streams and tables using *push queries*, which run continuously and emit/push results to clients whenever new data is available. Under the hood, push queries are compiled into Kafka Streams applications and are ideal for *event-driven microservices* that need to observe and react to events quickly.
- Create *materialized views* from streams and tables, and query these views using *pull queries*. Pull queries are akin to the way keyed-lookups work in traditional SQL databases, and under the hood, they leverage Kafka Streams and state stores.

Pull queries can be used by clients that need to work with ksqlDB in a synchronous/on-demand workflow.

- Define *connectors* to integrate ksqlDB with external data stores, allowing you to easily read from and write to a wide range of data *sources* and *sinks*. You can also combine connectors with tables and streams to create end-to-end *streaming ETL[1] pipelines*.

We'll explore each of these capabilities in detail over the following chapters. But it's worth noting that since ksqlDB is built on the mature bones of Kafka Connect and Kafka Streams, you get the stability and power of those tools for free, but also all of the benefits of a friendlier interface. We'll discuss the benefits of using ksqlDB in the next section, which will inform our decision of when to use it.

When to Use ksqlDB

It's no surprise that higher-level abstractions are often easier to work with than their lower-level counterparts. However, if we were to just say, "SQL is easier to write than Java," we'd be glossing over the many benefits of using ksqlDB that stem from its simpler interface and architecture. These benefits include:

- *More interactive workflows*, thanks to a managed runtime that can compose and deconstruct stream processing applications on demand using an included CLI and REST service for submitting queries.

- *Less code to maintain* since stream processing topologies are expressed using SQL instead of a JVM language.

- *Lower barrier to entry* and fewer new concepts to learn, especially for those who are familiar with traditional SQL databases but new to stream processing. This improves project onboarding for new developers and also maintainability.

- *Simplified architecture*, since the interface for managing connectors (which integrate external data sources into Kafka) and transforming data are combined into a single system. There's also an option for running Kafka Connect from the same JVM as ksqlDB.[2]

- *Increased developer productivity* since it takes less code to express a stream processing application, and complexities of lower-level systems are hidden beneath new layers of abstraction. Also, the interactive workflow translates to quicker

---

1 Extract, transform, load.

2 Whether or not you should run with this setup in production depends on your workload. For serious workloads, you'll probably want to run Connect externally so that you can scale these components independently, as we'll discuss in Chapter 9. However, the combined setup is extremely convenient for development purposes.

feedback loops and there is an included test harness that makes query verification extremely simple.[3] This makes for an enjoyable and productive development experience.

- *Cross-project consistency.* Thanks to SQL's declarative syntax, stream processing applications that are expressed in SQL are less likely to suffer from speciation (i.e., developing unique features that differentiate them from otherwise similar projects). Kafka Streams does a great job of this already by introducing a standard set of DSL operators for working with event streams, but there's still a lot of freedom when managing the rest of the application code, which can lead to applications that are more like pets than cattle.

- *Easy setup and turnkey deployments* thanks to several distribution options, including officially supported Docker images. For those who really want a streamlined path to production, there are also fully managed, cloud-based offerings of ksqlDB (e.g., Confluent Cloud (*https://oreil.ly/WeY4r*)).

- *Better support for data exploration.* ksqlDB makes it easy to list and print the contents of topics, and to quickly create and query materialized views of the data. These kinds of data exploration use cases are much better fitted for ksqlDB.

Now that we've discussed some of the benefits of using ksqlDB, let's look at when you should use ksqlDB over Kafka Streams. The most common answer you'll hear is to use ksqlDB whenever your stream processing applications can be expressed using SQL. However, I think this version of the answer is incomplete. Instead, I suggest that you use ksqlDB whenever your project could leverage any of the preceding benefits stated *and* when your stream processing applications can be expressed *naturally and simply* using SQL.

For example, one of ksqlDB's greatest and most powerful features is its ability for users to extend the built-in function library with custom, Java-based functions. You may want to leverage this feature on a regular basis, but if you find yourself operating at the JVM level frequently for a specific application/query set, it's worth evaluating whether or not you're operating at the proper abstraction level (e.g., it may make more sense to use Kafka Streams).

There are some additional use cases that are better suited for Kafka Streams. For example, if you need lower-level access to your application state, need to run periodic functions against your data, need to work with data formats that aren't supported in ksqlDB, want more flexibility with application profiling/monitoring (e.g., distributed tracing, custom metric collection, etc.), or have a lot of business logic that isn't easily expressed in SQL, then Kafka Streams is a better fit.

---

3 Note that testing Kafka Streams applications is also very easy, as we'll see in Chapter 12.

We've discussed when to use ksqlDB and what benefits it offers, so now we'll get a better understanding of the individual integrations (Kafka Streams and Kafka Connect) by looking at how ksqlDB evolved and improved these integrations over time.

Evolution of a New Kind of Database

It's helpful to understand how ksqlDB evolved over time and which capabilities it gained along the way. While ksqlDB's evolution is interesting, this section serves a larger purpose than to simply provide a look at its history. Since ksqlDB used to be known by a different name (KSQL), knowing when certain features were introduced can help you distinguish between different generations of this technology.

Let's kick off this section with how ksqlDB has evolved its Kafka Streams integration over time, and how Kafka Streams supports one of the most fundamental capabilities of ksqlDB: querying data.

Kafka Streams Integration

For the first two years of its life, ksqlDB was known as *KSQL*. Early development focused on its core feature: a streaming SQL engine that could parse and compile SQL statements into full-blown stream processing applications. In this early evolutionary form, KSQL was conceptually a mix between a traditional SQL database and Kafka Streams, borrowing features from relational databases (RDBMS) while using Kafka Streams to do the heavy lifting in the stream processing layer. This is shown in Figure 8-1.

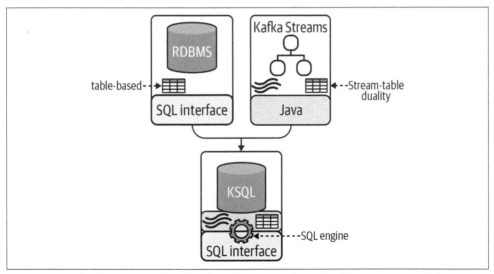

Figure 8-1. The first phase of ksqlDB's evolution combined Kafka Streams with features of traditional SQL databases, including a SQL interface

The most notable feature KSQL borrows from the RDBMS branch of the evolutionary tree is the SQL interface. This removed a language barrier for building stream processing applications in the Kafka ecosystem, since users were no longer required to use a JVM language like Java or Scala in order to use Kafka Streams.

Why SQL

SQL itself is the product of many rounds of product development and simplification. Retrieving data from persistent data stores used to require writing lengthy programs in complex languages. However, by using mathematical notations and declarative constructs, relational languages became much more compact and efficient. Additional rounds of linguistic optimization allowed a new language, SQL, to read more like natural English.[4] What we've ended up with after all of these rounds of simplification is a highly accessible language for querying persistent data stores that enjoys widespread popularity to this day. By adapting SQL to streaming use cases, ksqlDB immediately realizes the same benefits of using classical SQL:

- Succinct and expressive syntax that reads like English
- Declarative programming style
- A low learning curve

While the SQL grammar is inspired by ANSI SQL, a special SQL dialect was needed to model data in both streams *and* tables. Traditional SQL databases are primarily concerned with the latter, having no native support for unbounded datasets (streams). This manifests more generally as two types of statements in classical SQL:

- Classical DDL (Data Definition Language) statements are focused on creating and destroying database objects (usually tables, but sometimes databases, views, etc.):

```
CREATE TABLE users ...;
DROP TABLE users;
```

- Classical DML (Data Manipulation Language) statements are focused on reading and manipulating data in tables:

```
SELECT username from USERS;
INSERT INTO users (id, username) VALUES(2, "Izzy");
```

The SQL dialect implemented in KSQL (and subsequently ksqlDB) extends classical SQL to support streams. The next chapter will explore the extended DDL and DML

---

4 D. D. Chamberlin, "Early History of SQL," in IEEE Annals of the History of Computing, vol. 34, no. 4, pp. 78–82, Oct.–Dec. 2012.

statements in detail, but as you might expect, CREATE TABLE and DROP TABLE statements have stream equivalents (CREATE STREAM, DROP STREAM), and the extended DML supports querying both streams and tables.

With regards to the evolution of ksqlDB, it's important to note that the earlier form of this technology, KSQL, primarily used Kafka Streams to support push queries. These are continuously running queries that can be executed against a stream or table, and they emit (or *push*) results to a client whenever new data becomes available. The flow of data for a push query is shown in Figure 8-2.

At the time, queries in KSQL weren't referred to as push queries. The terminology was developed later on, though we still use this term to describe the earlier form of KSQL queries in this book since it is sufficiently descriptive for how these queries push results to clients.

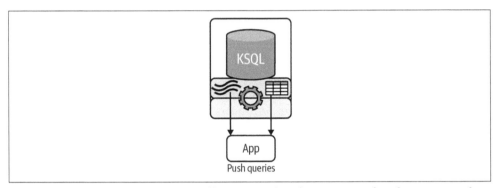

Figure 8-2. Push queries automatically emit results whenever new data becomes available; this allows applications/clients to listen for new data

Over time, the SQL engine became more advanced, and when KSQL was renamed ksqlDB, an important feature came with the name change: the ability to perform *pull queries*. The life cycle of a pull query is more similar to what you will find in traditional databases, since they are short-lived queries that are used to perform keyed-lookups of data. Under the hood, they leverage Kafka Streams and state stores. As you may recall from Chapter 4, state stores are locally embedded key-value stores that are usually powered by RocksDB. Figure 8-3 shows the flow of data for both push and pull queries, which are available in ksqlDB.

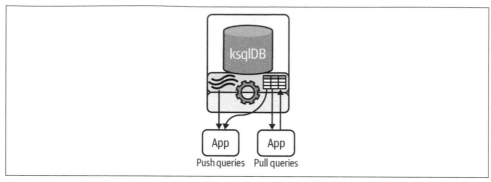

Figure 8-3. ksqlDB supports both push and pull queries

Both types of queries rely heavily on Kafka Streams and also ksqlDB's own SQL engine, which we'll get a deeper look at in "Architecture" on page 251. But now that we've looked at the Kafka Streams integration, let's look at ksqlDB's Kafka Connect integration and learn how it addresses a different set of streaming use cases than the Kafka Streams integration.

Connect Integration

As we learned in Chapter 2, Kafka Streams applications read from and write to Kafka topics. Therefore, if the data you want to process is external to Kafka, or if you want to sink the output of your Kafka Streams application to an external data store, you need to build a data pipeline to move data to and from the appropriate systems. These ETL processes are usually handled by a separate component of the Kafka ecosystem: Kafka Connect. So when you use vanilla Kafka Streams, you need to deploy Kafka Connect and the appropriate sink/source connectors yourself.

The early form of the product, KSQL, imposed the same limitations as vanilla Kafka Streams. Integrating non-Kafka data sources required you to absorb additional architectural complexities and operational overhead, since connector management needed to be handled by a separate system. However, when KSQL evolved into the more advanced form, ksqlDB, it brought with it some new ETL capabilities. It accomplished this by adding a Kafka Connect integration to its feature list. This integration includes the following:

- Additional SQL constructs for defining source and sink connectors. We'll provide more code examples in the next chapter's tutorial, but an initial look at the augmented DDL is shown here:

```
CREATE SOURCE CONNECTOR `jdbc-connector` WITH (
    "connector.class"='io.confluent.connect.jdbc.JdbcSourceConnector',
    "connection.url"='jdbc:postgresql://localhost:5432/my.db',
    "mode"='bulk',
```

```
      "topic.prefix"='jdbc-',
      "table.whitelist"='users',
      "key"='username'
);
```

- The ability to manage and execute connectors in an externally deployed Kafka Connect cluster, or run a distributed Kafka Connect cluster alongside ksqlDB for an even simpler setup.

The Kafka Connect integration allows ksqlDB to support the full ETL life cycle of an event stream, instead of just the transformation part of an ETL process, which is handled by the Kafka Streams integration. An updated look at ksqlDB, with both data integration and transformation capabilities, is shown in Figure 8-4.

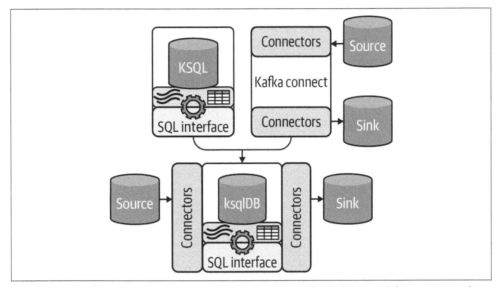

Figure 8-4. ksqlDB evolved into a system that supports both data transformation and integration

With both a Kafka Streams integration that drives ksqlDB's querying capabilities and a Kafka Connect integration that helps us make additional data sources available for querying, we can begin to see how powerful ksqlDB is.

How Does ksqlDB Compare to a Traditional SQL Database?

Now that we've seen how ksqlDB evolved into a new kind of database (an *event streaming database*), let's explore how it compares to a traditional SQL database. After all, when your database admin hears that you're running queries that may continue executing for months (push queries), they're going to want answers. First, let's start by looking at the similarities between ksqlDB and a traditional SQL database.

Similarities

Despite its focus on streaming, ksqlDB has many characteristics of a traditional SQL database. These similarities include the following:

A SQL interface
> Like a traditional SQL database, ksqlDB includes a SQL grammar, a parser, and an execution engine. This means interacting with data in either type of system can be accomplished using a high-level declarative language: SQL. ksqlDB's SQL dialect contains the language constructs you would expect, including SELECT for projection, FROM for defining sources, WHERE for filtering, JOIN for, well, joining, etc.

DDL and DML statements
> DDL and DML are the two broad categories of statements supported in both traditional SQL databases and ksqlDB. DDL statements are responsible for manipulating database objects (e.g., tables in traditional databases, tables and streams in ksqlDB), while DML statements are used to read and manipulate data.

Network service and clients for submitting queries
> If you have worked with traditional SQL databases, you have likely come to expect two things: you can connect to the database over a network and there are default client implementations (e.g., a CLI) for submitting queries. ksqlDB includes these features as well, with the network service being implemented as a REST API and a ksqlDB CLI and UI for submitting queries interactively. There is also a Java client (*https://oreil.ly/s6dDf*) that can be used for interacting with a ksqlDB server.

Schemas
> The collections you interact with contain schema definitions, which include field names and types. Furthermore, like some of the more flexible database systems (e.g., Postgres), ksqlDB supports user-defined types as well.

Materialized views
> To optimize for read performance in traditional databases, users sometimes create materialized views, which are named objects that contain the results of a query. In traditional systems, however, these views can be updated either *lazily* (the update to the view is queued for later or must be applied manually) or *eagerly* (whenever new data arrives). An eagerly maintained view is similar to how ksqlDB represents data, and updates to streams and tables are made immediately when new data becomes available.

Built-in functions and operators for data transformation
> Like many traditional SQL databases, ksqlDB includes a rich set of functions and operators for working with data. We will discuss functions and operators in detail

in "Functions and Operators" on page 337, but for now, suffice it to say there is a wide range of string functions, mathematical functions, time functions, table functions, geospatial functions, and more. Several operators are included as well (+,-,/,*,%,||, etc.), and there's even a pluggable interface for defining your own functions using Java.

Data replication

Most traditional databases leverage leader-based replication, where data written on the *leader* node is propagated to a *follower* (or replica) node. ksqlDB inherits this replication strategy (*https://oreil.ly/k92Sd*) from both Kafka (for the underlying topic data) and Kafka Streams (for stateful table data, via standby replicas, as discussed in "Standby Replicas" on page 180). In interactive mode, ksqlDB also uses *statement-based replication* by writing queries to an internal topic called the *command topic*, which ensures multiple nodes in a single ksqlDB cluster are able to process and run the same query.

As you can see, ksqlDB has many characteristics of a traditional SQL database. Now, let's explore the *differences* between ksqlDB and other database systems. This will help you explain to your database administrator friend that polling a traditional database in an infinite loop is not the same as using an event streaming database like ksqlDB, which has first-class support for unbounded datasets. It will also help you understand what use cases are better served by other systems.

Differences

Despite the many similarities between ksqlDB and traditional SQL databases, there are also some major differences. These include:

Enhanced DDL and DML statements

Classical DDL and DML statements that are supported in traditional databases are focused on modeling and querying data in tables. However, as an event streaming database, ksqlDB has a different view of the world. It recognizes the stream/table duality discussed in "Stream/Table Duality" on page 57, and therefore its SQL dialect supports modeling and querying data in streams and tables. It also introduces a new database object not typically found in other systems: *connectors*.

Push queries

The query pattern in most traditional SQL databases is to issue a query against the current snapshot of data, and to terminate the query as soon as the request is fulfilled or errors out. These short-lived, lookup-style queries are supported in ksqlDB, but since ksqlDB operates on unbounded event streams, it also supports continuous queries that can run for months or even years, emitting results whenever new data is received. This means out of the gate, ksqlDB has better support for clients who want to subscribe to changes in data.

Simple query capabilities

ksqlDB is a highly specialized database for querying eagerly maintained materialized views, either continuously via push queries or interactively via pull queries. It doesn't attempt to provide the same query capabilities as analytical stores (e.g., Elasticsearch), relational systems (e.g., Postgres, MySQL), or other types of specialized data stores.[5] Its query patterns are tailored to a specific set of use cases, including streaming ETL, materialized caches, and event-driven microservices.

More sophisticated schema management strategies

Schemas can be defined as you would expect using SQL itself. However, they can also be stored in a separate schema registry (Confluent Schema Registry), which has a few benefits, including schema evolution support/compatibility guarantees, reduced data size (by replacing the schema with a schema identifier in serialized records), automatic column name/data type inference, and easier integration with other systems (since downstream applications can also retrieve the record schema from the registry to deserialize the data processed by ksqlDB).

ANSI-inspired SQL, but not fully compliant

Attempts to standardize streaming SQL are still relatively new, and the SQL dialect used by ksqlDB introduces constructs that aren't found in the SQL standard.

High availability, fault tolerance, and failover operate much more seamlessly

These aren't separate add-ons or enterprise features like they are with some systems. They are built into ksqlDB's DNA, and are highly configurable.[6]

Local and remote storage

The data surfaced by ksqlDB lives in Kafka, and when using tables, is materialized in local state stores. This has a couple of interesting notes. For example, synchronization/commit acking is handled by Kafka itself, and your storage layer can be scaled independently from your SQL engine. Also, you get the performance benefits of colocating compute with the data (i.e., state stores) while taking advantage of Kafka's own distributed storage layer for more durable and scalable storage.

Consistency model

ksqlDB adheres to an eventually consistent and async consistency model, while many traditional systems adhere more closely to the Atomicity, Consistency, Isolation, Durability (ACID) model.

---

5 For more, see Jay Kreps's "Introducing ksqlDB" on Confluent. (*https://oreil.ly/lo9LY*)

6 For example, hot standbys are supported via Kafka Streams standby replica configs.

So now that we've looked at both the similarities and differences between ksqlDB and traditional SQL databases, what's our final verdict? Well, ksqlDB has many characteristics of a more traditional database, but it doesn't aim to replace them. It's a highly specialized tool that can be used for streaming use cases, and when you need the capabilities of another system, ksqlDB's Kafka Connect integration will help you move any enriched, transformed, or otherwise processed data to a data store of your choice.

Before we install ksqlDB, let's get a brief view of its architecture.

Architecture

Since ksqlDB is built on top of Kafka Streams, you can review the streaming architecture discussion in Chapter 2 for a lower-level understanding of how the Kafka Streams integration works. This section focuses on the ksqlDB-specific components of the architecture, which are broken into two main groups: the ksqlDB servers and ksqlDB clients.

ksqlDB Server

ksqlDB servers are responsible for running your stream processing applications (which in the ksqlDB sense would be a set of queries that work together to solve a business problem). Each server is conceptually similar to a single instance of a Kafka Streams application, and workloads (created by the query set) can be distributed across multiple ksqlDB servers with the same `ksql.service.id` configuration. Like Kafka Streams applications, ksqlDB servers are deployed separately from the Kafka cluster (usually on separate machines/containers from the brokers themselves).

A group of cooperating ksqlDB servers is called a *ksqlDB cluster*, and it's generally recommended to isolate workloads for a single application at the cluster level. For example, Figure 8-5 shows two ksqlDB clusters, each with a different service ID running isolated workloads that can be scaled and managed independently of each other.

When you need to add capacity to your ksqlDB cluster, you can deploy more ksqlDB servers. You can also scale the cluster down by removing ksqlDB servers at any time. Since ksqlDB servers with the same service ID are members of the same consumer group, Kafka automatically handles the reassignment/distribution of work as new ksqlDB servers are added or removed (removal could be manual or automatic, e.g., due to a system fault).

Each ksqlDB server is made up of two subcomponents: the SQL engine and the REST service. We'll discuss each of these separate components in the following sections.

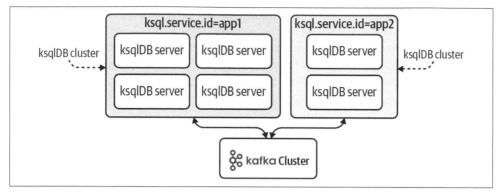

Figure 8-5. Two ksqlDB clusters processing data from Kafka independently

SQL engine

The SQL engine is responsible for parsing a SQL statement, converting it into one or more Kafka Streams topologies, and ultimately running the Kafka Streams applications. A visualization of this process is shown in Figure 8-6.

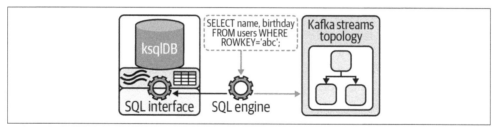

Figure 8-6. The SQL engine converts SQL statements into Kafka Streams topologies

The parser itself uses a tool called ANTLR (*https://antlr.org*), which converts a SQL statement into an Abstract Syntax Tree (AST) (*https://oreil.ly/8ScW6*), where each node in the tree represents a recognized phrase or token in the input query. ksqlDB visits each node in the parse tree and builds a Kafka Streams topology using the tokens it finds. For example, if you include a `WHERE` clause in your query, ksqlDB knows it needs to use the stateless `filter` operator when building the underlying Kafka Streams topology for your query. Similarly, if your query includes a join condition (e.g., `LEFT JOIN`), ksqlDB will add the `leftJoin` operator to the topology for you. Source processors are determined by looking at the `FROM` value, and the `SELECT` statement is used for projection.

Once the engine has created the necessary processor topologies required to run the query, it will actually run the resulting Kafka Streams application. Now, let's take a look at the component that is required to pass queries to the SQL engine: the REST service.

REST service

ksqlDB includes a REST interface that allows clients to interact with the SQL engine. It is primarily used by the ksqlDB CLI, ksqlDB UI, and other clients to submit queries to the engine (i.e., DML statements that begin with SELECT), execute other types of statements (e.g., DDL statements), check the cluster status/health, and more. By default, it listens on port 8088 and communicates over HTTP, but you can change the endpoint using the listeners config, and enable communication over HTTPS using the ssl configs. Both sets of configs are shown here:

```
listeners=http://0.0.0.0:8088
ssl.keystore.location=/path/to/ksql.server.keystore.jks
ssl.keystore.password=...
ssl.key.password=...
```

The REST API is optional, and depending on the mode of operation (see "Deployment Modes" on page 255), it may be disabled entirely. However, running the API is needed when working with ksqlDB interactively, whether you're using one of the default clients (e.g., the ksqlDB CLI and UI, which we will discuss in the following section) or a custom client. You can even issue requests using curl, as shown here:

```
curl -X "POST" "http://localhost:8088/query" \
    -H "Content-Type: application/vnd.ksql.v1+json; charset=utf-8" \
    -d $'{
  "ksql": "SELECT USERNAME FROM users EMIT CHANGES;",
  "streamsProperties": {}
}'
```

When interacting with the API directly, you should consult the most up-to-date REST API reference in the ksqlDB docs (*https://oreil.ly/J_wNH*). ksqlDB is still undergoing rapid evolution, and I expect this to be one area that sees changes in the future, based on some design proposals (*https://oreil.ly/iqyjz*) that have been submitted to the ksqlDB project. Most of the examples in this book will use the API indirectly via one of the officially supported clients, which we'll discuss next.

ksqlDB Clients

In the previous section, we learned that ksqlDB servers include a REST interface for submitting queries and retrieving information about the ksqlDB cluster. We also learned that we could interact with the REST service using curl or custom clients, but for most use cases, you will likely want to use one of the official clients for interacting with ksqlDB servers. In this section, we will learn about these clients, starting with the ksqlDB CLI.

ksqlDB CLI

The ksqlDB CLI is a command-line application that allows you to interact with a running ksqlDB server. It's an excellent tool for experimenting with ksqlDB, as it allows you to submit queries, inspect topics, adjust ksqlDB configurations, and more in an interactive fashion. It is distributed as a Docker image (`confluentinc/ksqldb-cli`) and also as part of Confluent Platform (*https://oreil.ly/eMqcJ*) (fully managed on Confluent Cloud, or through a self-managed deployment).

Invoking the CLI involves running the `ksql` command and specifying the host/port combination for the ksqlDB server (this corresponds to the `listeners` config, as discussed in "REST service" on page 253):

```
ksql http://localhost:8088
```

When you run the `ksql` command, you will be dropped into a prompt that looks similar to the following:

```
===============================================
=                 _          _ ___ ___        =
=                | |____   __| |  _ \   )      =
=                | |/ / _|/ _` | | | | | _ \   =
=                |  <\_ \ (_| | | |_| | |_) |  =
=                |_|\_\___/\__, |_|___/|___/   =
=                          |_|                 =
=        Event Streaming Database purpose-built =
=             for stream processing apps       =
===============================================

Copyright 2017-2020 Confluent Inc.

CLI v0.14.0, Server v0.14.0 located at http://ksqldb-server:8088
Server Status: RUNNING

Having trouble? Type 'help' (case-insensitive) for a rundown of how things work!

ksql>
```

In this book, the preceding prompt will be our launching point as we explore the SQL dialect and work through tutorials. Before we start using the CLI, let's look at another client: the ksqlDB UI.

ksqlDB UI

Confluent Platform also includes a UI for interacting with ksqlDB. The UI is a commercial feature, so you will find the UI in the commercially licensed version of Confluent Platform and also on Confluent Cloud (which runs Confluent Platform in a fully managed cloud environment). In addition to being able to submit queries from a web-based editor, you can also visualize the flow of data, create streams and tables using web forms, view a list of running queries, and more. A screenshot of the ksqlDB UI is shown in Figure 8-7.

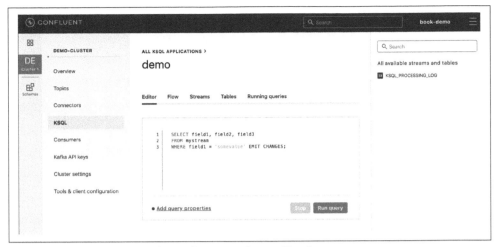

Figure 8-7. ksqlDB UI, as shown from Confluent Cloud

Deployment Modes

ksqlDB supports two different deployment modes, depending on the level of interactivity you want to allow with the running ksqlDB servers. This section will describe each of these deployment nodes and discuss when you might use each.

Interactive Mode

When running ksqlDB in *interactive mode*, clients can submit new queries anytime by using the REST API. As the name suggests, this leads to an interactive experience, allowing the ksqlDB server to create and tear down streams, tables, queries, and connectors at will.

A depiction of ksqlDB running in interactive mode is shown in Figure 8-8. One key characteristic of interactive mode is that all queries submitted to the SQL engine (via the REST API) are written to an internal topic called the *command topic*. This topic is autocreated and managed by ksqlDB, and is used to achieve statement-based replication, allowing all ksqlDB servers in the cluster to execute and run the query.

Interactive mode is the default deployment mode for ksqlDB, and you don't need any special configuration to run in this mode. However, if you want to disable interactive mode, you will need to run in headless mode, which does require a special configuration. We'll discuss headless mode in the next section.

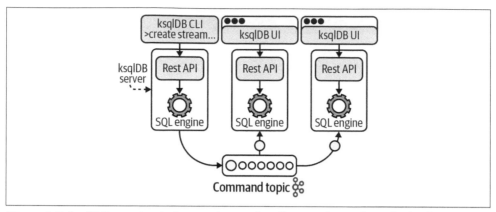

Figure 8-8. ksqlDB running in interactive mode, allowing clients (e.g., the ksqlDB CLI, UI, the Java client, or even curl) to submit queries via the REST API

Headless Mode

In some cases, you may not want clients interactively submitting queries against your ksqlDB cluster. For example, if you want to lock down a production deployment, you can run it in headless mode (which disables the REST API) to ensure no changes are made to the running queries. In order to run in headless mode, you simply need to create a file containing any persistent queries you want the SQL engine to execute, and specify the path to this file using the `queries.file` ksqlDB server config. For example:

```
queries.file=/path/to/query.sql ❶
```

❶ The path to the file containing the queries you want to run in your ksqlDB server is specified using the `queries.file` property.

A depiction of ksqlDB running in headless mode is shown in Figure 8-9. Note that unlike the interactive deployment, headless mode does not utilize a command topic for statement-based replication. However, it does write some internal metadata to a config topic.

For most of the tutorials in this book, we will be running in *interactive mode*. Next, let's finally get our feet wet with an initial "Hello, world" style tutorial for ksqlDB.

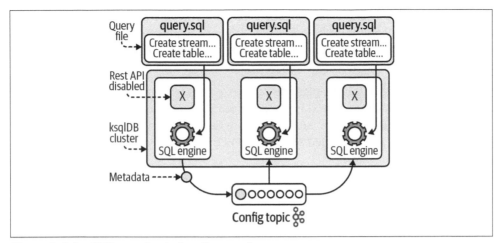

Figure 8-9. ksqlDB running in headless mode

Tutorial

In this section, we'll work through a very simple "Hello, world" tutorial. This will involve building a simple stream processing application with ksqlDB, which will say hello to each user that we write to a Kafka topic called users. Let's start by learning how to install ksqlDB.

Installing ksqlDB

There are a few different ways to start working with ksqlDB. The most popular options are listed in the following table:

Install method	Link	Notes
Download Confluent Platform	*https://www.confluent.io/download*	ksqlDB is a community-licensed software component in the self-managed version of Confluent Platform
Use Confluent Cloud	*https://confluent.cloud*	No download is necessary, you just need to create an account
Download and run the official Docker images	Images for both the ksqlDB server and CLI • *https://hub.docker.com/r/confluentinc/ksqldb-server* • *https://hub.docker.com/r/confluentinc/ksqldb-cli*	This will require you to run all dependencies and related software separately (Kafka, Schema Registry, the ksqlDB CLI)
Clone the open source repository on GitHub and build from source	*https://github.com/confluentinc/ksql*	This is the most involved option

The easiest method listed in the table is to use the official Docker images. The code repository for this book includes a Docker Compose deployment that stands up each of the related services using the appropriate Docker images. Refer to the full instructions on GitHub (*https://oreil.ly/Mk4Kt*).

The rest of the code in this chapter will reference the raw commands that are needed to start the ksqlDB server, the CLI, precreate our Kafka topic, etc. Where applicable, we have added instructions for how to execute these commands with Docker Compose, though these are annotated separately since they are more specific to a Docker Compose–based workflow.

With ksqlDB installed, it's time to start running a ksqlDB server. We'll learn how to do that in the next section.

Running a ksqlDB Server

Once you've installed ksqlDB, you need to create the configuration for the ksqlDB server. There are several configuration properties at your disposal, but for now, let's just save the two most important configs to a file named *ksql-server.properties*:

```
listeners=http://0.0.0.0:8088 ❶
bootstrap.servers=kafka:9092 ❷
```

❶ The REST API endpoint for the ksqlDB server. This will bind to all IPv4 interfaces.

❷ A list of host and port pairs corresponding to one or more Kafka brokers. This will be used to establish a connection to the Kafka cluster.

With our ksqlDB server configuration saved to a file, we can start the ksqlDB server with the following command:

```
ksql-server-start ksql-server.properties ❶
```

❶ In a Docker Compose workflow, this command is set in the *docker-compose.yml* file. See this chapter's code repository (*https://oreil.ly/i0F4T*) for more information.

After running the preceding command, you should see a lot of information get printed to the console as ksqlDB boots up. Among the other lines in the output, you should see something similar to the following:

```
[2020-11-28 00:53:11,530] INFO ksqlDB API server listening on http://0.0.0.0:8088
```

As you recall from our discussion in "Deployment Modes" on page 255, the default deployment mode is *interactive mode*, and since we didn't set the `queries.file` config in our *ksql-server.properties* file, the REST service is running inside our ksqlDB

---

server, and we can now use one of the default clients to submit queries to the ksqlDB server. In this tutorial, we'll submit our queries via the ksqlDB CLI, as we'll see next.

Precreating Topics

In the following chapters, we'll learn how ksqlDB can autocreate topics if we set certain parameters in our SQL statements. For this tutorial, we will simply pre-create our users topic by running the following command:

```
kafka-topics \ ❶
  --bootstrap-server localhost:9092 \
  --topic users \
  --replication-factor 1 \
  --partitions 4 \
  --create
```

❶ If running from Docker Compose, prefix this command with docker-compose exec kafka.

Now we're ready to start using the ksqlDB CLI.

Using the ksqlDB CLI

It's time to build our "Hello, world" streaming processing application by creating a set of queries for the ksqlDB server to run. Since we'll be using the CLI to submit our queries, the first thing we need to do is run the ksql command with the REST endpoint of our ksqlDB server, as shown here:

```
ksql http://0.0.0.0:8088 ❶
```

❶ If running with Docker Compose, run docker-compose exec ksqldb-cli ksql http://ksqldb-server:8088.

This will drop you in the CLI. From here, you can run various queries and statements. You can also adjust various ksqlDB configurations from the CLI. For example, run the following SET statement to ensure our queries read from the beginning of the underlying Kafka topics:

```
SET 'auto.offset.reset' = 'earliest';
```

Since we precreated our users topic, we can use the SHOW TOPICS command to verify its presence and view some of the topic's underlying configuration (e.g., partition and replica counts).

This command is shown in the following code block:

```
ksql> SHOW TOPICS ;

Kafka Topic | Partitions | Partition Replicas
-----------------------------------------------
 users       | 4          | 1
-----------------------------------------------
```

Now, let's model the data in the `users` topic as a stream using the `CREATE STREAM` DDL statement in ksqlDB. Among other things, this gives ksqlDB some information about the data types and format it can expect to find in this topic, and also creates a stream that we can query:

```
CREATE STREAM users (
    ROWKEY INT KEY, ❶
    USERNAME VARCHAR ❷
) WITH ( ❸
    KAFKA_TOPIC='users', ❹
    VALUE_FORMAT='JSON' ❺
);
```

❶ `ROWKEY` corresponds to the Kafka record key. Here, we specify the type as `INT`.

❷ Here, we specify that the records in the `users` topic will have a field called `USERNAME`. The data type for this field is `VARCHAR`.

❸ The `WITH` clause is used to pass in additional properties. There are several additional properties that we'll discuss in "With Clause" on page 291.

❹ Our stream reads from the `users` topic, which we specify in the `KAFKA_TOPIC` property in the `WITH` clause.

❺ Specify the serialization format of the record values in Kafka.

Once you run the `CREATE STREAM` statement, you should see confirmation that the stream was created in the console, as shown here:

```
Message
----------------
 Stream created
----------------
```

Before we query the `users` stream, let's insert some test data in this stream using ksqlDB's `INSERT INTO` statement:

```
INSERT INTO users (username) VALUES ('izzy');
INSERT INTO users (username) VALUES ('elyse');
INSERT INTO users (username) VALUES ('mitch');
```

Now that the stream has been created and has been populated with test data, we can create a push query that will create a greeting for every user that appears in the users stream. Run the statement in Example 8-1 to create a continuous, transient (i.e., not persistent)[7] push query.

Example 8-1. A Hello, world–style push query

```
SELECT 'Hello, ' + USERNAME AS GREETING
FROM users
EMIT CHANGES; ❶
```

❶ By including EMIT CHANGES here, we are telling ksqlDB to run a push query, which will automatically emit/push changes to the client (in this case, the CLI) whenever new data is available.

Because we inserted some test data in our users stream, you should see the following output immediately printed to the console, since we set auto.offset.reset to earliest and there is already data available in the topic:

```
+--------------------+
|GREETING            |
+--------------------+
|Hello, izzy         |
|Hello, elyse        |
|Hello, mitch        |
```

Note that the SELECT query will continue to run even after the initial set of results have been emitted. As mentioned before, this is characteristic of push queries, which will continue to run and emit results until you terminate the query (or, if you include a LIMIT clause in your query, will continue to run until the record limit is reached).

You can also open another CLI session and run additional INSERT INTO statements to generate more data in the users stream. Whenever a new record is inserted, the push query (represented by the SELECT statement issued earlier) will continue to emit results to the console.

This completes our simple tutorial for this chapter, but this represents only the tip of the iceberg of what ksqlDB can do. Over the next few chapters, we will explore the query language in more detail and work through some interesting tutorials to get you even more familiar with ksqlDB.

---

7 Transient means the results of this query will not be written back to Kafka. We will explore persistent queries in the next chapter.

Summary

We have gotten an initial look at ksqlDB's history, learned why it was built and when to use it, seen how it compares with traditional databases, and taken a peek at its architecture. In the next chapter, we'll continue our journey of learning about ksqlDB by exploring how to integrate it with external data sources.

## CHAPTER 9

Data Integration with ksqlDB

The first step of building a stream processing application with ksqlDB is to consider where the data you want to process currently lives, and where the enriched/transformed data will eventually be written. Since ksqlDB leverages Kafka Streams under the hood, the *direct* input and outputs of the application you build will always be Kafka topics. ksqlDB makes it simple to integrate other data sources as well, including from popular third-party systems like Elasticsearch, PostgreSQL, MySQL, Google PubSub, Amazon Kinesis, MongoDB, and hundreds of others.

Of course, if your data already lives in Kafka and you don't plan on writing the processed results to an external system, then working with ksqlDB's data integration features (which are driven by Kafka Connect) isn't required. However, should you ever need to read from/write to external systems, this chapter will provide the necessary foundations to help you connect the appropriate data sources and sinks using ksqlDB and Kafka Connect.

This chapter isn't a comprehensive guide on Kafka Connect, which is a separate API in the Kafka ecosystem and, accordingly, a topic about which much can and has been written. We will provide enough background to get you started, and look at ksqlDB's high-level abstractions for working with the Connect API. Some of the topics we will explore in this chapter include:

- A quick Kafka Connect overview
- Kafka Connect integration modes
- Configuring Kafka Connect workers
- Installing source and sink connectors
- Creating, dropping, and introspecting source and sink connectors in ksqlDB

- Introspecting source and sink connectors using the Kafka Connect API
- Viewing connector schemas in Confluent Schema Registry

By the end of this chapter, you will understand two of the three tasks for performing *Streaming ETL* (extract, transform, and load) operations with ksqlDB:

- *Extracting* data from external systems into Kafka
- *Loading* data from Kafka to an external system

The missing piece of the ETL abbreviation, *transforming*, will be covered in the next two chapters since transforming data relates more closely with stream processing than data integration. We'll start with a quick overview of Kafka Connect to learn about the technology that actually powers the data integration features in ksqlDB.

Kafka Connect Overview

Kafka Connect is one of five APIs in the Kafka ecosystem,[1] and it is used to connect external data stores, APIs, and filesystems to Kafka. Once the data is in Kafka, we can process, transform, and enrich it using ksqlDB. The primary components of Kafka Connect are as follows:

Connectors
> Connectors are packaged pieces of code that can be installed on workers (we'll discuss workers in a moment). They facilitate the flow of data between Kafka and other systems, and can be broken into two categories:
>
> - *Source connectors* read data from an external system to Kafka
> - *Sink connectors* write data to an external system from Kafka

Tasks
> Tasks are the units of work inside a connector. The number of tasks is configurable, allowing you to control how much work a single worker instance can perform.

Workers
> Workers are the JVM processes that execute the connectors. Multiple workers can be deployed to help parallelize/distribute the work, and to achieve fault tolerance in the event of partial failure (e.g., one worker goes offline).

---

1 The Consumer, Producer, Streams, and Admin APIs are the other four.

Converters

Converters are the code that handles the serialization/deserialization of data in Connect. A default converter (e.g., the `AvroConverter`) must be specified at the worker level, but you can also override the converter at the connector level.

Connect cluster

A connect cluster refers to one or more Kafka Connect workers, working together as a group to move data to and from Kafka.

A visualization of how these components work together is shown in Figure 9-1.

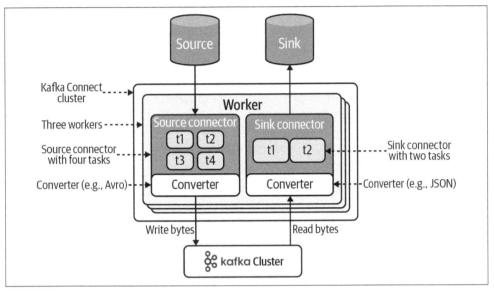

Figure 9-1. Kafka Connect architecture

It may seem like a lot to keep track of now, but as we work our way through the chapter, you will see that ksqlDB simplifies the mental model for working with Kafka Connect quite a bit. Now, let's see our options for deploying Kafka Connect for use with ksqlDB.

External Versus Embedded Connect

In ksqlDB, the Kafka Connect integration can run in two different modes. This section describes each mode and when to use them. We'll start by looking at external mode.

External Mode

If you already have a Kafka Connect cluster running, or if you want to create and manage a separate deployment of Kafka Connect outside of ksqlDB, then you can run the Kafka Connect integration in *external mode*. This involves pointing ksqlDB to the URL of the Kafka Connect cluster using the `ksql.connect.url` property. ksqlDB will make requests to the external Kafka Connect cluster directly in order to create and manage connectors. An example configuration for enabling external mode is shown in the following code (this would be saved to your ksqlDB server properties file):

```
ksql.connect.url=http://localhost:8083
```

When running in external mode, any source/sink connectors your application requires will need to be installed on the external workers themselves. Note that the workers are generally *not colocated with the ksqlDB server when running in external mode,* since one of the main benefits of running in this mode is that you don't need to share machine resources with ksqlDB. A diagram of Kafka Connect running in external mode is shown in Figure 9-2.

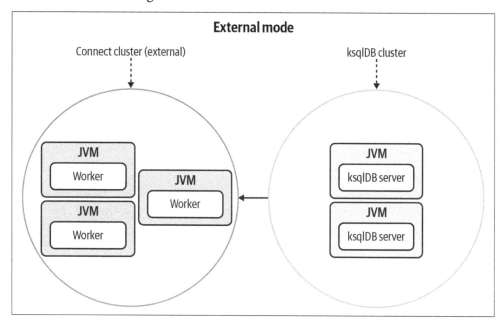

Figure 9-2. Kafka Connect running in external mode

Some reasons you may want to run Kafka Connect in external mode include:

- You want to scale your stream processing and data ingress/egress workloads independently and/or want resource isolation for these different types of workloads.
- You expect high throughput on the source/sink topics.
- You already have an existing Kafka Connect cluster.

Next, let's look at embedded mode, which is the mode we'll be using for the tutorials in this book.

Embedded Mode

In *embedded mode*, a Kafka Connect worker is executed in the same JVM as the ksqlDB server. The worker runs in Kafka Connect's distributed mode,[2] meaning work can be distributed across multiple cooperating worker instances. The number of Kafka Connect workers coincides with the number of ksqlDB servers in your ksqlDB cluster. You should use embedded mode when:

- You want to scale your stream processing and data ingress/egress workloads together.
- You expect low to medium throughput on the source/sink topics.
- You want to support data integration very simply, you don't want to manage a separate deployment of Kafka Connect, and you don't have a need to scale data integration/transformation workloads independently.
- You don't mind your Kafka Connect workers being restarted whenever you restart your ksqlDB servers.
- You don't mind sharing compute/memory resources between ksqlDB and Kafka Connect.[3]

Since ksqlDB servers are colocated with Kafka Connect workers in embedded mode, you'll need to install any source/sink connectors your application requires on the same node that your ksqlDB servers run on. A diagram of Kafka Connect running in embedded mode is shown in Figure 9-3.

---

2 Kafka Connect has its own deployment modes (distributed and standalone), which shouldn't be confused with ksqlDB's Kafka Connect integration modes (external and embedded).

3 See the ksqlDB documentation (*https://oreil.ly/fK6WQ*) for more.

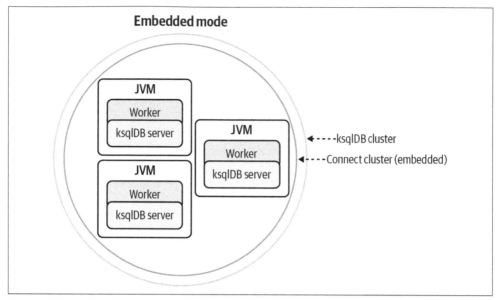

Figure 9-3. Kafka Connect running in embedded mode

To run in embedded mode, you'll need to set the `ksql.connect.worker.config` property in the ksqlDB server configuration. The value of this property is the path to the Kafka Connect worker configs (remember, the workers are the Kafka Connect processes that actually execute the source and sink connectors). An example of how this property can be configured in a ksqlDB server's properties file is shown here:

```
ksql.connect.worker.config=/etc/ksqldb-server/connect.properties
```

So what should live in the worker configuration file referenced by the `ksql.connect.worker.config` property? We'll take a look at that next.

Configuring Connect Workers

Kafka Connect is highly configurable, and the official Apache Kafka documentation (*https://oreil.ly/UWnW3*) covers the available configuration properties in detail. However, this section will cover some of the more important parameters by looking at an example Kafka Connect worker config. If you're running it in embedded mode, this should be saved to a file (e.g., *connect.properties*), and referenced in the *ksql.connect.worker.config* properties in the ksqlDB server configuration. If you're running in external mode, the worker configuration is supplied as an argument when starting Kafka Connect. The example configuration is shown in the following code block:

```
bootstrap.servers=localhost:9092    ❶
group.id=ksql-connect-cluster    ❷
```

```
key.converter=org.apache.kafka.connect.storage.StringConverter ❸
value.converter=org.apache.kafka.connect.storage.StringConverter ❹

config.storage.topic=ksql-connect-configs ❺
offset.storage.topic=ksql-connect-offsets
status.storage.topic=ksql-connect-statuses

errors.tolerance=all❻

plugin.path=/opt/confluent/share/java/ ❼
```

❶ A list of host/port pairs of the Kafka brokers that should be used for establishing an initial connection to the Kafka cluster.

❷ A string identifier that corresponds with the Connect cluster this worker belongs to. Workers that are configured with the same `group.id` belong to the same cluster, and can share the workload for executing connectors.

❸ "Converter class used to convert between Kafka Connect format and the serialized form that is written to Kafka. This controls the format of the *keys* in messages written to or read from Kafka, and since this is independent of connectors it allows any connector to work with any serialization format. Examples of common formats include JSON and Avro." (Connect docs (*https://oreil.ly/08AW5*))

❹ "Converter class used to convert between Kafka Connect format and the serialized form that is written to Kafka. This controls the format of the *values* in messages written to or read from Kafka, and since this is independent of connectors it allows any connector to work with any serialization format. Examples of common formats include JSON and Avro." (Connect docs)

❺ Kafka Connect uses a few topics to store information related to connector and task configurations. Here, we just use the standard names for these topics, prefixed by `ksql-` since we will be running in embedded mode (meaning the workers will be executed in the same JVM as our ksqlDB server instances).

❻ The `errors.tolerance` property allows you to configure the default error handling policy in Kafka Connect. Valid values include `none` (fail immediately when an error occurs) and `all` (either ignore errors completely, or, when used with the `errors.deadletterqueue.topic.name` property, route all errors to the Kafka topic of your choice).

❼ A comma-separated list of filesystem paths where plug-ins (connectors, converters, transformations) are expected to be installed. We'll see how to install connectors later in this chapter.

As you can see, most of the worker configurations are pretty straightforward. However, one set of configurations that are worth digging into further, since they relate to the important task of data serialization, are the converter properties (`key.converter` and `value.converter`). Let's take a deeper look at converters and serialization formats in the next section.

Converters and Serialization Formats

The converter classes we use in Kafka Connect play an important role in how data is serialized and deserialized in both Kafka Connect and ksqlDB. In our "Hello, world" tutorial in the previous chapter (see "Tutorial" on page 257), we used the statement in Example 9-1 to create a stream in ksqlDB.

Example 9-1. Create a stream that reads from the users topic

```
CREATE STREAM users (
    ROWKEY INT KEY,
    USERNAME VARCHAR
) WITH (
    KAFKA_TOPIC='users',
    VALUE_FORMAT='JSON'
);
```

In the preceding statement, we tell ksqlDB that the users topic (`KAFKA_TOPIC= 'users'`) contains records with JSON-serialized record values (`VALUE_FORMAT= 'JSON'`). If you have a custom producer that is writing JSON-formatted data to a topic, then it's pretty easy to reason about the format. But what if you're using Kafka Connect to, say, stream data from a PostgreSQL database to Kafka? Which format does the data from PostgreSQL get serialized to when it is written to Kafka?

This is where the converter configurations come into play. To control the serialization format of both the record keys and values that Kafka Connect handles, we can set the `key.converter` and `value.converter` properties to the appropriate converter class. Table 9-1 shows the most common converter classes and the corresponding ksqlDB serialization format (i.e., the value you would provide for the `VALUE_FORMAT` property when creating a stream or table, as we saw in Example 9-1).

Table 9-1 also denotes which converters rely on Confluent Schema Registry to store the record schemas, which is useful when you want a more compact message format (Schema Registry allows you to store record schemas, i.e., field names/types, outside of the messages themselves).

Table 9-1. The most common converter classes that can be used with Kafka Connect, and their corresponding serialization type in ksqlDB

Type	Convert class	Requires Schema Registry?	ksqlDB serialization type
Avro	`io.confluent.connect.avro.Avro Converter`	Yes	AVRO
Protobuf	`io.confluent.connect.protobuf.Protobuf Converter`	Yes	PROTOBUF
JSON (with Schema Registry)	`io.confluent.connect.json.JsonSchema Converter`	Yes	JSON_SR
JSON	`org.apache.kafka.connect.json.Json Converter`[a]	No	JSON
String	`org.apache.kafka.connect.stor age.StringConverter`	No	KAFKA[b]
DoubleConverter	`org.apache.kafka.connect.convert ers.DoubleConverter`	No	KAFKA
IntegerConverter	`org.apache.kafka.connect.convert ers.IntegerConverter`	No	KAFKA
LongConverter	`org.apache.kafka.connect.convert ers.LongConverter`	No	KAFKA

[a] When using the `JsonConverter` that ships with Kafka Connect, you may want to also set the following configuration in your Connect worker configs: `value.converter.schemas.enable`. Setting this value to `true` will tell Connect to embed its own schema in the JSON record (this does not use Schema Registry, and by including the schema in each record, message sizes can be quite large). Alternatively, you can set this value to `false` and ksqlDB will determine the field type using the data type hints you define when creating a stream or table. We'll explore this later.

[b] The KAFKA format indicates that a record key or value was serialized using one of Kafka's built-in Serdes (see Table 3-1).

For each converter in Table 9-1 that requires Schema Registry, you will need to add an additional configuration property: `{ key | value }.converter.schema.regis try.url`. For example, in this book, we'll be mostly working with Avro data, so if we want our connectors to write values in this format, we can update our worker configuration as shown in Example 9-2:

Example 9-2. Worker configuration that uses an AvroConverter for record values

```
bootstrap.servers=localhost:9092
group.id=ksql-connect-cluster

key.converter=org.apache.kafka.connect.storage.StringConverter
value.converter=io.confluent.connect.avro.AvroConverter ❶
value.converter.schema.registry.url=http://localhost:8081 ❷

config.storage.topic=ksql-connect-configs
offset.storage.topic=ksql-connect-offsets
```

```
status.storage.topic=ksql-connect-statuses

plugin.path=/opt/confluent/share/java/
```

❶ Use the `AvroConverter` to ensure that Kafka Connect serializes values in Avro format.

❷ The Avro converter requires Confluent Schema Registry to store record schemas, so we need to specify the URL where Schema Registry is running using the `value.converter.schema.registry.url` property.[4]

Now that we have learned how to specify the data serialization format in Kafka Connect, and we have prepared the Kafka Connect worker configuration (Example 9-2), let's work through a tutorial to actually install and use some connectors.

Tutorial

In this tutorial, we will use a JDBC source connector to stream data from PostgreSQL to Kafka. Then, we will create an Elasticsearch sink connector to write data from Kafka to Elasticsearch. Refer to the code for this tutorial, and instructions (*https://oreil.ly/7ImWJ*) for setting up the environment (including a PostgreSQL and Elasticsearch instance), on GitHub.

We'll start by installing the connectors.

Installing Connectors

There are two primary ways of installing source and sink connectors:

- Manual installation
- Automated installation via Confluent Hub

Manual installation can vary across connector implementations, and is dependent on how the connector maintainer chooses to distribute the artifact (a connector artifact usually includes one or more JAR files). However, it usually involves downloading the artifact directly from a website or an artifact repository like Maven Central or Artifactory. Once the connector is downloaded, the JAR files are placed in the location specified by the `plugin.path` configuration property.

An easier method for downloading connectors, and the method we'll use in this book, allows us to install connectors using a CLI tool developed by Confluent. This CLI,

---

4 It is also possible to use Schema Registry–dependent converters for record keys. In this case, you would need to set the `key.converter.schema.registry.url` property in your worker configs.

called `confluent-hub`, can be installed using the instructions in the Confluent documentation (*https://oreil.ly/31Sd9*). Once you've installed Confluent Hub, you can install connectors very easily. The command syntax for installing a connector is as follows:

```
confluent-hub install <owner>/<component>:<version> [options]
```

For example, to install the Elasticsearch sink connector, we could run the following command:

```
confluent-hub install confluentinc/kafka-connect-elasticsearch:10.0.2 \
    --component-dir /home/appuser \ ❶
    --worker-configs /etc/ksqldb-server/connect.properties \ ❷
    --no-prompt ❸
```

❶ The directory where the connector should be installed.

❷ Location of the worker configs. The install location (specified by `--component-dir`) will be appended to the `plugin.path` if it is not already included.

❸ Bypass interactive steps (e.g., install confirmations, software license agreements, etc.) by allowing the CLI to proceed with the recommended/default values. This is useful for scripted installs.

Similarly, the PostgreSQL source connector can be installed with the following command:

```
confluent-hub install confluentinc/kafka-connect-jdbc:10.0.0 \
    --component-dir /home/appuser/ \
    --worker-configs /etc/ksqldb-server/connect.properties \
    --no-prompt
```

Note that if you are running in embedded mode, you will need to restart the ksqlDB server if you want to use any connectors that were installed after the ksqlDB server instance was started. Once you've installed the connectors required by your application, you can create and manage connector instances in ksqlDB. We'll discuss this in the next section.

Creating Connectors with ksqlDB

The syntax for creating a connector is as follows:

```
CREATE { SOURCE | SINK } CONNECTOR [ IF NOT EXISTS ] <identifier> WITH(
    property_name = expression [, ...]);
```

Assuming you have a PostgreSQL instance running at `postgres:5432`, we can install a source connector to read from a table called *titles* by running the following command in ksqlDB:

```
CREATE SOURCE CONNECTOR `postgres-source` WITH( ❶
    "connector.class"='io.confluent.connect.jdbc.JdbcSourceConnector', ❷
    "connection.url"=
        'jdbc:postgresql://postgres:5432/root?user=root&password=secret', ❸
    "mode"='incrementing', ❹
    "incrementing.column.name"='id', ❺
    "topic.prefix"='', ❻
    "table.whitelist"='titles', ❼
    "key"='id'); ❽
```

❶ The WITH clause is used to pass in the connector configuration (this varies by connector, so you'll need to look at the connector's documentation for a list of available configuration properties).

❷ The Java class for the connector.

❸ The JDBC source connector requires a connection URL for connecting to the data store (in this case, a PostgreSQL database).

❹ There are various modes you can run the JDBC source connector in. Since we want to stream any new records that get added to the titles table, and have an auto-incrementing column, we can set the mode to incrementing. This mode, and the other modes supported by this connector, are detailed in the connector's documentation (*https://oreil.ly/w8Grb*).

❺ The name of the auto-incrementing column that our source connector will use to determine which rows it has seen already.

❻ Each table is streamed to a dedicated topic (e.g., the titles table will be streamed to the titles topic). We can optionally set a prefix for the topic name (e.g., a prefix for ksql- would stream the titles data into the ksql-titles topic). In this tutorial, we won't use a prefix.

❼ A list of tables to stream into Kafka.

❽ The value that will be used as the record key.

Once you've executed the CREATE SOURCE CONNECTOR statement, you should see a message like the following:

```
Message
-----------------------------------
Created connector postgres-source
-----------------------------------
```

Now, let's create the sink connector for writing the output of our application to Elasticsearch. This is pretty similar to creating a source connector:

```
CREATE SINK CONNECTOR `elasticsearch-sink` WITH(
    "connector.class"=
        'io.confluent.connect.elasticsearch.ElasticsearchSinkConnector',
    "connection.url"='http://elasticsearch:9200',
    "connection.username"='',
    "connection.password"='',
    "batch.size"='1',
    "write.method"='insert',
    "topics"='titles',
    "type.name"='changes',
    "key"='title_id');
```

As you can see, the connector-specific configurations vary across connectors. Most of the preceding configurations are self-explanatory, but we'll leave it as an exercise for the reader to learn more about the ElasticsearchSinkConnector configurations, which can be found in the Elasticsearch Sink Connector's configuration reference (*https://oreil.ly/o8h7j*). Again, you should see some confirmation that the preceding statement worked after executing the CREATE SINK CONNECTOR statement:

```
Message
---------------------------------------
Created connector elasticsearch-sink
---------------------------------------
```

Once the connector instances have been created in ksqlDB, we can interact with them in various ways. We'll look at some use cases in the following sections.

Showing Connectors

In interactive mode, it is sometimes helpful to list all of the running connectors and their statuses. The syntax for listing connectors is as follows:

```
{ LIST | SHOW } [ { SOURCE | SINK } ] CONNECTORS
```

In other words, we can show all connectors, just source connectors, or just sink connectors. Since we've created both a source and sink connector at this point, let's use the following variation to list both:

```
SHOW CONNECTORS ;
```

You should see both connectors listed in the output:

```
Connector Name      | Type   | Class | Status
-----------------------------------------------------------------
postgres-source     | SOURCE | ...   | RUNNING (1/1 tasks RUNNING)
elasticsearch-sink  | SINK   | ...   | RUNNING (1/1 tasks RUNNING)
-----------------------------------------------------------------
```

The SHOW CONNECTORS command prints some useful information about the active connectors, including their status. In this case, both connectors have a single task in the RUNNING state. The other states you might see include UNASSIGNED, PAUSED, FAILED, and DESTROYED. If you see a state like FAILED, you might want to investigate. For example, if your `postgres-source` connector lost its connection to the configured PostgreSQL database (which you can simulate in this tutorial by simply killing your PostgreSQL instance), then you will see something like this:

```
Connector Name  | Type   | Class | Status
-------------------------------------------------------------
postgres-source | SOURCE | ...   | FAILED
-------------------------------------------------------------
```

So how do you get more information about the connector, e.g., if you want to investigate failed tasks? This is where ksqlDB's ability to describe connectors comes into play. Let's take a look at that next.

Describing Connectors

ksqlDB makes it easy to retrieve the status of connectors using the DESCRIBE CONNECTOR command. For example, if our `postgres-source` connector lost its connection to the underlying data store, as we discussed in the previous section, you could describe the connector to glean some additional information about its state. For example:

```
DESCRIBE CONNECTOR `postgres-source` ;
```

If an error is present, you should see an error trace in the output. A truncated version is shown here:

```
Name        : postgres-source
Class       : io.confluent.connect.jdbc.JdbcSourceConnector
Type        : source
State       : FAILED
WorkerId    : 192.168.65.3:8083
Trace       : org.apache.kafka.connect.errors.ConnectException ❶

 Task ID | State  | Error Trace
-------------------------------------------------------------
   0     | FAILED | org.apache.kafka.connect.errors.ConnectException ❷
```

❶ The stack trace in this example is truncated, but in the event of an actual failure, you should see the full stack trace of the exception.

❷ The task-specific breakdown. Tasks can be in different states (e.g., some may be RUNNING, while others are UNASSIGNED, FAILED, etc.).

More often than not, however, you should see tasks in a healthy state. An example output for the DESCRIBE CONNECTOR command is shown here:

```
Name               : postgres-source
Class              : io.confluent.connect.jdbc.JdbcSourceConnector
Type               : source
State              : RUNNING
WorkerId           : 192.168.65.3:8083

Task ID | State   | Error Trace
-------------------------------
0       | RUNNING |
-------------------------------
```

Now that we've seen how to create and describe connectors, let's learn how to remove them.

Dropping Connectors

Dropping connectors is required for reconfiguring previously registered connectors, or permanently deleting a connector. The syntax for dropping a connector is:

```
DROP CONNECTOR [ IF EXISTS ] <identifier>
```

For example, to drop our PostgreSQL connector, we could run the following command:

```
DROP CONNECTOR `postgres-source` ;
```

Whenever you drop a connector, you should see some verification that the connector was actually dropped. For example:

```
Message
-------------------------------------
Dropped connector "postgres-source"
-------------------------------------
```

Verifying the Source Connector

One quick way to verify that the PostgreSQL source connector is working is to write some data to our PostgreSQL database and then print the contents of the topic. For example, let's create a table called titles in our Postgres instance, and prepopulate this table with some data:

```
CREATE TABLE titles (
    id          SERIAL PRIMARY KEY,
    title       VARCHAR(120)
);

INSERT INTO titles (title) values ('Stranger Things');
```

```
INSERT INTO titles (title) values ('Black Mirror');
INSERT INTO titles (title) values ('The Office');
```

 The preceding statement is a PostgreSQL statement, not a ksqlDB statement.

Our PostgreSQL source connector should populate the data from this table to the `titles` topic automatically. We can use the PRINT statement in ksqlDB to verify this:

```
PRINT `titles` FROM BEGINNING ;
```

ksqlDB should print output similar to the following:

```
Key format: JSON or KAFKA_STRING
Value format: AVRO or KAFKA_STRING
rowtime: 2020/10/28 ..., key: 1, value: {"id": 1, "title": "Stranger Things"}
rowtime: 2020/10/28 ..., key: 2, value: {"id": 2, "title": "Black Mirror"}
rowtime: 2020/10/28 ..., key: 3, value: {"id": 3, "title": "The Office"
```

Note in the first two lines in the output, ksqlDB tries to infer both the key and value format of the records in the `titles` topic. Since we're using the `StringConverter` for record keys and the `AvroConverter` for record values (see Example 9-2), this is the expected output.

Similarly, verifying the sink connector requires us to produce data to the sink topic, and then query the downstream data store. We'll leave this as an exercise for the reader (the code repository (*https://oreil.ly/gs18X*) also shows how to do this). Now, let's look at how to interact with the Kafka Connect cluster directly, and explore use cases for why we might want to do that.

Interacting with the Kafka Connect Cluster Directly

In some cases, you may want to interact with the Kafka Connect cluster directly, outside of ksqlDB. For example, the Kafka Connect endpoints sometimes expose information that isn't available in ksqlDB, and they allow you to perform some important operational tasks like restarting failed tasks. Providing a comprehensive guide of the Connect API is beyond the scope of this book, but some example queries you may want to execute against your Connect cluster are shown in the following table:

Use case	Example query
Listing connectors	`curl -XGET localhost:8083/connectors`
Describing a connector	`curl -XGET localhost:8083/connectors/elasticsearch-sink`
Listing tasks	`curl -XGET -s localhost:8083/connectors/elasticsearch-sink/tasks`

Use case	Example query
Getting task status	`curl -XGET -s localhost:8083/connectors/elasticsearch-sink/tasks/0/status`
Restarting a failed task	`curl -XPOST -s localhost:8083/connectors/elasticsearch-sink/tasks/0/restart`

Finally, let's learn how to inspect schemas when using serialization formats that leverage Confluent Schema Registry.

Introspecting Managed Schemas

Table 9-1 showed several data serialization formats, some of which required Confluent Schema Registry for storing the record schemas. Now, Kafka Connect will automatically store schemas in Confluent Schema Registry for you. Table 9-2 shows some example queries that you can make to a Schema Registry endpoint to introspect the managed schemas.

Table 9-2. Example Schema Registry queries

Use case	Example query
Listing schema types	`curl -XGET localhost:8081/subjects/`
Listing versions of a schema	`curl -XGET localhost:8081/subjects/titles-value/versions`
Getting the version of a schema	`curl -XGET localhost:8081/subjects/titles-value/versions/1`
Getting the latest version of a schema	`curl -XGET localhost:8081/subjects/titles-value/versions/latest`

A full API reference can be found in the Schema Registry API reference (*https://oreil.ly/Q26Si*).

Summary

You've now learned how to integrate external systems with ksqlDB. With a basic understanding of Kafka Connect, along with our knowledge of various ksqlDB statements for managing connectors, you are ready to learn how to process, transform, and enrich data using ksqlDB. In the next chapter, we will look at a stream processing use case at Netflix and explore some additional ksqlDB statements for building stream processing applications using SQL.

## CHAPTER 10

Stream Processing Basics with ksqlDB

In this chapter, we will learn how to use ksqlDB to perform some common stream processing tasks. The topics we will explore include:

- Creating streams and tables
- Leveraging ksqlDB data types
- Filtering data using simple Boolean conditions, wildcards, and range filters
- Reshaping data by flattening complex or nested structures
- Using projection to select a subset of the available fields
- Using conditional expressions to handle NULL values
- Creating derived streams and tables, and writing the results back to Kafka

By the end of this chapter, you will be well prepared to handle basic data pre-processing and transformation tasks using ksqlDB's SQL dialect. Furthermore, while the SQL constructs we explored in the preceding chapter leveraged ksqlDB's Kafka Connect integration under the hood, all of the SQL statements we will use in this chapter will leverage ksqlDB's Kafka Streams integration. This is where we will really start to see how powerful ksqlDB is, since with just a few lines of SQL, we will be able to build full-blown stream processing applications. As usual, we will explore this chapter's topics by building an application that leverages the related language constructs. So without further ado, let's introduce our tutorial.

Tutorial: Monitoring Changes at Netflix

Netflix invests billions of dollars in video content every year. With so many film and television shows in production at once, communicating updates to various systems when a production change occurs (e.g., release date changes, financial updates, talent scheduling, etc.) is important to keeping things running smoothly. Historically, Netflix has used Apache Flink for its stream processing use cases. But in collaboration with Nitin Sharma, an engineer at Netflix, we have decided to tackle this problem using ksqlDB instead.[1]

The goal of this application is simple. We need to consume a stream of production changes, filter and transform the data for processing, enrich and aggregate the data for reporting purposes, and ultimately make the processed data available to downstream systems. It sounds like a lot of work, but with ksqlDB, the implementation will be very straightforward.

The type of change we'll be focusing on in this tutorial will be changes to a show's season length (for example, *Stranger Things*, Season 4 may originally be slated for 12 episodes, but could be reworked into an 8-episode season, causing a ripple effect in various systems, including talent scheduling, cash projection, etc.). This example was chosen because it not only models a real-world problem, but also touches on the most common tasks you will tackle in your own ksqlDB applications.

The architectural diagram for the change-tracking application we'll be building is shown in Figure 10-1. Descriptions of each step can be found after the diagram.

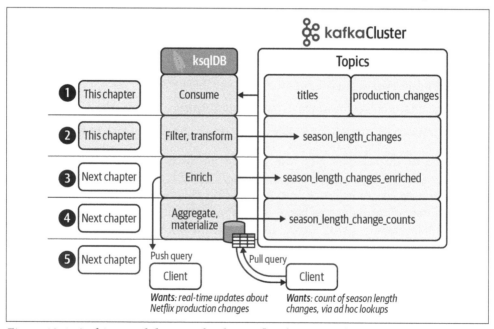

Figure 10-1. Architectural diagram for the Netflix change-tracking application

---

1 Note: this is not a production application at Netflix, but a demonstration of how to model a Netflix use case with ksqlDB.

❶ Our application will read from two topics:

- The `titles` topic is a compacted topic containing metadata (title name, release date, etc.) for films and television shows (collectively referred to as *titles* throughout this tutorial) that are hosted on the Netflix service.

- The `production_changes` topic is written to whenever there is a talent scheduling, budgetary, release date, or season length change to a title that is currently in production.

❷ After consuming the data from our source topics, we need to perform some basic preprocessing (e.g., filtering and transformation) in order to prepare the `production_changes` data for enrichment. The preprocessed stream, which will contain only changes to a title's episode count/season length after it has been filtered, will be written to a Kafka topic named `season_length_changes`.

❸ We will then perform some data enrichment on the preprocessed data. Specifically, we will join the `season_length_changes` stream with the `titles` data to create a combined record from multiple sources and dimensions.

❹ Next, we will perform some windowed and nonwindowed aggregations to count the number of changes in a five-minute period. The resulting table will be materialized, and made available for lookup-style pull queries.

❺ Finally, we will make the enriched and aggregated data available to two different types of clients. The first client will receive continuous updates via push queries, using a long-lived connection to ksqlDB. The second client will perform point lookups using short-lived pull queries that are more akin to traditional database lookups.

Given the sheer number of concepts we will be introducing in this example, our tutorial will span two chapters. This chapter will focus on creating streams and tables, as well as the basic data preprocessing and transformation steps (i.e., steps 1–2). The next chapter will focus on data enrichment, aggregation, and push/pull queries (though we will explore push queries in this chapter as well, since they are needed for step 2).

Project Setup

The code for this chapter is located at *https://github.com/mitch-seymour/mastering-kafka-streams-and-ksqldb.git*.

If you would like to reference the code as we work our way through each topology step, clone the repo and change to the directory containing this chapter's tutorial. The following command will do the trick:

```
$ git clone git@github.com:mitch-seymour/mastering-kafka-streams-and-ksqldb.git
$ cd mastering-kafka-streams-and-ksqldb/chapter-10/
```

This tutorial uses Docker Compose to spin up each component needed for this application, including:

- Kafka
- Schema Registry
- ksqlDB server
- ksqlDB CLI

Simply run the following command after cloning the repo to start each component:

```
docker-compose up
```

The SQL statements we discuss in this chapter will be executed in the ksqlDB CLI. You can log in to the ksqlDB CLI using the following command:

```
docker-compose exec ksqldb-cli \ ❶
    ksql http://ksqldb-server:8088 ❷
```

❶ Use `docker-compose exec` to run a command in the `ksqldb-cli` container. The command we will run is shown on the next line.

❷ `ksql` is the name of the CLI executable. The `http://ksqldb-server:8088` argument is the URL of our ksqlDB server.

Now that the CLI is running, let's begin our tutorial.

Source Topics

So you have data in a Kafka topic and you want to process it using ksqlDB. Great! Where do you start?

The most logical place to begin is by looking at the data in your source topics, and then determining how to model the data in ksqlDB. In this tutorial, we have two primary source topics: `titles` and `production_changes`. An example record in each source topic is shown in Table 10-1.

Table 10-1. Example record in each source topic

Source topic	Example record
`titles`	```{ "id": 1, "title": "Stranger Things", "on_schedule": false }```
`production_change`	```{ "uuid": 1, "title_id": 1, "change_type": "season_length", "before": { "season_id": 1, "episode_count": 12 }, "after": { "season_id": 1, "episode_count": 8 }, "created_at": "2021-02-08 11:30:00" }```

In the previous chapter, we discussed *record-level* serialization formats that are supported in ksqlDB. These include popular formats such as `AVRO`, `JSON`, `PROTOBUF`, `DELIMITED`, and single-value primitives (e.g., `String`, `Double`, `Integer`, and `Long` types, which are collectively grouped under the `KAFKA` format). For example, since the data in our `titles` topic is formatted as JSON, we know that we can use `JSON` as our record serialization format.

What we haven't covered yet are the field-level *data types*. For example, the `titles` record in Table 10-1 contains three fields (`id`, `title`, `on_schedule`), each with different *types* of values (integer, string, and Boolean, respectively). Before we create any streams or tables to model the data in our topics, we need to consider which data type is associated with each field. ksqlDB includes many built-in data types for us to use, which we will explore in the next section.

Data Types

The available data types in ksqlDB are shown in Table 10-2.

Table 10-2. Built-in data types

Type	Description
`ARRAY<element-type>`	A collection of elements of the same type (e.g., ARRAY<STRING>)
`BOOLEAN`	A Boolean value

Type	Description
INT	32-bit signed integer
BIGINT	64-bit signed integer
DOUBLE	Double precision (64-bit) IEEE 754 floating-point number
DECIMAL(precision, scale)	A floating-point number with a configurable number of total digits (*precision*) and digits to the right of the decimal point (*scale*)
MAP<key-type, element-type>	An object that contains keys and values, each of which coincides with a data type (e.g., MAP<STRING,INT>)
STRUCT<field-name field-type [, ...]>	A structured collection of fields (e.g., STRUCT<FOO INT, BAR BOOLEAN>)
VARCHAR or STRING	A unicode character sequence (UTF8)

One interesting thing about ksqlDB data types is that for some serialization formats, they are optional. This includes any serialization format that relies on Confluent Schema Registry, including AVRO, PROTOBUF, and JSON_SR. This is because Schema Registry already stores field names and types, so specifying the data types again in a CREATE statement is redundant (ksqlDB can just pull the schema information from Schema Registry).

The exception to this is when you need to specify a *key column*. In ksqlDB, you can use the PRIMARY KEY (for tables) or KEY (for streams) identifier to tell ksqlDB which column to read for the message key.

Therefore, we only need to specify a *partial schema* that contains the PRIMARY KEY column, which tells ksqlDB to read this column for the message key. However, the value columns (e.g., title) can be derived from the schema. For example, if our *titles* data was instead formatted as AVRO, and the related Avro schema was stored in Schema Registry, we could use *either* of the following CREATE statements to create our titles table:

Explicit types	Inferred types[a]

<pre>CREATE TABLE titles (
    id INT PRIMARY KEY,
    title VARCHAR
) WITH (
    KAFKA_TOPIC='titles',
    VALUE_FORMAT='AVRO',
    PARTITIONS=4
);</pre>
	<pre>CREATE TABLE titles (
	    id INT PRIMARY KEY
	)
	WITH (
	    KAFKA_TOPIC='titles',
	    VALUE_FORMAT='AVRO',
	    PARTITIONS=4
	);</pre>

[a] Only available for serialization formats that use Schema Registry.

This book will use the explicit version to improve the clarity of our examples, even when the short-form version would suffice. We will also explain the CREATE { STREAM | TABLE } syntax in more detail shortly, but let's first continue our discussion of data types by learning how we can create our own custom types in ksqlDB.

Custom Types

Custom types (similar to composite types in PostgreSQL) allow us to specify a group of field names and their associated data types, and then later reference the same collection of fields using a name of our choosing. Custom types are especially useful for reusing complex type definitions. For example, our application needs to capture changes to a season length, which could have a *before* and *after* state that are structurally identical. The following record demonstrates this:

```
{
    "uuid": 1,
    "before": { ❶
        "season_id": 1,
        "episode_count": 12
    },
    "after": {
        "season_id": 1,
        "episode_count": 8
    },
    "created_at": "2021-02-08 11:30:00"
}
```

❶ The structure of the before field is identical to the after field. This is a good use case for a custom type.

We could specify separate STRUCT definitions for the before and after fields, or we could simply create a custom type that can be reused. In this tutorial, we'll opt for the latter since it will improve readability of our SQL statements. The various operations for working with custom types, as well as the related SQL syntax, are shown in the following table:

Operation	Syntax
Create a custom type	CREATE TYPE <type_name> AS <type>;
Show all registered custom types	{ LIST	SHOW } TYPES
Drop a custom type	DROP TYPE <type_name>

Let's create a custom type named season_length using the following statement:

```
ksql> CREATE TYPE season_length AS STRUCT<season_id INT, episode_count INT> ;
```

Once the type has been created, you can use the SHOW TYPES query to view it:

```
ksql> SHOW TYPES ;

Type Name     | Schema
------------------------------------------------------------------
SEASON_LENGTH | STRUCT<SEASON_ID INTEGER, EPISODE_COUNT INTEGER>
------------------------------------------------------------------
```

If we wanted to drop our custom type, we could execute the following statement:

```
ksql> DROP TYPE season_length;
```

This tutorial will make use of the season_length custom type, so if you dropped it, be sure to re-create it before proceeding. Now that we've learned about the various data types in ksqlDB, we can start creating the streams and tables needed by our application. We'll explore this topic in the next section.

Collections

Streams and tables are the two primary abstractions at the heart of both Kafka Streams and ksqlDB. In ksqlDB, they are referred to as *collections*. We got our first look at streams and tables in "Streams and Tables" on page 53, but we'll quickly review the differences again before we look at the ksqlDB syntax for creating them.

Tables can be thought of as a snapshot of a continuously updating dataset, where the latest state or computation (in the case of an aggregation) of each unique key in a Kafka topic is stored in the underlying collection.[2] They are backed by compacted topics and leverage Kafka Streams state stores under the hood.

A popular use case for tables is join-based data enrichment, in which a so-called lookup table can be referenced to provide additional context about events coming through a stream. They also play a special role in aggregations, which we will explore in the next chapter.

Streams, on the other hand, are modeled as an immutable sequence of events. Unlike tables, which have mutable characteristics, each event in a stream is considered to be independent of all other events. Streams are stateless, meaning each event is consumed, processed, and subsequently forgotten.

To visualize the difference, consider the following sequence of events (keys and values are shown as <key, value>):

---

2 These collections are backed by RocksDB state stores, as we discussed in "State Stores" on page 98.

Sequence of events
<K1, V1>
<K1, V2>
<K1, V3>
<K2, V1>

A stream models the full history of events, while a table captures the latest state of each unique key. The stream and table representations of the preceding sequence are shown here:

Stream	Table
<K1, V1>	<K1, V3>
<K1, V2>	<K2, V1>
<K1, V3>	
<K2, V1>	

There are a couple of ways of creating streams and tables in ksqlDB. They can either be created directly on top of Kafka topics (we refer to these as *source collections* in this book) or derived from other streams and tables (referred to as *derived collections*). We'll look at both types of collections in this chapter, but we'll start our discussion with source collections since they are the starting point for all stream processing applications in ksqlDB.

Creating Source Collections

Before we can start working with data in ksqlDB, we need to create the source collections on top of our Kafka topics. This is because in ksqlDB, we don't query Kafka topics directly. We query collections (i.e., streams and tables). The syntax for creating streams and tables is here:

```
CREATE [ OR REPLACE ] { STREAM | TABLE } [ IF NOT EXISTS ] <identifier> (
    column_name data_type [, ... ]
) WITH (
    property=value [, ... ]
)
```

In this tutorial, we need to create both a stream and a table. Our `titles` topic, which contains metadata about films and television shows (we'll refer to both of these entities as *titles* going forward), will be modeled as a table since we only care about the current metadata associated with each title. We can create our table using the following statement:

```
CREATE TABLE titles (
    id INT PRIMARY KEY, ❶
    title VARCHAR
) WITH (
```

```
    KAFKA_TOPIC='titles',
    VALUE_FORMAT='AVRO',
    PARTITIONS=4 ❷
);
```

❶ PRIMARY KEY specifies the key column for this table, and this is derived from the record key. Remember that tables have mutable, update-style semantics, so if multiple records are seen with the same primary key, then only the latest will be stored in the table. The exception to this is if the record key is set but the value is NULL. In this case, the record is considered to be a *tombstone* and will trigger a deletion of the related key. Note that for tables, ksqlDB will ignore any record whose key is set to NULL (this is not true for streams).

❷ Since we're specifying the PARTITIONS property in our WITH clause, ksqlDB will create the underlying topic for us if it does not already exist (in this case, the topic will be created with four partitions). We could also set the replication factor of the underlying topic here using the REPLICAS property. We'll explore the WITH clause in more detail in the next section.

Furthermore, we'll model the production_changes topic as a stream. This is the ideal collection type for this topic since we don't need to track the latest state of each change event; we simply need to consume and process each value. Therefore, we can create our source stream using the following statement:

```
CREATE STREAM production_changes (
    rowkey VARCHAR KEY, ❶
    uuid INT,
    title_id INT,
    change_type VARCHAR,
    before season_length, ❷
    after season_length,
    created_at VARCHAR
) WITH (
    KAFKA_TOPIC='production_changes',
    PARTITIONS='4',
    VALUE_FORMAT='JSON',
    TIMESTAMP='created_at', ❸
    TIMESTAMP_FORMAT='yyyy-MM-dd HH:mm:ss'
);
```

❶ Unlike tables, streams do not have a primary key column. Streams have immutable, insert-style semantics, so uniquely identifying records is not possible. However, the KEY identifier can be used to alias the record key column (which corresponds to the Kafka record key).

❷ Here, we're using our custom type, season_length, to reuse the type definition for both the before and after fields, which are complex objects[3] that are structurally identical.

❸ This tells ksqlDB that the created_at column contains the timestamp that ksqlDB should use for time-based operations, including windowed aggregations and joins (which we'll explore in the next chapter). The TIMESTAMP_FORMAT property on the next line specifies the format of the record timestamps. More information about the TIMESTAMP and TIMESTAMP_FORMAT properties will be covered in the next section.

The WITH clause that is available in CREATE { STREAM | TABLE } statements supports several properties that we haven't explored yet. Let's explore these in the next section before continuing our discussion of streams and tables.

With Clause

When creating a stream or table, you can configure several properties using ksqlDB's WITH clause. Some of the more important properties you will likely make use of are shown in Table 10-3:

Table 10-3. Properties that are supported in the WITH clause

Property name	Description	Required?
KAFKA_TOPIC	The Kafka topic that contains the data you want to consume.	Yes
VALUE_FORMAT	The serialization format of the data in the source topic (e.g., AVRO, PROTOBUF, JSON, JSON_SR, KAFKA).	Yes
PARTITIONS	Specify this property if you want ksqlDB to create the source topic with the configured number of partitions.	No
REPLICAS	Specify this property if you want ksqlDB to create the source topic with the configured number of replicas.	No

---

3 Here, *complex* refers to a nonprimitive type. In this case, both the before and after fields are represented using a STRUCT, which we alias using our custom type. MAP and ARRAY are also complex types.

Property name	Description	Required?
TIMESTAMP	The name of the column that contains the timestamp that ksqlDB should use for time-based operations (e.g., windowed operations). If you do not set this property, ksqlDB will use the timestamp embedded in the record metadata. If the column is a BIGINT type, then ksqlDB will know how to parse the timestamp without additional configuration. If the column is a VARCHAR type, you should also set the TIMESTAMP_FORMAT property, which we'll discuss next.	No
TIMESTAMP_FORMAT	The format of the timestamp. Any format supported by java.time.format.DateTimeFormatter is valid (e.g., yyyy-MM-dd HH:mm:ss).	No
VALUE_DELIMITER	The character that acts as the field delimiter when VALUE_FOR MAT='DELIMITED'. Commas (,) are the default delimiter, but 'SPACE' and 'TAB' are also valid values.	No

Let's continue our discussion of streams and tables by learning how to inspect them once they have been created.

Working with Streams and Tables

In interactive mode, it's often useful to view and describe the collections you have created. In some cases, you may even want to delete a collection because you no longer need it, or because you want to re-create another stream or table with the same name. This section will discuss each of these use cases and show example responses for the related SQL statements. First, let's look at how to show the active streams and tables defined in your application.

Showing Streams and Tables

Sometimes, you may want to view some information about *all* of the currently registered streams and tables. ksqlDB includes a couple of statements to help with this, and the syntax is as follows:

```
{ LIST | SHOW } { STREAMS | TABLES } [EXTENDED];
```

While LIST and SHOW are interchangable, we will use the SHOW variation in this book.

For example, we have created both the source stream and table needed for our tutorial. Let's now use the SHOW statement to view some information about these collections in the ksqlDB CLI. The output of each statement is shown directly after the command in the following code block:

```
ksql> SHOW TABLES ;

 Table Name | Kafka Topic | Format | Windowed
----------------------------------------------
 TITLES     | titles      | AVRO   | false
----------------------------------------------

ksql> SHOW STREAMS ;

 Stream Name        | Kafka Topic        | Format
------------------------------------------------------------------
 PRODUCTION_CHANGES | production_changes | JSON
------------------------------------------------------------------
```

As you can see, the output for listing streams and tables is pretty minimal. If you need more information about the underlying collections, you can use the EXTENDED variation of the SHOW statement, as shown here:

```
ksql> SHOW TABLES EXTENDED; ❶

Name              : TITLES
Type              : TABLE
Timestamp field   : Not set - using <ROWTIME>
Key format        : KAFKA
Value format      : AVRO
Kafka topic       : titles (partitions: 4, replication: 1)
Statement         : CREATE TABLE titles (...) ❷

 Field | Type
-----------------------------------------
 ID    | INTEGER        (primary key)
 TITLE | VARCHAR(STRING)
-----------------------------------------

Local runtime statistics ❸
------------------------
messages-per-sec:   0.90   total-messages:   292   last-message: 2020-06-12...

(Statistics of the local KSQL server interaction with the Kafka topic titles)
```

❶ SHOW STREAMS EXTENDED is also supported, but we have omitted a streams-specific example since the output format is similar.

❷ The full DDL statement is shown in the actual output, but has been truncated here for brevity.

❸ The runtime statistics include additional fields not shown here, including consumer-total-message-bytes, failed-messages-per-sec, last-failed, and more. This is useful to get a high-level glance at the throughput and error rates (e.g., deserialization errors) of your streams and tables. Note that these statistics will be omitted if none are available (e.g., if there's no activity on the stream or table).

Since SHOW commands are used to view data for all of the streams/tables in the ksqlDB cluster, the preceding output would be repeated for each stream/table that is currently registered.

Now that you know how to show all of the streams and tables in your cluster, let's see how to describe specific streams and tables, one at a time.

Describing Streams and Tables

Describing collections is similar to the SHOW command, but it operates on a single stream or table instance at a time. The syntax for describing a stream or table is as follows:

```
DESCRIBE [EXTENDED] <identifier> ❶
```

❶ <identifier> is the name of a stream or table. Note the lack of a STREAM or TABLE keyword in this command. Since ksqlDB doesn't allow you to create a stream and table using the same name, it doesn't need to distinguish between the collection type in this command. It simply needs to know the unique identifier of the stream or table you wish to describe.

For example, we could describe the titles table using the following statement:

```
ksql> DESCRIBE titles ;

Name                 : TITLES
 Field | Type
-----------------------------------------
 ID    | INTEGER          (primary key)
 TITLE | VARCHAR(STRING)
-----------------------------------------
```

If we wanted more information, e.g., about the runtime statistics, we could use the DESCRIBE EXTENDED variation, as shown in the following code snippet. We have omitted the output for the DESCRIBE EXTENDED command, since it was identical to the SHOW { STREAMS | TABLES } EXTENDED output at the time of writing, except it only shows the output for the specified stream/table, and not all of the streams and tables currently registered by the ksqlDB cluster:

```
ksql> DESCRIBE EXTENDED titles ;
```

Another common task in more traditional databases is to drop database objects you no longer need. Similarly, ksqlDB allows you to drop streams and tables, as we will see in the next section.

Altering Streams and Tables

Sometimes you may want to alter an existing collection. ksqlDB includes an ALTER statement that makes this possible. The syntax is shown in the following snippet:

```
ALTER { STREAM | TABLE } <identifier> alterOption [,...]
```

As of ksqlDB version 0.14.0, the only operation that can be performed with the ALTER statement is adding columns, although this may be expanded in the future. An example of how to add a column using the ALTER statement is shown in the following:

```
ksql> ALTER TABLE titles ADD COLUMN genre VARCHAR;  ❶

 Message
 ---------------------
 Table TITLES altered.
 ---------------------
```

❶ Add a VARCHAR column named genre to the titles table

Dropping Streams and Tables

My parents used to say, "I brought you into this world, and I can take you out of it." Similarly, if you brought a stream or table into the world and want to take it out again (maybe it was supposed to be home by 10 p.m., but didn't get home until 11 p.m. and then lied about it), you can use the DROP { STREAM | TABLE } command. The full syntax is as follows:

```
DROP { STREAM | TABLE } [ IF EXISTS ] <identifier> [DELETE TOPIC]
```

For example, if we wanted to drop our production_changes stream *and* the underlying topic, you could execute the following statement:[4]

```
ksql> DROP STREAM IF EXISTS production_changes DELETE TOPIC ;

 Message
 ----------------------------------------------------------------------
 Source `PRODUCTION_CHANGES` (topic: production_changes) was dropped.
 ----------------------------------------------------------------------
```

Be careful with the optional DELETE TOPIC clause, since ksqlDB will promptly delete the topic if this is included. You can exclude DELETE TOPIC if you simply want to delete the table and not the topic itself.

At this point, we have covered a lot about how to work with collections at a high level. For example, we can assert their presence and inspect their metadata using ksqlDB's

---

4 If you are following along with the tutorial and decide to run this statement, be sure to re-create the production_changes stream before proceeding with the rest of the tutorial.

`SHOW` and `DESCRIBE` statements, and we can bring them in and out of this world using `CREATE` and `DROP` statements. Let's now look at some additional ways to work with streams and tables by exploring some basic stream processing patterns and their related SQL statements.

Basic Queries

In this section, we'll look at some basic ways of filtering and transforming data in ksqlDB. Recall that at this point, our change-tracking application is consuming data from two different Kafka topics: `titles` and `production_changes`. We have already completed step 1 of our application (see Figure 10-1) by creating source collections for each of these topics (a `titles` table and a `production_changes` stream). Next, we will tackle step 2 of our application, which requires us to filter the `production_changes` stream for season-length changes only, to transform the data into a simpler format, and to write the filtered and transformed stream to a new topic called `season_length_changes`.

Let's get started by looking at a statement that is particularly useful for development purposes: the `INSERT VALUES` statement.

Insert Values

Inserting values into a stream or table is extremely useful when you need to pre-populate a collection with data. If you are familiar with traditional databases, the insert semantics are slightly different than what you're used to. For both streams and tables, the record is appended to the underlying Kafka topic, but tables only store the latest representation of each key, so it acts as more of an *upsert* operation for tables (which is why there isn't a separate `UPDATE` statement in ksqlDB).

We'll prepopulate both our `titles` table and our `production_changes` stream in this tutorial with some test data to facilitate experimentation with various types of SQL statements. The syntax for inserting values into a collection is as follows:

```
INSERT INTO <collection_name> [ ( column_name [, ...]] ) ]
VALUES (
    value [,...]
);
```

Our application is only interested in changes to a title's season length, so let's insert the following record:

```
INSERT INTO production_changes (
    uuid,
    title_id,
    change_type,
    before,
    after,
```

```
        created_at
) VALUES (
    1,
    1,
    'season_length',
    STRUCT(season_id := 1, episode_count := 12),
    STRUCT(season_id := 1, episode_count := 8),
    '2021-02-08 10:00:00'
);
```

Since we'll need to filter out all other types of changes, let's insert a release date change as well. This will be useful to test our filter conditions later on. We'll use a slightly different variation of the INSERT statement this time, by also specifying values for ROWKEY and ROWTIME, which are special pseudo columns that are automatically created by ksqlDB:

```
INSERT INTO production_changes (
    ROWKEY,
    ROWTIME,
    uuid,
    title_id,
    change_type,
    before,
    after,
    created_at
) VALUES (
    '2',
    1581161400000,
    2,
    2,
    'release_date',
    STRUCT(season_id := 1, release_date := '2021-05-27'),
    STRUCT(season_id := 1, release_date := '2021-08-18'),
    '2021-02-08 10:00:00'
);
```

Finally, for good measure, let's insert some data into our titles table as well. We'll use another variation of INSERT INTO VALUES here, which omits the column names. Instead, we'll provide values for each column in the order they were defined (e.g., the first value will specify the id, and the second value will correspond to the title):

```
INSERT INTO titles VALUES (1, 'Stranger Things');
INSERT INTO titles VALUES (2, 'Black Mirror');
INSERT INTO titles VALUES (3, 'Bojack Horseman');
```

Now that we have prepopulated our table and stream with some test data, let's get to the exciting part: running queries against our collections.

Simple Selects (Transient Push Queries)

The simplest form of query we can run is called a transient (i.e., not persistent) push query. These are simple `SELECT` statements with an `EMIT CHANGES` clause at the end. The syntax for transient push queries is as follows:

```
SELECT select_expr [, ...]
FROM from_item
[ LEFT JOIN join_collection ON join_criteria ]
[ WINDOW window_expression ]
[ WHERE condition ]
[ GROUP BY grouping_expression ]
[ PARTITION BY partitioning_expression ]
[ HAVING having_expression ]
EMIT CHANGES
[ LIMIT count ];
```

Let's start by selecting all of the records from the `production_changes` stream:

```
ksql> SET 'auto.offset.reset' = 'earliest'; ❶
ksql> SELECT * FROM production_changes EMIT CHANGES ; ❷
```

❶ This allows us to read from the beginning of our topics, which is useful since we've already inserted some test data.

❷ Run a transient query.

Unlike persistent queries, which we will explore at the end of this chapter, transient push queries like the preceding one will not survive restarts of your ksqlDB server.

If we run the preceding query, we will see the initial query output printed to the screen, and the query will continue to run, waiting for new data to arrive. The output of the query is shown in Example 10-1.

Example 10-1. Output of our transient push query

```
+------+----+--------+------------+--------------------+--------------------+------------+
|ROWKEY|UUID|TITLE_ID|CHANGE_TYPE |BEFORE              |AFTER               |CREATED_AT  |
+------+----+--------+------------+--------------------+--------------------+------------+
|2     |2   |2       |release_date|{SEASON_ID=1,       |{SEASON_ID=1,       |2021-02-08...|
                                   EPISODE_COUNT=null}  EPISODE_COUNT=null}

|null  |1   |1       |season_length|{SEASON_ID=1,       |                    |            |
                                    EPISODE_COUNT=12}   |{SEASON_ID=1,       |2021-02-08...|
                                                        EPISODE_COUNT=8}
```

If you were to open another CLI session and execute another `INSERT VALUES` statement against the `production_changes` stream, the output of the results would be updated automatically.

Transient push queries against tables work the same way. We can verify by running a SELECT statement against our `titles` table:

```
ksql> SELECT * FROM titles EMIT CHANGES ;
```

Again, the initial contents of the table would be emitted, as shown in the following code. Furthermore, as new data arrived, the output would be updated accordingly:

```
+----+-----------------+
|ID  |TITLE            |
+----+-----------------+
|2   |Black Mirror     |
|3   |Bojack Horseman  |
|1   |Stranger Things  |
```

Simple SELECT statements like the ones we've explored in this section are a useful starting point for building stream processing applications, but processing data often requires us to transform data in different ways. We'll explore some basic data transformation tasks in the next couple of sections.

Projection

Perhaps the simplest form of data transformation involves selecting a subset of the available columns in a stream or table, and thereby simplifying the data model for downstream operations. This is called *projection*, and simply requires us to replace the SELECT * syntax with the explicit column names we want to work with. For example, in this tutorial, we need to work with the `title_id`, `before`, `after`, and `created_at` columns in the `production_changes` stream, so we can write the following statement to project these columns into a new, simplified stream:

```
SELECT title_id, before, after, created_at
FROM production_changes
EMIT CHANGES ;
```

The output of this query shows the simplified stream:

```
+---------+--------------------+--------------------+-------------+
|TITLE_ID |BEFORE              |AFTER               |CREATED_AT   |
+---------+--------------------+--------------------+-------------+
|2        |{SEASON_ID=1,       |{SEASON_ID=1,       |2021-02-08...|
|             EPISODE_COUNT=null}   EPISODE_COUNT=null}              |

|1        |{SEASON_ID=1,       |{SEASON_ID=1,       |2021-02-08...|
|             EPISODE_COUNT=12}     EPISODE_COUNT=8}                 |
```

As you can see, our stream still includes some records we don't actually need for our application. We're only interested in `season_length` changes, but the record with TITLE_ID=2 is a `release_date` change, as we saw in Example 10-1. Let's explore ksqlDB's filtering capabilities to see how we can address this use case.

Filtering

ksqlDB's SQL dialect includes the ubiquitous WHERE clause, which can be used for filtering streams and tables. Since our application is only interested in a certain kind of production change at Netflix (season_length changes), we can use the statement in Example 10-2 to filter the relevant records.

Example 10-2. A ksqlDB statement that uses the WHERE clause to filter records

```
SELECT title_id, before, after, created_at
FROM production_changes
WHERE change_type = 'season_length'
EMIT CHANGES ;
```

The output of this query is shown in Example 10-3.

Example 10-3. The filtered result set

```
+---------+--------------------+----------------------------------+
|TITLE_ID |BEFORE              |AFTER             |CREATED_AT    |
+---------+--------------------+----------------------------------+
|1        |{SEASON_ID=1,       |{SEASON_ID=1,     |2021-02-08...|
          EPISODE_COUNT=12}    EPISODE_COUNT=8}
```

Now, let's explore some variations of the WHERE statement before we move forward.

 In addition to the variations of the WHERE statement that we'll discuss later, there is also an IN predicate that is currently supported for pull queries (which we'll look at in the next chapter). The IN predicate is expected to be supported for push queries sometime in the future as well. The purpose of the IN predicate is to match multiple values (e.g., WHERE id IN (1, 2, 3)). If you are using a version of ksqlDB greater than 0.14.0, you can check the ksqlDB changelog (*https://oreil.ly/QkAJm*) to see if your version of ksqlDB supports the IN predicate for push queries.

Wildcards

Wildcard filtering is also supported in ksqlDB, and is useful for cases when we want to match only part of a column value. In this case, the LIKE operator with the % character, which represents zero or more characters, can be used for a more powerful filtering condition, as shown here:

```
SELECT title_id, before, after, created_at
FROM production_changes
WHERE change_type LIKE 'season%' ❶
EMIT CHANGES ;
```

❶ Match any record where the `change_type` column begins with the word *season*.

Logical operators

Multiple filter conditions can be provided using AND/OR *logical operators*. You can also use parentheses to group multiple filter conditions as a single logical expression. Conditions can be negated using the NOT operator. The following variation of our SQL statement demonstrates each of these concepts:

```
SELECT title_id, before, after, created_at
FROM production_changes
WHERE NOT change_type = 'release_date' ❶
AND ( after->episode_count >= 8 OR after->episode_count  <=20 ) ❷
EMIT CHANGES ;
```

❶ Include only records where the `change_type` is set to any value *except* `release_date`.

❷ The two conditions in the parentheses are evaluated together. In this case, we are filtering for any change where the new episode count is between 8 and 20 (inclusive).

Finally, while the second filtering condition is capturing records where the episode count falls within a certain range (8 to 20), there is a better option for implementing range filters, which we will explore in the next section.

Between (range filter)

If you need to filter for records within a certain numeric or alphanumeric range, you can use the BETWEEN operator. The range is *inclusive*, meaning BETWEEN 8 AND 20 will match values *between* 8 and 20, *including* 8 and 20. An example SQL statement is:

```
SELECT title_id, before, after, created_at
FROM production_changes
WHERE change_type = 'season_length'
AND after->episode_count BETWEEN 8 AND 20
EMIT CHANGES ;
```

For our tutorial, the filtering condition shown in Example 10-2 will suffice, but you should now have a good idea how to use other types of filtering conditions as well.

Our stream is now filtered, but as you can see from the output in Example 10-3, two of the columns (`before` and `after`) contain complex, multivariate structures (e.g., {SEASON_ID=1, EPISODE_COUNT=12}). This highlights another common use case in data transformation and preprocessing: flattening/unnesting complex structures into simpler structures. We'll take a look at this use case next.

Flattening/Unnesting Complex Structures

Flattening values involves breaking out nested fields in a complex structure (e.g., a STRUCT) into top-level, single-value columns. Like projection, it is a useful way of simplifying the data model for downstream operations.

For example, in the previous section, we saw the following complex value in the after column for a single record:

```
{SEASON_ID=1, EPISODE_COUNT=8}
```

We can access nested struct fields using the -> operator, and pull these values into separate columns using the following query:

```
SELECT
    title_id,
    after->season_id,
    after->episode_count,
    created_at
FROM production_changes
WHERE change_type = 'season_length'
EMIT CHANGES ;
```

As you can see from the following output, this has a flattening effect since the once multivariate datapoint ({SEASON_ID=1, EPISODE_COUNT=8}) is now represented in two separate columns:

```
+----------+-----------+---------------+-------------------+
|TITLE_ID  |SEASON_ID  |EPISODE_COUNT  |CREATED_AT         |
+----------+-----------+---------------+-------------------+
|1         |1          |8              |2021-02-08 10:00:00|
```

We're well on our way to creating a transformed version of the production_changes stream that we can use for more advanced operations later on, but before we write the results back to Kafka, let's take a look at another type of expression that is useful in basic stream processing use cases: conditional expressions.

Conditional Expressions

ksqlDB also supports several conditional expressions. There are many different uses for these expressions, but one common use case is to address potential data integrity issues in a stream or table by supplying alternate values for NULL columns.

As an example, say we want to address a potential data integrity issue in our production_changes stream, where the season_id is sometimes NULL in one of the before or after columns, but not the other. In this case, we can use one of three different types of conditional expressions to handle this error case, and fallback to an alternate season_id value when necessary. Let's start by looking at the COALESCE function.

Coalesce

The COALESCE function can be used to return the first non-NULL value in a list of values. The function signature of COALESCE is as follows:

```
COALESCE(first T, others T[])
```

For example, to implement some fallback logic to select a non-NULL *season_id*, we could update our SELECT statement like this:

```
SELECT COALESCE(after->season_id, before->season_id, 0) AS season_id
FROM production_changes
WHERE change_type = 'season_length'
EMIT CHANGES ;
```

In this case, if after->season_id is NULL, then we fallback to before->season_id. If before->season_id is also NULL, then we will fallback to a default value of 0.

IFNULL

The IFNULL function is similar to COALESCE, except it only has a single fallback value. The function signature of IFNULL is as follows:

```
IFNULL(expression T, altValue T)
```

If we want to fallback to before->season_id in the event after->season_id is NULL, we could update our statement like this:

```
SELECT IFNULL(after->season_id, before->season_id) AS season_id
FROM production_changes
WHERE change_type = 'season_length'
EMIT CHANGES ;
```

Case Statements

Of all the conditional expressions in ksqlDB, the CASE statement is the most powerful. It allows us to evaluate any number of Boolean conditions and return the first value where the condition evaluates to true. Unlike COALESCE and IFNULL, the conditions evaluated in a CASE statement are not limited to simple NULL checks.

The syntax for CASE statements is as follows:

```
CASE expression
    WHEN condition THEN result [, ...]
    [ELSE result]
END
```

For example, the following code shows how to use a CASE statement that includes multiple fallback conditions, and return 0 if both the after->season_id and before->season_id values are NULL:

```
SELECT
  CASE
    WHEN after->season_id IS NOT NULL THEN after->season_id
    WHEN before->season_id IS NOT NULL THEN before->season_id
    ELSE 0
  END  AS season_id
FROM production_changes
WHERE change_type = 'season_length'
EMIT CHANGES ;
```

If you're performing a simple NULL check, as we are, it makes more sense to use COALESCE or IFNULL. In this tutorial, we'll use the IFNULL variation.

Now we're finally ready to write our filtered and transformed production_changes stream back to Kafka.

Writing Results Back to Kafka (Persistent Queries)

Up until this point, we've been working with transient queries. These queries begin with SELECT and the output is returned to the client, but not written back to Kafka. Furthermore, transient queries do not survive server restarts.

ksqlDB also allows us to create so-called persistent queries, which write the results to Kafka and also survive server restarts. This is useful when you want to make your filtered, transformed, and/or enriched stream available to other clients. In order to write the results of a query back to Kafka, we can create *derived collections*. We'll discuss what these are in the next section.

Creating Derived Collections

Derived collections are the product of creating streams and tables from other streams and tables. The syntax varies slightly from the way we create *source collections*, since we don't specify the column schemas and there is an added AS SELECT clause. The full syntax for creating derived collections is as follows:

```
CREATE { STREAM | TABLE } [ IF NOT EXISTS ] <identifier>
WITH (
    property=value [, ... ]
)
AS SELECT select_expr [, ...]
FROM from_item
[ LEFT JOIN join_collection ON join_criteria ]
[ WINDOW window_expression ]
[ WHERE condition ]
[ GROUP BY grouping_expression ]
[ PARTITION BY partitioning_expression ]
[ HAVING having_expression ]
EMIT CHANGES
[ LIMIT count ];
```

The queries for creating derived streams are often referred to by one of two acronyms:

- *CSAS* (pronounced *sē-sas*) queries (CREATE STREAM AS SELECT) are used to create *derived streams*.

- CTAS (pronounced *sē-tas*) queries (CREATE TABLE AS SELECT) are used to create *derived tables*.

Let's apply the filter conditions, data transformations, and conditional expressions we've learned about so far to create a derived stream named season_length_changes, which will contain only the types of changes we need for our application:

```
CREATE STREAM season_length_changes ❶
WITH ( ❷
    KAFKA_TOPIC = 'season_length_changes', ❸
    VALUE_FORMAT = 'AVRO',
    PARTITIONS = 4,
    REPLICAS = 1
) AS SELECT ❹
    ROWKEY, ❺
    title_id, ❻
    IFNULL(after->season_id, before->season_id) AS season_id, ❼
    before->episode_count AS old_episode_count, ❽
    after->episode_count AS new_episode_count,
    created_at
FROM production_changes
WHERE change_type = 'season_length' ❾
EMIT CHANGES ;
```

❶ Creating derived collections is syntactically similar to creating source collections (e.g., CREATE STREAM and CREATE TABLE).

❷ The WITH clause is also supported when creating derived collections.

❸ Write the derived stream to the season_length_changes topic.

❹ The AS SELECT part of the statement is where we define the query to populate the derived stream or table.

❺ You must include the key column in the projection. This tells ksqlDB what value it should use for the key in the underlying Kafka record.

❻ By specifying individual columns, we are using *projection* to reshape the original stream or table.

❼ Using the `IFNULL` conditional expression allows us to handle certain types of data integrity issues. We also use the `AS` statement here (and in the two lines that follow) to provide explicit names for our column.

❽ Flattening nested or complex values will make our collection easier to work with for downstream processors and clients.

❾ Filtering the stream allows us to capture a specific subset of records, which is another common stream processing use case.

Once you've created the derived collection, you should see confirmation that a query was created:

```
Message
--------------------------------------------------
 Created query with ID CSAS_SEASON_LENGTH_CHANGES_0
--------------------------------------------------
```

As you can see, ksqlDB created a continuous/persistent query when we ran the preceding CSAS statement. The queries that ksqlDB creates (for example, `CSAS_SEASON_LENGTH_CHANGES_0`) are essentially Kafka Streams applications that were dynamically created by ksqlDB in order to process the provided SQL statement. Before we close out this chapter, let's quickly explore some of the statements you can run to interact with the underlying query.

Showing queries

Whether you've created a derived collection or are running a simple transient query, it is sometimes useful to view the active queries in your ksqlDB cluster and their current state.

The syntax for viewing the active queries is as follows:

```
{ LIST | SHOW } QUERIES [EXTENDED];
```

Now that we've created a derived stream that contains our filtered and transformed `season_length` changes, we can view some information about the underlying query by executing the following statement:

```
ksql> SHOW QUERIES;

 Query ID                      | Query Type | Status    | ....  ❶
------------------------------------------------------------
 CSAS_SEASON_LENGTH_CHANGES_0 | PERSISTENT | RUNNING:1 | ....  ❷
------------------------------------------------------------
```

❶ Some columns in the SHOW QUERIES output were truncated for brevity. However, more information appears in the output, including the Kafka topic that the persistent query is writing to, the original query string, and more.

❷ The query ID (CSAS_SEASON_LENGTH_CHANGES_0) is needed for certain operations (for example, terminating and explaining queries). The query type will show as PERSISTENT if you run a CSAS or CTAS statement, or PUSH if the query is transient (e.g., begins with SELECT instead of CREATE). Finally, the status of this query indicates that it is in a RUNNING state. Other valid query states include ERROR and UNRESPONSIVE.

Explaining queries

When we need even more information about an active query than the SHOW QUERIES statement provides, we can explain queries. The syntax for explaining a query is as follows:

```
EXPLAIN { query_id | query_statement }
```

For example, to explain the query we created in the previous section, we could execute the following statement:

```
ksql> EXPLAIN CSAS_SEASON_LENGTH_CHANGES_0 ;
```

You could also explain a hypothetical query that is not actually running. For example:

```
ksql> EXPLAIN SELECT ID, TITLE FROM TITLES ;
```

In either case, the output is extremely verbose, so we will leave this as an exercise for the reader. Among the information included, however, are the field names and types included in the query, the status of the ksqlDB servers that are running the query (unless you are explaining a hypothetical query), and a description of the underlying Kafka Streams topology that is being used to actually run the query.

Terminating queries

Earlier in this chapter, we learned how to drop running streams and tables. However, if you were to drop our newly created season_length_changes stream, you would see an error:

```
ksql> DROP STREAM season_length_changes ;

Cannot drop SEASON_LENGTH_CHANGES.
The following queries read from this source: [].
The following queries write into this source: [CSAS_SEASON_LENGTH_CHANGES_0].
You need to terminate them before dropping SEASON_LENGTH_CHANGES.
```

The error text is pretty self-explanatory: you cannot drop a collection when a query is currently accessing it (e.g., reading from or writing to it). Therefore, we first need to terminate the underlying query.

The syntax for terminating a query is as follows:

```
TERMINATE { query_id | ALL }
```

If we had multiple queries, we could stop all of them at once by running TERMINATE ALL. Furthermore, if we wanted to only stop the query we created earlier (with an ID of CSAS_SEASON_LENGTH_CHANGES_0), we could execute the following statement:

```
TERMINATE CSAS_SEASON_LENGTH_CHANGES_0 ;
```

Once the query has been terminated and no other queries are accessing the stream or table, you can drop the collection using the DROP { STREAM | TABLE } statement discussed in "Dropping Streams and Tables" on page 295.

Putting It All Together

We've explored a lot of different stream processing use cases and SQL statements in this chapter, but the actual code needed to build steps 1 and 2 of our stream processing application is pretty succinct. The full query set needed to complete this part of the tutorial is shown in Example 10-4.

Example 10-4. The query set for steps 1–2 in our Netflix-inspired change-tracking application

```
CREATE TYPE season_length AS STRUCT<season_id INT, episode_count INT> ;

CREATE TABLE titles (
    id INT PRIMARY KEY,
    title VARCHAR
) WITH (
    KAFKA_TOPIC='titles',
    VALUE_FORMAT='AVRO',
    PARTITIONS=4
);

CREATE STREAM production_changes (
    rowkey VARCHAR KEY,
    uuid INT,
    title_id INT,
    change_type VARCHAR,
    before season_length,
    after season_length,
    created_at VARCHAR
) WITH (
    KAFKA_TOPIC='production_changes',
```

```
    PARTITIONS='4',
    VALUE_FORMAT='JSON',
    TIMESTAMP='created_at',
    TIMESTAMP_FORMAT='yyyy-MM-dd HH:mm:ss'
);

CREATE STREAM season_length_changes
WITH (
    KAFKA_TOPIC = 'season_length_changes',
    VALUE_FORMAT = 'AVRO',
    PARTITIONS = 4,
    REPLICAS = 1
) AS SELECT
    ROWKEY,
    title_id,
    IFNULL(after->season_id, before->season_id) AS season_id,
    before->episode_count AS old_episode_count,
    after->episode_count AS new_episode_count,
    created_at
FROM production_changes
WHERE change_type = 'season_length'
EMIT CHANGES ;
```

In the next chapter, we will continue with our tutorial by learning how to enrich, aggregate, and materialize data using ksqlDB (steps 3–5 in Figure 10-1).

Summary

We have now learned how to perform many important stream processing tasks with ksqlDB, including filtering data, flattening complex structures, using conditional expressions, and more. We have also learned about several SQL statements that are especially helpful for introspecting the state of our streams, tables, and queries, and of course the related statements for creating and dropping each of these entities.

While this chapter focused on data preprocessing and transformation, there is still a whole other world yet to be discovered in ksqlDB. Specifically, a world focused on data enrichment and aggregation. In the next chapter, we will explore these topics in detail, and in doing so, learn about a more powerful set of SQL statements and constructs that are available in ksqlDB.

## CHAPTER 11

Intermediate and Advanced Stream Processing with ksqlDB

In the last chapter, we learned how to perform basic data preprocessing and transformation tasks using ksqlDB. The SQL statements we discussed were stateless, and they allowed us to filter data, flatten complex or nested structures, use projection to reshape data, and more. In this chapter, we will deepen our understanding of ksqlDB by discussing some data enrichment and aggregation use cases. Most of the statements we will discuss are stateful (e.g., involve multiple records, which is required with joins and aggregations) and time-based (e.g., windowed operations), making them more complex under the hood, but also more powerful.

Some of the topics we will cover in this chapter include:

- Using joins to combine and enrich data
- Performing aggregations
- Executing pull queries (i.e., point lookups) against materialized views using the CLI
- Working with built-in ksqlDB functions (`scalar`, `aggregate`, and `table` functions)
- Creating user-defined functions using Java

We will use the Netflix change-tracking tutorial from the previous chapter to introduce many of these concepts (see "Tutorial: Monitoring Changes at Netflix" on page 281 if you need a recap). However, some topics, including ksqlDB functions, will be introduced as standalone discussions near the end of the chapter.

Let's get started by reviewing the project setup steps.

Project Setup

If you would like to reference the code (*https://github.com/mitch-seymour/mastering-kafka-streams-and-ksqldb.git*) as we work our way through each topology step, clone the repo and change to the directory containing this chapter's tutorial. The following command will do the trick:

```
$ git clone git@github.com:mitch-seymour/mastering-kafka-streams-and-ksqldb.git
$ cd mastering-kafka-streams-and-ksqldb/chapter-11/
```

As discussed in the previous chapter, we will use Docker Compose to spin up each component that is needed for this tutorial (e.g., Kafka, ksqlDB server, the CLI, etc.). Simply run the following command after cloning the repo to start each component:

```
docker-compose up
```

Unless otherwise noted, the SQL statements we discuss in this chapter will be executed in the ksqlDB CLI. You can log in to the ksqlDB CLI using the following command:

```
docker-compose exec ksqldb-cli \
    ksql http://ksqldb-server:8088 --config-file /etc/ksqldb-cli/cli.properties
```

So far, the setup has been nearly identical to Chapter 10. However, this chapter builds on the previous chapter's tutorial, so we actually need to set up our ksqlDB environment where the last chapter left off. This brings us to a very important ksqlDB statement, which we will discuss in the next section.

Bootstrapping an Environment from a SQL File

We have already worked through part of the tutorial to build the Netflix change-tracking application, and therefore, we have a set of previously created queries that we need to rerun in order to pick up from where we left off. This may seem specific to this tutorial, but running a set of queries to set up your environment is a common development workflow, and ksqlDB includes a special statement that makes this easy.

The syntax of this statement is as follows:

```
RUN SCRIPT <sql_file> ❶
```

❶ The SQL file can contain any number of queries to execute.

For example, we can place all of the queries for the previous chapter (see Example 10-4) in a file called */etc/sql/init.sql*, and then run the following command to re-create the collections and queries that we were working with previously:

```
ksql> RUN SCRIPT '/etc/sql/init.sql' ;
```

When RUN SCRIPT is executed, the output of every statement that was included in the SQL file will be returned to the client. In the case of the CLI, the output is simply printed to the screen. An example of the truncated output for the Chapter 10 queries is shown here:

```
CREATE TYPE season_length AS STRUCT<season_id INT, episode_count INT> ;

------------------------------
 Registered custom type ...
------------------------------

CREATE TABLE titles ...

----------------
 Table created
----------------

CREATE STREAM production_changes ...

------------------
 Stream created
------------------

CREATE STREAM season_length_changes ...
-----------------------------------------------------
 Created query with ID CSAS_SEASON_LENGTH_CHANGES_0
-----------------------------------------------------
```

As you can see, RUN SCRIPT is a useful time-saving mechanism for iterating on a ksqlDB application. We can experiment with statements in the CLI, and checkpoint our progress to a file that can be executed later on. When we're ready to deploy our queries to production, we can use the same SQL file to run ksqlDB in headless mode (see Figure 8-9).

To visualize which steps RUN SCRIPT executed for us, and to get our bearings for the additional steps we'll be tackling in this chapter, see Figure 11-1.

The next step we need to tackle is step 3, which requires us to enrich the filtered and transformed data in our season_length_changes stream. We'll take a look at this in the next section.

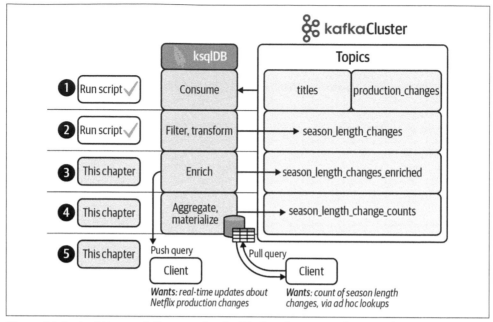

Figure 11-1. Architectural diagram for the Netflix change-tracking application; steps 1 and 2 were completed in the previous chapter, and re-executed using the RUN SCRIPT statement

Data Enrichment

Data enrichment refers to the process of improving or enhancing raw data. It goes beyond simple data transformation, which is usually focused on changing the format or structure of data. Instead, enrichment involves *adding information* to data, and one of the most widely used enrichment techniques in the database world are *joins*.

In step 3 of our application, we will enrich our `season_length_changes` stream with information from the `titles` table. We'll explore how to do this in the next section.

Joins

Joining data involves combining related records from multiple data sources using a *join predicate* (a Boolean expression that resolves to true when a related record is found, otherwise false). Joins are common in both the relational and streaming worlds, since data is often scattered across many sources and needs to be brought together for processing and analysis.

There are many types of joins in ksqlDB, and the variations can be expressed using two dimensions:

- The join expression that is being used (INNER JOIN, LEFT JOIN, and FULL JOIN)
- The type of collections that are being joined (STREAM, TABLE)

Let's start with the first bullet point. Table 11-1 provides a description of each of the available join types in ksqlDB.

Table 11-1. Join expressions that are available in ksqlDB

SQL expression	Description
INNER JOIN	An inner join is triggered when the input records on both sides of the join share the same key.
LEFT JOIN	A left join is triggered when a record on the *left side* of the join is received. If there is no matching record with the same key on the right side of the join, then the right value is set to null.
FULL JOIN	A full join is triggered when a record on *either side* of the join is received. If there is no matching record with the same key on the opposite side of the join, then the corresponding value is set to null.

If you've worked with traditional databases before, the preceding join expressions should feel familiar. However, while traditional databases are capable of joining tables, ksqlDB supports joins across two types of collections: tables and streams. Furthermore, the type of join expression you can use (INNER JOIN, LEFT JOIN, or FULL JOIN) depends on which collections (STREAM or TABLE) are the subject of your join. Table 11-2 provides a summary of the available combinations, with an extra column (*Windowed*) to indicate whether or not the join must also be time-constrained.

Table 11-2. Join types in ksqlDB

Join type	Supported expressions	Windowed
Stream-Stream	• INNER JOIN • LEFT JOIN • FULL JOIN	Yes
Stream-Table	• INNER JOIN • LEFT JOIN	No
Table-Table	• INNER JOIN • LEFT JOIN • FULL JOIN	No

As you can see, Stream-Stream joins are windowed. Since streams are unbounded, we must confine the search of related records to a user-defined time range. Otherwise, we'd be left with the infeasible task of searching two or more unbounded, continuous streams for related records, which is why ksqlDB imposes a windowing requirement for this type of join.

Prerequisites for Joining Data Across Collections

Before we start writing our join query, it's important to note that there are some pre-requisites for joining data across collections. These include:

- All columns referenced in the join expression must be of the same data type (STRING, INT, LONG, etc.).

- The partition count on each side of the join must be the same.[1]

- The data in the underlying topics must have been written using the same partitioning strategy (usually, this means the producers will use the default parti-tioner, which creates a hash based on the input record's key).

With these requirements in mind, let's write a join query. In our tutorial, our pre-processed data stream, season_length_changes, includes a column called title_id. We'd like to use this value to look up more information about a title (including the title name, e.g., Stranger Things or Black Mirror, which is stored in the titles table). If we wanted to express this as an inner join, we could execute the SQL state-ment shown in Example 11-1:

Example 11-1. A SQL statement that joins two collections

```
SELECT
    s.title_id,
    t.title,
    s.season_id,
    s.old_episode_count,
    s.new_episode_count,
    s.created_at
FROM season_length_changes s
INNER JOIN titles t ❶
ON s.title_id = t.id ❷
EMIT CHANGES ;
```

❶ Use INNER JOIN since we only want the join to be triggered when a correspond-ing record in the titles table can be found.

❷ Streams can specify any column to use for the join. Tables must be joined on the column that was designated as the PRIMARY KEY. The latter requirement can be understood when we consider that tables are key-value stores. As new records

---

1 This is checked when you execute a SQL statement containing a join. If the partition count doesn't match, you will see an error similar to Can't join S with T since the number of partitions don't match.

from the stream come in, we need to execute a point lookup in the table's underlying key-value store to see if there's a related record. Using the PRIMARY KEY is the most efficient way to do this, since records are already keyed by this value in the underlying state store. This also guarantees that no more than one record in the table will be matched to the stream record, since the key is a unique constraint on the table.

The output of the preceding statement shows the new enriched record, which contains the title name (see the TITLE column):

```
+---------+----------------+-----------+------------------+------------------+-------------+
|TITLE_ID |TITLE           |SEASON_ID  |OLD_EPISODE_COUNT |NEW_EPISODE_COUNT |CREATED_AT   |
+---------+----------------+-----------+------------------+------------------+-------------+
|1        |Stranger Things |1          |12                |8                 |2021-02-08...|
```

The preceding join was very simple, in part because all of the join prerequisites were already met in this tutorial. However, the join prerequisites for real-world applications may not be so conveniently satisfied. Let's quickly explore some slightly more complicated situations that will require additional steps in order to perform a join.

Casting a column to a new type

In some cases, the data sources you are joining may specify different data types on the join attribute. For example, what if s.title_id was actually encoded as a VARCHAR, but you needed to join it against the ROWKEY, which is encoded as an INT? In this case, you could use the built-in CAST expression to convert s.title_id to an INT type, and thus satisfy the first prerequisite for joining data, as discussed in "Joins" on page 314:

```
SELECT ... ❶
FROM season_length_changes s
INNER JOIN titles t
ON CAST(s.title_id AS INT) = t.id ❷
EMIT CHANGES ;
```

❶ The column names here were omitted for brevity.

❷ In this hypothetical example, if s.title_id was encoded as a VARCHAR, then we'd need to cast s.title_id to the same type as t.id (INT) in order to satisfy the first join prerequisite.

Repartitioning data

Let's now consider a situation that would require us to repartition data before executing a join. This could arise if either of the last two join prerequisites described in "Prerequisites for Joining Data Across Collections" on page 316 isn't met. For example, what if the titles table had eight partitions, and the season_length_changes table had four partitions?

In this case, you would need to repartition one of the collections in order to perform the join. This can be accomplished by creating a new collection with the PARTITIONS property, as shown in the SQL statement in Example 11-2.

Example 11-2. Example of how to repartition data using the PARTITIONS property

```
CREATE TABLE titles_repartition
WITH (PARTITIONS=4) AS ❶
SELECT * FROM titles
EMIT CHANGES;
```

❶ By default, this will create a new topic with the same name as the collection (TITLES_REPARTITION). You could also provide the KAFKA_TOPIC property if you want to specify a custom name for the repartition topic.

Once you've repartitioned the data to ensure the partition count matches on both sides of the join, you can join on the repartitioned collection (titles_repartition) instead.

Persistent joins

Now that we've learned how to satisfy the various prerequisites for joining data, let's continue implementing step 3 of our tutorial. The starting point for our join query will be Example 11-1 since the join prerequisites were already satisfied for our Netflix change-tracking application.

As discussed in the previous chapter, queries beginning with SELECT are not persistent, meaning they do not survive server restarts and the results are not written back to Kafka. So if we want to actually persist the results of our join query instead of simply printing the output to the CLI console, we need to use a CREATE STREAM AS SELECT (aka CSAS) statement.

The following SQL statement shows a persistent version of our join query, which will write the enriched records to a new topic called season_length_changes_enriched (see step 3 in Figure 11-1):

```
CREATE STREAM season_length_changes_enriched ❶
WITH (
    KAFKA_TOPIC = 'season_length_changes_enriched',
    VALUE_FORMAT = 'AVRO',
    PARTITIONS = 4,
    TIMESTAMP='created_at', ❷
    TIMESTAMP_FORMAT='yyyy-MM-dd HH:mm:ss'
) AS
SELECT ❸
    s.title_id,
    t.title,
    s.season_id,
```

```
        s.old_episode_count,
        s.new_episode_count,
        s.created_at
    FROM season_length_changes s
    INNER JOIN titles t
    ON s.title_id = t.id
    EMIT CHANGES ;
```

❶ Use CREATE STREAM to make our original query persistent.

❷ This tells ksqlDB that the created_at column contains the timestamp that
    ksqlDB should use for time-based operations, including windowed aggregations
    and joins.

❸ Our original SELECT statement starts on this line.

We have now learned how to join data using ksqlDB, and have completed step 3 of
our tutorial. Before we wrap up our discussion of joins, let's talk about another type of
join that is commonly used in stream processing applications.

Windowed Joins

In this tutorial, we don't need to perform a windowed join. But we'd be remiss if we
didn't at least mention them in this book, since they are required for Stream-Stream
joins. Windowed joins are different than unwindowed joins (e.g., the join we created
in the previous section) since they include an additional join attribute: *time*.

We have an entire chapter dedicated to windows and time, so a deep dive of these
topics will require a visit to Chapter 5. But as mentioned in that chapter, windowed
joins use something called *sliding windows* under the hood, which group records that
fall within a configured time boundary, as shown in Figure 11-2.

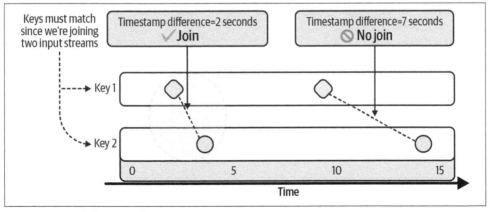

Figure 11-2. Sliding window

To create a windowed join, you need to include the WITHIN expression in your join clause. The syntax is as follows:

```
WITHIN <number> <time_unit>
```

The supported time units, including both the singular and plural forms, are:

- DAY, DAYS
- HOUR, HOURS
- MINUTE, MINUTES
- SECOND, SECONDS
- MILLISECOND, MILLISECONDS

For example, let's step away from our tutorial for a minute (which doesn't require a windowed join) and consider another use case. You're working at Netflix, and you've decided to capture all shows or movies that get less than two minutes of watch time before the user ends their watch session. In our fictional example, the start-watching and stop-watching events are written to separate Kafka topics. This is a great use case for a windowed join since we need to join each record using a session_id (which identifies the watch session) *and* the event time. Translating this example into SQL, let's first create our two source streams using the DDL in Example 11-3.

Example 11-3. Create two separate streams for start- and stop-watching events

```
CREATE STREAM start_watching_events ( ❶
    session_id STRING, ❷
    title_id INT,
    created_at STRING
)
WITH (
    KAFKA_TOPIC='start_watching_events',
    VALUE_FORMAT='JSON',
    PARTITIONS=4,
    TIMESTAMP='created_at',
    TIMESTAMP_FORMAT='yyyy-MM-dd HH:mm:ss' ❸
);

CREATE STREAM stop_watching_events ( ❹
    session_id STRING,
    title_id INT,
    created_at STRING
)
WITH (
    KAFKA_TOPIC='stop_watching_events',
    VALUE_FORMAT='JSON',
    PARTITIONS=4,
    TIMESTAMP='created_at',
```

```
TIMESTAMP_FORMAT='yyyy-MM-dd HH:mm:ss'
);
```

❶ Create a source stream for start-watching events. This stream will see a new record each time a user starts watching a new show or movie.

❷ The `session_id` is one of our join attributes. It represents a single watch session and is referenced in both of our source streams.

❸ The optional `TIMESTAMP_FORMAT` allows us to specify a format string that represents the format of the timestamps in this Kafka topic, which can be any value supported by the `DateTimeFormatter` class (*https://oreil.ly/A4v62*) in Java.

❹ Create a source stream for the stop-watching events. This stream will see a new record each time a user stops watching a show or movie.

Now, let's insert a couple of start- and stop-watching events for two different watch sessions (you can think of this as two different viewers watching two different shows). The first session, `session_123`, will have a total watch time of 90 seconds. The second session, `session_456`, will have a total watch time of 25 minutes:

```
INSERT INTO start_watching_events
VALUES ('session_123', 1, '2021-02-08 02:00:00');

INSERT INTO stop_watching_events
VALUES ('session_123', 1, '2021-02-08 02:01:30');

INSERT INTO start_watching_events
VALUES ('session_456', 1, '2021-02-08 02:00:00');

INSERT INTO stop_watching_events
VALUES ('session_456', 1, '2021-02-08 02:25:00');
```

Finally, let's capture the watch sessions that were less than two minutes long using a windowed join. At a high level, we're simply asking the following question with our query: which watch sessions were terminated (as indicated by the stop-watching timestamp) within two minutes of their start time (as indicated by the start-watching timestamp)? The following SQL statement demonstrates how to ask this question in ksqlDB:

```
SELECT
  A.title_id as title_id,
  A.session_id as session_id
FROM start_watching_events A
INNER JOIN stop_watching_events B
WITHIN 2 MINUTES ❶
ON A.session_id = B.session_id
EMIT CHANGES ;
```

❶ Join records from the `start_watch_events` and `stop_watching_events` streams with timestamps that are less than two minutes apart, and where the `session_id` is the same across both streams (the latter condition is expressed on the next line). This will capture all watch sessions that were less than two minutes long.

You should see the following output, since `session_123` had only 90 seconds of watch time:

```
+-------------+--------------+
|TITLE_ID     |SESSION_ID    |
+-------------+--------------+
|1            |session_123   |
```

Now that we have a good grasp of both windowed and unwindowed joins, let's continue our primary tutorial (the Netflix change-tracking application) by learning how to aggregate data in ksqlDB.

Aggregations

Working with a single record at a time in ksqlDB is useful for certain tasks, including filtering data, transforming the structure of data, or even performing event-at-a-time enrichment. However, some of the most powerful insights we can glean from our data require us to group and then aggregate related records. For example, counting the number of season-length changes at Netflix over a period of time may help improve planning processes around new television shows or films, or provide an indicator of projects that are experiencing operational hiccups.

Aggregations can be computed over both streams and tables, but they always return a table. This is because aggregate functions are applied to a *group of related records*, and the result of our aggregate function (e.g., COUNT) needs to be saved to some mutable structure that can easily be retrieved and updated whenever new records come in.[2]

There are two broad categories of aggregations: windowed and unwindowed. In this tutorial, we will use a windowed aggregation to compute the `season_length_change_counts` table (see step 4 in Figure 11-1). But first, let's take a look at the basics of aggregating data in the next section.

---

2 In the case of a COUNT operation, the value for a given key will be initialized to 0, and then incremented by 1 whenever a new record comes in with the same key. As we've mentioned previously, these kinds of mutable semantics require a stateful table structure under the hood, instead of a stream.

Aggregation Basics

There are two primary steps for aggregating data in ksqlDB:[3]

- Construct a SELECT expression that leverages some *aggregate function*.
- Group related records using the GROUP BY clause. The aggregate function will be applied to each group.

An example aggregation query is shown in Example 11-4.

Example 11-4. Example usage of an aggregate function (COUNT) and the GROUP BY clause

```
SELECT
  title_id,
  COUNT(*) AS change_count, ❶
  LATEST_BY_OFFSET(new_episode_count) AS latest_episode_count ❷
FROM season_length_changes_enriched
GROUP BY title_id ❸
EMIT CHANGES ;
```

❶ Use the built-in COUNT aggregate function to count the number of records for each title_id.

❷ Use the built-in LATEST_BY_OFFSET aggregate function to get the latest episode count for each title_id.

❸ Group the records in this stream by the title_id column.

The query in Example 11-4 uses the built-in COUNT function, but ksqlDB includes many aggregate functions, including AVG, COUNT_DISTINCT, MAX, MIN, SUM, and many more. Aggregations aren't even always mathematical. Two prominent examples include the EARLIEST_BY_OFFSET and LATEST_BY_OFFSET aggregate functions, which return the oldest and newest value for a column (computed by offset), respectively. At the end of this chapter, we'll show you how to list all of the available aggregate functions in ksqlDB, and discuss how to write your own functions should the need arise. But for now, suffice it to say you have a lot of different built-in functions to choose from in ksqlDB.

The second requirement involves grouping records using the GROUP BY clause. This places records into distinct buckets based on the columns you specify in this clause.

---

3 As we'll see in the next section, there is an optional third step that involves specifying a time window over which the aggregation should be computed.

For example, the query shown in Example 11-4 will group all items with the same title_id in the same group.

Finally, your SELECT expression can include additional columns as well. For example, let's add the title_id and season_id columns to our query:

```
SELECT
  title_id,
  season_id, ❶
  COUNT(*) AS change_count,
  LATEST_BY_OFFSET(new_episode_count) AS latest_episode_count
FROM season_length_changes_enriched
GROUP BY title_id, season_id ❷
EMIT CHANGES ;
```

❶ Add a new nonaggregate column (season_id) to our query.

❷ Add the season_id column to the GROUP BY clause.

Note that when performing aggregations, if you want to include a nonaggregate column in your SELECT expression, it must also be included in the GROUP BY clause. For example, say you ran the following query:

```
SELECT
  title_id,
  season_id, ❶
  COUNT(*) AS change_count,
  LATEST_BY_OFFSET(new_episode_count) AS latest_episode_count
FROM season_length_changes_enriched
GROUP BY title_id ❷
EMIT CHANGES ;
```

❶ We've included season_id in the SELECT expression (i.e., the projection)…

❷ …but not the GROUP BY clause.

You would get an error like this:

```
Non-aggregate SELECT expression(s) not part of GROUP BY: SEASON_ID
Either add the column to the GROUP BY or remove it from the SELECT
```

Despite the error message, there is a third option to resolve this issue: apply an aggregation function to the column that isn't included in the GROUP BY clause.

Each field that you include in the GROUP BY clause becomes part of the key in the underlying table. For example, GROUP BY title_id will create a table that is keyed by each unique title_id. If you group by multiple columns, e.g., GROUP BY title_id, season_id, then the underlying table will contain composite keys, where each column value is separated by |+| (e.g., 1|+|2).

This is important to remember when you execute pull queries against the materialized table, since if you are querying a table with composite keys, you need to include the separator in your query (e.g., SELECT * FROM T WHERE COL='1|+|2'). Future versions of ksqlDB will likely improve how composite keys are queried, but the behavior we documented here was present in at least version 0.14.0.

Each of the preceding aggregations is an example of an unwindowed aggregation. They are considered unwindowed since the records are only bucketed by the fields in the GROUP BY clause, and not using a separate time-based windowing condition. However, ksqlDB also supports windowed aggregations, which we will explore in the next section.

Windowed Aggregations

Sometimes, you may want to compute an aggregation over a certain period of time. For example, we may want to know how many season-length changes occurred over a 24-hour period. This adds another dimension to our aggregation: time. Luckily for us, ksqlDB supports *windowed aggregations*, which were designed for this use case.

In Chapter 5, we discussed the three different types of windows in Kafka Streams (see "Window Types" on page 154 if you need a recap). The same window types are available in ksqlDB, and each window type and the corresponding ksqlDB expression is shown in Table 11-3.

Table 11-3. ksqlDB window types

Window type	Example
Tumbling windows	WINDOW TUMBLING (SIZE 30 SECONDS)

Hopping windows	WINDOW HOPPING (
	    SIZE 30 SECONDS,
	    ADVANCE BY 10 SECONDS
	)

Session windows	WINDOW SESSION (60 SECONDS)

In order to incorporate a window expression in a query, you simply need to include the window expressions before the GROUP BY clause, as shown here:

```
SELECT
  title_id,
  season_id,
  COUNT(*) AS change_count,
  LATEST_BY_OFFSET(new_episode_count) AS latest_episode_count
FROM season_length_changes_enriched
WINDOW TUMBLING (SIZE 1 HOUR) ❶
GROUP BY title_id, season_id ❷
EMIT CHANGES ;
```

❶ Group records into one-hour-long buckets.

❷ Records are grouped by `title_id` and `season_id`.

The preceding query will produce the following results:

```
+-----------+----------+-------------+--------------------+
|TITLE_ID   |SEASON_ID |CHANGE_COUNT |LATEST_EPISODE_COUNT |
+-----------+----------+-------------+--------------------+
|1          |1         |1            |8
```

Of course, while windowing is pretty easy using ksqlDB's windowing expressions, the added dimension of time requires additional considerations around the following:

- When should data be emitted to downstream processors?
- How can we handle delayed/out-of-order data?
- How long should we retain each window?

We'll address each of these considerations in the following sections.

Delayed data

When we talk about the delayed arrival of data in ksqlDB or Kafka Streams, we aren't exclusively talking about an event being delayed according to the wall clock time. For example, if an event occurs at 10:02 a.m., but isn't processed by your stream processing application until 10:15 a.m., you may consider it delayed in the traditional sense of the word.

However, as we learned in Chapter 5, Kafka Streams (and, by extension, ksqlDB) keeps an internal clock called the *stream time*, which is an always-increasing value that is extracted from the timestamps of consumed records. The timestamps can be extracted from the record metadata, or from an embedded value within a record using the TIMESTAMP and TIMESTAMP_FORMAT properties, as we saw in Example 11-3.

When records are consumed out of timestamp order, then any record that arrives with a timestamp less than the current stream time is considered delayed. And when it comes to windowed aggregations, delayed records are of particular interest since you can control whether or not they are admitted to a window (which allows them to be computed in the aggregation) or if they are simply ignored after a certain amount of time has elapsed (at this point, they are considered *late* and are not admitted to the window). The allowed delay is called the *grace period*, and the syntax for defining a grace period in ksqlDB is as follows:

```
WINDOW <window_type> ( ❶
    <window_properties>, ❷
    GRACE PERIOD <number> <time_unit> ❸
)
```

❶ The *window type* can be HOPPING, TUMBLING, or SESSION.

❷ See Table 11-3 for the required windowing properties needed for constructing each window type.

❸ Define a grace period. Note that the same time units we discussed for sliding windows are also supported for grace periods. See "Windowed Joins" on page 319.

For example, if we want to apply a windowed aggregation that tolerates up to 10 minutes of delay, and ignores any record that arrives after this threshold, we could use the following query:

```
SELECT
    title_id,
    season_id,
    COUNT(*) AS change_count,
    LATEST_BY_OFFSET(new_episode_count) AS episode_count
FROM season_length_changes_enriched
WINDOW TUMBLING (SIZE 1 HOUR, GRACE PERIOD 10 MINUTES) ❶
GROUP BY title_id, season_id
EMIT CHANGES ;
```

❶ Group records into 1-hour-long buckets, and tolerate delays of up to 10 minutes.

With the preceding grace period defined as 10 MINUTES, we can produce some records in another tab (while the previous query is running) to see explicitly the effect it has on stream time, and whether or not the record will be admitted to an open window. Example 11-5 shows the statements we will execute to produce these records.

Example 11-5. In another CLI session, produce records with various timestamps to observe the effect on stream time

```
INSERT INTO production_changes VALUES (
    '1', 1, 1, 'season_length',
    STRUCT(season_id := 1, episode_count := 12),
    STRUCT(season_id := 1, episode_count := 8),
    '2021-02-24 10:00:00' ❶
);

INSERT INTO production_changes VALUES (
    '1', 1, 1, 'season_length',
    STRUCT(season_id := 1, episode_count := 8),
    STRUCT(season_id := 1, episode_count := 10),
    '2021-02-24 11:00:00' ❷
);

INSERT INTO production_changes VALUES (
    '1', 1, 1, 'season_length',
    STRUCT(season_id := 1, episode_count := 10),
    STRUCT(season_id := 1, episode_count := 8),
    '2021-02-24 10:59:00' ❸
);

INSERT INTO production_changes VALUES (
    '1', 1, 1, 'season_length',
    STRUCT(season_id := 1, episode_count := 8),
    STRUCT(season_id := 1, episode_count := 12),
    '2021-02-24 11:10:00' ❹
);

INSERT INTO production_changes VALUES (
    '1', 1, 1, 'season_length',
    STRUCT(season_id := 1, episode_count := 12),
    STRUCT(season_id := 1, episode_count := 8),
    '2021-02-24 10:59:00' ❺
);
```

❶ Stream time is set to 10 a.m., and this record will be added to the (10 a.m.–11 a.m.) window.

❷ Stream time is set to 11 a.m., and this record will be added to the (11 a.m.–12 p.m.) window.

❸ Stream time is unchanged, because this record's timestamp is less than the current stream time. The record will be added to the (10 a.m.–11 a.m.) window because the grace period is still active.

❹ Stream time is set to 11:10 a.m., and this record will be added to the (11 a.m.– 12 p.m.) window.

❺ This record does not get added to a window, since this record is 11 minutes late. In other words, `stream_time (11:10 a.m.) – current_time (10:59 a.m.) = 11 minutes`, which is greater than the grace period of 10 minutes.

When a record is skipped because it arrives late (for example, the last record in Example 11-5), you should see some helpful information included in the ksqlDB server logs, as shown here:

```
WARN Skipping record for expired window.
key=[Struct{KSQL_COL_0=1|+|1}]
topic=[...]
partition=[3]
offset=[5]
timestamp=[1614164340000] ❶
window=[1614160800000,1614164400000) ❷
expiration=[1614164400000] ❸
streamTime=[1614165000000] ❹
```

❶ The current timestamp associated with this record is `2021-02-24 10:59:00`.

❷ The window this record would have been grouped in has a range of `2021-02-24 10:00:00 – 2021-02-24 11:00:00`.

❸ The expiration time translates to `2021-02-24 11:00:00`. This is calculated by subtracting the grace period (10 minutes) from the stream time (see the next bullet).

❹ The stream time, which is the highest timestamp seen by ksqlDB, translates to `2021-02-24 11:10:00`.

Setting a grace period is optional (though highly recommended), so it really depends on how you want to handle out-of-order/delayed data. If you don't set a grace period, the window will remain open until its retention has expired and the window has been closed.

Window retention is also configurable, and it plays another role in ksqlDB since it controls how long windowed data can be queried. So, let's look at how to control the retention of windows in the next section.

Window retention

If you plan to query the results of a windowed aggregation, as we do, you may want to control the retention period of old windows in ksqlDB. Once a window is removed, you can no longer query it. Another motivation for explicitly setting the retention period of windows is to keep your state stores small. The more windows you keep around, the larger your state stores will become. As we learned in Chapter 6, keeping state stores small can reduce the impact of rebalancing and also the resource utilization of your application.[4]

In order to set the retention of a window, you simply need to specify the RETENTION property in the WINDOW expression. The syntax is as follows:

```
WINDOW { HOPPING | TUMBLING | SESSION } ( ❶
    <window_properties>, ❶
    RETENTION <number> <time_unit> ❷
)
```

❶ See Table 11-3 for the required windowing properties needed for constructing each window type.

❷ Specify the window retention period. Note that the same time units we discussed for sliding windows are also supported for window retention settings. See "Windowed Joins" on page 319.

 The window retention period must be greater than or equal to the window size plus the grace period. Also, the retention is a lower bound for how long windows should be maintained. The window will most likely not be removed at the exact time the retention period expires.

For example, let's refactor our query to set a window retention of two days. The SQL statement in Example 11-6 shows how we can accomplish this.

Example 11-6. A ksqlDB statement that explicitly sets the retention period for the underlying window

```
SELECT
    title_id,
    season_id,
    LATEST_BY_OFFSET(new_episode_count) AS episode_count,
    COUNT(*) AS change_count
FROM season_length_changes_enriched
WINDOW TUMBLING (
    SIZE 1 HOUR,
    RETENTION 2 DAYS, ❶
    GRACE PERIOD 10 MINUTES
```

---

4 By default, state stores leverage an embedded key-value store called RocksDB, which stores data in memory and can optionally spill to disk when the keyspace is large. Therefore, you should be conscious of disk and memory utilization when maintaining large state stores.

```
)
GROUP BY title_id, season_id
EMIT CHANGES ;
```

❶ Set a window retention period of two days.

One important thing to note here is that the retention period is driven by Kafka Streams and ksqlDB's internal clock: stream time. It does not reference wall clock time.

Example 11-6 gets us extremely close to being able to wrap up step 4 of our tutorial (see Figure 11-1). The last thing we need to do is create a materialized view from this query. We'll explore this in the next section.

Materialized Views

Materialized views have existed in the database world for a long time, and they are used to store the results of a query (this is called *materialization*). The precomputed results of a query are then made available for querying, and are ideal for improving the performance of expensive queries in traditional databases, which operate on many rows at a time in a batch-like manner.

ksqlDB also has the concept of materialized views, which maintain some of the same properties of their traditional counterparts:

- They are derived from a query against another collection.
- They can be queried in a lookup-style manner (called pull queries in ksqlDB).

Materialized views in ksqlDB are also different in some important ways:

- At the time of this writing, materialized views in ksqlDB could only be computed from aggregate queries.
- They are refreshed automatically as new data comes in. Compare this with traditional systems, where refreshes can be scheduled, issued on demand, or non-existent.

When we talk about materialized views in ksqlDB, we are actually talking about a certain kind of TABLE that we can execute pull queries against. As we've already seen in this book, tables can be created directly on top of Kafka topics (see "Creating Source Collections" on page 289) or from nonaggregate queries (e.g., Example 11-2). At the time of this writing, ksqlDB did not support keyed-lookups (pull queries) against these kinds of tables (though this limitation may not be around in future versions of ksqlDB).

However, we can execute pull queries against materialized views, which are TABLE objects that are constructed from an aggregate query.[5] All we need to do is create a derived table collection (see "Creating Derived Collections" on page 304) using an aggregate query.

For example, let's create a materialized view from our windowed aggregation query that we created in Example 11-6. The SQL statement shown in Example 11-7 demonstrates how to do this.

Example 11-7. Create a materialized view using an aggregate query

```
CREATE TABLE season_length_change_counts
WITH (
    KAFKA_TOPIC = 'season_length_change_counts',
    VALUE_FORMAT = 'AVRO',
    PARTITIONS = 1
) AS
SELECT
    title_id,
    season_id,
    COUNT(*) AS change_count,
    LATEST_BY_OFFSET(new_episode_count) AS episode_count
FROM season_length_changes_enriched
WINDOW TUMBLING (
    SIZE 1 HOUR,
    RETENTION 2 DAYS,
    GRACE PERIOD 10 MINUTES
)
GROUP BY title_id, season_id
EMIT CHANGES ;
```

We now have a materialized view named season_length_change_counts that we can query. This completes step 4 of our tutorial (see Figure 11-1), and we are ready to proceed with the final step: executing queries against our data using various clients.

Clients

The final step of our tutorial is to ensure the data we've processed with ksqlDB can be queried by various clients. Let's now walk through the process of executing queries against our materialized view (season_length_change_counts) and push queries against our enriched stream (season_length_changes_enriched). We'll explore each type of query using both the CLI and curl.

---

5 The *view* nomenclature was adopted from traditional systems, but there isn't a separate *view* object in ksqlDB. So when you hear the word *view* in relation to ksqlDB, you should just think of a table collection that can be used for lookup-style pull queries.

We use `curl` not with the expectation that you will build production clients using this command-line utility, but because it will be a useful reference point when implementing a RESTful client in the language of your choice. We owe this to `curl`'s simple syntax, which conveys the HTTP method type being used for the request, the HTTP client headers, and the request payload. Furthermore, you can analyze the raw response returned by `curl` for a clear understanding of the response format returned by ksqlDB.

 At the time of this writing, an initial version of a Java client had also been released. The source code for this chapter contains an example of how to use this client as well. We have omitted it here due to uncertainty around how the Java client interface will change in the near future. Furthermore, a ksqlDB improvement proposal (KLIP) (*https://oreil.ly/TOurV*) was also under discussion at the time of this writing, which mentioned potential changes to the Java client, the ksqlDB REST API, and even the possible introduction of new, official clients written in Python or Go.

Let's explore pull queries in more detail.

Pull Queries

With our materialized view in place, we can execute pull queries against the view. The syntax for executing a pull query is as follows:

```
SELECT select_expr [, ...]
FROM from_item
WHERE condition
```

As you can see, pull queries are very simple. At the time of this writing, neither joins nor aggregations were supported in the pull query itself (though you can perform both of these operations when creating the materialized view, as shown in Example 11-7). Instead, pull queries can be thought of as simple lookups that reference a key column, and for windowed views, they can also optionally reference the `WINDOWSTART` pseudo column, which contains the lower boundary for a given window's time range (the upper boundary is stored in another pseudo column called `WINDOWEND`, but this latter column is not queryable).

So, what is the name of the key column that we can perform lookups against? It depends. When grouping by a single field in the `GROUP BY` clause, the name of the key column will match the name of the grouped field. For example, suppose your query included the following expression:

```
GROUP BY title_id
```

We could execute a pull query that performed a lookup against the `title_id` column. However, our query references two columns in the GROUP BY clause:

```
GROUP BY title_id, season_id
```

In this case, ksqlDB will generate a key column for us in the format of KSQL_COL_? (this is another artifact of the current implementation of ksqlDB that may be changing in the future). You can retrieve the column name from the DESCRIBE output:

```
ksql> DESCRIBE season_length_change_counts ;

Name                    : SEASON_LENGTH_CHANGE_COUNTS
 Field          | Type
-------------------------------------------------------------------
 KSQL_COL_0     | VARCHAR(STRING)  (primary key) (Window type: TUMBLING)
 EPISODE_COUNT  | INTEGER
 CHANGE_COUNT   | BIGINT
-------------------------------------------------------------------
```

In this case, we can perform a lookup against the `season_length_change_counts` view using the pull query in Example 11-8.

Example 11-8. An example pull query

```
SELECT *
FROM season_length_change_counts
WHERE KSQL_COL_0 = '1|+|1' ; ❶
```

❶ When grouping by multiple fields, the key is a composite value where the value of each column is separated by `|+|`. If we were only grouping by one field (e.g., `title_id`), then we would use WHERE `title_id=1`.

> The IN predicate can also be used in pull queries to match multiple possible keys (e.g., WHERE KSQL_COL_0 IN ('1|+|1', '1|+|2')).

If we execute the preceding query from the CLI, we will see the following output:

```
+------------+----------------+----------------+---------------+---------------+
|KSQL_COL_0  |WINDOWSTART     |WINDOWEND       |CHANGE_COUNT   |EPISODE_COUNT  |
+------------+----------------+----------------+---------------+---------------+
|1|+|1       |1614160800000   |1614164400000   |2              |8              |
|1|+|1       |1614164400000   |1614168000000   |2              |12             |
```

As you can see, the two pseudo columns, WINDOWSTART and WINDOWEND, are included in the output. We can query the WINDOWSTART column as well, using either the Unix timestamp or a more readable datetime string. The following two statements demonstrate both types of queries:

```
SELECT * FROM
season_length_change_counts
WHERE KSQL_COL_0 = '1|+|1'
AND WINDOWSTART=1614164400000;

SELECT *
FROM season_length_change_counts
WHERE KSQL_COL_0 = '1|+|1'
AND WINDOWSTART = '2021-02-24T10:00:00';
```

In this case, the output of the preceding queries is the same:

```
+-----------+---------------+---------------+---------------+---------------+
|KSQL_COL_0 |WINDOWSTART    |WINDOWEND      |CHANGE_COUNT   |EPISODE_COUNT  |
+-----------+---------------+---------------+---------------+---------------+
|1|+|1      |1614160800000  |1614164400000  |2              |8              |
```

When it comes time to query the data in your materialized views, you will likely want to issue queries using a client other than the CLI. Let's explore how to issue a pull query using `curl`, since a `curl` example could easily be extended to a custom client written in Python, Go, or some other language.

Curl

Perhaps the easiest way to query a ksqlDB server outside of the CLI is with the widely used command-line utility `curl`. The following command shows how to execute the same pull query we created in Example 11-8 from the command line:

```
curl -X POST "http://localhost:8088/query" \   ❶
    -H "Content-Type: application/vnd.ksql.v1+json; charset=utf-8" \   ❷
    --data $'{   ❸
  "ksql":"SELECT * FROM season_length_change_counts WHERE KSQL_COL_0=\'1|+|1\';",
  "streamsProperties": {}
}'
```

❶ We can execute a pull query by submitting a POST request to the `/query` endpoint.

❷ The content type includes the API version `v1` and serialization format (`json`).

❸ Pass the pull query in the POST data. The query is nested in a JSON object, under a key named `ksql`.

The output of the preceding command is shown here. It includes both the column names (see `header.schema`) and one or more rows:

```
[
  {
    "header": {
      "queryId": "query_1604158332837",
      "schema": "`KSQL_COL_0` STRING KEY, `WINDOWSTART` BIGINT KEY, `WINDOWEND`
        BIGINT KEY, `CHANGE_COUNT` BIGINT, `EPISODE_COUNT` INTEGER"
    }
  },
  {
    "row": {
      "columns": [
        "1|+|1",
        1614160800000,
        1614164400000,
        2,
        8
      ]
    }
  },
  ... ❶
]
```

❶   Additional rows have been omitted for brevity.

As you can see, it's very simple to query a ksqlDB server, even outside of the CLI. Now, let's learn more about executing push queries.

Push Queries

We've already seen many examples of push queries in this book. For example, executing a query against the `season_length_change_counts` stream from the CLI is as simple as running the following SQL statement:

```
ksql> SELECT * FROM season_length_changes_enriched EMIT CHANGES ;
```

So this section will focus on executing push queries from `curl`.

Push Queries via Curl

Executing a push query using `curl` is similar to executing a pull query. For example, we can issue a push query using the following command:

```
curl -X "POST" "http://localhost:8088/query" \
    -H "Content-Type: application/vnd.ksql.v1+json; charset=utf-8" \
    -d $'{
  "ksql": "SELECT * FROM season_length_changes_enriched EMIT CHANGES ;",
  "streamsProperties": {}
}'
```

An example response is shown here:

```
[{"header":{"queryId":"none","schema":"`ROWTIME` BIGINT, `ROWKEY` INTEGER,
  `TITLE_ID` INTEGER, `CHANGE_COUNT` BIGINT"}},


{"row":{"columns":[1,"Stranger Things",1,12,8,"2021-02-24 10:00:00"]}},
{"row":{"columns":[1,"Stranger Things",1,8,10,"2021-02-24 11:00:00"]}},
{"row":{"columns":[1,"Stranger Things",1,10,8,"2021-02-24 10:59:00"]}},
{"row":{"columns":[1,"Stranger Things",1,8,12,"2021-02-24 11:10:00"]}},
{"row":{"columns":[1,"Stranger Things",1,12,8,"2021-02-24 10:59:00"]}},

]
```

Note: if you don't see any output, the consumer offset is likely set to `latest`, so you may need to rerun the statements in Example 11-5 to verify.

Unlike pull queries, the connection does not terminate immediately after executing the query. The output is streamed to the client in a series of chunks, over a long-lived connection that will continue to emit responses when new data becomes available. This is possible via HTTP's chunked transfer encoding.

Now that we know how to query enriched and aggregated data in ksqlDB, we have completed the last step of our Netflix change-tracking tutorial. Before we close out this chapter, let's explore one final topic: functions and operators.

Functions and Operators

ksqlDB includes a rich set of functions and operators that can be used for working with data. First, let's take a quick look at some of the operators.

Operators

ksqlDB includes several operators that can be included in your SQL statements:

- Arithmetic operators (+,-,/,*,%)
- String concatenation operators (+,||)
- Subscript operators for accessing array indices or map keys ([])
- Struct dereference operators (->)

We've already seen some of these in action (see Example 8-1). We won't spend a lot of time looking at the operators in this book, but a full operator reference and example usage can be found in the official ksqlDB documentation (*https://docs.ksqldb.io*). Now, let's turn to the more interesting part of this discussion: functions.

Showing Functions

One of the most interesting features of ksqlDB is its built-in function library. We've already seen one example of a function, COUNT, but there are many more and the function library is always growing. To list the available functions, we can use the SHOW FUNCTIONS statement.

For example:

```
ksql> SHOW FUNCTIONS ;
```

The output of the SHOW FUNCTIONS command is quite large, but a truncated example is shown here:

```
Function Name          | Type
-----------------------------------
...

AVG                    | AGGREGATE
CEIL                   | SCALAR
CHR                    | SCALAR
COALESCE               | SCALAR
COLLECT_LIST           | AGGREGATE
COLLECT_SET            | AGGREGATE
CONCAT                 | SCALAR
CONCAT_WS              | SCALAR
COUNT                  | AGGREGATE
COUNT_DISTINCT         | AGGREGATE
CUBE_EXPLODE           | TABLE
DATETOSTRING           | SCALAR
EARLIEST_BY_OFFSET     | AGGREGATE
ELT                    | SCALAR
ENCODE                 | SCALAR
ENTRIES                | SCALAR
EXP                    | SCALAR
EXPLODE                | TABLE
...
```

When viewing the list of built-in ksqlDB functions, you'll notice three different categories listed in the TYPE column. A description of each type is shown in the following table:

Function type	Description
SCALAR	A stateless function that operates on a single row at a time, and returns one output value.
AGGREGATE	A stateful function that is used to aggregate data. These functions also return one output value.
TABLE	A stateless function that takes one input and produces 0 or more outputs. This is similar to the way flatMap works in Kafka Streams.

As you're looking through the function library, you may want more information about a particular function. We'll see how to accomplish this in the next section.

Describing Functions

If you want more information about a ksqlDB function, you can always visit the official documentation on the ksqlDB website (*https://ksqldb.io*). However, you don't need to navigate away from the CLI to describe a function, because ksqlDB includes a special statement that will provide the information you need. The syntax for this statement is as follows:

```
DESCRIBE FUNCTION <identifier>
```

For example, if you want more information about the built-in `EARLIEST_BY_OFFSET` function, you could run the SQL statement in Example 11-9.

Example 11-9. An example of how to describe a function in ksqlDB

```
ksql> DESCRIBE FUNCTION EARLIEST_BY_OFFSET ;

Name        : EARLIEST_BY_OFFSET
Author      : Confluent
Overview    : This function returns the oldest value for the column,
              computed by offset. ❶
Type        : AGGREGATE ❷
Jar         : internal ❸
Variations  : ❹

        Variation   : EARLIEST_BY_OFFSET(val BOOLEAN)
        Returns     : BOOLEAN
        Description : return the earliest value of a Boolean column

        Variation   : EARLIEST_BY_OFFSET(val INT)
        Returns     : INT
        Description : return the earliest value of an integer column

        ...
```

❶ The description of the function.

❷ The type of function (see Table 11-3 for a list of the available function types).

❸ When viewing a built-in function that is included in ksqlDB, the `Jar` value will show as `internal`. We'll see how to build our own functions in the next section, which will contain a path to the actual `Jar` on disk.

❹ The variations section will contain a list of all of the valid method signatures for a function. This section was truncated for brevity's sake, but you can see that there are at least two variations of this function: one variation accepts a `BOOLEAN` argument and returns a `BOOLEAN` value, while another variation accepts and returns an `INT`.

ksqlDB has an impressive number of built-in functions, but it also gives you the freedom to implement your own functions whenever the need arises. So if you scroll through the output of `SHOW FUNCTIONS` and don't find anything that fits your use case, don't fret. We'll explain how to create your own function in the next section.

Creating Custom Functions

Sometimes, you may want to create a custom function to use in your ksqlDB queries. For example, you may want to apply a specialized mathematical function to a column, or invoke a machine learning model using inputs from your data stream. Regardless of how simple or complex your use case is, ksqlDB includes a Java interface that gives you the power to extend the built-in function library with your own set of user-defined functions.

There are three different types of user-defined functions in ksqlDB, each one relating to a built-in function type that we discussed in the previous section (scalar, aggregate, and table functions). A summary of the user-defined function types is shown in the following table:

Type	Description
User-defined functions, or *UDFs*	These are custom SCALAR functions. UDFs are stateless and return exactly one value.
User-defined Aggregate functions, or *UDAFs*	These are custom AGGREGATE functions. UDAFs are stateful and return exactly one value.
User-defined Table functions, or *UDTFs*	These are custom TABLE functions. UDTFs are stateless and return zero or more values.

To get a better idea of how custom functions work, we will implement a UDF that removes stop words from a string of text. An example UDAF and UDTF are also available in the source code for this chapter (*https://oreil.ly/rJN5s*), but have been omitted from the text since the development and deployment process is largely the same no matter which type of function you decide to implement. There are some subtle differences in how UDFs, UDAFs, and UDTFs are implemented, and we have highlighted these differences in the source code for the chapter.

Now let's learn how to create a user-defined function.

Stop-word removal UDF

A common data preprocessing task is to remove so-called stop words from a string of text. Stop words are common words (such as "a," "and," "are," "but," "or," "the," etc.) that don't add a lot of meaning to the underlying text. If you have a machine learning or natural language model that attempts to extract information from text, it is common to remove stop words from the model input first. Therefore, we will create a UDF called `REMOVE_STOP_WORDS`. The process of creating any type of user-defined function is simple. Here are the steps to follow:

1. Create a Java project that will contain the code of our function.

2. Add the `io.confluent.ksql:ksql-udf` dependency to our project, which contains annotations that we need for our UDF class.

3. Add any other dependencies we need to implement our function. For example, if there is a third-party Maven dependency that you want to leverage in your code, add it to your build file.

4. Write the logic for our UDF, using the appropriate annotations (we'll cover these shortly).

5. Build and package the code as an uber JAR, which combines the source code of your function, and all of the third-party code it depends on, into a single JAR file.

6. Copy the uber JAR to the ksqlDB extensions directory. This is a configurable file path on the ksqlDB server, which can be defined using the `ksql.extension.dir` configuration property.

7. Restart the ksqlDB server. When the ksqlDB server comes back online, it will load the new function, making it available for use in your SQL statements.

Now, let's implement our function using these instructions to show how this works. First, let's create a new Java project using Gradle's `init` command. The following code shows how to do this:

```
mkdir udf && cd udf

gradle init \
  --type java-library \
  --dsl groovy \
  --test-framework junit-jupiter \
  --project-name udf \
  --package com.magicalpipelines.ksqldb
```

Let's add the `ksql-udf` dependency to our build file (*build.gradle*). This dependency lives in Confluent's Maven repository, so we need to update the `repositories` block as well:

```
repositories {
    // ...
    maven {
        url = uri('http://packages.confluent.io/maven/')  ❶
    }
}
```

```
dependencies {
    // ...
    implementation 'io.confluent.ksql:ksqldb-udf:6.0.0' ❷
}
```

❶ Add the Confluent Maven repository, which is where the `ksql-udf` dependency lives.

❷ Add the `ksql-udf` dependency to our project. This artifact contains all of the annotations we need to add to our code, as we'll see shortly.

Our UDF doesn't require any third-party code, but if it did, we could have updated the `dependencies` block with any other artifacts required by our UDF.[6] OK, it's time to implement the business logic of our function. In this case, we can create a file called *RemoveStopWordsUdf.java*, and add the following code:

```java
public class RemoveStopWordsUdf {

    private final List<String> stopWords =
        Arrays.asList(
            new String[] {"a", "and", "are", "but", "or", "over", "the"});

    private ArrayList<String> stringToWords(String source) { ❶
        return Stream.of(source.toLowerCase().split(" "))
            .collect(Collectors.toCollection(ArrayList<String>::new));
    }

    private String wordsToString(ArrayList<String> words) { ❷
        return words.stream().collect(Collectors.joining(" "));
    }

    public String apply(final String source) { ❸
        ArrayList<String> words = stringToWords(source);
        words.removeAll(stopWords);
        return wordsToString(words);
    }
}
```

❶ This method converts a string of text to a list of words.

❷ This method converts a list of words back into a string.

❸ This method contains the implementation of our business logic, which removes a list of stop words from a source string. You can name this method whatever you like, but it should be nonstatic and have `public` visibility.

---

6 The dependencies will need to be packaged into an uber JAR, using a plug-in like the `com.github.johnren` `gelman.shadow` plug-in. See the UDF documentation (*https://oreil.ly/1g847*) for more information.

Now that we have the business logic written for our UDF, we need to add the annotations that are included in the `ksql-udf` dependency. These annotations are read by ksqlDB when it loads the JAR, and provides ksqlDB with more information about the function, including its name, description, and parameters. As you'll see shortly, the values we provide in our annotations will be viewable in the DESCRIBE FUNCTION output:

```
@UdfDescription( ❶
    name = "remove_stop_words", ❷
    description = "A UDF that removes stop words from a string of text",
    version = "0.1.0",
    author = "Mitch Seymour")
public class RemoveStopWordsUdf {
  // ...

  @Udf(description = "Remove the default stop words from a string of text") ❸
  public String apply(
      @UdfParameter(value = "source", description = "the raw source string") ❹
      final String source
  ) { ... }
}
```

❶ The `UdfDescription` annotation tells ksqlDB that this class contains a ksqlDB function that should be loaded into the ksqlDB library on startup. If you are implementing a UDAF or UDTF, the `UdafDescription`/`UdtfDescription` should be used instead.

❷ The name of our function, as it should appear in the function library. The rest of the properties (`description`, `version`, and `author`) will appear in the DESCRIBE FUNCTION output.

❸ The `Udf` annotation should be applied to a public method that can be invoked by ksqlDB. You can have multiple methods with the `Udf` annotation in a single UDF, and each one will be considered a separate variation of the function, as we discussed when looking at the EARLIEST_BY_OFFSET function (see Example 11-9). Note that UDTFs and UDAFs use different annotations here as well (`Udtf` and `UdafFactory`). See this chapter's source code for details (*https://oreil.ly/rJN5s*).

❹ The `UdfParameter` can be used to provide helpful information for each parameter in your UDF. This is also surfaced in the DESCRIBE FUNCTION output, in the `Variations` section.

Once you've written the business logic for your UDF and have added the class-level and method-level annotations, it's time to build the uber JAR. With Gradle, this can be accomplished with the following command:

```
./gradlew build --info
```

The preceding command will create a JAR at the following location, relative to the root directory of your Java project:

```
build/libs/udf.jar
```

In order to tell ksqlDB about our new UDF, we need to place this JAR in the location specified by the `ksql.extension.dir` configuration parameter. You can define this parameter in the ksqlDB server configuration file. For example:

```
ksql.extension.dir=/etc/ksqldb/extensions
```

Once we have the location of the ksqlDB extension directory, we can copy the JAR to this location and restart the ksqlDB server, as shown here:

```
cp build/libs/udf.jar /etc/ksqldb/extensions

ksql-server-stop
ksql-server-start
```

Upon restart, we should be able to see our UDF in the output of the SHOW FUNCTIONS command:

```
ksql> SHOW FUNCTIONS ;

 Function Name          | Type
---------------------------------
 ...
 ...
 REMOVE_STOP_WORDS      | SCALAR ❶
 ...
 ...
```

❶ The name of our function, defined by the `UdfDescription` annotation, will appear in the alphabetized function list.

We can also describe our custom function using the same SQL statement that is used to describe built-in functions:

```
ksql> DESCRIBE FUNCTION REMOVE_STOP_WORDS ;

Name        : REMOVE_STOP_WORDS
Author      : Mitch Seymour
Version     : 0.1.0
Overview    : A UDF that removes stop words from a string of text
Type        : SCALAR
Jar         : /etc/ksqldb/extensions/udf.jar ❶
Variations  :

        Variation   : REMOVE_STOP_WORDS(source VARCHAR)
        Returns     : VARCHAR
```

```
        Description : Remove the default stop words from a string of text
        source      : the raw source string
```

❶ Note that the `Jar` value now points to the physical location of the UDF JAR on disk.

Finally, we can use our function just like any of the built-in functions in ksqlDB. Let's create a stream called `model_inputs`, and insert some test data that we can run our function against:

```
CREATE STREAM model_inputs (
    text STRING
)
WITH (
    KAFKA_TOPIC='model_inputs',
    VALUE_FORMAT='JSON',
    PARTITIONS=4
);

INSERT INTO model_inputs VALUES ('The quick brown fox jumps over the lazy dog');
```

Now, let's apply our function:

```
SELECT
  text AS original,
  remove_stop_words(text) AS no_stop_words
FROM model_inputs
EMIT CHANGES;
```

As you can see from the following output, our new function works as expected:

```
+-------------------------------------------+------------------------------+
|ORIGINAL                                   |NO_STOP_WORDS                 |
+-------------------------------------------+------------------------------+
|The quick brown fox jumps over the lazy dog|quick brown fox jumps lazy dog|
```

Additional Resources for Custom ksqlDB Functions

Creating custom ksqlDB functions is a huge topic, and we could have easily dedicated multiple chapters to it. However, I have spent a lot of time speaking and even writing about ksqlDB functions elsewhere, and the official documentation also contains some great information about this feature. Please check out the following resources for more information about custom ksqlDB functions:

- "The Exciting Frontier of Custom KSQL Functions" (*https://oreil.ly/HTb-F*) (Mitch Seymour, Kafka Summit 2019)

- "ksqlDB UDFs and UDAFs Made Easy" (*https://oreil.ly/HMU9F*) (Mitch Seymour, Confluent Blog)

- Official ksqlDB Documentation (*https://oreil.ly/qEafS*)

Summary

Despite having a simple interface, ksqlDB supports many intermediate to advanced stream processing use cases, including joining data in different collections, aggregating data, creating materialized views that can be queried using keyed-lookups, and more. Furthermore, ksqlDB gives us an extensive built-in function library that we can use for tackling a wide range of data processing and enrichment use cases. Whether you are looking for common mathematical functions (`AVG`, `COUNT_DISTINCT`, `MAX`, `MIN`, `SUM`, etc.), string functions (`LPAD`, `REGEXP_EXTRACT`, `REPLACE`, `TRIM`, `UCASE`, etc.), or even geospatial functions (`GEO_DISTANCE`), ksqlDB has you covered.

But where ksqlDB really shines is in its ability to provide this high-level interface, while still giving developers the option to extend the built-in function library with their own custom Java functions. This is incredibly important, as it allows you to continue building stream processing applications using a simple SQL dialect, even if your application requires custom business logic. This veers into more advanced usage since it requires knowledge of Java, but as demonstrated in this chapter, even this process has been made simple by ksqlDB.

Now that you know how to tackle basic, intermediate, and advanced stream processing use cases with ksqlDB, let's move on to the final chapter in this book, where we will learn how to test, deploy, and monitor our Kafka Streams and ksqlDB applications.

## PART IV

The Road to Production

## CHAPTER 12

Testing, Monitoring, and Deployment

In the previous chapters, we learned how to build a variety of stream processing applications with Kafka Streams and ksqlDB. In this final chapter, we will learn some steps we'll need to take in order to ship our applications to a production environment. You may be wondering why we decided to unify the chapter on productionizing Kafka Streams and ksqlDB applications. Despite some differences, specifically with respect to testing, the process is largely the same, and simplifying our mental model for how we productionize software will improve its maintainability in the long run (especially in hybrid environments where we use both Kafka Streams and ksqlDB).

Some of the questions we will answer in this chapter include:

- How can we test Kafka Streams applications and ksqlDB queries?
- How can we run benchmarks against a Kafka Streams topology?
- Which types of monitoring should we have in place?
- What is the process for accessing the built-in JMX metrics in Kafka Streams and ksqlDB?
- How can we containerize and deploy our Kafka Streams and ksqlDB applications?
- What are some of the operational tasks we are likely to encounter?

Let's start by learning how to test our stream processing applications.

Testing

Once the initial development of your ksqlDB queries or Kafka Streams application is complete, you will likely continue shipping updates to your code over time. For example, a change in business requirements may require an update to your code, you may identify a bug or performance issue that needs to be fixed, or you may just be updating software versions.

Each time you make a change, however, you should take steps to ensure you don't accidentally introduce a *regression* that could impact the correctness or performance of your application. The best way to do this is by establishing good testing practices. In this section, we will discuss several testing strategies that will help you ensure a smooth evolutionary path for your stream processing applications.

Testing ksqlDB Queries

Testing ksqlDB queries is very straightforward. The maintainers of ksqlDB have built a tool called `ksql-test-runner`, which takes three arguments:

- A file containing one or more SQL statements to be tested
- A file that specifies the data inputs for one or more source topics
- A file that specifies the expected outputs of one or more sink topics

Let's run through an example to see how this works. First, we'll create a set of SQL statements that read data from the `users` topic and convert each row into a greeting. The queries we'll be working with are shown in the following code block, which we will save to a file called *statements.sql*:

```
CREATE STREAM users (
  ROWKEY INT KEY,
  USERNAME VARCHAR
) WITH (kafka_topic='users', value_format='JSON');

CREATE STREAM greetings
WITH (KAFKA_TOPIC = 'greetings') AS
SELECT ROWKEY, 'Hello, ' + USERNAME AS "greeting"
FROM users
EMIT CHANGES;
```

Once our ksqlDB queries have been created, we need to specify the inputs that should be used for our tests. In this example, we have a single source topic called `users`. Therefore, we'll save the following content to a file called *input.json*, which will instruct the `ksql-test-runner` to insert two records into the `users` topic when running our test:

```json
{
  "inputs": [
    {
      "topic": "users",
      "timestamp": 0,
      "value": {"USERNAME": "Isabelle"
      },
      "key": 0
    },
    {
      "topic": "users",
      "timestamp": 0,
      "value": {"USERNAME": "Elyse"
      },
      "key": 0
    }
  ]
}
```

Finally, we need to specify the expected outputs of our ksqlDB queries. Since our queries write to a topic called `greetings`, we will make assertions about what should appear in this output topic (after our queries handle the test data) by saving the following lines to a file called *output.json*:

```json
{
  "outputs": [
    {
      "topic": "greetings",
      "timestamp": 0,
      "value": {
        "greeting": "Hello, Isabelle"
      },
      "key": 0
    },
    {
      "topic": "greetings",
      "timestamp": 0,
      "value": {
        "greeting": "Hello, Elyse"
      },
      "key": 0
    }
  ]
}
```

With our three files created, we can now run the tests using the following command:

```
docker run \
    -v "$(pwd)":/ksqldb/ \
    -w /ksqldb \
    -ti confluentinc/ksqldb-server:0.14.0 \
    ksql-test-runner -s statements.sql -i input.json -o output.json
```

At the time of this writing, the output of the test tool was quite verbose, but you should see the following text somewhere in the output:

```
>>> Test passed!
```

If you accidentally introduce a breaking change later on, the tests will fail. For example, let's change the way the greeting column is created. Instead of greeting users with Hello, we will greet them with Good morning:

```
CREATE STREAM greetings
WITH (KAFKA_TOPIC = 'greetings') AS
SELECT ROWKEY, 'Good morning, ' + USERNAME AS "greeting"
FROM users
EMIT CHANGES;
```

If we rerun our tests again, they will fail. Of course, this is expected since we changed our query without changing the assertions in *output.json*:

```
>>>>> Test failed: Topic 'greetings', message 0:
  Expected <0, {"greeting":"Hello, Isabelle"}> with timestamp=0
  but was  <0, {greeting=Good morning, Isabelle}> with timestamp=0
```

This example is trivial, but the overarching idea is important. Testing your ksqlDB queries in this way will prevent accidental regressions and is highly advisable before shipping code changes to production.

> If you are leveraging custom ksqlDB functions (i.e., UDFs, UDAFs, and/or UDTFs), you will likely want to set up unit tests for the underlying Java code. The process is very similar to the unit testing strategy we cover a little later in Example 12-1, but for more information, please see my article, "ksqlDB UDFs and UDAFs Made Easy" on the Confluent blog (*https://oreil.ly/PUmD7*).

Now, let's look at how to test Kafka Streams applications, which is a little more involved (but still relatively simple).

Testing Kafka Streams

When you test a Kafka Streams application, you will need an automated testing framework for executing your tests. Which framework you work with is ultimately up to you, but the examples in this section will use JUnit for running the tests, and AssertJ for improving the readability of our assertions.

In addition to a testing framework, you will want to include the kafka-streams-test-utils library that is maintained and published as part of the official Kafka project. This library includes:

- A simulated runtime environment for executing Kafka Streams topologies
- Helper methods for reading and writing data in test Kafka topics
- Mock objects that can be used for unit testing processors and transforms

As usual with Kafka Streams projects, using third-party packages is simply a matter of updating our project's build file (*build.gradle*) with the appropriate dependencies. Therefore, in order to pull each of the aforementioned items into our Kafka Streams project (the testing framework and helper libraries), we can update our build file as follows:

```
dependencies {
  testImplementation "org.apache.kafka:kafka-streams-test-utils:${kafkaVersion}"
  testImplementation 'org.assertj:assertj-core:3.15.0'
  testImplementation 'org.junit.jupiter:junit-jupiter:5.6.2'
}

test {
  useJUnitPlatform()
}
```

With our test dependencies pulled into our project, we are ready to start writing some tests. Since there are many ways to test a Kafka Streams application, we will break this section into smaller subsections, each focused on a different testing strategy. Unless otherwise specified, the tests we will be creating will live in the *src/test/java*[1] directory of our project, and can be executed using the following command:

```
./gradlew test --info
```

Unit tests

Unit testing involves testing individual pieces of code. When you build a Kafka Streams topology, the *units* you will most commonly want to test are the individual processors that compose your topology. Since processors can be defined in different ways depending on whether you are using the DSL or the Processor API, your tests will differ depending on which API you are using. First, let's look at unit testing stream processors in the DSL.

DSL. When using the DSL, a common practice is to pass a lambda to one of the built-in Kafka Streams operators. For example, in the following topology definition, the logic for the `selectKey` operator is defined inline using a lambda function:

```
public class MyTopology {
  public Topology build() {
```

---

[1] For example, a topology test could be defined in a file called *src/test/java/com/magicalpipelines/GreeterTopologyTest.java*.

```
StreamsBuilder builder = new StreamsBuilder();
builder
    .stream("events", Consumed.with(Serdes.String(), Serdes.ByteArray()))
    .selectKey(
        (key, value) -> {   ❶
            // ...  ❷
            return newKey;
        })
    .to("events-repartitioned");

    return builder.build();
    }
}
```

❶ The selectKey logic has been defined inside a lambda.

❷ The logic has been omitted for brevity.

When the code inside the lambda is succinct and straightforward, this works well. However, for larger or more complicated pieces of code, you can improve the testability of your application by breaking out the logic into a dedicated method. For example, let's assume the logic we want to define for our selectKey operation spans many lines, and that we want to test this logic in isolation from the larger topology. In this case, we can replace the lambda with a method reference, as shown in the following code:

```
public class MyTopology {
    public Topology build() {
        StreamsBuilder builder = new StreamsBuilder();
        builder
            .stream("events", Consumed.with(Serdes.String(), Serdes.ByteArray()))
            .selectKey(MyTopology::decodeKey)  ❶
            .to("events-repartitioned");

    return builder.build();
    }

    public static String decodeKey(String key, byte[] payload) {
        // ...  ❷
        return newKey;
    }
}
```

❶ The lambda has been replaced by a method reference.

❷ The logic that was initially defined in the lambda has been moved to a dedicated method. This greatly improves the testability of our code. Once again, the actual logic has been omitted for brevity.

After the logic has been moved to a dedicated method, it is much easier to test. In fact, we don't even need the `kafka-streams-test-utils` package to test this code, since we can just use our testing framework to unit test this method, as shown in Example 12-1.

Example 12-1. A simple unit test for the selectKey topology step, which relies on a dedicated method called MyTopology.decodeKey

```
class MyTopologyTest {
  @Test
  public void testDecodeId() {
    String key = "1XRZTUW3";
    byte[] value = new byte[] {};
    String actualValue = MyTopology.decodeKey(key, value);  ❶
    String expectedValue = "decoded-1XRZTUW3";  ❷
    assertThat(actualValue).isEqualTo(expectedValue);  ❸
  }
}
```

❶ Our test will invoke the same method that we use in our `selectKey` processor. Here, we pass in a hardcoded key and value. We could also use a feature of JUnit called parameterized tests (*https://oreil.ly/0FYD9*) if we want to execute several iterations of this method using different key-value pairs.

❷ We define our expectations for what the output of our method should be.

❸ We use AssertJ to assert that the actual value that was returned by the `MyTopol ogy.decodeKey` method matches what we expect.

By testing our processing logic in this way, we can have very detailed and narrow test cases to help us identify and prevent regressions in our code. Furthermore, Kafka Streams applications are often composed of more than just a collection of processors. You may have various helper methods, utility classes, or custom Serdes implementations that support the topology in other ways. In this case, it's important to test these units of code as well, using the same approach we describe here.

This form of testing works really well with applications that use the DSL. However, when we're using the Processor API, there are some additional considerations with how we structure and execute our tests. We'll cover this in the next section.

Processor API. With the Processor API, we don't typically work with lambdas or method references when we define the logic for our stream processors. Instead, we work with classes that implement the `Processor` or `Transformer` interfaces. So our testing strategy is a little different because we need to mock the underlying

`ProcessorContext` that Kafka Streams passes to these lower-level stream processors when they are first initialized.

 When we refer to stream processors, we are not referring to the `Processor` interface. We are using this term in the broader sense to refer to any code that is responsible for applying data processing/ transformation logic to an input stream. When using the Processor API, a stream processor can either be an implementation of the `Pro cessor` or `Transformer` interface. If you need a refresher on the differences between these interfaces, please see "Processors and Transformers" on page 231.

To demonstrate how we can test a lower-level stream processor, let's implement a stateful transformer that tracks the number of records it has seen for each unique key. The implementation for the transformer we will be testing is shown in the following code block:

```java
public class CountTransformer
    implements ValueTransformerWithKey<String, String, Long> {

  private KeyValueStore<String, Long> store;

  @Override
  public void init(ProcessorContext context) { ❶
    this.store =
        (KeyValueStore<String, Long>) context.getStateStore("my-store"); ❷
  }

  @Override
  public Long transform(String key, String value) { ❸
    // process tombstones
    if (value == null) {
      store.delete(key);
      return null;
    }

    // get the previous count for this key,
    // or set to 0 if this is the first time
    // we've seen this key
    Long previousCount = store.get(key);
    if (previousCount == null) {
      previousCount = 0L;
    }

    // calculate the new count
    Long newCount = previousCount + 1;
    store.put(key, newCount);
    return newCount;
  }
```

```
  @Override
  public void close() {}
}
```

❶ Processor and Transformer implementations have an initialization function that accepts a `ProcessorContext`. This context is used for various tasks, like retrieving state stores and scheduling periodic functions.

❷ This transformer is stateful since it needs to remember the count for each unique key it sees, so we'll save a reference to the state store.

❸ The `transform` method contains the logic for this stream processor. The comments in this code block discuss the implementation details.

With our transformer in place, we can begin writing our unit test. Unlike the simple method-level tests we implemented in the previous section, this test will require us to use some helpers in the `kafka-streams-test-utils` package. Among other things, this package allows us to create `MockProcessorContext` objects, which enable us to access state and schedule punctuations without actually running our topology.

A common approach is to create the `MockProcessorContext` within a setup function, which runs before the unit tests are executed. If your processor is stateful, you will also need to initialize and register your state store. Furthermore, while your topology may use a persistent state store, it is recommended to use an in-memory store for unit tests. An example of how to set up a `MockProcessorContext` and register a state store is shown in the following code block:

```
public class CountTransformerTest {
  MockProcessorContext processorContext; ❶

  @BeforeEach ❷
  public void setup() {
    Properties props = new Properties(); ❸
    props.put(StreamsConfig.APPLICATION_ID_CONFIG, "test");
    props.put(StreamsConfig.BOOTSTRAP_SERVERS_CONFIG, "dummy:1234");
    processorContext = new MockProcessorContext(props); ❹

    KeyValueStore<String, Long> store = ❺
        Stores.keyValueStoreBuilder(
                Stores.inMemoryKeyValueStore("my-store"),
                Serdes.String(), Serdes.Long())
            .withLoggingDisabled()
            .build();

    store.init(processorContext, store); ❻
    processorContext.register(store, null);
  }
}
```

❶ We will save the `MockProcessorContext` object as an instance variable so that we can reference it later on in our tests.

❷ Our setup method is annotated with JUnit's `BeforeEach` annotation, which will cause this code block to execute before each test.

❸ In order to create a `MockProcessorContext`, we need to provide some Kafka Streams properties. Here, we only provide the two required properties.

❹ Instantiate a `MockProcessorContext` instance.

❺ Our transformer is stateful, so we create an in-memory state store for it to use.

❻ Initialize and register the state store, which primes it for use in our tests.

Once the `MockProcessorContext` has been created, you can simply instantiate and initialize your `Processor` or `Transformer` class using this context object, and then perform the unit tests. In the code block that follows, we show how to test our `Count Transformer` using this approach. Our test covers the basic counting behavior, and also the tombstone-processing behavior:

```
public class CountTransformerTest {
  MockProcessorContext processorContext;

  @BeforeEach
  public void setup() {
    // see the previous section
  }

  @Test ❶
  public void testTransformer() {
      String key = "123";
      String value = "some value";

      CountTransformer transformer = new CountTransformer(); ❷
      transformer.init(processorContext); ❸

      assertThat(transformer.transform(key, value)).isEqualTo(1L); ❹
      assertThat(transformer.transform(key, value)).isEqualTo(2L);
      assertThat(transformer.transform(key, value)).isEqualTo(3L);
      assertThat(transformer.transform(key, null)).isNull(); ❺
      assertThat(transformer.transform(key, value)).isEqualTo(1L);
  }
}
```

❶ JUnit's `Test` annotation signals that this method executes a test.

❷ Instantiate our `CountTransformer`.

❸ Initialize our `CountTransformer` instance with the `MockProcessorContext` that we initialized in the `setup` method.

❹ Test the behavior of our transformer. Since our `CountTransformer` counts the number of times it has seen each key, we perform a series of tests to ensure the count increments as expected.

❺ Our transformer also contains logic for processing tombstones (records with a key and a null value). In Kafka Streams, tombstones are used to signal that a record should be deleted from a state store. This line, and the one that follows it, ensures that the tombstone was processed correctly.

There are additional testing capabilities that the `MockProcessorContext` enables as well. For example, you can also test processors that rely on a punctuator function for flushing records to downstream processors. For more examples of how to unit test a lower-level processor, please see the official documentation (*https://oreil.ly/3YAbM*).

Behavioral Tests

Unit testing is helpful, but a Kafka Streams topology is usually composed of a collection of processors that work together. So how can we test the behavior of an entire topology? The answer, once again, is provided by the `kafka-streams-test-utils` package. This time, we will leverage a simulated runtime environment that is included in this library.

For demonstration purposes, let's create a very simple topology that we can use to build some tests.

The following code block shows a simple Kafka Streams topology that reads usernames from a topic called `users`, and produces a greeting for each user into a topic called `greetings`. However, there is one exception: if the user's name is Randy, we do not generate a greeting. This filtering condition will give us a slightly more interesting test scenario (and is not meant to offend anyone named Randy):

```
class GreeterTopology {

  public static String generateGreeting(String user) {
    return String.format("Hello %s", user);
  }

  public static Topology build() {
    StreamsBuilder builder = new StreamsBuilder();

    builder
        .stream("users", Consumed.with(Serdes.Void(), Serdes.String()))
        .filterNot((key, value) -> value.toLowerCase().equals("randy"))
        .mapValues(GreeterTopology::generateGreeting)
```

```
      .to("greetings", Produced.with(Serdes.Void(), Serdes.String())));

    return builder.build();
  }
}
```

Next, let's write a unit test that uses a test driver included in the Kafka Streams library called the *topology test driver*. This test driver allows us to pipe data into a Kafka Streams topology (in this case, the `GreeterTopology` we just defined), and to analyze the resulting data that is appended to the output topics. We'll start by defining a setup and teardown method for creating and destroying test driver instances, as shown here:

```
class GreeterTopologyTest {
  private TopologyTestDriver testDriver;
  private TestInputTopic<Void, String> inputTopic;
  private TestOutputTopic<Void, String> outputTopic;

  @BeforeEach
  void setup() {
    Topology topology = GreeterTopology.build(); ❶

    Properties props = new Properties(); ❷
    props.put(StreamsConfig.APPLICATION_ID_CONFIG, "test");
    props.put(StreamsConfig.BOOTSTRAP_SERVERS_CONFIG, "dummy:1234"); ❸

    testDriver = new TopologyTestDriver(topology, props); ❹

    inputTopic =
        testDriver.createInputTopic( ❺
            "users",
            Serdes.Void().serializer(),
            Serdes.String().serializer());

    outputTopic =
        testDriver.createOutputTopic( ❻
            "greetings",
            Serdes.Void().deserializer(),
            Serdes.String().deserializer());
  }

  @AfterEach
  void teardown() {
    testDriver.close(); ❼
  }
}
```

❶ Build the Kafka Streams topology.

❷ Configure Kafka Streams by supplying the two required configuration parameters.

❸ Since our topology will be running in a simulated runtime environment, the bootstrap servers don't need to be resolvable.

❹ Create a topology test driver. Test drivers contain several helper methods that make testing topologies very easy.

❺ The test driver includes a helper method for creating an input topic. Here, we create the users topic.

❻ The test driver also includes a helper method for creating an output topic. Here, we create the greetings topic.

❼ Make sure resources are cleaned up properly after each test by calling the TopologyTestDriver.close() method.

With a TopologyTestDriver instance being created for each test case, we can now write the topology tests. This simply involves piping messages to our input topic, and checking the output topic for the expected records. An example of this strategy is shown here:

```
class GreeterTopologyTest {
  // ...

  @Test
  void testUsersGreeted() {
    String value = "Izzy"; ❶

    inputTopic.pipeInput(value); ❷

    assertThat(outputTopic.isEmpty()).isFalse(); ❸

    List<TestRecord<Void, String>> outRecords =
      outputTopic.readRecordsToList(); ❹
    assertThat(outRecords).hasSize(1); ❺

    String greeting = outRecords.get(0).getValue(); ❻
    assertThat(greeting).isEqualTo("Hello Izzy");
  }
}
```

❶ Our test case will create a record to pipe into our input topic.

❷ Pipe the test record to our input topic. There is also an overloaded version of the pipeInput method that accepts a key and a value.

❸ Use the isEmpty() method to assert that the output topic contains at least one record.

❹ There are various ways to read the records in the output topic. Here, we read all of the output records into a list using the `readRecordsToList()` method. Some other methods you may want to check out include `readValue()`, `readKey Value()`, `readRecord()`, and `readKeyValuesToMap()`.

❺ Assert that there was only one output record (topologies that use `flatMap` operators may have a 1:N ratio of input to output records).

❻ Read the value of the output record. There are additional methods for accessing more record data, including `getKey()`, `getRecordTime()`, and `getHeaders()`.

The `TestOutputTopic.readRecordsToList()` method is useful when working with streams since it contains the entire sequence of output events. On the other hand, `TestOutputTopic.readKeyValuesToMap()` is useful when working with tables as opposed to streams, since it only contains the latest representation of each key. In fact, we've already discussed the close relationship between streams and lists (both of which use insert semantics) and tables and maps (both of which use update semantics) in "Stream/Table Duality" on page 57, and the relationship is modeled in these methods as well.

Benchmarking

While ksqlDB takes care of composing the underlying Kafka Streams topology for you, the freedom that comes with using the Kafka Streams DSL or Processor API directly introduces more vectors for potential performance regressions. For example, if you accidentally introduce a slow computational step, or rework your topology in a way that makes it less efficient, it will be much less painful to troubleshoot if you catch the regression before you ship the change to production.

To protect ourselves against performance regressions, we should run benchmarks against our code whenever we make changes to our Kafka Streams application. Luckily for us, we can combine the simulated runtime environment that the `kafka-streams-test-utils` package provides with a benchmarking framework like JMH to achieve this.

The first thing we need to do is simply add the `me.champeau.gradle.jmh` plug-in to our *build.gradle* file, and configure the `jmh` task that this plug-in creates. An example of how to do both is shown in the following code block:

```
plugins {
  id 'me.champeau.gradle.jmh' version '0.5.2'
}

jmh { ❶
  iterations = 4
```

```
    benchmarkMode = ['thrpt']
    threads = 1
    fork = 1
    timeOnIteration = '3s'
    resultFormat = 'TEXT'
    profilers = []

    warmupIterations = 3
    warmup = '1s'
}
```

❶ The jmh plug-in supports several configuration parameters. For a full list and description of these parameters, see the plug-in's documentation (*https://oreil.ly/vBYCb*).

Now, let's create a class for executing the benchmarks. Unlike the other Kafka Streams test code we've developed so far, the benchmarking code is expected to be in the *src/jmh/java* directory. Our benchmarking class is shown here:

```
public class TopologyBench {
  @State(org.openjdk.jmh.annotations.Scope.Thread)
  public static class MyState {
    public TestInputTopic<Void, String> inputTopic;

    @Setup(Level.Trial) ❶
    public void setupState() {
      Properties props = new Properties();
      props.put(StreamsConfig.APPLICATION_ID_CONFIG, "test");
      props.put(StreamsConfig.BOOTSTRAP_SERVERS_CONFIG, "dummy:1234");
      props.put(StreamsConfig.CACHE_MAX_BYTES_BUFFERING_CONFIG, 0);

      // build the topology
      Topology topology = GreeterTopology.build();

      // create a test driver. we will use this to pipe data to our topology
      TopologyTestDriver testDriver = new TopologyTestDriver(topology, props);

      testDriver = new TopologyTestDriver(topology, props);

      // create the test input topic
      inputTopic =
          testDriver.createInputTopic(
              "users", Serdes.Void().serializer(), Serdes.String().serializer());
    }
  }

  @Benchmark ❷
  @BenchmarkMode(Mode.Throughput) ❸
  @OutputTimeUnit(TimeUnit.SECONDS)
  public void benchmarkTopology(MyState state) {
    state.inputTopic.pipeInput("Izzy"); ❹
```

```
    }
}
```

❶ The `Setup` annotation is used to signal that this method should be executed before the benchmark. We use this method to set up the `TopologyTestDriver` instance and the input topics. The `Level.Trial` argument tells JMH that this method should be executed before each run of the benchmark. (Note: this does *not* mean the setup will be executed before each iteration.)

❷ The `Benchmark` annotation signals JMH that this is a benchmark method.

❸ Here, we set the benchmark mode to `Mode.Throughput`. This will measure the number of times, per second, this benchmarking method could be executed.

❹ Pipe a test record to the input topic.

Now that the benchmarking code has been created, we can execute the benchmarks with Gradle, using the following command:

```
$ ./gradlew jmh
```

You should see output similar to the following:

```
Benchmark                        Mode  Cnt     Score       Error  Units
TopologyBench.benchmarkTopology  thrpt    4  264794.572 ± 39462.097  ops/s
```

Does this mean your application can handle >264k messages per second? Not exactly. Remember that, like our topology tests in the previous section, our benchmarks are being executed in a simulated runtime environment. Furthermore, we aren't making any network calls to an external Kafka cluster like a production application would, and benchmarks are often executed on different hardware (e.g., a continuous integration server) than production workloads run on. Therefore, these numbers should only be used to establish a performance baseline for your topology, and to compare future benchmarking results against.

Kafka Cluster Benchmarking

Whether you're working with Kafka Streams or ksqlDB, you may also want to run performance tests at the Kafka cluster level. Kafka includes a couple of console scripts that can help with this, which allow you to measure read/write throughput, execute load and stress tests against your cluster, and determine how certain client settings (batch size, buffer memory, producer acks, consumer thread count) and input characteristics (record size, message volume) impact the performance of your cluster.

If you want to analyze the performance of producing data to a topic, you can use the `kafka-producer-perf-test` command. There are many available options, and the following example demonstrates several of them:

```
kafka-producer-perf-test \
  --topic users \
  --num-records 1000000 \
  --record-size 100 \
  --throughput -1 \
  --producer-props acks=1 \
  bootstrap.servers=kafka:9092 \
  buffer.memory=67108864 \
  batch.size=8196
```

Another useful version of this command involves specifying a payload file. The records in this file will be produced to the specified Kafka topic. The following code block will write three test records to a file called *input.json*:

```
cat <<EOF >./input.json
{"username": "Mitch", "user_id": 1}
{"username": "Isabelle", "user_id": 2}
{"username": "Elyse", "user_id": 3}
EOF
```

Now we can replace the `--record-size` flag with the `--payload-file input.json` argument to run the performance test using our hardcoded input records:

```
kafka-producer-perf-test \
  --topic users \
  --num-records 1000000 \
  --payload-file input.json \
  --throughput -1 \
  --producer-props acks=1 \
  bootstrap.servers=kafka:9092 \
  buffer.memory=67108864 \
  batch.size=8196
```

An example performance report is shown here:

```
1000000 records sent, 22166.559528 records/sec (0.76 MB/sec),
58.45 ms avg latency, 465.00 ms max latency,
65 ms 50th, 165 ms 95th, 285 ms 99th, 380 ms 99.9th.
```

There is also a console script for running consumer performance tests. An example invocation is shown in the following code:

```
kafka-consumer-perf-test \
  --bootstrap-server kafka:9092 \
  --messages 100000 \
  --topic users \
  --threads 1

# example output (modified to fit)
start.time              end.time               data.consumed.in.MB
2020-09-17 01:23:41:932 2020-09-17 01:23:42:817 9.5747

MB.sec    data.consumed.in.nMsg   nMsg.sec
10.8189   100398
```

Final Thoughts on Testing

Consider setting up an automated workflow for running tests whenever you make a change to your code. An example workflow is as follows:

- All code changes are pushed to a separate branch in your version control system (e.g., GitHub, Bitbucket).

- When a developer wants to merge a code change, they should open a pull request.

- When the pull request is opened, the tests are executed automatically using a system like Jenkins, Travis, GitHub Actions, etc.

- If one or more tests fail, merging should be blocked. Otherwise, if the checks pass, your code is ready for review.

Workflows like this one may be second nature for many readers. But automated tests play an important role in avoiding code regressions, so it's worth reviewing our testing practices and workflows on a regular basis.

Now that we've learned how to test ksqlDB and Kafka Streams applications, let's take a look at another important prerequisite for shipping software to production: monitoring.

Monitoring

Monitoring is a huge topic, and often involves many different technologies. Therefore, this section will not attempt to cover every approach in detail, but will provide a checklist for the different types of monitoring you will want to have in place and some example technologies that you may want to use.

However, there is one piece of the Kafka Streams and ksqlDB monitoring puzzle that we will cover in technical detail. Both technologies include a set of built-in JMX metrics,[2] and being able to extract these metrics will greatly enhance the observability of our applications and queries. We will cover metric extraction in technical detail a little later. But first, let's look at the monitoring checklist.

---

2 JMX stands for *Java Management Extensions*, and it is used for monitoring and managing resources. The Kafka Streams library registers and updates a set of JMX metrics, which provide insight into how the application is performing. Since ksqlDB is built on top of Kafka Streams, it gets these JMX metrics for free.

Monitoring Checklist

The following table shows some monitoring strategies you will likely want to have in place for your production Kafka Streams and ksqlDB applications:

Monitoring strategy	What should you monitor?	Example technology
Cluster monitoring	• Under-replicated partitions • Consumer lag • Offset advancement • Topic throughput	kafka_exporter[a]
Log monitoring	• Total log rate • Error log rate	ELK, ElastAlert, Cloud Logging
Metric monitoring	• Consumption rate • Production rate • Process latency • Poll time	Prometheus
Custom instrumentation[b]	• Business metrics	OpenCensus
Profiling	• Deadlocks • Hot spots	YourKit
Visualizations	• All of the above	Grafana
Alerting	• SLOs (service-level objectives)	Alertmanager

[a] See *https://github.com/danielqsj/kafka_exporter*.
[b] Primarily used for Kafka Streams.

Extracting JMX Metrics

Both Kafka Streams and ksqlDB expose metrics via Java Management Extensions (JMX). When you run a Kafka Streams application or ksqlDB server, you can access these metrics using something called JConsole, and this is the direction most tutorials take. If you are running JConsole on the same machine as Kafka Streams and/or ksqlDB, you can simply run the `jconsole` command without any arguments to inspect the JMX metrics.

For example, the following code snippet shows how to set various system properties for enabling remote JMX monitoring (*https://oreil.ly/JK4pg*), and run ksqlDB with JMX enabled:

```
docker-compose up ❶

MY_IP=$(ipconfig getifaddr en0); ❷

docker run \ ❸
    --net=chapter-12_default \ ❹
    -p 1099:1099  \
    -v "$(pwd)/ksqldb":/ksqldb \
```

```
    -e KSQL_JMX_OPTS="\ ❺
        -Dcom.sun.management.jmxremote \
        -Djava.rmi.server.hostname=$MY_IP \
        -Dcom.sun.management.jmxremote.port=1099 \
        -Dcom.sun.management.jmxremote.rmi.port=1099 \
        -Dcom.sun.management.jmxremote.authenticate=false \
        -Dcom.sun.management.jmxremote.ssl=false" \
    -ti confluentinc/ksqldb-server:0.14.0 \
    ksql-server-start /ksqldb/config/server.properties ❻
```

❶ The source code includes a Docker Compose setup for running a Kafka cluster. Our ksqlDB server instance that we'll run a couple of lines down will talk to this Kafka cluster.

❷ Save your IP to an environment variable. We will reference this in the JMX properties further down so that we can expose the JMX metrics over this IP.

❸ Run a ksqlDB server instance with JMX enabled.

❹ Since we're running our ksqlDB server manually outside of Docker Compose, we can connect to the Docker network using the --net flag.

❺ Set the system properties needed to access the JMX metrics.

❻ Start the ksqlDB server instance.

You can open JConsole with the following command:

```
jconsole $MY_IP:1099
```

If you click the MBeans tab, you will see all of the available metrics that are exposed by your Kafka Streams or ksqlDB application. For example, Figure 12-1 shows the metric list for a ksqlDB server. Since ksqlDB is built on top of Kafka Streams, and since Kafka Streams is built on top of the lower-level Kafka Consumer and Kafka Producer clients, you will see metrics reported by each of the underlying libraries.

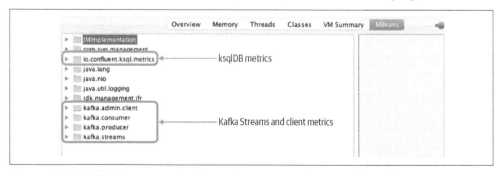

Figure 12-1. Kafka Streams–related metric groups as shown in JConsole

You can drill down into each group to view some metadata and the values for each metric, as shown in Figure 12-2.

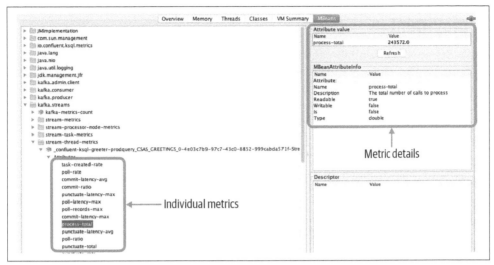

Figure 12-2. A more detailed view of some of the Kafka Streams metrics

While JConsole is great for inspecting metrics on the fly in a testing or development environment, when it's time to deploy your software to production, you'll want a more robust solution that is capable of storing historical datasets, performing queries against your data, and integrating with alerting systems.

At the time of this writing, the technology that I recommend for working with Kafka Streams and ksqlDB JMX metrics is Prometheus. In order to get metrics into Prometheus, you need an exporter that will expose the metrics over an HTTP endpoint. Setting up the exporter for both Kafka Streams and ksqlDB instances is similar. You'll need to:

- Download the Prometheus JMX exporter JAR (*https://oreil.ly/t-7Lg*).
- Start Kafka Streams or ksqlDB with the following flag:

      -javaagent:./jmx_prometheus_javaagent-0.14.0.jar=8080:config.yaml

- Configure Prometheus to scrape the HTTP endpoint, which is the IP address or hostname where your Kafka Streams or ksqlDB application is running, followed by the port number that was configured to expose the JMX metrics.

The source code for this chapter includes a full example of using Prometheus with Kafka Streams and ksqlDB. We have omitted the technical details of Prometheus from this text since it's an implementation detail, but the main takeaway is that regardless of whether you use Prometheus or another monitoring system, you should export the built-in JMX metrics provided by Kafka Streams and ksqlDB to an external system to improve the observability of your application.

Deployment

Kafka Streams and ksqlDB can run on bare-metal machines, inside VMs, or using containers. The recommended path, however, is to containerize your application using Docker. Some of the benefits of this approach include:

- Containers provide a lightweight, isolated runtime environment for your code to run in.

- Storing, managing, sharing, and maintaining multiple versions of containers is extremely easy using both private and public container registries.[3]

- Containers allow you to decouple the underlying infrastructure from your code. This means you can easily run the same container on-premise, on colocated servers, on a multitude of cloud platforms, or even on your local machine.

Let's take a look at how to work with both technologies using containers.

ksqlDB Containers

Confluent has already published official container images for both the ksqlDB server and CLI. When you are ready to deploy your queries to production, you can use the official ksqlDB server container image (`confluentinc/ksqldb-server`) or a derivative image if you need to make adjustments to the runtime environment.[4]

The official ksqlDB server image allows you to specify virtually any of the ksqlDB configuration properties using an environment variable. However, this has a few downsides:

- Configuration should be version controlled. Setting all of your ksqlDB properties using environment variables makes this difficult.

- The commands for running the container image can become large and unwieldy for configuration-heavy applications.

- Setting environment variables is a shortcut for mounting an actual configuration file inside a container, but if you are running ksqlDB in headless mode or using

---

3 Docker Hub, Artifactory, and Google Container Registry are some popular container registries.

4 A derivative image would simply specify the official ksqlDB image as the base image using the FROM instruction at the top of the Dockerfile. Any customizations to the environment would be specified in the Dockerfile.

certain data integration features, you will still need to mount files inside the container.

Therefore, instead of relying purely on environment variables to configure production ksqlDB server instances, I recommend mounting a version-controlled configuration file inside the container. For example, let's save our ksqlDB server configuration to a file called *config/server.properties* on our local machine. We'll keep the contents of this file simple for demonstration purposes, but you can include any of the available ksqlDB properties in your configuration file (see Appendix B):

```
bootstrap.servers=kafka:9092
ksql.service.id=greeter-prod
```

We can mount this configuration inside the official container image, and invoke the `ksql-server-start` command:

```
docker run \
  --net=chapter-12_default \ ❶
  -v "$(pwd)/config":/config \ ❷
  -ti confluentinc/ksqldb-server:0.14.0 \
  ksql-server-start /config/server.properties ❸
```

❶   This flag is specific to our tutorial, and allows us to connect to the Kafka cluster running in our Docker Compose environment.

❷   Mount a configuration from our host system to the running container.

❸   Start the ksqlDB server instance with the mounted configuration file.

Recall that there are a couple of ksqlDB configurations that reference another file path:

`ksql.connect.worker.config`
> An optional configuration that specifies the location of the Kafka Connect worker configs if running Kafka Connect in embedded mode (see Figure 9-3).

`queries.file`
> When running ksqlDB server in headless mode, this config specifies the location of the queries file to execute.

Whenever your configuration includes either of these properties, you'll need to mount the file referenced by these configs inside your container as well. Now, let's see how to run Kafka Streams applications inside containers.

Kafka Streams Containers

Running Kafka Streams inside a container is slightly more involved, but it's still pretty simple. You could easily create your own Docker image using a lower-level base image.[5] However, a simpler option is to use a popular image builder called Jib (*https:// oreil.ly/xjvpR*), which was developed by Google and simplifies the way Java applications are containerized and distributed.

In order to use Jib, you'll need to add the Jib dependency to your build file. Since we've been using Gradle as our build system in this book, we'll add the following to our *build.gradle* file:

```
plugins {
  id 'com.google.cloud.tools.jib' version '2.1.0'
}

jib {
  to {
    image = 'magicalpipelines/myapp:0.1.0'
  }
  container {
    jvmFlags = []
    mainClass = application.mainClassName
    format = 'OCI'
  }
}
```

We can use a variety of different naming schemes for our image, depending on whether or not we want Jib to automatically push our image to a container registry, and which container registry we want our Docker image pushed to. The official Jib documentation (*https://oreil.ly/3C-09*) is the best resource for the available container registries and naming schemes, but at the time of this writing, the following container registries were supported:

- Docker Hub
- Google Container Registry (GCR)
- Amazon Elastic Container Registry (ECR)
- Azure Container Registry (ACR)

Once your build file has been updated, you can execute one of the following tasks:

---

5 An example of a suitable base image is `openjdk:8-jdk-slim`.

```
./gradlew jib
```
> This task will build your container image *and* push the resulting container image to a container registry. You must be authenticated to the desired container registry for this to work.

```
./gradlew jibDockerBuild
```
> This task will build your container image using the local Docker daemon, and will *not* push your image to a container registry. This is the easiest way to test that your image can be built.

For demonstration purposes, we'll simply build the Docker image locally by executing the following command:

```
./gradlew jibDockerBuild
```

You should see output similar to the following:

```
Built image to Docker daemon as magicalpipelines/myapp:0.1.0
```

The Docker image tag referenced in the output contains our Kafka Streams application, and can be executed on any machine that is capable of running containers. This brings us on par with ksqlDB at this point since we now have the ability to run either ksqlDB or Kafka Streams workloads using a container. So how should we execute these containers? We'll provide one recommendation in the next section.

Container Orchestration

We strongly believe that the best way to run a Kafka Streams or ksqlDB application is to use a container orchestration system, like Kubernetes. This has the following benefits:

- If the node your container is running on fails, then the orchestrator will automatically move the container to a healthy node.

- It's easy to scale your workloads by increasing the replica count for your containers.

- The underlying infrastructure is abstracted away. However, in cases where you still want some control over where your containers run, you can use *node selectors* or *affinity* rules to gain more control.

- You can easily deploy so-called *sidecar* containers, which run alongside your Kafka Streams or ksqlDB containers, to provide services like:

  — Collecting and exporting metrics to monitoring systems

  — Log shipping

  — Communication proxies (for example, if you want to put an authentication layer in front of a Kafka Streams app where interactive queries are enabled;

this is much easier than building an authentication and authorization layer inside your Kafka Streams application)

- It's easy to coordinate rolling restarts of your application when you push a code update.

- Support for StatefulSet resources provide persistent and stable storage for stateful topologies.

Exploring Kubernetes in detail is beyond the scope of this book, but there are many great resources on this topic, including *Kubernetes: Up and Running* by Brendan Burns et al. (O'Reilly) (*https://oreil.ly/3YzEh*).

Operations

In this last section, we will cover a few operational tasks that you are likely to encounter while maintaining a Kafka Streams or ksqlDB application.

Resetting a Kafka Streams Application

In some cases, you may need to reset a Kafka Streams application. A common use case is if you discover a bug in your system and need to reprocess all or a subset of the data in your Kafka topics. To facilitate this, the maintainers of Kafka built an application reset tool, which is distributed with the Kafka source (*https://oreil.ly/zNwrL*).

This tool can theoretically be used for ksqlDB as well. However, you need to know the consumer group in order to use this tool. In Kafka Streams, there is a direct mapping between the `applica tion.id` config and the consumer group ID. However, in ksqlDB, there is *not* a direct mapping between the `service.id` and the consumer group.

Therefore, if you adapt these instructions to reset a ksqlDB application, please be extra careful and ensure that you identify the correct consumer group for your application (the `kafka-consumer-groups` console script can help with this).

This tool does a few things:

- Updates the consumer offset to the specified position on the *source topics*
- Skips to the end of *intermediate topics*
- Deletes *internal changelog and repartition topics*

Special care must be taken when using this tool with stateful applications, since this tool does not reset application state. Please be sure to read the following instructions in their entirety so you don't miss the crucial step.

In order to use the reset tool, follow these steps:

1. Stop all instances of your application. Do not proceed to the next step until the consumer group is inactive. You can determine whether or not the group is inactive by running the following command. Inactive consumer groups will show the state as Empty in the output:

   ```
   kafka-consumer-groups \
       --bootstrap-server kafka:9092 \ ❶
       --describe \
       --group dev \ ❷
       --state
   ```

   ❶ Update the bootstrap server with the host/port pair of one of your brokers.

   ❷ The group is specified by the application.id setting in Kafka Streams. If you are resetting a ksqlDB application, there unfortunately isn't a direct correlation between ksqlDB's service.id parameter and the consumer group name.

2. Run the application reset tool with the appropriate parameters. A full list of parameters and detailed usage information can be viewed by running the following command:

   ```
   kafka-streams-application-reset --help
   ```

   For example, if we wanted to reset the greeter application we created earlier in this chapter, we could run the following:

   ```
   kafka-streams-application-reset \
       --application-id dev \
       --bootstrap-servers kafka:9092 \
       --input-topics users \
       --to-earliest
   ```

   The output will look similar to the following:

   ```
   Reset-offsets for input topics [users]
   Following input topics offsets will be reset to (for consumer group dev)
   Topic: users Partition: 3 Offset: 0
   Topic: users Partition: 2 Offset: 0
   Topic: users Partition: 1 Offset: 0
   Topic: users Partition: 0 Offset: 0
   Done.
   ```

```
Deleting all internal/auto-created topics for application dev
Done.
```

3. If your application is *stateless*, you can restart your application instances after running the `kafka-streams-application-reset` command. Otherwise, if your application is stateful, you will need to reset your application's state *before restarting*. There are two ways to reset your application state:

   - Manually remove each state directory.

   - Invoke the `KafkaStreams.cleanUp` method in your code (Kafka Streams only). You should only do this the first time you restart your application after the reset tool has been executed.

Once your application state has been cleaned up using either of the preceding methods, you can restart your application.

Rate-Limiting the Output of Your Application

Kafka Streams and ksqlDB are capable of high throughput, but you may find yourself in a situation where the downstream systems that are processing your output topics can't keep up with the volume. In this case, you may want to rate-limit the output of your application using the *record cache*.

When using the Kafka Streams DSL or ksqlDB, the record cache can help reduce the number of output records that are written to state stores and also the number of records that are forwarded to downstream processors. When using the Processor API, the record cache is only capable of reducing the number of records that are written to state stores.

Each stream thread (controlled by the `num.stream.threads` parameter) is allocated an even share of the total cache size. So if your total cache size is `10485760` (i.e., 10 MB) and your application is configured to run with 10 threads, then each thread will be allocated approximately 1 MB of memory for its record cache.

This setting is extremely important in improving the performance of not only your application, but also downstream systems that rely on the data your application produces to Kafka. To understand why, let's consider a topology that needs to count the number of messages it sees per key. If you have the following sequence of events:

- `<key1, value1>`
- `<key1, value2>`
- `<key1, value3>`

Then a topology that performs a count aggregation without the record cache disabled (i.e., with `cache.max.bytes.buffering` set to 0) would produce the following sequence of aggregations:

- `<key1, 1>`
- `<key1, 2>`
- `<key1, 3>`

However, if this sequence of updates occurs quickly enough (e.g., within a few milliseconds or seconds of each other), do you really need to know about every single intermediate state (`<key1, 1>` and `<key1, 2>`)? There isn't a right or wrong answer to this question, it just depends on your use case and the semantics you wish to achieve. If you want to rate-limit the application and reduce the number of intermediate states you see, then you may want to use the record cache.

If you allocate some memory for a record cache using this config, then Kafka Streams and ksqlDB could potentially reduce the original sequence of aggregations to simply:

- `<key1, 3>`

The record cache may not always be able to reduce the output records completely since there are multiple items at play here, including when the cache is flushed and when the messages arrive. However, this is an important lever that can be used to reduce the output of your application. When your application writes less, downstream processors in the topology itself, and downstream systems that operate on the data outside of Kafka Streams and ksqlDB, have less data to process.

Please see the official documentation (*https://oreil.ly/ddP7x*) for more information about this important setting.

Upgrading Kafka Streams

At the time of this writing, Apache Kafka (including Kafka Streams) was on a time-based release plan. Therefore, you should expect a new version of Kafka Streams to be released every four months. The versioning strategy is shown here:

```
major.minor.bug-fix
```

In most cases, the four-month release cadence applies to minor versions. For example, `2.5.0` was released in April 2020, and `2.6.0` was released four months later, in August 2020. In rare cases, you may see a major version bump for more impactful changes (e.g., changes to the Kafka message format or major changes to the public API) or when significant milestones are reached in the project. Bug fixes are common and can occur at any time.

Whenever you upgrade Kafka Streams, it's important to follow the upgrade guide that is published to the official Kafka website (*https://oreil.ly/DohxP*) for each release. In some cases, you may be required to set the `upgrade.from` parameter to the older version, and then perform a series of restarts to make sure the upgrade is performed safely. This is especially true if you wait a while before upgrading (e.g., if you are upgrading from `2.3.0` to `2.6.0`).

There are a few options for staying informed of new releases:

- Sign up for one or more of the official mailing lists (*https://oreil.ly/LkcYH*) to receive release announcements.

- Visit the official GitHub repository for Apache Kafka, and "watch" the project (there's a Releases Only option if you want to cut down on the noise). You can also star the project while you're at it to support the people who work on Kafka Streams and the wider Kafka ecosystem.

- Follow @apachekafka on Twitter (*https://oreil.ly/3cblY*).

Upgrading ksqlDB

ksqlDB is rapidly evolving, and is likely to have breaking changes from time to time that make the upgrade path a little more precarious. Taken from the official ksqlDB documentation:

> Until version 1.0 of ksqlDB, each minor release will potentially have breaking changes in it, which means that you can't simply update the ksqlDB binaries and restart the server(s).
>
> The data models and binary formats used within ksqlDB are in flux. This means data local to each ksqlDB node and stored centrally within internal Kafka topics may not be compatible with the new version you're trying to deploy.
>
> —ksqldb.io

In fact, the documentation even goes so far as to discourage upgrades after you've deployed to production, *until* backward compatibility can be promised.[6] However, this doesn't mean you *shouldn't* upgrade; it just highlights the uncertainty around what some upgrades entail, how they should be performed, and what (if any) potential breaking changes a certain upgrade will bring. You should always consult the official ksqlDB documentation (*https://docs.ksqldb.io*) before upgrading a ksqlDB cluster.

---

6 The exact quote from the documentation is: "If you're running ksqlDB in production, and you don't yet need the features or fixes the new version brings, consider delaying any upgrade until either another release has features or fixes you need, or until ksqlDB reaches version 1.0 and promises backward compatibility."

Summary

Both Kafka Streams and ksqlDB include testing utilities that allow us to build confidence in our code before shipping it to production, and help us avoid unintended code regressions as we continue to make changes and improvements to our applications over time. Furthermore, no matter which technology you are using, it's easy to maintain visibility about how the application is operating using the built-in JMX metrics. We can also make our applications highly portable by running them in a containerized environment, whether that involves building our own application-specific Docker images for Kafka Streams applications or using Confluent-maintained images for running our ksqlDB server and CLI instances.

The additional tips we provided about monitoring, benchmarking, rate-limiting, and resetting your applications will help you productionize and maintain your stream processing applications. I am confident that this knowledge, alongside the rest of the information offered in this book, will help you solve a wide range of business problems using two of the best technologies in the stream processing space.

Congratulations, you've made it to the end of this book.

Kafka Streams Configuration

Kafka Streams is highly configurable, and the available parameters, as well as their default values, are a moving target. Therefore, the configuration properties listed in this appendix should be used as a starting point for familiarizing yourself with the various configuration parameters, but please refer to the official documentation (*https://oreil.ly/-dIwr*) for the latest information.

Configuration Management

In this book, we've been configuring Kafka Streams applications by creating a `Proper ties` instance, and setting the various configuration parameters manually. An example of this strategy is shown in the following code:

```
class App {

  public static void main(String[] args) {
    Topology topology = GreeterTopology.build();

    Properties config = new Properties();
    config.put(StreamsConfig.APPLICATION_ID_CONFIG, "dev-consumer");
    config.put(StreamsConfig.BOOTSTRAP_SERVERS_CONFIG, "kafka:9092");

    KafkaStreams streams = new KafkaStreams(topology, config);

    // ....
  }
}
```

However, when it's time to ship your application to production, you should consider loading your configuration from a file, instead of hardcoding the values directly in your application. Being able to make configuration changes without touching code is less error-prone, and if the configuration file can be overridden at runtime (e.g., via a system flag), then it's extremely easy to manage multiple deployments of your application.[1]

A full discussion of configuration management strategies for Java applications (including Kafka Streams) is beyond the scope of this book, but the source code for this appendix shows how to manage multiple configurations for a single Kafka Streams application using a library called Typesafe Config (*https://oreil.ly/i42AO*).

Regardless of how you *manage* your configurations, the values you provide for the configuration parameters in either Kafka Streams or ksqlDB can impact the performance of your application. Therefore, most of this section will focus on the configuration parameters themselves. Let's start by looking at the Kafka Streams-specific parameters.

Configuration Properties

First of all, two parameters are required when configuring your Kafka Streams application:

application.id
> A unique identifier for your Kafka Streams application. You can run multiple *application instances* with the same application.id to distribute the workload across many machines/processes. Under the hood, this identifier is used for several things, including:
>
> - The consumer group ID
> - A prefix for internal topic names (i.e., repartition and changelog topics created by Kafka Streams)
> - The default client.id prefix for the underlying producers and consumers used by the Kafka Streams library
> - A subdirectory for persistent state stores (see Example 6-1)

bootstrap.servers
> A list of host and port pairs corresponding to one or more Kafka brokers. This will be used to establish a connection to the Kafka cluster.

There are also several optional parameters:

acceptable.recovery.lag
> The maximum amount of lag (i.e., number of unread records) a Kafka Streams task can have on the input partition in order to be considered "warm" and ready

---

[1] You may have multiple deployments if your application needs to process data in multiple Kafka clusters, or if your application needs to be deployed to different environments (e.g., staging, QA, production).

for a task assignment. When a stateful application instance needs to recover part or all of its state, you may not want Kafka Streams to assign it work while it's recovering. If this is the case, then you can set this parameter to allow application instances to only receive a task assignment when their lag falls beneath this threshold.

`cache.max.bytes.buffering`

This controls the size of the record cache in Kafka Streams. We talk about the record cache in more detail in "Rate-Limiting the Output of Your Application" on page 376. Setting this to a value greater than 0 will enable the record cache, and can have the effect of rate-limiting the output of your application.

`default.deserialization.exception.handler`

The class that should be used for handling deserialization errors. We discuss this in a tip on "Handling Deserialization Errors in Kafka Streams" on page 75. Built-in options include `LogAndContinueExceptionHandler` and `LogAndFailExceptionHandler`. The former is more permissive and allows Kafka Streams to continue processing records if a deserialization error occurs. The latter will cause Kafka Streams to log the exception and cease processing. You can also implement the `DeserializationExceptionHandler` interface, which is included in the Kafka Streams library, to define a custom handler.

`default.production.exception.handler`

The class that should be used for handling errors related to producing data to Kafka. For example, if a record is too large, the underlying producer will throw an exception that needs to be handled in some way. By default, the built-in `DefaultProductionExceptionHandler` class is used, which will cause Kafka Streams to fail and shut down. Another option is to use the `AlwaysContinueProductionExceptionHandler` class, which will allow Kafka Streams to continue processing data, or to implement `ProductionExceptionHandler` interface if you want to provide your own, custom logic.

`default.timestamp.extractor`

A class that should be used for associating a given record with a timestamp. We discuss this in detail in "Timestamp Extractors" on page 150.

`default.key.serde, default.value.serde`

The default class to be used for serializing and deserializing record keys (`default.key.serde`) and values (`default.value.serde`). In this book, we have mostly defined our Serdes classes inline. For example:

```
KStream<byte[], Tweet> stream =
    builder.stream(
        "tweets",
        Consumed.with(Serdes.ByteArray(), JsonSerdes.Tweet()));  ❶
```

❶ Both the key Serdes (`Serdes.ByteArray()`) and the value Serdes (`Json Serdes.Tweet()`) are defined inline in this example.

We could have instead set the default Serdes classes using these two configuration parameters, and omitted the `Consumed.with(...)` line, which would have prompted Kafka Streams to use the default classes specified by these parameters.

`max.task.idle.ms`
> The maximum amount of time a streams task should wait for all of its partition buffers to contain data. Higher values could increase latency but could prevent out-of-order data when a task is reading from multiple input partitions (e.g., in the case of a join).

`max.warmup.replicas`
> The number of replicas (in addition to the `num.standbys`) that can be used for warming up a task.

`metrics.recording.level`
> The level of granularity for metrics that are captured by Kafka Streams. This defaults to `INFO`, but you can override this to `DEBUG` if you want more visibility into your application. Metrics are reported via Java Management Extensions (JMX), and we discuss how to capture these metrics in "Extracting JMX Metrics" on page 367.

`num.standby.replicas`
> The number of replicas to create for each state store. This helps reduce downtime, since if a stateful task goes offline, Kafka Streams can reassign the work to another application instance that has the replicated state, thus avoiding the expensive operation of rebuilding a task's state from scratch. We talk about standby replicas in depth in "Standby Replicas" on page 180.

`num.stream.threads`
> As you may recall from "Tasks and Stream Threads" on page 41, stream threads are what execute the Kafka Streams tasks. Increasing the thread count can help you take full advantage of the available CPU resources on your machine, and will improve performance. For example, if your Kafka Streams application is reading from a single topic that contains eight partitions, then it will create eight tasks. You can execute these tasks across one, two, or even four threads if you want (the number is up to you, as long as it's less than or equal to the number of tasks), but if you're running on a machine that has eight cores, then increasing the thread count to eight will allow you to parallelize work across all of the available cores.
>
> This configuration is especially important for maximizing the throughput of your application.

`processing.guarantee`

Supported values include:

`at_least_once`

Records may be redelivered during certain failure conditions (e.g., networking issues or broker failures that cause a producer to resend a message to a source topic). However, records are never lost. This is the default processing guarantee in Kafka Streams and is ideal for latency-sensitive applications whose correctness is not impacted by reprocessing duplicate records.

`exactly_once`

Records are processed exactly once using a transactional producer and an embedded consumer with a `read_committed` isolation level.[2] Your application may be more susceptible to consumer lag with this processing guarantee (there is a relatively small performance penalty for transactional writes), but the correctness of some applications requires exactly-once processing. This option requires your brokers to be on version 0.11.0 or higher.

`exactly_once_beta`

This option enables exactly-once processing guarantees (see preceding bullet) with improved scalability and reduced overhead for the Streams application.[3] This option requires your brokers to be on version 2.5 or higher.

`replication.factor`

The replication factor for internal changelog or repartition topics created by Kafka Streams. Remember that not all topologies will result in an internal topic being created, but if you rekey any records or perform a stateful aggregation (and have explicitly disabled change logging), then an internal topic will be created (the name of the topic will be prefixed by the `application.id`). The recommended setting is 3, which will allow you to tolerate up to two broker failures.

`rocksdb.config.setter`

A custom class to be used for configuring RocksDB state stores. This configuration may be of interest for those who are fine-tuning a stateful application. Configuring RocksDB using a custom class is generally not needed, but the official documentation (*https://oreil.ly/AdQah*) provides an example in case you are interested. This is usually not the first knob you will turn when trying to optimize for performance, but we include it here because you should know it's an

---

2 This isolation level ensures the consumer will not read any messages from failed/aborted transactions.

3 `exactly_once` will create a transactional producer per input partition. `exactly_once_beta` will create a transactional producer per streams thread. The ability to achieve exactly-once semantics with less producers (using the `exactly_once_beta` option) can reduce the application's memory footprint and reduce the number of network connections to the brokers.

option for situations where you need to squeeze more performance out of your application and have identified RocksDB as the bottleneck.

state.dir
> A directory name (expressed as an absolute path, e.g., */tmp/kafka-streams*) where state stores should be created. We discuss this configuration in "Persistent Store Disk Layout" on page 176. The important thing to remember is to never have multiple application instances with the same `application.id` writing to the same state store directory.

topology.optimization
> Set this to `all` (i.e., `StreamsConfig.OPTIMIZE`) if you want Kafka Streams to perform some internal optimizations (e.g., reducing the number of repartition topics, which can save network trips, or preventing unnecessary creation of changelog topics when a `KTable` is created from a source topic) to make your code run more efficiently. At the time of this writing, topology optimization was disabled by default.

upgrade.from
> This parameter is used when upgrading Kafka Streams. We discuss this in more detail on "Upgrading Kafka Streams" on page 377.

Consumer-Specific Configurations

You can also configure the different consumers used by Kafka Streams by using the following configuration prefixes:

main.consumer.
> Use this prefix to configure the *default consumer* used for stream sources.

restore.consumer.
> Use this prefix to configure the *restore consumer*, which is used for recovering state stores from changelog topics.

global.consumer.
> Use this prefix to configure the *global consumer*, which is used for populating `GlobalKTable`'s.

ksqlDB Configuration

ksqlDB accepts most Kafka Streams and Kafka Client (i.e., producer and consumer) configurations. The recommended pattern is to prefix all Kafka Streams and Kafka Client configs with `ksql.streams`. For example, if you want to configure a record cache using the `cache.max.bytes.buffering` parameter in Kafka Streams, you would set the `ksql.streams.cache.max.bytes.buffering` parameter in your *server.properties* file. Furthermore, if you want to configure the `auto.offset.reset` Kafka Consumer configuration, this would also be prefixed the same way, and would become `ksql.streams.auto.offset.reset`. Technically, the prefix is optional, but comes as a recommendation from the creators of ksqlDB (Confluent).

In addition to the standard Kafka Streams and Kafka Client configs, ksqlDB also allows you to specify a Kafka Connect configuration if you are using ksqlDB's data integration features (e.g., whenever you are executing a `CREATE {SOURCE|SINK} CON NECTOR` statement). We've already discussed this in "Configuring Connect Workers" on page 268, so please see that section for more detail.

Finally, there are several configurations that are specific to ksqlDB. We have grouped some of the most important configurations into two categories: query configurations and server configurations. This page should be used as a starting point for configuring ksqlDB. Please refer to the official documentation for a full list of ksqlDB configuration parameters.[1]

---

1 The official documentation is here: *https://docs.ksqldb.io*. Some of the configuration descriptions included in this appendix were derived directly from this documentation.

Query Configurations

The following configurations control various aspects of how ksqlDB actually executes queries:

`ksql.service.id`

This *required* property serves a similar purpose as Kafka Streams' `application.id` parameter: it identifies a group of cooperating applications and allows work to be distributed across all instances that share the same identifier. Unlike Kafka Streams' `application.id`, however, there is not a direct correlation between ksqlDB's `service.id` and the consumer group ID.

Default: no default

`ksql.streams.bootstrap.servers`

This *required* property specifies a list of host/port pairs of the Kafka brokers that should be used for establishing an initial connection to the Kafka cluster.

Default: no default

`ksql.fail.on.deserialization.error`

Set this to `true` if you want ksqlDB to stop processing data if it can't deserialize a record. By default, this is set to `false`, which tells ksqlDB to log the deserialization error and continue processing. If this sounds similar to Kafka Streams' `default.deserialization.exception.handler`, that's because it is. ksqlDB's configuration is used to set the appropriate exception handler class under the hood.

Default: `false`

`ksql.fail.on.production.error`

In rare cases, you may encounter an issue when producing data to a Kafka topic. For example, a transient networking issue can cause a producer exception. If you want to keep processing data when a producer exception occurs (not recommended for most use cases), set this parameter to `false`. Otherwise, keep the default.

Default: `true`

`ksql.schema.registry.url`

If your queries use a data serialization format that requires Confluent Schema Registry (see Table 9-1 for a list of these serialization formats), you will need to set this parameter to the URL where your Schema Registry instance is running.

Default: no default

`ksql.internal.topic.replicas`

The replication factor for the internal topics used by the ksqlDB server. For production environments, it is recommended that this value be >= 2.

Default: 1

`ksql.query.pull.enable.standby.reads`

When standby replicas are >=1,[2] this parameter controls whether or not a standby can be used for serving read requests when the active task (which would normally handle read traffic) is dead. Setting to `true` can help ensure high availability for pull queries.

Default: `false`

`ksql.query.pull.max.allowed.offset.lag`

Controls the maximum amount of lag (i.e., the number of offsets that haven't been read for a particular partition) tolerated by a pull query against a table. This applies to both active and standby tasks. This configuration is only activated when `ksql.lag.reporting.enable` is set to `true`.

Default: `Long.MAX_VALUE`

Server Configurations

The following properties are used to configure ksqlDB server instances:

`ksql.query.persistent.active.limit`

The maximum number of persistent queries that may be running at the same time in interactive mode. If the limit is reached, then users will need to terminate one of the running persistent queries to start a new one.

Default: `Integer.MAX_VALUE`

`ksql.queries.file`

If you want to run ksqlDB in headless mode, set this configuration to an absolute file path that contains the queries you want to run in your ksqlDB server. See "Deployment Modes" on page 255 for more information.

Default: no default

---

2 This is controlled by a Kafka Streams config, and can be set using the `ksql.streams.num.standby.replicas` parameter.

`listeners`
> The REST API endpoint for the ksqlDB server to listen at.
>
> *Default*: The default listeners is *http://0.0.0.0:8088*, which binds to all IPv4 inter-faces. Set listeners to http://[::]:8088 to bind to all IPv6 interfaces. Update this to a specific interface to bind only to a single interface.

`ksql.internal.listener`
> The address to bind for internode communication. This is useful if you want to bind a separate address for internal and external endpoints (for example, if you want to secure the different endpoints separately at the network level).
>
> *Default*: The first listener defined by the `listeners` property

`ksql.advertised.listener`
> The listener this node will share with other ksqlDB nodes in the cluster for inter-nal communication. In IaaS environments, this may need to be different from the interface to which the server binds.
>
> *Default*: The `ksql.internal.listener` value or, if not set, the first listener defined by the `listeners` property

`ksql.metrics.tags.custom`
> A list of tags to be included with emitted JMX metrics, formatted as a string of key-value pairs separated by commas. For example, `key1:value1,key2:value2`.
>
> *Default*: no default

Security Configurations

With ksqlDB rapidly evolving, and security being an area where it's important to ref-erence the most up-to-date information available, we will not attempt to capture the entire breadth of security configurations in this text. Instead, please see the official documentation (*https://oreil.ly/7RVCJ*) for a look at ksqlDB's security features.

Index

A

Abstract Syntax Tree (AST), 252
abstractions, 44
    abstraction levels of Kafka Streams APIs, 45
access modes for state stores, 100
ACID model, 250
active Kafka Streams instances, 200
active segments, 191
adders (aggregate and reduce operators), 123
    Aggregator interface, 125
AGGREGATE function type, 338
aggregate operator, 97, 123
aggregations, 123
    aggregating streams, 123
        adder, 125
        Initializer interface, 124
    aggregating tables, 126
        subtractor, 126
    in ksqlDB, 322-331
        aggregate queries producing material-
            ized views, 331
        basics of, 323
        windowed aggregations, 325-331
    operators for, 97
    using sliding aggregation windows, 158
    windowed, 159
alerts sink, 170
allMetadataForStore method, 139
allowed lateness of events, 163
ALTER statement, 295
AND/OR/NOT logical operators, 301
annotations for UDF in ksqlDB, 343
ANSI SQL, 244
    in ksqlDB vs. traditional SQL databases, 250

Apache Beam, 32
    comparison to Kafka Streams, 33
Apache Flink, 25, 30, 32
Apache Kafka (see Kafka)
Apache Spark, 25, 30, 32
APIs
    abstraction levels of Kafka Streams APIs, 45
    moving data to and from Kafka, 23
append-only logs, 6
APPLICATION_SERVER_CONFIG parame-
    ter, 135
arithmetic operators, 337
AS SELECT clause, 304
asynchronous communication, benefits of, 5
AVG function, 323
Avro
    data class for enriched tweets, 83
    improving readability of data with kafka-
        avro-console-consumer script, 93
    serializing Avro data into byte arrays, 87-90
        Schema Registry–aware Avro Serdes, 88
    use in Kafka community, 83
AVRO serialization format, 285
AvroConverter class, 270, 278
    worker configuration using for record val-
        ues, 271

B

batch processing, micro-batching, 31
Beam, 32
behavioral tests, 359-362
behaviors
    capturing with accumulation of facts, 97
    differences between facts and, 96

DROP { STREAM | TABLE }, 295, 308
DSL (domain-specific language)
    building a Topology instance, 211
    combining with Processor API in IoT digital
        twin service, 230-231
    example for Kafka Streams Hello Streams
        tutorial, 48
    high-level DSL versus low-level Processor
        API in Kafka Streams, 44
    Kafka Streams high-level DSL, 203
    operators specifying Serdes instance, 210
    processors and transformers, 231-235
    refactor of IoT digital twin service, 235-236
    representations of topics in Kafka Streams
        DSL, 53

E

eager rebalancing, 186
EARLIEST_BY_OFFSET function, 323, 339
elasticity (Kafka Streams), 29
Elasticsearch, 250, 263
    writing data from Kafka to, 272
        creating sink connector, 275
        installing Elasticsearch sink connector,
            273
        showing connectors, 275
embedded mode, Kafka Connect integration
    with ksqlDB, 267, 273
embedded state stores, 99
EMIT CHANGES statement, 261
    using in SELECT statement, 298
emitEarlyWhenFull, 165
entities, 85
EntitySentiment class (Avro-based), 86
ephemeral stores, 178
error handling, configuring for Kafka Connect,
    269
ETL (extract, transform, load)
    capabilities in ksqlDB, 246
    streaming ETL, 264
    streaming ETL pipelines, 241
event streaming database, 240
event time, 147
    benefits of using, 149
    embedded event timestamp, 148
event-driven microservices, 240
events, 5, 11
    effects of observer on processing, 114

event-at-a-time processing with Kafka
    Streams, 31
event-first thinking, 96
    stateful stream processing and, 95
    streams modeled as immutable sequence of
        events, 288
EXPLAIN statements, 307
EXTENDED variation of SHOW statement,
    293
external mode, Kafka Connect integration with
    ksqlDB, 266
extracting data from external systems into
    Kafka, 264

F

facts
    events as immutable facts, 95
    events representing, 96
FailOnInvalidTimestamp extractor, 150
failover, 250
fault tolerance
    fault tolerant state stores, 100
    in ksqlDB and traditional SQL databases,
        250
    stateful applications, 177-180
        changelog topics, 178
        standby replicas, 180
faults, handling by Kafka Streams, 29
field-level data types, 285
filter operator, 76
filtering data, 63, 75-77
    in derived streams, 306
    filtering and rekeying windowed KTables,
        166
    in INSERT INTO statement in ksqlDB, 297
    ksqlDB statement using WHERE clause, 300
        BETWEEN operator, 301
        logical operators, 301
        wildcards, 300
    pull query filtering windowstart value in
        ksqlDB, 335
filterNot operator, 76
flatMap operator, 64, 85, 216
flatMapValues operator, 85
    verification of results, 93
flattening values, 302, 306
flatTransform operator, 232
flatTransformValues operator, 232
flowing state (of data), 1

example aggregation query in ksqlDB, 323
simple, differing capabilities in ksqlDB and traditional SQL databases, 250
queries.file ksqlDB server config, 256
QueryableStoreTypes class, 131
queryMetadataForKey method, 137

R
range scans, 132
    key + window range, 170
    window range, 171
ranges, inclusive, 301
rate limiting
    of application output, 376
    of updates, 164
rebalancing, 175
    effects on interactive queries to state stores, 200
    enemy of the state store, 180
    and interactive queries to state stores, 200
    preventing unnecessary rebalances, 185
    reducing impact of, 186-194
        controlling state size, 189
        incremental cooperative rebalancing, 187
record caches, 376
    deduplicating writes to state stores with, 195
record schemas, 83
record stream, 53
records
    generic or specific, using with Avro, 83
    metadata, accessing in Processor API, 223
    serialization formats supported by ksqlDB, 285
reduce operator, 97, 123
redundant state stores, 100
registration
    registering streams with timestamp extractor, 153
    streams and tables, 110
registryless Avro Serdes, 88
regressions (see performance regressions)
rekeying records, 115
    in windowed KTables, 166
relational databases, 243
relationships between data in separate tables and streams, 111
reliability of Kafka Streams, 29
remote queries, 134-142, 173

REMOVE_STOP_WORDS UDF, creating in ksqlDB, 341-345
removing connectors, 277
repartition operator, 90
repartition topic, 119
replayable communication, 3
REPLICAS property, 291
replication of data (see data replication)
reported and desired state on digital twins, 205
REST APIs
    query submission to ksqlDB via, 255
    REST endpoint of ksqlDB server, 259
    REST service in ksqlDB, 253, 259
    service to expose digital twin records, 226
    service/client for remote queries, 134
RETENTION property in WINDOW expressions, 330
RocksDB, 99
    number of entries queries on, 133
ROWKEY pseudo columns, 297
ROWTIME pseudo columns, 297
RPCs (remote procedure calls), service/client for remote queries, 134
RUN SCRIPT statement, 312
runners (execution engines) in Apache Beam, 32
Running state, applications, 201

S
scalability of Kafka Streams, 28
SCALAR functions, 338
schemas
    Avro, 83
        in serialization of Avro data, 87
    converters' storage of record schemas, 270
    introspecting managed schemas in Confluent Schema Registry, 279
    for ksqlDB and traditional SQL databases, 248
    more sophisticated management in ksqlDB vs. traditional SQL databases, 250
    running Schema Registy instance, 91
    Schema Registry–aware Avro Serdes, 88
season_length custom type, 287
segments (topic), 191
SELECT statements, 72, 298
    aggregate functions in, 323
    for Hello, World query in ksqlDB, 261
    joins and, 117

custom, 152
registering streams with, 153
TIMESTAMP property, 291, 321, 326
support by WITH clause, 292
TimestampExtractor interface, 150, 152
TIMESTAMP_FORMAT property, 291, 321, 326
support by WITH clause, 292
to operator, 90
tombstones, 189
topics, 4
aggressive compaction of, 191
configurations for more frequent log cleaning/compaction, 192
configurations reducing writes to state stores and downstream processors, 195
creating, Hello Kafka example, 16
defined, 11
events stored in topic partitions, 11
homogeneous and heterogeneous, 9
internal topics created from KStream-KTable join, 119
partitions in, 9
partitions spread across multiple brokers, 12
precreating in ksqlDB, 259
representations in Kafka Streams DSL, 53
SHOW TOPICS statement, 259
stream-like nature of, 6
topologies
SQL engine converting SQL statements into Kafka Streams topologies, 252
testing Kafka Streams topology, 359-362
topology (processor), 36
Topology instance, 51
instantiating directly, 211
Topology#addStateStore method, 218, 233
Topology#connectProcessorAndState method, 218
Topology.addProcessor method, 51
Topology.addSource method, 51
TopologyTestDriver, 360-362
transform operator, 231
transformers, 231-235
transformValues operator, 232
transient push queries, 298
translating tweets, 79-81
tumbling windows, 155, 325
TUMBLING window type in ksqlDB, 327

Twitter stream, processing (see processing a Twitter stream tutorial)
types, 285
(see also data types)

U

UI (ksqlDB), 254
UNION query (SQL), 81
unit tests
for Java code in ksqlDB custom functions, 352
for Kafka Streams, 353-359
Processor API, 355-359
URL of Kafka Connect cluster, 266
users topic
modeling data as stream in ksqlDB, 260
pre-creating, 259

V

value joiners, 117
value.converter property, 270
ValueTransformerWithKey interface, 233
VALUE_DELIMITER property, 292
VALUE_FORMAT property, 291
VARCHAR type, 260, 292
casting to INT for a join, 317
video game leaderboard tutorial
adding source processors, 106-110
GlobalKTable, 109
KStream, 106
KTable, 107
aggregations, 123
aggregating streams, 123
aggregating tables, 126
data models, 104-105
grouping records, 121
grouping streams, 121
grouping tables, 122
interactive queries, 129-142
accessing read-only state stores, 131
local queries, 134
materialized state stores, 129
querying non-windowed key-value stores, 131
remote queries, 134-142
introduction to, 102-104
joins, 111-121
KStream-GlobalKTable join, 120
KStream-KTable join, 119

About the Author

Mitch Seymour is a staff engineer and tech lead on the Data Services team at Mailchimp. Using Kafka Streams and ksqlDB, he has built several stream processing applications that process billions of events per day with sub-second latency. He is active in the open source community, has presented about stream processing technologies at international conferences (Kafka Summit London, 2019), speaks about Kafka Streams and ksqlDB at local meetups, and is a contributor to the Confluent blog.

Colophon

The animal on the cover of *Mastering Kafka Streams and ksqlDB* is a paradise fish (*Macropodus opercularis*). The paradise fish can be found in the wild in most types of fresh water in East Asia, and it is a popular aquarium fish as well, being one of the first ornamental fish made available to western aquarium keepers.

These aggressive small fish have forked tails and are banded with vividly colored stripes of red or orange alternating with blue or green, which may change color when the fish are in a fight or get exposed to other stimuli. Their ventral fins are always orange. They can grow up to 6.7 cm long, although they are more commonly about 5.5 cm in length. Paradise fish can survive in a wide range of water conditions, although they are most commonly found in vegetation-dense shallow water.

Paradise fish are predators, eating insects, invertebrates, and fish fry. They are combative and will harass and attack each other as well as other small fish. Their aggressive behaviors have been observed to increase as they travel farther from their homes. As a still-common aquarium fish, the paradise fish's conservation status is "Least Concern," although river pollution has threatened some regional populations. Many of the animals on O'Reilly covers are endangered; all of them are important to the world.

The cover illustration is by Karen Montgomery, based on a black-and-white engraving from *Encyclopedie D'Histoire Naturelle*. The cover fonts are Gilroy Semibold and Guardian Sans. The text font is Adobe Minion Pro; the heading font is Adobe Myriad Condensed; and the code font is Dalton Maag's Ubuntu Mono.

O'REILLY®

There's much more where this came from.

Experience books, videos, live online training courses, and more from O'Reilly and our 200+ partners—all in one place.

Learn more at oreilly.com/online-learning

©2019 O'Reilly Media, Inc. O'Reilly is a registered trademark of O'Reilly Media, Inc. | 175

Milton Keynes UK
Ingram Content Group UK Ltd.
UKHW051350180224
437974UK00003BA/5

9 781492 062493